A Guide to 65 Tests for Special Education

Contributing Authors

Joan Bisagno
M.S., Learning Disability Specialist

Polly Bredt
M.A., C.C.C., Speech and Language Pathologist

Barbara Fourt
OTR, Registered Occupational Therapist

Donna Minkler
M.A., C.C.C., Speech and Language Pathologist

Karen Travis
M.A., C.C.C., Speech and Language Pathologist
and Bilingual Consultant

A Guide to 65 Tests for Special Education

Carolyn Compton, Ph.D.
Educational Director
Children's Health Council
Palo Alto, California

Fearon Education
a division of
PITMAN LEARNING, INC.
Belmont, California

Project director: Robert G. Bander, Ph.D.
Project editor: Janet Joers
Designer: McQuiston & Daughter
Cover designer: McQuiston & Daughter

ISBN–0–8224–3580–2
Library of Congress Catalog Card Number: 79–54761
Printed in the United States of America.
1 9 8 7 6 5 4 3 2

Contents

List of Figures

Preface

For the last 15 years, educational testing has been a rapidly growing field. Gone are the days when reading-readiness tests given at the end of kindergarten and group intelligence and achievement tests given every other year constituted the school testing program. Now there are tests for everything—from walking on a balance beam to reading calendars. Three major educational trends have all added to the push toward testing. The focus on individualized instruction requires measurement of individual skills as a basis for program planning. The concept of accountability demands more attention to careful measurement of pupil progress. And the rapidly expanding field of learning disabilities has created a need for more specialized diagnostic tests.

As with all trends, opinions on the subject of educational testing are polarized. For some teachers, test performance is the final word on every decision from A to R, acceleration to retention; others view all tests as instruments of the devil. Teacher A says, "I can't put Johnny in a reading group until he gets tested." Teacher G says, "No, I didn't read that 10-page test report; it's all hogwash."

Regardless of where you are on this continuum, educational testing is here to stay. The purpose of this book is not to defend testing—but to make it a usable tool for teachers. The book is intended for educators working with students in the primary and intermediate grades, although many of the tests that are reviewed can be used with junior high school students. A special section (Part II) discusses tests for preschool children.

A Guide to 65 Tests for Special Education has three functions: (1) to enable the teacher to understand and interpret students' test results based on knowledge of the test's format and limitations; (2) to help the teacher, psychologist, or administrator plan a testing program by providing basic information about the tests available in each major skill area; and (3) to provide a means for improved communication among teachers, diagnosticians, and parents about the purposes, procedures, and results of testing.

The first function might be described as the receptive function of *65 Tests*. Many educators have had the experience of sitting in a school planning meeting, listening to a child's test results, and wondering what is being said: "Her auditory analysis of Test A was two standard devia-

tions below the mean, but her figure-ground discrimination on the TAP was a standard score of 100. How does she perform in the classroom in that area, Classroom Teacher?" Or, a child has moved into the district with a stack of reports documenting test performance in many areas and the recommendation for a special class placement: "Special Education Teacher, please review the reports and determine an appropriate placement for this student." This book is intended to be a resource on such occasions. Tests are grouped according to the types of skills they assess, and enough information is given to allow you to find out what each test measures, how it measures it, and what the tests mean. The Glossary provides more information on the meaning of common testing terms.

The second function of *65 Tests* is to provide a resource for planning a testing program for your special education department. No book of test reviews can ever be complete, and this guide should certainly not be considered unabridged. Nevertheless, enough information is given about each test to enable you to review several of the commonly used tests in a given skill area and to determine which are the most appropriate and useful in your setting. *65 Tests* also is not intended to give you enough information to administer the test; that can be obtained only from the examiner's manual, practice, and experience. Rather, this guide is intended to be an introduction to the test, to familiarize teachers with the test's format, its strengths, and its limitations. Thus each test review includes the test's salient characteristics, which are important to consider when you are planning a testing program.

The third function of *65 Tests* is to improve communication among the people giving tests, the people using test results, and the parents. Educational jargon often reaches a peak of ridiculousness in the words used to describe test performance. The Glossary is intended to increase your knowledge of test terminology and to provide some clearer ways to explain test results to anyone who is inexperienced in educational testing.

Following an overview of assessment processes in the Introduction, the test reviews are organized into three parts. Part I contains the skill area tests, specifically tests dealing with academic achievement and ability, perception and memory, speech and language, and gross motor skills.

Part II discusses preschool and kindergarten tests, focusing on assessment tools for the child from birth to 6 years old. In Part III, general intelligence tests and developmental scales are reviewed. The ordering of the tests within each chapter is explained in the opening pages for that chapter.

All of the tests reviewed in *65 Tests* have been used in our clinic. We all work as diagnosticians at the Children's Health Council, a private multidisciplinary clinic in Palo Alto, California, serving children of all ages who have mild-to-severe learning, language, and emotional disorders. This book is written from our experience as clinicians and from our familiarity with testing instruments and procedures. A survey of friends in various parts of the United States indicates that the tests we have reviewed are widely used in diagnostic clinics and public-school programs throughout the country. They are often spoken and written about by professionals in the field.

We have purposefully omitted two areas of testing. Personality assessment, specifically projective testing, is a field of its own. This type of assessment is usually done outside the public schools, and teachers need ongoing consultation in order to use the information in planning a particular student's educational program. And prevocational and vocational assessment, although extremely important areas of assessment, require a different set of skills and materials, which are outside the scope of this book.

In addition, because bilingual language tests have only recently been developed, it seemed premature to review them extensively here. Some tests have not yet been published, some have been described in trade journals only, and many lack normative data. However, these tests are presented in shortened form in Appendix F.

We are not researchers or statisticians, and although we have included some comments about the technical characteristics of the tests, our expertise is clearly in their clinical use. We hope that the form used to describe each test will aid you in developing a systematic approach when you evaluate the usefulness of other tests. *65 Tests* is our attempt to limit the misuse of tests. We hope our experience is helpful to you.

Acknowledgments

Grateful acknowledgment is made to the following authors and publishers for their permission to reprint copyrighted sample test materials and illustrative matter.

LLOYD DUNN and FREDERICK MARKWARDT, JR., for Figure 4, from *Peabody Individual Achievement Test*. Circle Pines, Minn.: American Guidance Service, Inc., 1970.

ALBERT H. BRIGANCE, for Figures 7a, 7b, and 8, from *Brigance Diagnostic Inventory of Basic Skills*. Woburn, Mass.: Curriculum Associates, Inc., 1976. By permission of the author and publisher.

RICHARD W. WOODCOCK, for Figure 9, from *Woodcock Reading Mastery Tests*. Circle Pines, Minn.: American Guidance Service, Inc., 1973.

A. I. GATES and W. H. MACGINITIE, for Figures 10–14. Reprinted by permission of the publisher from *Gates-MacGinitie Reading Tests*. New York: Teachers College Press, © 1964 by Teachers College, Columbia University.

HELMER R. MYKLEBUST, for the photograph on page 64, from *Development and Disorders of Written Language* vol. 1. New York: Grune & Stratton, Inc., 1965. By permission of the author and publisher.

A. CONNOLLY, W. NACHTMAN, and E. M. PRITCHETT, for Figure 16, from *KeyMath Diagnostic Arithmetic Test*. Circle Pines, Minn.: American Guidance Service, Inc., 1971.

H. J. BAKER and B. LELAND, for Figures 17–25, from *Detroit Tests of Learning Aptitude*. Copyright © 1958, 1959, 1967 by The Bobbs-Merrill Co., Inc. Reprinted with permission.

M. FROSTIG, for Figures 26–30, from *Frostig Developmental Test of Visual Perception*. Palo Alto, Calif.: Consulting Psychologists Press, Inc., 1966.

RONALD COLARUSSO and DONALD HAMMILL, for Figures 31–35, from *Motor Free Visual Perception Test*. Novato, Calif.: Academic Therapy Publications, 1972. By permission of the authors and publisher.

LAURETTA BENDER, for Figure 36, from *A Visual Motor Gestalt Test and Its Clinical Use*. Research Monograph no. 3, American Orthopsychiatric Association, Inc., New York, 1938. By permission of the author and publisher.

KEITH E. BEERY and NORMAN A. BUKTENICA, for Figures 38a, 38b, and 38c, from *Developmental Test of Visual-Motor Integration*. Copyright © 1967 by Keith E. Beery and Norman A. Buktenica. Used by permission of Follett Publishing Company, Chicago.

H. B. FISHER and J. A. LOGEMANN, for Figures 39 and 40, from *Fisher-Logemann Test of Articulation Competence*. Boston: Houghton Mifflin Company, 1971.

RONALD GOLDMAN and MACALYNE FRISTOE, for Figure 41, from *The Goldman-Fristoe Test of Articulation*. Circle Pines, Minn.: American Guidance Service, Inc., 1972.

ARTHUR J. COMPTON and STANLEY HUTTON, for Figure 42, from *Compton-Hutton Phonological Assessment*. San Francisco: Carousel House, 1978.

SAMUEL A. KIRK, JEAN J. MCCARTHY, and WINIFRED D. KIRK, for Figures 43–47, from *Illinois Test of Psycholinguistic Abilities*. Copyright © 1968 by the Board of Trustees of the University of Illinois. University of Illinois Press, Urbana.

ELIZABETH CARROW, for Figures 49a and 49b, from *Test for Auditory Comprehension of Language*. Copyright © 1973, by Elizabeth Carrow. Austin, Tex.: Learning Concepts, Inc., rev. 1977.

ANN E. BOEHM, for Figure 50. Reproduced from *Boehm Test of Basic Concepts* by permission. Copyright © 1969 by The Psychological Corporation, New York, N.Y. All rights reserved.

LAURA LEE, for Figures 51 and 52, from *Northwestern Syntax Screening Test*. Evanston, Ill.: Northwestern University Press, 1969, rev. 1971.

DOROTHY TYACK and ROBERT GOTTSLEBEN, for the blank forms used for Figures 53a–c, 54, and 55, from *Language Sampling, Analysis, and Training*. Palo Alto, Calif.: Consulting Psychologists Press, Inc., 1974.

A. J. AYRES, for the blank form used for Figure 56, from *Southern California Sensory Integration Tests*. Los Angeles: Western Psychological Services, 1972.

WILLIAM K. FRANKENBURG and JOSIAH B. DODDS, for Figure 57, from *Denver Developmental Screening Test*. Copyright © 1969 by William K. Frankenburg and Josiah B. Dodds. Denver: Ladoca Project and Publishing Foundation, Inc., 1970.

ALBERT H. BRIGANCE, for Figures 58 and 59, from
Brigance Inventory of Early Development. Woburn,
Mass.: Curriculum Associates, Inc., 1978. By permission
of the author and publisher.

BETH SLINGERLAND, for Figures 61–72 (blank forms only
for 67 and 69), from *Pre-Reading Screening Procedures*.
Cambridge, Mass.: Educators Publishing Service, 1977.

D. WECHSLER, for the blank forms used for Figures 79 and
80. Reproduced from *Wechsler Intelligence Scale for
Children—Revised* by permission. Copyright © 1974 by
The Psychological Corporation, New York, N.Y. All
rights reserved.

Introduction

Educational assessment, in its broadest sense, is the gathering of information about a student's performance in school. When the student's school performance is deemed inadequate, educational diagnosis is used to investigate and define the student's particular pattern of academic strengths and skill deficiencies and to translate them into an individualized program. The diagnostician uses many tools—observation, interview, diagnostic teaching, and testing. Testing, then, is just one part of educational assessment, a part that has recently received much applause and much criticism.

This book reviews the instruments of educational testing, and their uses and misuses, within the total process of educational assessment for students in academic difficulty because of learning disabilities and related problems.

PURPOSES OF TESTING
The general purpose of educational testing is to answer educationally relevant questions about a student. Broadly, these questions to be answered are:

- What is the student's current functioning level in basic skills?
- What are the student's specific skill deficiencies, if any?
- What are the student's strengths?
- What and how shall the student be taught?
- How well is the student progressing?

The general school testing program attempts to answer these questions through group achievement tests given periodically throughout the grades. Such tests as the Iowa Test of Basic Skills (Lindquist and Hieronymus 1956), the California Achievement Tests (Tiegs and Clark 1970), and the Sequential Tests of Basic Skills (1958) all give teachers and parents important information about students' progress from year to year and their academic relationship to other students at the same age and grade level.

But questions about an individual student's specific strengths and weaknesses are not easily answered by group achievement tests. Particularly for students with difficulties in academic areas, individual testing is essential to discover the pattern of strengths and weaknesses, which in turn leads to an individual instructional program. Educational tests for students in academic difficulty have four main functions: screening, diagnosis, program planning, and evaluation.

Screening
The first phase of the diagnostic process is screening. A test or series of tests is given to a group of students who have something in common—age, grade level, or signs of a special problem, such as deficient fine motor coordination or poor reading performance. The results from screening tests provide a first look at a group of students to determine temporary groupings or to identify students in need of further testing. Kindergarten screening, for example, is popular in many districts as a means of determining which children may have difficulty in first grade. The goal of any screening program is to identify students in need of further individual diagnostic testing. The essence of screening is its quickness. In addition, test items must be carefully selected to measure critical skills.

Because most students who are screened do not receive further testing, we must take care to ensure that the screening procedures will identify properly those students in need of further evaluation. False positives, students identified as having disabilities when they do not, and false negatives, students with difficulty who slip through the screening process, are both serious problems. False positives can be corrected by referrals for individual testing, but false negatives do not get that opportunity.

Diagnostic Testing

In contrast to screening, diagnostic testing is usually a lengthy individual process. A battery of tests assesses the student's functioning not only in basic academic skills but also in processes believed to be essential for all learning—perception, memory, concept development, visual-motor skills, language development, and expressive skills. These tests assess the primary modalities used in the learning process—auditory, visual, and kinesthetic or motor. Some attention is given to a possible cause for the academic problems, but much more attention is given to a description of their type and degree of severity. The result of diagnostic testing is usually a placement decision. Students are admitted to special programs, excluded from special programs, retained, placed in private schools, or referred for medical and psychological services on the basis of diagnostic testing. Thus it must be carried out thoughtfully by experienced professionals who understand the importance of careful diagnostic decisions.

Program Planning

Following the in-depth diagnostic process and the placement decision, program planning begins. The process of designing an instructional program for an individual student based on the results of diagnostic tests is called the *diagnostic-remedial process,* or *diagnostic-prescriptive teaching*. Salvia and Ysseldyke (1978) describe two different diagnostic-prescriptive teaching models: the ability-training model and the task-analysis model. Each of these models has its advocates and its critics.

In the *ability-training model,* the primary concern is the assessment of such learning processes as perception, memory, visual-motor skills, and concept development. The remedial program is designed to improve these abilities or to teach the student to compensate for deficiencies.

The *task-analysis model* attempts to identify skill deficiencies by breaking down a complex academic task (such as word recognition) into its many subparts; the parts that the student has not mastered are analyzed. The remedial program is then designed to teach the student those subskills.

Program planning is usually done by the remedial teacher. In order to plan appropriate remedial programs, the remedial teacher needs information on the student's learning abilities and academic skill deficiencies.

Evaluation

The final function of educational testing is evaluation. It is of two major types: evaluation of individual pupil progress and program evaluation. Measuring pupil progress includes pre- and posttesting on formal and informal tests, daily charting of performance on specific tasks, and observing student performance in the classroom. Program evaluation attempts to measure the progress of groups of students participating in special remedial programs as compared with similar students not receiving specialized assistance. Standardized tests and rating scales are usually used for this purpose.

Testing, in the best of situations, is a time-consuming, expensive process. Is it worth it? This is the critical question that must be asked of every person involved in planning and implementing a testing program. If the educational questions presented earlier are posed carefully, then educational testing (as a part of the total assessment process) becomes not only helpful but also essential in program planning and instruction.

ABUSES AND MISUSES OF TESTS

Many of the criticisms of educational tests are legitimate; in many instances tests have been abused and misused. One problem area in educational testing is the confusion of terms. As mentioned earlier, *assessment* is the total process of gathering information about a student's performance in school; *diagnosis* is one part of that process, and the diagnostician uses *testing* as one tool. Basing educational decisions on test results alone, without using the other tools of the diagnostician—observation, interview, and diagnostic teaching—is a misuse of tests. Viewing diagnosis as a once-only process rather than a continuous procedure is also a common error.

Anastasiow (1973, p. 349) describes four other consistent abuses of tests:

• Generalizing the interpretation of test scores to groups not represented in the norming sample

• Overinterpreting scores, say by focusing on a five-point gain in IQ score when five points is not statistically significant

• Teaching the answers to test questions in the belief that an improved test score alone will demonstrate pupil progress

• Violating students' confidentiality and privacy by revealing test scores to persons not directly involved with the educational program

Wallace and Larsen (1978, p. 22) add one other abuse to the list:

• Overgeneralizing the findings of a test, either by making decisions about an individual student based on performance on a group test or labeling students on the basis of single test scores

Salvia and Ysseldyke, in *Assessment in Special and*

Remedial Education (1978), discuss the misuses of tests extensively. They divide testing errors into three types: (1) the wrong test, (2) the wrong interpretation, and (3) "dumb" mistakes. A test may be wrong if it is technically inadequate, that is, invalid or unreliable. A test may be wrong if it is used for the wrong purpose, such as using the Reading subtest of the Wide Range Achievement Test as if it were a measure of total reading. A test may be wrong when it is used with the wrong child—a child whose characteristics differ greatly from the norming sample.

The wrong interpretation of test scores, according to Salvia and Ysseldyke, is easily done. Two common errors are inferring causation from a student's test behavior and assigning a student to a group of students with similar test behavior on the basis of that test behavior alone. A good test can elicit performance that will define a student's skill deficiencies—but not the cause of them. Also, a student whose test performance is similar to that of retarded children is not necessarily retarded.

"Dumb" mistakes described by Salvia and Ysseldyke include such things as equating IQ scores on different tests and clerical errors in scoring. Another "dumb" mistake is repeating the same test too frequently.

Testing is simply one diagnostic tool. When tests are part of a well-designed assessment procedure, planned and implemented by sensitive professionals, they provide important information about a student. But tests selected, administered, and interpreted incorrectly are worse than useless. They lead to incorrect and inappropriate placements and programs for children.

TYPES OF TESTS

There are many types of tests. To plan an appropriate testing program, one must understand the essential characteristics of each type.

Formal and Informal Tests

Formal tests are more appropriately called *standardized tests*. They may be group or individual tests. They have standardized procedures for administration, timing, and scoring. They are normed on a representative sample of students and provide age-level and grade-level scores or percentiles that allow the educator to compare a student with other students of the same age and grade. Once the standardized procedure has been altered, the norms are no longer valid, and legitimate comparisons cannot be made. (Another term for formal or standardized tests is *norm-referenced tests*.)

Informal testing does not produce normed scores. Informal tests are structured observations that appraise the student's performance without reference to other students. Informal tests are usually administered individually. Because there are no norms, the teacher can modify the test format,

the timing, and the administration procedures to allow the student the best opportunity to demonstrate his or her skills. Test items can be selected to best reflect the curriculum being taught. Because the tests are not normed, interpretation of the results is very dependent on the skills of the examiner.

Individual tests generally allow the student more opportunity to demonstrate skills. The examiner can establish rapport with the student and provide breaks to decrease anxiety or fatigue. The examiner also has more opportunity to clarify instructions and to encourage the student who has a poor self-image. If presented skillfully, the tests can hold the student's interest and elicit cooperation without deviating from standardized procedures. For these reasons, individual tests are usually recommended for the diagnosis of learning disabilities and other academic problems.

Diagnostic and Achievement Tests

Diagnostic and achievement tests can be either standardized or informal, group or individual. Diagnostic tests are designed to determine whether a student has a specific learning disability and, if so, in what skill area or learning process it occurs. Some diagnostic tests, such as the Gates-McKillop Reading Diagnostic Tests, measure one specific academic skill area in depth. Others, such as the Marianne Frostig Developmental Test of Visual Perception, attempt to assess several subskills of an important learning process, such as visual perception. In diagnostic testing, observations of how the student does the task and the types of errors made are as important as the score. For this reason, individual diagnostic tests are usually more valuable than group tests in determining which students may have learning disabilities and in planning their instruction.

Achievement tests are designed to measure the student's present functioning level in basic academic skills. Items are selected to represent typical curriculum materials at specific grade levels. For example, a spelling test would include a graded list of words to be dictated by the examiner and written by the student. The score would reflect the student's present functioning level in spelling and suggest the instructional level. Evaluation of the student's error pattern on an achievement test is possible but not as easy as on a diagnostic test designed for that purpose. Achievement tests are often group tests, usually standardized and norm-referenced. They reflect curriculum content in a single area such as mathematics or in multiple areas such as reading, mathematics, and spelling.

Criterion-Referenced Tests

Relative newcomers to the field of testing, criterion-referenced tests (CRTs) were designed by educators who were dissatisfied with norm-referenced, standardized achievement tests. Standardized tests determine a student's rank in comparison to others of the same age or grade but do not assess how much or what the student knows. CRTs tell what the student is able to do and allow the educator to judge the student as an individual in relation to a set of skills in an academic area. The items either are arranged developmentally or follow the order of a specific curriculum.

The score on a CRT can be expressed as a ratio:

$$\frac{\text{Number of skills learned}}{\text{Number of skills required}} = \text{Score in percent}$$

For example, if Susan has mastered 190 words out of a 200-word spelling list, her score would be 190/200, or 95 percent (Smith, Smith, and Brink 1977, p. 2). The score on a CRT can also be translated into a statement of the student's expected performance. On the Woodcock Reading Mastery Tests, the relative mastery score permits such statements as "David can be expected to perform with 53 percent accuracy on tasks in word comprehension at a seventh-grade level." Some tests, such as the Woodcock Reading Mastery Tests, are both norm-referenced and criterion-referenced, yielding grade-level and percentile scores as well as ratios and percentages.

Criterion-referenced testing carefully identifies the specific skills mastered by a student. Because the test items have been arranged in developmental order, it is easy to see which skills must be mastered next, and they become the teaching objectives. CRTs, then, lead directly to individual instructional planning. Increasing numbers of commercial curriculum materials are including CRTs that assess the specific skills taught in that curriculum.

THE DIAGNOSTIC BATTERY
A major group of students for whom educational assessment is needed are those in academic difficulty because of suspected learning disabilities. The task of the diagnostician is to determine whether the student's academic problems are related to learning disabilities and, if so, what type of instructional program is needed.

In designing a diagnostic testing battery for a student with suspected learning disabilities, the diagnostician must take into consideration three factors: academic skill areas, learning processes and modalities, and the time and personnel available for testing.

Academic Skill Areas
If time and personnel are not an issue, what academic skill areas should be assessed in a complete educational evaluation? Table 1 serves as a guide to the major academic skill areas and their subgroups. In Appendix A, the tests reviewed in this book are matched with the academic skill areas listed in Table 1.

Table 1. Academic Skill Areas

Reading

Decoding
  Phonic skills
  Sight-word recognition
  Oral paragraph reading
Comprehension
  Oral reading
  Silent reading
  Listening
  Comprehension in specific content areas

Writing

Penmanship
  Manuscript
  Cursive
Written Expression
  Fluency
  Syntax
  Mechanics
  Content

Spelling

Written
  Phonic words
  Irregular words
Recognition of Sight Words
Oral

Arithmetic

Concepts
Computation
  Addition
  Subtraction
  Multiplication
  Division
Word Problems
  Oral
  Written

Oral Language

Receptive
  Vocabulary
  Listening comprehension
Expressive
  Articulation
  Morphology
  Syntax
  Semantics

Each of these major areas could be further broken down into multiple subskills. Testing, from the point of view of the student and the teacher who referred the student, can go on forever. Fortunately, the constraints of time and personnel force some decisions about what areas should be assessed. Such decisions should be made by considering the following factors:

- *The concerns of the teacher or the parent in the referral or testing request.* If a student is referred because of difficulties in reading and spelling but exhibits superior math skills, the diagnostician may do a quick math screening but focus the evaluation in the areas of reading, writing, and spelling.
- *The age and grade of the student.* If the student is in first or second grade, the reading evaluation will focus on phonic skills, sight-word recognition, and oral reading rather than advanced word analysis skills or silent reading comprehension.
- *Relevance of the area to classroom performance.* Oral spelling and oral math are often omitted because of their low frequency as classroom tasks. Similarly, written expression, an essential skill, should always be included.

Learning Processes and Modalities

The second factor to consider in designing the diagnostic testing battery is the basic learning processes and the primary sensory modalities in which they occur. Table 2 provides an outline for assessing the basic learning processes in the three modalities, or sensory channels, most commonly used in classroom learning. The chart incorporates some of the categories of the Illinois Test of Psycholinguistic Abilities, namely reception, association, memory, and expression. A general category of perception was added to cover such processes as closure, figure-ground discrimination, and spatial relationships. Appendix B fills in the chart with the names of the tests reviewed in this book that are appropriate for assessing each area.

Modality assessment has repeatedly been criticized on several counts:

- There is no clear agreement about the precise meaning of such terms as *reception* and *perception*.
- There is little evidence that we can assess strengths and weaknesses in these learning processes with reliability and validity.
- There is little evidence that specific programs designed to remediate deficiencies in these processes affect academic progress.

Despite these criticisms, process and modality testing—as part of the total assessment process—can provide important information about a student. For example, if a student does consistently poorly on all tasks involving figure-ground discrimination, the diagnostician may recommend that the teacher provide a quiet working space for the student and simplify the format of the curriculum materials used. Or the diagnostic information that a student consistently performs better on tasks of kinesthetic memory than visual memory may be used by the teacher to plan a spelling program that incorporates kinesthetic tracing techniques.

Again, the learning processes selected for assessment should be based on the individual student's needs. If the teacher reports that the student has great difficulty following oral classroom instructions and giving oral reports, tests that assess auditory reception, auditory memory, and verbal expression will be selected. If the academic testing reveals confusion between words such as *boy* and *day* or *came* and *come*, tests in the area of visual perception would have high priority. Selection of tests to answer specific educational questions is more appropriate than administering a standard battery to all students; the latter frequently results in excessive testing (Wallace and Larsen 1978, p. 71).

Table 2. Process-Modality Chart

Modality	Process				
	Reception (initial receiving of information)	**Perception** (initial organizing of information)	**Association** (relating new information to other information)	**Memory** (short-term, sequential memory)	**Expression** (output)
Auditory (primary stimuli are auditory)					Verbal expression
Visual (primary stimuli are visual)					Written expression
Tactile/Kinesthetic (primary stimuli accompanied by motoric input)					Motoric expression other than written or verbal

Process and modality tests are simply one part of the assessment process; they are neither perfect nor useless. But they often provide information about the tasks a student can do well—a part of the diagnostic process too often omitted.

Time and Personnel Available
The practicalities of time and personnel clearly affect the selection of tests in the diagnostic battery. Two hours of individual educational testing is generally considered a minimum amount of time for a basic educational evaluation; three to four hours would be more usual. Students with major learning disabilities, students who work slowly, or students who need frequent breaks and much encouragement often need several short testing sessions. Overtesting should be avoided; not only is it time-consuming, but it rarely leads to significantly more educationally relevant information.

Educational assessment is frequently done by a diagnostic team. The psychologist usually administers general intelligence tests and often tests of visual-motor development. The language therapist assesses receptive and expressive language skills, articulation, and auditory processing. The educational diagnostician tests academic performance and related learning processes. A perceptual-motor specialist examines gross and fine motor skills. When the educational diagnostician is a one-person team, the test battery must include a broader range of tests, particularly in the areas of concept development, language, and motor skills.

TEST SELECTION
Most educators have little trouble identifying the academic areas or learning processes to be tested. The chief problem is choosing the specific tests to be used. Too often, tests are ordered rather than selected. Test selection should be based on the following criteria:
- Does the test answer the educational question being asked?
- Is the test valid?
- Is the test reliable?
- Are the design and format appropriate for the student being tested?
- Is the content or skill area being measured appropriate for the age and grade of the student?
- Is the test economical in terms of time and money?

Educational Relevance
The most important question to ask in selecting a test is, What type of educational information do I need? Clearly, some tests should be given to every student, whereas other tests should be used only in highly specific situations. Screening tests should be quick and include items carefully selected to measure critical skills. Diagnostic tests must be thoughtful and yield information upon which placement

decisions can be made and individualized program plans formulated. Tests used to measure pupil progress must be sensitive to the curriculum being taught. Random selection of tests without careful consideration of the type of educational information the tests will yield often results in overtesting or in trying to force a set of test scores to answer questions they were not intended to answer. The following examples illustrate this point.

Sycamore School District arranged with a local college to have education students administer the Illinois Test of Psycholinguistic Abilities, a lengthy and highly specialized language test, to all 400 incoming kindergarteners. The kindergarten teachers were not instructed in how to use the data, so 600 hours of testing was of little value.

Maple School District decided to give a group standardized math test to all elementary-level students in the learning disability program in October and May to measure pupil progress in math. The test measured standard computation skills, but the curriculum being used was an experimental, "new math" approach. Few students showed progress in math between October and May. Teachers had to spend spring parent conferences explaining that Johnny actually had made progress despite his test scores.

Validity and Reliability
Once the purposes of testing have been defined and specific educational questions have been posed, test selection should consider the validity and reliability of the tests available. Validity is the primary consideration. Does the test measure the skill area well? There are many types of validity.
- *Content validity* considers whether the skills being measured are critical to the academic task and whether the test reflects the curriculum.
- *Concurrent validity* asks if the test correlates well with other accepted criteria of performance in that subject or skill area.
- *Predictive validity* asks how well the scores correlate with some criterion for future success. Predictive validity is of particular importance for screening instruments.
- *Construct validity* questions the theory and assumptions under which the test was constructed.
- *Discriminate validity* considers whether each of the subtests does, in fact, measure a separate, distinct skill.

Consideration of test validity is of critical importance in all test selection. For some tests, studies of validity are readily available in the examiner's manual; for others, library research is necessary; for some, no evidence of validity is offered.

Another aspect of validity is the composition of the norming sample for standardized tests. The test author selects a population of students to whom he or she administers the new test. The performance of this group of students becomes the "norm." It is the author's responsibility to describe that population of students in depth—number of students represented in each age level, sex, racial background, socioeconomic level, intelligence level, and so forth. Examiners must learn to look for and pay attention to the composition of the norming sample to determine if that sample included students of the type being tested. Making judgments about a student's performance on a test with an inappropriate norming population is not a valid decision-making process and is one of the misuses of tests (Anastasiow 1973).

Reliability is second only to validity in importance as a criterion for test selection. The consistency with which a test measures what it measures is a critical variable. Many factors influence a student's score on a test. Some of them are within the student—attention, motivation, physical condition, anxiety, and so forth. The good diagnostician takes these factors into account when interpreting test scores. But other factors affecting reliability are part of the test itself—the length of the test, the clarity of instructions, the objectivity of the scoring, and others. The diagnostician must also learn to study the reliability data on a test and to select the most reliable test that yields the needed educational information. Reliable answers to educational questions not asked are of little value, but unreliable answers to critical educational questions can cause placement and instructional errors.

Design and Format
The design and format of a test should also be considered in selection. Students with learning disabilities and other academic problems need tests that are simple in design, are clearly printed, and have easy-to-understand instructions. Whether a test is timed or untimed should also be considered. Sometimes it is important to know how rapidly a student can perform a given task. Reading, for example, is not a usable tool until it becomes fluent. Speed is also a critical variable in measuring writing ability. When speed is a factor, a timed test that will yield a score based on both accuracy and speed should be selected. Just as often, we need to know how much a student can do in a skill area when no time constraints are imposed. Untimed tests, or power tests, allow students to continue working until they reach a ceiling or complete the tests. When students are first learning a skill, untimed tests are usually more appropriate.

Careful consideration should be given to the type of response required by the tests; the format of a test should not penalize a particular type of student. Students with learning disabilities frequently have a short attention span, little motivation for school tasks, great anxiety about testing, and difficulty following directions. These characteristics frequently result in an impulsive style of test taking. Tests with multiple-choice or yes-or-no responses often lead to impulsive guessing with little monitoring of answers and are therefore often less appropriate with these students. Other tests place a high demand on auditory memory. Because auditory memory is frequently a weak area for students with learning disabilities, selection of a test that does not focus on this skill will yield more meaningful results.

Appropriateness of Content
Another factor in test selection is the appropriateness of the test content for the age and grade level of the student. Perceptual tests are much more appropriate at the primary grade levels, when perceptual skills are normally developing. Only the most impaired secondary students will demonstrate difficulties on perceptual tests. Bright students will have developed compensation techniques; their continued perceptual problems will be seen more clearly through error analysis of academic tasks. Oral reading tests are also more appropriate for primary and intermediate students. During those grades, oral reading is an important classroom skill. As the student gets older, oral reading tests give information about word recognition skills but may not yield accurate information about silent reading comprehension of content material—the more essential classroom task.

Time and Money
Economics must also be considered in test selection. Students with academic problems are often tested extensively during the identification, diagnostic, and placement phases and then again to measure progress. Group tests save time in administration and scoring and may appropriately be used in screening and in some types of progress evaluations. But generally, students with academic difficulties benefit more from individual or small group tests. Consumable tests (those in which the student writes on the test booklet rather than an answer sheet), although more expensive, are much easier for the student with learning problems, are more reliable, and provide more diagnostic information for the teacher. To save time, the examiner should use the most valid and reliable tests available, because if the examiner has confidence in the diagnostic information, "backup" tests may not have to be administered. Some tests, such as the Illinois Test of Psycholinguistic Abilities or the KeyMath Diagnostic Arithmetic Test, take longer to administer and score but yield information that translates more directly into instructional programming. Others, such as the Wide Range Achievement Test, are quick to administer and score but need considerable time and expertise to translate into individual programs. A testing program that gains maximum information from minimum student time is essential. Teachers must have time to teach and students need time to learn—not just to be tested.

Inservice Training

Test selection should involve the full team of administrators, diagnosticians, and teachers. Available tests should be reviewed, and their validity and reliability should be studied. But careful test selection will be of little value unless it is followed by inservice training in administration and scoring procedures, test interpretation, and explanation of results to parents. Professionals involved in testing who do not take part in inservice training often use tests without critiquing their value. Inservice training sessions should serve as an ongoing evaluation of each test being given and its usefulness in providing answers to specific educational questions.

SPECIAL ISSUES IN TESTING

Evaluating Progress

Evaluating pupil progress is an essential part of every program for students with academic difficulties. Accountability (one of the new ''buzz'' words in education) demands that educators evaluate programs in terms of pupil progress, but measuring an individual student's growth is often not a simple process. The selection of tests that will not only provide valuable diagnostic information but also prove to be effective measures of pupil progress takes forethought and planning. The following factors may serve as general guidelines.

• Selecting tests that have equivalent alternate forms for retesting purposes may not be critical in determining student progress. Research studies regarding a ''practice effect'' on achievement tests are inconclusive. Curr and Gorlay (1960, pp. 155–167) reported a high practice effect in ninth-grade students tested in the mechanics of reading and reading comprehension at one-, three-, and six-month intervals. In contrast, Karlin and Jolly (1965, pp. 187–191) tested fourth through eighth graders in September and May in reading. Whether the same test was readministered or an alternate form was used, they found no differences between the results. These results give mixed information about the practice effect in normal students. Even less is known about the practice effect in students with learning disabilities. However, because the concept of practice effect is based on the assumption that the student will remember the first test's content, it is likely that students with learning disabilities will be less affected by the practice effect than normal students will be.

• Selecting an individual test, such as the Wide Range Achievement Test, or a coordinated series of tests, such as the Gates-MacGinitie Silent Reading Tests, that covers a wide age range allows for a measure of progress from year to year.

• Selecting tests with an appropriate level of difficulty for students is necessary in determining student progress. A test that is too hard or too easy gives little information on

growth. (This particularly difficult issue for students with reading problems is discussed in the following section.)

• Issues of validity are important in measuring pupil progress. The test must reflect the curriculum content. As the example of the Maple School District (p. 6) demonstrates, tests that do not measure the skills being taught show little pupil progress and require much explanation. Another example deals with oral reading tests. Tests of oral reading usually include a high percentage of sight words. If the student has been taught all year in a systematic phonics program, the retest score may not reflect his or her progress, because exposure to sight words has been minimal. In this case, a measure of phonic skills that reflects the curriculum should be included in the retesting procedures. Testing oral reading with a timed test when speed of reading has not been emphasized by the classroom teacher is another example of an impractical way to measure student progress.

For severely impaired students with learning disabilities, even the format of the test items should be familiar. Shifting from math computation in the vertical format

$$\frac{2}{+6}$$

to the horizontal format ($2 + 6 = $ _____) may be enough to confuse the student so that the test score does not reflect progress in math computation.

• Reliability is a critical factor in selecting measures of pupil progress. In addition to the factors within the student and the test that affect reliability (discussed on p. 7), the teacher needs to be aware of several other reliability factors that affect measurement of progress. Difference scores are frequently used to document pupil progress; that is, a student is given a test in September and the same test (or its equivalent form) in May. The lower score (hopefully September's) is subtracted from the higher score, and the resulting difference score is used as an indication of growth or lack of progress. But several precautions are needed for this procedure. First, grade scores and percentile scores are not based on an equal-interval scale and should not be used for calculating differences. Raw scores or standard scores should be used. Second, difference scores are the most unreliable of test scores, because they combine the measurement errors of both test scores. Small gains or losses in achievement may not be reliable or statistically significant. Finally, difference scores that do reach statistical significance may not make any practical difference in instructional level and should not be overplayed.

• Tests with many subtests are particularly difficult to interpret in terms of student progress. Changes in the total test score often are used to document progress. However, total test scores are usually obtained by summing several subtest scores. Such a procedure often obscures progress in certain skills and lack of progress in others.

• Measuring progress in specific skill areas, such as auditory memory or math computation, often needs to be done at two intervals: immediately following the unit of instruction and a few months later. Immediate scores are often very high, whereas the later scores are lower but reflect the critical skills of retention and generalization.

The problems of evaluating pupil progress by test results are many, and clearly the reevaluation process should include less formal but in many ways more important data from the teacher. Anecdotal records and observational data on social-emotional skills, work habits, and attention are often the primary indicators of progress. Many curriculum materials now provide records of continuous progress in specific skills. These ongoing records of progress are the most important tools in future program planning. They provide measures of such behaviors as rate of learning and retention rate—critical factors that are not assessed in standardized, norm-referenced tests.

Standardized tests are also weak in another important area. Although they may be valid and reliable measurements of specific academic skills, they do not assess the degree to which those skills have been generalized to other curriculum areas and new learning situations. A good example is the student who makes a three-year gain on a test of listening comprehension but still cannot follow the flow of conversation in a classroom. Systematic observation of the student learning new materials and in larger instructional groups is an important part of the reevaluation process.

Who should do the pre- and posttesting on students in special programs? In some school districts the teacher does the testing; the rationale is that the teacher who does the testing gets information about the student's performance firsthand rather than through a diagnostician's translation. Having the teacher retest for progress gives the student the advantage of being tested by the most familiar person— presumably a less anxiety-producing situation. However, it is more desirable for someone other than the teacher, such as an administrator or diagnostician, to do the post-testing, for a number of reasons. First, the teacher has a great deal of personal need for the student to do well; the skill of the teacher is validated by the success of the students. In this situation, it is very difficult to be objective; in very subtle and unknowing ways the teacher may give the student more cues or more time. Second, having the teacher do the testing may in fact prove to be more stressful for a student. The student and the teacher often have a very close relationship, and the student may not want to disappoint the teacher. Although having a relative stranger do the testing may initially be stressful for the student, usually the neutral relationship results in less anxiety.

There are other advantages to having someone other than the teacher do the testing. A diagnostician, in the process of testing the whole class, gains an overall view of the group that may lead to suggestions for new groupings, materials, or instructional techniques. Because testing is time-consuming, this procedure allows the teacher to continue teaching—the teacher's most important responsibility.

Testing the Student with Reading Problems

Particular problems arise in evaluating the progress of students with significant reading problems. Standardized reading tests are designed to assess "normal" readers; students with identified reading problems are usually excluded from the norming sample. It is questionable practice to apply the norms of the "normal" population to students with reading problems, but we have no choice: One purpose of reading testing is to compare the poor reader with other students. It is that comparison that determines the degree of reading retardation.

One question that always arises is what level of test should be given to the student with reading problems—the level that is appropriate for the student's age and grade or the level that fits the student's reading functioning? Do you give Susan, a sixth grader reading at the third-grade level, a sixth-grade test that you know she cannot read? Or a third-grade test that will only tell you how she compares with third graders? This question only occurs on such tests as the Wide Range Achievement Test, the Gates-MacGinitie Silent Reading Tests, and the Slingerland Screening Tests for Identifying Children with Specific Language Disability, which specify different forms for different grade levels. Many reading tests use the same form for all age levels, and through a basal and ceiling procedure, ask the student to read only passages appropriate for his or her skill level.

When it is necessary to select a test level for a below-grade-level reader, the educational question being asked again determines which level to use. Here are three examples of when the below-grade-level reader should be given the test for his or her age and grade level:

1. If a standardized achievement test is being used to measure the progress of all the students in a special program, retarded readers must be given the test level for their age and grade, no matter how difficult it is for them. Otherwise, their scores cannot be included with the group.

2. Sometimes it is necessary to demonstrate that a student cannot do the academic work required in a regular classroom. In such cases, giving the student a test appropriate for that grade level clearly demonstrates skill deficiencies and makes the student eligible for special assistance.

3. Important clinical information is often acquired by giving a student a test that is too difficult. In the individual setting, the examiner can observe the student's reactions to stress. Does the student stop working or begin to guess wildly? How much encouragement does the student need to continue working? Such information is helpful to the diagnostician in program planning.

When a student is given a test that is obviously too difficult, other testing should be done both to provide a success experience for the student and to provide valid testing information. If the student achieves a score below the norms on the test for his or her grade level, then a lower-lever test that the student can do well should be administered. Readministration of both levels of the test is necessary for the progress report. For diagnostic purposes, you may choose to use several other tests to assess specific skills taught during the year, and these will form additional measures of progress.

As discussed earlier, the usual procedure for measuring pupil progress is through difference scores (posttest minus pretest score). Given the unreliability of difference scores, what is the best way to measure growth? Bliesmer (1962, pp. 344–350) compared three methods of evaluating progress in retarded readers:

1. Determining gains by the usual pretest-and-posttest difference method
2. Comparing yearly gains in the remedial program with average yearly gains before entering the remedial program
3. Comparing the reading achievement–reading potential gaps at the beginning and end of a remedial program

Bliesmer found that the third method did not demonstrate significant improvement, probably because as reading achievement improved, reading potential as measured by listening comprehension also improved. The first method did demonstrate gains, but the students with reading disabilities gained at the same rate as normal readers. When the second method was used and difference scores were compared to an average of difference scores in previous years, the growth of the students in the special program was more dramatic. This concept of determining the achievement rate of a student before the remedial program begins and comparing it to the achievement rate in the program holds the most promise for effectively reporting pupil progress (see Table 3).

Another problem inherent in assessing progress in disabled readers is the ''regression toward the mean'' phenomenon. There is a high probability that the students with the lowest scores on a pretest will score nearer the mean on subsequent retests (Farr 1969, p. 145). Students are frequently selected for remedial programs because they are significantly below average in reading. Consequently, when retested, their scores have a tendency to move closer to the mean, thus inflating the amount of progress they appear to have made. This issue is clouded by the fact that the lowest-functioning students often make strong initial gains in a structured remedial program; it becomes difficult to sort out what is ''true'' gain and what can be attributed to the statistical regression phenomenon.

In some school districts, students are selected for

Table 3. Measuring Pupil Progress in Reading*

Actual Grade Level	Grade Score
First	K.4
Second	1.3
Second (retained)	1.5
Third	2.0
Fourth	2.8
Fifth (special program)	3.8

*For Sam Green, a hypothetical fifth-grade student, whose progress has been measured with the Wide Range Achievement Test. His growth, during 10 months in the special program at grade 5, has been the equivalent of 10 months, or one school year. In the 50 school months before he entered the special program, he achieved only 28 months' progress. Thus, before Sam entered the special program, his average growth in reading ability per school year was 5.6 months (28 ÷ 5).

remedial reading programs on the basis of their intellectual functioning; that is, students with high intellectual ability have higher priority for the programs. This policy is based on the assumption that bright students will make more progress in remedial programs. Such an assumption does not take into account the fact that the student's intellectual functioning may be depressed by reading disabilities or that research studies often report the greatest gains from students with lower intellectual functioning.

Measuring long-term gains in a remedial program is also a difficult task. Remedial programs often create a Hawthorne effect; that is, the individualized work, small class size, highly structured program, concerned teacher, students' reduced fear of failure, and other characteristics of the program result in improved performance within the program, which unfortunately has little carry-over into other settings and few long-term gains. Some school districts have now introduced ''watch and consult'' programs in which students who leave the remedial program to return to regular classes are carefully monitored to ensure continued success.

Given the difficulties of measuring reading progress by administering standardized tests to students with reading disabilities, teachers must develop continuous monitoring systems and charts that graph students' work on a daily basis. These are more reliable measures of growth.

Measuring Reading Comprehension
For many students with reading disabilities at the upper-elementary and secondary school levels, the reading problem is not decoding, or word reading, but reading comprehension. Tests available in the area of reading comprehension, oral or silent, yield grade-level or percentile scores but offer little diagnostic information about the types of reading comprehension problems that the student demon-strates. Many skills make up reading comprehension —

decoding, knowing word meanings, understanding content, organizing, recognizing tone and mood, inferring meaning, and many others. We badly need a task analysis of the reading comprehension process and developmental studies of the progression of skills involved. From these data, criterion-referenced tests can be designed. Meanwhile, diagnosticians need to remember that many factors of the test affect reading comprehension scores:

- Level of material read (too easy or too difficult)
- Type of questions asked (specific facts or inferential questions)
- Type of response required (written, oral, multiple-choice, or essay)
- Length of time between reading and responding (immediate or delayed recall)
- Speed factor (timed or untimed)
- Instructions to the student

No global score can accurately reflect a student's reading comprehension. The conditions of the test must be considered.

Teachers who are designing individual programs to remediate reading comprehension should also consider the following factors in the student that may cause poor reading comprehension:

- *Poor decoding skills*. The most usual explanation for poor comprehension is that the student is reading material too difficult for his or her decoding skills.
- *Deficits in underlying language skills*. Weaknesses in vocabulary and sentence comprehension, due to inadequate language comprehension, is a frequent cause of low reading comprehension.
- *Experiential deficits*. Students may not have the experience to understand the concepts being presented in the reading material.
- *Memory deficits*. Diagnosticians and teachers too often attempt to teach comprehension skills to students who already comprehend but who cannot recall the material.
- *Deficits in expressive skills*. Reading comprehension is often assessed by asking the student to express understanding of a passage verbally or in writing. The problem may not be in the comprehension but in the expressive part of this process.
- *Specific comprehension deficits*. Many students need to be taught such specific skills as finding the main idea, recognizing mood and tone, and so forth.

When planning individualized reading programs, the teacher must study the diagnostic test information and the student's classroom performance to determine which of the above factors are contributing to the student's reading comprehension difficulties. The remediation program should be very different for the student who has significant language disabilities and for the student who needs to be taught specific comprehension skills.

In addition, predicting students' silent reading skills from their oral reading performance is risky. The average reader usually has better comprehension in silent reading, but the student with learning disabilities frequently reads aloud with greater accuracy and comprehension. Oral reading increases this student's attention, and hearing himself or herself read, often improves comprehension. Measures of both kinds of reading should be included in a full diagnostic evaluation.

Determining Instructional Level

Deciding where to begin classroom instruction in a given subject is not always clear from test scores, as the following example from reading will illustrate:

David's score on the Gilmore Oral Reading Test was 2.1 (second grade, first month) in accuracy; this means instruction should begin in the beginning second grade reader. Right? Not necessarily.

Grade scores on tests cannot be translated directly into instructional level. Grade scores are a translation of a student's total raw score into a score that corresponds with an average performance for students at that grade level. However, those raw score points may have been gathered in many ways. For example:

David reads a primer paragraph with 2 errors, a first-grade paragraph with 4 errors, a second-grade paragraph with 4 errors, and a third-grade paragraph with 14 errors. This performance on one test yields a raw score of 20 and a grade-equivalent score of 2.1.

Jane reads the primer paragraph with no errors, the first-grade paragraph with no errors, the second-grade paragraph with 18 errors, and the third-grade paragraph with 30 errors. Her raw score on the same test is 20, yielding an identical grade-equivalent score of 2.1.

For David, a beginning second-grade reader may be appropriate; for Jane, it is much too difficult. She needs the transition of more instruction in a difficult first-grade reader.

In 1946, Betts (pp. 445–454) divided reading levels into four categories depending on the student's accuracy rate. These categories are still our best guide for determining instructional level.

1. *Basal or independent level*. Student reads with 99 percent accuracy and 90 percent comprehension. Oral reading is fluent and well phrased. The student is free from tension and free to think about the content, because he or she is totally in control of the vocabulary, the sentence construction, and the content.

2. *Probable instructional level*. Student reads with 95 percent accuracy and 75 percent comprehension. He or she can use word analysis skills and makes good progress with teacher guidance.

3. *Frustration level.* Student reads with less than 90 percent accuracy and less than 50 percent comprehension. He or she becomes easily bogged down, tense, distractable, and sometimes resistive.

4. *Probable capacity.* Student comprehends material read aloud with 75 percent accuracy and can discuss it with good vocabulary.

It is questionable whether listening comprehension is a valid measure of reading capacity (see the review of the Durrell Listening-Reading Series, p. 52). However, Betts's other three categories are very relevant for planning classroom instruction. Many, many students are being instructed in materials at their frustration level; that is, they are misreading more than 1 word in every 10. Halting and struggling over every word, they become very tense. This is not instruction; it is frustration.

Students with good phonics instruction will often read with approximately the same accuracy rate in materials at a wide range of grade levels, like David in the previous example. In such cases, instructional level should be the highest level at which the student has 75 percent comprehension. Students with reading disabilities of the dyslexic type often make errors on little words (*the, he, they, from*). Their accuracy rate may also be the same across several grade levels, and they should be instructed at the highest level of good (75 percent) comprehension.

The Diagnostic Report

For many diagnosticians, the written report is the most difficult part of the educational assessment process. Describing a student's behavior during testing and analyzing the student's performance on several tests is a very difficult task. The written diagnostic report ranges in length from a 12-page dissertation about the student's performance (which few people take the time or make the effort to read) to a 1-page listing of test scores. Between these extremes is a thoughtfully prepared 3- or 4-page report that helps the teacher, parent, or doctor understand more fully the student's classroom performance.

The following general outline has been useful in preparing a written report.

1. Identifying data
2. Reason for referral
3. Behavioral observations during testing
4. Tests administered
5. Test results
6. Analysis of test results
7. Summary
8. Recommendations

Appendix C contains two examples of completed diagnostic reports using a similar format.

Identifying Data
The identifying data include such information as the student's name, birthdate, chronological age, grade, school, examiner's name, and date of testing.

Reason for Referral
This should be a brief statement of the present problem. It is helpful to know who referred the student, what behaviors were of concern, and the purpose of the testing.

Behavior during Testing
A most important section of the report is the description of the student's behavior during testing. Statements about the student's cooperation, attention, persistence, anxiety level, and response to the testing are important in assessing the validity of the tests. Although the comments are subjective, based on the examiner's observation of the student, they do describe the student in the individual testing situation. The student may behave very differently from in the class-room—more attentive and cooperative or less so, more nervous and hyperactive or less so. The student's behavior may account for differences in performance and may provide clinical information critical to the assessment process.

Tests Administered
These tests are often listed separately or combined with test results. Whenever possible, a brief description of the test itself should be included for readers who are unfamiliar with the test format. Some diagnosticians prefer to describe the tests on a separate page attached to the test report.

Analysis of Test Results
The essence of the test report is in the analysis of the test results. The examiner discusses the student's performance on each test, summarizes the student's strengths and weaknesses in skills, and analyzes the various learning processes assessed. Examples are given to illustrate the kinds of errors the student made. The examiner describes in detail the specific tasks the student has not mastered and summarizes the error pattern.

Summary Statement
The summary reviews the essential information about the student, reason for referral, behavior, and test performance.

Recommendations
These typically include a placement recommendation as well as teaching suggestions. In a well-written report, the recommendations flow logically from the description of the behavior and the performance. The suggestions for teaching are based on task analysis and error analysis. They should incorporate analyses of the student's interests and strengths. They lead the teacher directly into curriculum planning.

This section should also specify a date for reevaluation.

The written report described in this section is similar in format to those prepared by many psychologists and educational diagnosticians. In recent years, shorter standardized forms have been devised that allow test results to be written in quickly with little or no narrative concerning the student's behavior or performance. But description of 16 separate tests with no analysis of their interrelationships is of little value. Such report forms, although expedient, often lead to stereotyped recommendations that do not follow logically from the student's behavior. The purpose of the written report is to communicate information about a student's performance that will enable teachers to plan and implement an appropriate instructional program and to communicate information to parents about their child's performance. As such, it is a critical document, deserving of time and effort in preparation.

Communicating Test Results to Parents

In addition to providing information to the student's classroom teacher, the assessment process should help parents understand their child. Conveying the results of the diagnostic assessment to parents is usually the responsibility of the special education administrator, teacher, or psychologist. Conducting a parent conference that conveys clear and helpful information to parents is a very important skill.

Parents want and have the right to know whatever you know about their child's abilities and disabilities. They have the right to know your concerns and to express theirs. They need to have all of the information necessary to participate knowledgeably in any decisions being made about their child's placement and program. This means that professionals involved in the assessment process have the responsibility to convey clear and accurate information. This does not mean giving the parents a list of numerical scores that have little meaning for them. Nor does it mean describing in detail a child's problems in terms like "perceptual disturbance" or "auditory closure." Nor does it mean talking with parents in such generalities ("Yes, Tom is a little behind in math") that they leave the office uncertain of the results of the assessment. The balance between being too technical and too general is very difficult, but essential, to achieve.

Some parents ask for specific numbers and terms. What is their child's IQ? What grade level is he or she reading at? Is the child dyslexic? Brain-damaged? Others ask few questions. But beneath the specific questions and the unasked questions, parents of all levels of sophistication are basically asking, "Is something the matter with my child? What is it? Is the child going to be all right? What is the school going to do? How can we help?"

The following guidelines can be used in preparing for a parent conference:

• Think about the most important information you want to share with the parents about their child. Be sure that the information is presented clearly and does not get lost in a morass of numbers and descriptions of behavior.

• Be certain you know what your recommendations will be. If the assessments have been done by a team, come to an agreement about recommendations before the parent conference. Parents want to hear the professional recommendations—not four conflicting views.

• Have all the information ready for the parent conference. Come prepared to answer such questions as Who is the teacher of the special class? When can we observe? Do you know a good math tutor? How do we go about getting some counseling?

In a recent study titled "What Parents of the Learning Disabled Really Want from Professionals," Dembinski and Mauser (1977, p. 53) found that parents wanted professionals (teachers, psychologists, and physicians) to use terminology they could understand. They overwhelmingly disapproved of professional jargon. But the use of educational and psychological jargon is such a part of the professional role that teachers and psychologists must make a conscious effort not to overwhelm the parents with "jargonese." The following techniques have proven helpful:

• Review with the parents the reasons for referral and the school's concerns about the child. If the parents initiated the assessment, ask them to restate their concerns. Review the assessment process. Name the professionals who worked with the child and explain what they did. Be certain the parents know the names and understand the roles of all the people involved in the assessment process.

• Show the parents a few of the actual test items to demonstrate the task the student was asked to perform and the performance. Be certain to include examples of both the student's strengths and deficits. Rockowitz and Davidson (1979, p. 6) found it was better to present information about the child's strengths early in the conference. Too often, parents cannot hear the good news after a discussion of problems.

• Illustrate with examples how the student's skill deficiencies may be noted in the classroom, at home, and with friends.

• Encourage parent questions and comments by your manner. Try to draw both parents into the discussion. Be certain to schedule enough time for questions and discussion.

• Don't avoid using terms such as *mental retardation, learning disability, dyslexia,* or *aphasia* if your evaluation clearly supports the diagnosis. Rockowitz and Davidson (1979, p. 6) echo the finding of several researchers that parents need a name for their child's problem.

• Give parents a written report. With some parents it is

better to discuss the report point by point; with others it is better to just talk about the assessment results and have them read the report later. Explain clearly and note in the report which scores are age equivalents and which are grade equivalents. It makes a great deal of difference to clarify whether the student is performing at the 4-year-old level or a fourth-grade level.

• Before concluding, ask the parents to restate what they have learned from the conference. This gives the professional a chance to clarify any misconceptions.

• End the conference with a clear plan of what will happen next and whose responsibility it is to carry out each part of the process. Be aware of parents' feelings, and don't press them to make decisions until they have had a chance to think it over and talk to others.

THE TEST REVIEWS

The remaining chapters of this book present critical reviews of some of the most commonly used instruments in educational diagnosis. Each test is introduced with a data sheet that presents the essential data about the test. The purpose of the test, the major areas tested, and the age or grade range of the test are stated. Possible classifications for those who usually administer the test, as well as types of tests and scores obtained, are shown below.

The data sheet also indicates whether the student's performance is timed, the amount of testing time required, and the amount of scoring/interpretation time necessary. If available, information on the norming sample is given. The data sheet also indicates whether a test has alternate forms for test-retest purposes.

Following the data sheet, the format of the test is described, and a critical review of the test's strengths and limiting factors is presented. Guidelines are given for the use of each test to minimize abuses and misuses of the test and to provide information for the diagnostician regarding administration and interpretation. But *65 Tests* is not intended to teach the reader how to administer any test. Even a person who is experienced in diagnostic testing needs to study the examiner's manuals and practice administering the test before using it with a student referred for testing.

Testing is one part of the educational assessment process—an important part but not the only part. The educational diagnostician must work with parents, teachers, and others who know the student to gather information that will answer important educational questions accurately. This, after all, is the goal of educational assessment—a field of challenges and responsibilities.

Usually Given By	Classroom teacher Special education teacher Occupational therapist Remedial reading teacher Doctor Nurse	Counselor Physical therapist Motor therapist Psychologist Physical education teacher	Speech/language clinician Paraprofessional Administrator Principal Any trained person
Type of Test	Individual Group	Informal Standardized	Norm-referenced Criterion-referenced
Scores Obtained	Age level Perceptive age Mastery age Mental age Standard Percentile Stanine	Ratio Quality scale Rating scale Relative mastery Achievement index Scaled	Test age IQ Verbal IQ Performance IQ Full-scale IQ Perception quotient (PQ)

PART I
Skill Area Tests

Most tests used in special education assess one or more specific skill areas. The tests reviewed in Part I are grouped into four chapters according to the type of skills they assess. These chapters are: Academic Tests, Perception and Memory Tests, Speech and Language Tests, and Gross Motor Tests. While it is difficult to categorize tests that cover a wide range of skills, two major considerations determined the placement of such tests in Part I: (1) when a test is commonly used to evaluate a particular skill or learning process, and/or (2) when the majority of a test's subtests relate to a particular skill or learning process.

The assessment of skills in basic academic areas is one of the primary purposes of educational testing. Chapter One contains 15 representative tests that assess student functioning in the basic academic skill areas. General achievement tests, as well as specific tests of reading, spelling and written language, and mathematics are included.

Ten tests of perception and memory are reviewed in Chapter Two. These tests are commonly used in conjunction with tests that assess basic academic skills. "Comprehensive tests," that is, tests that assess more than one of the primary modalities used in the learning process—auditory, visual, and kinesthetic or motor—are included as well as tests that principally assess either auditory perception and memory or visual and visual-motor perception and memory.

The 13 speech and language tests reviewed in Chapter Three include both tests that measure articulation or speech production and tests that measure receptive and expressive language skills. All of the tests in this chapter are designed for use with preschool children as well as those in the elementary grades. In addition to these language assessment

tools, Appendix F includes information on ten bilingual tests for Spanish-speaking children.

Chapter Four contains four test batteries whose primary contribution is the assessment of motor skills. Because developmental delays in physical coordination may be associated with learning disorders, these tests yield information valuable in the planning of many students' educational programs.

Academic Tests

The assessment of skills in basic academic areas is one of the primary purposes of educational testing. This chapter contains 15 representative tests that assess student functioning in the basic academic skills of reading, writing, spelling, and mathematics.

The first section reviews three multiple-subject tests of academic achievement. The Wide Range Achievement Test is probably the best-known and most widely used individual achievement test. It assesses a student's skills in reading, spelling, and mathematics. The Peabody Individual Achievement Test, a more recent addition to the field of testing, includes those three areas as well as reading comprehension and general information. A very new test, the Brigance Diagnostic Inventory of Basic Skills, is a comprehensive criterion-referenced instrument.

The second section of the chapter contains eight tests specific to the field of reading. Two very similar and well-known standardized tests of oral reading, the Gray Oral Reading Tests and the Gilmore Oral Reading Test, are reviewed. Next are four more-extensive batteries of reading skills: the Spache Diagnostic Reading Scales, the Durrell Analysis of Reading Difficulty, the Gates-McKillop Reading Diagnostic Tests, and the Woodcock Reading Mastery Tests. The section concludes with two tests of silent reading, the older and well-known Gates-MacGinitie Silent Reading Tests and the newer Durrell Listening-Reading Series, which also includes comparative measures of listening comprehension. For a complete overview of the reading tests, see Appendix D.

In the spelling and written language section of this chapter, there are three tests. The Larsen-Hammill Test of Written Spelling provides a norm-referenced spelling instrument, and a very new test, Diagnostic Word Patterns by Evelyn Buckley, is an informal criterion-referenced tool. An individual diagnostic test of written language, Myklebust's Picture Story Language Test, concludes this section.

Because mathematics is included in the three multiple-subject tests, only one individual diagnostic test for mathematics is reviewed in this chapter. The KeyMath Diagnostic Arithmetic Test assesses a wide range of math concepts and computation skills. The Kraner Preschool Math Inventory and the Brigance Diagnostic Inventory of Early Development, which both include counting and other beginning math skills, are reviewed in Part II: Preschool and Kindergarten Tests.

Some tests are difficult to categorize. The Slingerland Screening Tests for Identifying Children with Specific Language Disability and the Malcomesius Specific Language Disability Test are clearly tools for assessing academic skills. They include sections related to writing, spelling, and phonics. However, the primary contribution of these tests to educational assessment is in the area of perception and memory, so they are reviewed in Chapter Two.

Achievement Tests

Wide Range Achievement Test (WRAT)

J. F. Jastak, S. R. Jastak, and S. W. Bijou
Guidance Associates of Delaware, Inc., 1937; revised 1965; Manual revised 1976
1526 Gilpin Ave., Wilmington, DE 19806

Purpose	To assess skills in reading (word recognition), written spelling, and arithmetic computation
Major Areas Tested	Reading, spelling, and arithmetic
Age or Grade Range	5 years–adult
Usually Given By	Classroom teacher Special education teacher Psychologist
Type of Test	Standardized Individual Group (some subtests)
Scores Obtained	Grade level Standard Percentile Stanine
Student Performance Timed?	Yes (some subtests)
Testing Time	20–30 minutes
Scoring/Interpretation Time	15 minutes
Normed On	A large sample of children and adults from all socioeconomic groups and all ranges of intellectual ability in seven states
Alternate Forms Available?	No

FORMAT

The materials for administering the Wide Range Achievement Test (WRAT) include the manual of instructions and individual student record forms.

The test is divided into two levels. Level I is for students between the ages of 5 years, 0 months and 11 years, 11 months. Level II is for students 12 years of age and older. The same manual and student record forms are used with both levels of the test.

Each level of the WRAT contains three subtests:

1. *Reading*. Recognizing and naming letters and pronouncing single words; no measure of context reading or comprehension
2. *Spelling*. Copying marks (X, ⌐ , ⊏), writing the name, and writing single words from dictation
3. *Arithmetic*. Counting dots, reading numerals, solving oral problems, and performing basic written computation skills; no measure of mathematical concepts

The three subtests can be given independently. When all three are given, no particular order is required. The WRAT usually is given individually, but group procedures for the Spelling and Arithmetic subtests are described in the manual.

In Level I, each of the subtests begins with some preacademic tasks. In the Reading section, the prereading skills assessed include naming letters in the student's name, matching 10 letters by form, and naming 13 letters of the alphabet. The prespelling test consists of copying 18 geometric marks and writing names. The prearithmetic test includes counting 15 dots, reading 5 digits, showing 3 and 5 fingers, identifying which number is more, and doing 3 oral addition and subtraction problems. Students between the ages of 5 and 7 years are routinely given the pretests. Older students are given the pretests only when they cannot achieve a basal level on the Reading, Spelling, or Arithmetic subtests. Level II students who cannot achieve a basal level are also given the pretests.

The items in each subtest are arranged in order of difficulty. The student continues working until a ceiling level is reached in Reading (12 consecutive errors) and Spelling (10 consecutive errors) or until the time limit expires in Arithmetic (10 minutes).

Raw scores are converted to grade scores immediately, using the norm tables printed on the student record forms. Standard scores and percentiles are available in the manual.

STRENGTHS OF THE WRAT

• The WRAT is undoubtedly the best known and most widely used quick measure of individual achievement in basic academic skills. Students of all ages and skill levels can be tested to get an estimate of academic performance that can serve as a first step in diagnostic evaluation.

Although equivalent forms of the WRAT are not available, the wide age range covered by the test makes it a valuable tool for assessing the progress of an individual student over several years. The WRAT is inexpensive in terms of materials and time. It is relatively quick to administer and score.

• Grade scores, standard scores, and percentiles are provided and should be reported. The use of these three types of scores makes interpretation of the student's performance clear to parents and teachers.

• Extensive research has been done on the WRAT, and reliability and validity data are presented in the manual.

• The manual also presents excellent discussions of such topics as the diagnostic evaluation, reading disability, speed reading, remedial techniques, and reading readiness, which are interesting to the teacher and helpful in test interpretation and program planning.

LIMITING FACTORS OF THE WRAT

• Because the WRAT is so easy to give and to score, it is frequently overused and misused. It must be viewed as an initial estimate of a student's basic academic skills and not as a complete diagnostic instrument. Too often students are admitted to or excluded from special programs on the basis of their WRAT scores alone. An investigation of the content of each of the WRAT subtests indicates that such a use of the test is not warranted.

The Reading subtest assesses word recognition only. The student simply reads aloud a list of single words. There is no measure of sentence reading, paragraph reading, or comprehension. Because the student can obtain 25 points for the prereading items, a reading grade score of 1.4 is obtained by reading three preprimer words. Overestimates of primary students' reading level consequently are quite common on the WRAT.

Similarly, in Spelling a student may obtain a grade score of 1.3 by copying 18 marks and writing 2 letters in his or her name correctly. The relationship between design copying and written spelling is not well documented and raises questions about the validity of including 18 points from such a task on a measure of spelling.

The Arithmetic subtest raises many content questions. Because it is a straight computation test, student performance depends on the curriculum that has been taught. Students who have not been taught skills in fractions cannot obtain a fourth-grade score. Students instructed totally in the "new math" may get unrealistically low scores. Also, there is only one example of many types of problems. For example, on Level I

$$\begin{array}{r} \$62.04 \\ -\ 5.30 \end{array}$$

is the only example of subtraction with regrouping; it clearly requires understanding of zeros and money as well. In addition, the 10-minute time limit on the arithmetic test affects the scores of older students, who may work slowly. If possible, they should be given an opportunity to complete as many problems as they can; then two scores should be reported, one within the 10-minute limit and one after the time limit was extended.

• A major limiting factor in the 1965 edition of the WRAT was the poor organization of its manual. Administration procedures were confusing, and examiner errors in administration and scoring were frequent. However, the most recent revision of the WRAT manual is well organized. Nevertheless, examiners who are new to the test are still cautioned to study the manual carefully and to practice giving the test several times before administering it to a student with academic difficulties.

• Although it is quick to administer and an easy source of grade scores, the WRAT is a limited diagnostic tool. Time should be taken to analyze a student's error pattern. Table 4 shows how an analysis of common WRAT spelling errors can be used to define a remedial program.

Table 4. Analysis of Spelling Errors

Word	Spelling	Error Type	Teaching Strategy
cat	*ɔat*	Letter reversal (kinesthetic)	Dictation, visual-motor training
boy	*doy*	*b/d* confusion (visual-kinesthetic)	Visual discrimination, visual-motor training
will	*well*	Vowel discrimination (auditory)	Auditory discrimination, word patterns (*ill*)
make	*mack*	Vowel error and visual recall	Silent-*e* rule, dictation
say	*sae*	Poor visual recall	Word patterns (*ay*), word tracing
grown *explain*	*grone* *explane*	Poor visual recall	Word tracing
enter *advice*	*inter* *edvice*	Vowel discrimination (auditory)	Auditory discrimination, dictation
surprise	*suprise*	Incorrect pronunciation (auditory)	Auditory-kinesthetic feedback, visual cuing, color coding
cut *cook*	*kut* *kook*	Poor visual recall	Word tracing
light *dress* *watch*	*lite* *dres* *woch*	Poor visual recall	Word tracing, color coding

Peabody Individual Achievement Test (PIAT)

Lloyd M. Dunn and Frederick C. Markwardt, Jr.
American Guidance Service, Inc., 1970
Publishers' Bldg., Circle Pines, MN 55014

Purpose	To provide a wide-range screening measure of reading, spelling, mathematics, and general achievement
Major Areas Tested	Mathematics, reading, spelling, and general achievement
Age or Grade Range	Grades K–12
Usually Given By	Classroom teacher Paraprofessional Special education teacher Any trained person Psychologist
Type of Test	Standardized Individual
Scores Obtained	Age level Grade level Standard Percentile
Student Performance Timed?	No
Testing Time	30–40 minutes
Scoring/Interpretation Time	20 minutes
Normed On	Public school children from 27 urban, suburban, and rural communities across the United States; sample balanced for sex, race, and parents' occupations
Alternate Forms Available?	No

FORMAT

The Peabody Individual Achievement Test (PIAT) materials consist of individual record booklets, the examiner's manual, and two easel kits that contain the test items, practice items, and instructions for administration. A training tape that provides a guide for acceptable pronunciation of reading and spelling words is also available.

The two easel kits are arranged as follows:

Volume I
    Subtest 1: Mathematics
    Subtest 2: Reading Recognition
Volume II
    Subtest 3: Reading Comprehension
    Subtest 4: Spelling
    Subtest 5: General Information

The PIAT was standardized on all five subtests given in the above order. However, it is possible to give selected subtests rather than the complete test. The PIAT combines short-answer and multiple-choice questions. No writing is required. Suggested starting points are given for each subtest, and the basal level is five consecutive correct responses. Testing continues until the student makes five errors in seven consecutive responses. With this procedure, students are tested only on items within their range of ability. The five subtests are:

1. *Mathematics*. This subtest contains 84 multiple-choice items, ranging from such kindergarten-level tasks as matching numbers to high school concepts in algebra and geometry. The questions are read to the student, who selects the answer from four visually-presented choices (see Figures 1 and 2). All computation must be done mentally.

2. *Reading Recognition*. This subtest contains 84 items, including 18 readiness tasks such as letter matching and letter naming. The remaining 66 items are single words that the student reads aloud (see Figure 3). The words were selected from basic reading series using both the "look-say" and phonic approaches.

3. *Reading Comprehension*. This subtest contains 66 multiple-choice items. On each one, the student is presented with a page that contains one sentence to be read silently; the second page has four pictures, and the student selects the picture that best illustrates the meaning of the sentence just read (see Figure 4).

4. *Spelling*. This subtest contains 84 multiple-choice items. The first 14 are readiness tasks, such as finding the "different" symbol in a group of four and letter recognition. The remaining 70 items require the student to select the correct spelling of a word pronounced by the examiner from four choices, as shown in Figures 5 and 6. No written spelling is required.

5. *General Information*. This subtest contains 84 questions that are read to the student and answered orally. The content includes science, social studies, fine arts, and sports. Examples of the test items might include the following:

How are birds and fish different?

Which boy has the least money?

David has three dimes and two pennies.	John has six nickles and one dime.
Jim has three quarters.	Bill has twenty cents.

Figure 1. PIAT Mathematics

Which set of lines are *not* parallel?

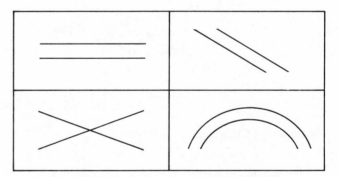

Figure 2. PIAT Mathematics

come	down	yellow	fast
huge	warm	century	artist
impede	caution	survey	knead

Figure 3. PIAT Reading Recognition

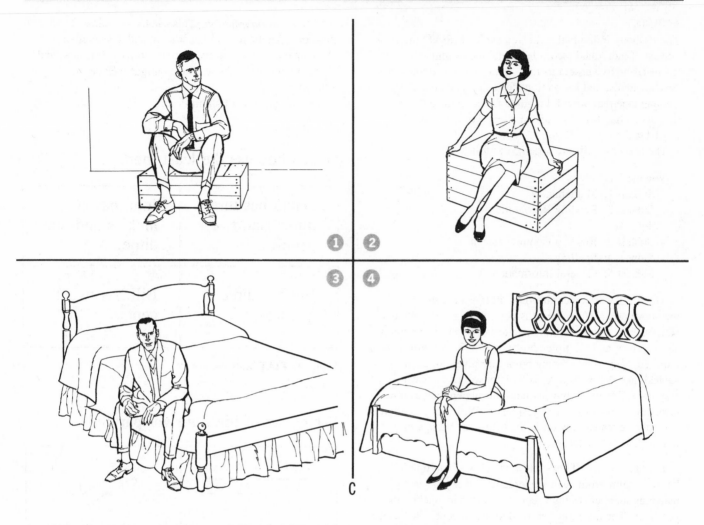

Mother sits on the bed.

Figure 4. PIAT Reading Comprehension

What do you call a large group of people who play musical instruments together?

By what process do the people select their government officials?

What is a common belief of the Catholic and Protestant religions as contrasted with Judaism?

Grade level, age level, percentile, and standard scores are obtained for each of the five subtests as well as for the total test. Using these derived scores, together with chronological and mental ages, a variety of types of profiles can be plotted to represent graphically a student's achievement in the five subtest areas.

Alternate forms for test-retest purposes are not available, but the wide age range of the PIAT makes it a usable test for documenting progress over time.

lok	loc
looke	look

Figure 5. PIAT Spelling

excillent	excellent
excelant	excellant

Figure 6. PIAT Spelling

STRENGTHS OF THE PIAT

• The PIAT provides a quick rough estimate of achievement levels. The multiple-choice format allows the test taker to move quickly, and the variety of items holds students' interest. The items appeal to a wide age range, which makes the PIAT very useful for underachieving secondary students.

• The subtests of the PIAT, used in conjunction with other diagnostic tests, can provide useful information. The Mathematics subtest includes items that assess a student's problem-solving skills more effectively than a straight computation test would. The picture format of the Reading Comprehension subtest is a unique way to measure the important skill of sentence comprehension. For students who have not previously had an intelligence test, the General Information subtest can provide a quick estimate of overall functioning.

• Perhaps most useful is a comparison of a student's Spelling score on the PIAT (which requires only recognition of the correct spelling) with written spelling performance on a test such as the Wide Range Achievement Test (p. 19) or the Larsen-Hammill Test of Written Spelling (p. 57). For example, suppose two sixth-grade students obtained the grade scores shown here:

	WRAT Spelling	PIAT Spelling
Student A	4.3	5.8
Student B	4.5	4.7

Both students are performing significantly below grade level on written spelling. Student A, however, has the ability to recognize correct spelling, as her PIAT score indicates, thus demonstrating some visual memory skills. The remedial program for Student A would attempt to capitalize on that visual memory, and the expectations for performance in such skills as proofreading and dictionary work would be higher than they would be for Student B.

LIMITING FACTORS OF THE PIAT

• The PIAT was not intended to be a comprehensive diagnostic instrument in any of the subtest areas. For students with academic problems, it should serve only as a guide for further in-depth testing.

• When interpreting a student's performance on the PIAT, it is necessary to keep in mind the exact task presented on each subtest. The broad general subtest names (Mathematics, Reading Recognition, Reading Comprehension, Spelling, and General Information) do not describe the tasks. For example, the examiner must be careful not to make general statements about a student's spelling based on the PIAT alone, because the task of recognizing correct spelling is quite different from written spelling (the more usual classroom task). Such a statement as "Student C is two years below grade level in math" may be very inaccurate if based on the PIAT alone; the student's computation skills may be excellent.

• The multiple-choice format used on the Mathematics, Reading Comprehension, and Spelling subtests is appropriate for a screening tool but may yield very inaccurate results for individual students. For example, the impulsive student often selects an answer without thinking, whereas the student with sophisticated test-taking skills may puzzle out an answer by the process of elimination without really knowing the information.

• As with any test made up of subtests, there is a tendency to focus attention on a comparison of subtest scores; that is, to discuss Student A's performance in spelling compared to her performance in math. The PIAT manual discusses the problems in this type of analysis and presents guidelines for interpreting differences between raw scores on subtests. The examiner should study these guidelines carefully to avoid overinterpretation of subtest differences.

• The arrangement of subtest materials in the easel kit is confusing; the examiner needs to practice locating materials quickly before administering the test. There is little room for writing comments in the individual record book.

• PIAT reliability varies with the subtest and the age of the students. In general, the Reading Recognition and Total Test scores are most reliable, and the Spelling and Reading Comprehension subtest scores are least reliable. The reliability of performance of kindergarten students is low, suggesting that the PIAT is not a good test for students at the preacademic level.

• Studies on the validity of the PIAT are notably lacking, again suggesting that the best use of the PIAT is as a quick screening device.

Brigance Diagnostic Inventory
of Basic Skills (Brigance)

Albert H. Brigance
Curriculum Associates, Inc., 1976
6 Henshaw St., Woburn, MA 01801

Purpose	To assess basic readiness and academic skills and to provide a systematic performance record to help teachers define instructional objectives and plan individualized educational programs
Major Areas Tested	Reading, language arts, and mathematics
Age or Grade Range	Grades K–6
Usually Given By	Classroom teacher Administrator Special education teacher Paraprofessional Psychologist
Type of Test	Informal Criterion-referenced Individual
Scores Obtained	Grade level on some tests
Student Performance Timed?	No
Testing Time	15–90 minutes (depending on purpose of testing)
Scoring/Interpretation Time	15–30 minutes
Normed On	Not normed, but field-tested in Northern California and Boston, Massachusetts
Alternate Forms Available?	No

FORMAT

The materials for the Brigance Diagnostic Inventory of Basic Skills (Brigance) consist of an examiner's notebook and individual student record books. The notebook is designed to lay flat on the table between the examiner and the student. It includes the directions for administering each subtest, the test items, scoring criteria, and instructional objectives in behavioral terms. A sample page from the examiner's notebook is shown in Figure 7a. Test items for this subtest are shown in Figure 7b.

The individual student record books provide a means of recording ongoing progress. The student's responses are recorded by the examiner in the record book in a different color each time the test is administered. A grade-level profile is charted after each administration to provide a graphic summary of student achievement, as shown in Figure 8. Observation of student behavior can also be noted.

The Brigance is an informal inventory. It gives administration directions, but the teacher or other examiner is encouraged to adjust the assessment procedures to meet the needs of the student. The only question being asked in each subtest is, Has the student mastered this skill adequately, or is additional instruction needed?

The Brigance covers a wide range of skill areas. The entire inventory may be given, or subtests may be selected to measure specific skills. In all, the inventory includes 141 subtests organized as follows:

1. *Readiness*. The 24 subtests in this skill area include color recognition, body parts, sentence memory, counting, and letter recognition.
2. *Reading*. The 33 subtests included here test for word

INITIAL CLUSTERS VISUALLY

SKILL: Can articulate correct sound when cluster is presented visually.

DIRECTIONS: Point to the first letters (sh).

Say: *Look at these letters. Tell me the sound they have when they are together at the beginning of a word.*

If the student does not understand, explain the first blend.

Say: *These letters have the sound of sh as in shock or shape.*

See *NOTE* #2 and the next page for alternate method of administration.

NOTES:

1. You may wish to check the student's understanding of the voiced and unvoiced "th."

   Say: *Can you tell me the other sound "th" makes?*, after the student has given one sound.

2. An alternate method of assessing this skill is to present the initial clusters in combination with a vowel. The results of the alternate method may have more validity if the student has been taught by a method which always presents the clusters in combination with a vowel such as Duggins or *Words in Color*. See next page for alternate administration.

DISCONTINUE: After three consecutive errors.

TIME: 10 seconds per response.

ACCURACY: Give credit for each correct response.

OBJECTIVE: When presented with a list of 33 blends and digraphs (clusters) listed in an order commonly taught, the student will indicate the sound____(quantity) of the consonants have or make in the initial position.

-56-

Initial Clusters Visually C-10

Figure 7a. Brigance Examiner's Notebook, Page 56

recognition, oral reading, word analysis, and vocabulary skills such as classification and analogies.

3. *Language Arts*. The 20 subtests assess handwriting, grammar, spelling, and reference skills.

4. *Math*. The 64 subtests in this skill area include number sequences, computation, measurement, time, and geometry.

The Brigance is a criterion-referenced test; derived scores such as age norms, stanines, or percentiles, which allow comparison of students, are not provided. However, the initial subtests in oral reading, spelling, and math do provide quick grade-level scores.

The Brigance is intended to be readministered at regular intervals, but alternate equivalent forms are not provided.

STRENGTHS OF THE BRIGANCE

• The Brigance is a helpful newcomer to the field of

informal inventories. The 141 subtests are appropriate for a wide age range and cover a variety of academic tasks. Several subtests cover areas omitted from other assessments, such as personal data responses, homonyms, alphabetical order, abbreviations, dictionary and reference book use, graphs, maps, and elementary geometry. Often the special class curriculum overlooks these skills, which are important for upper-elementary students.

• The Brigance administration manual is well organized, clear, and well written. Notes on each subtest give suggestions for varying the administration procedures and explain the rationale for each subtest. These notes, together with the flexibility of administration allowed in an informal test, make the Brigance a helpful instrument for the classroom teacher.

• The addition of the grade-level scores in reading,

sh →	wh	th (v)	th (u)	st
sw	gr	sp	fl	gl
sl	pl	cl	bl	tr
cr	sc	dr	ch	fr
pr	br	sm	sk	wr
qu	spr	thr	scr	shr
str	spl	squ		

Figure 7b. Brigance Examiner's Notebook, Test Items

spelling, and math add to the Brigance's usefulness as a screening device.

• The individual student record book provides an excellent measure of continuous pupil progress. Together with the instructional objectives written for each subtest, the Brigance offers a unique package of a wide-range assessment tool, instructional objectives leading directly to program planning, and a record of continuous pupil progress.

LIMITING FACTORS OF THE BRIGANCE

• The Brigance is a new test, and validity and reliability data are not available. The author is currently collecting data to document the predictive validity of the readiness tests with the California Test of Basic Skills. Other research is needed to establish the validity of the academic subtests.

• As with other informal tests, reliability is difficult to establish, because the test is not administered in a standardized manner. Therefore, the Brigance should not be the only measure of progress. A standardized test in the appropriate academic skills should be used with the Brigance if one of the purposes of testing is to measure progress.

• Starting points on some subtests are unclear, and ceilings can be arbitrary.

• The student record books do not provide a place to mark errors while the student is doing oral paragraph reading. A copy of the paragraphs for the examiner would allow for marking errors and later analyzing the error pattern.

Name		Birthdate		School

BRIGANCE™
STUDENT RECORD BOOK

Table of Contents

Recording Procedures and Color Code

Doing each evaluation in a different color develops a graphic profile of progress. CIRCLE responses for skills the student can do; UNDER-LINE with the **next color** skill objectives being set for the next evaluation. See the introduction of the **Inventory of Basic Skills** for further discussion.

Evalu-ation	Color	Date	Examiner
1st	Pencil		
2nd	Blue		
3rd	Red		
4th	Black		
5th	Green		
6th	Purple		

Grade Level Test Profile: The results of Grade Level Tests included in the *Inventory* may be indicated on the bar graph below to provide a summary of the student's progress. Use the color code.

TEST	Pr	1	2	3	4	5	6	7
Word Recognition —Page 3								
Comfortable Reading Level—Page 5								
Reading Comprehension Level—Page 5								
Spelling—Page 8								
Math—Page 9								

Testing Observations

Write the letters "S" or "N" and circle "Yes" or "No" in the designated box to describe the student's behavior/reaction during testing. Use a pencil or pen of the color indicated on the left.

S—Satisfactory   N—Needs to Improve

	Cooperative	Persistent	Attention Span	Concentration	Confidence	Rapport	Appeared to Hear Well	Appeared to See Well	Read with Expression
							Yes No	Yes No	Yes No
							Yes No	Yes No	Yes No
							Yes No	Yes No	Yes No
							Yes No	Yes No	Yes No
							Yes No	Yes No	Yes No
							Yes No	Yes No	Yes No

Figure 8. Brigance Student Record Book, Page 1

Reading Tests

Gray Oral Reading Tests (Gray Oral)

William S. Gray
Bobbs-Merrill Company, Inc., 1967
4300 W. 62nd St., Indianapolis, IN 46206

Purpose	To measure growth in oral reading and to aid in the diagnosis of oral reading problems
Major Areas Tested	Oral reading
Age or Grade Range	Grades 1–college
Usually Given By	Special education teacher Psychologist Diagnostician trained in reading disorders
Type of Test	Standardized Individual
Scores Obtained	Grade level
Student Performance Timed?	Yes
Testing Time	15–20 minutes
Scoring/Interpretation Time	15 minutes
Normed On	Public school children in two districts in Florida and in several schools in metropolitan and suburban Chicago, Illinois
Alternate Forms Available?	Yes

FORMAT

The Gray Oral Reading Tests (Gray Oral) consist of four equivalent forms—A, B, C, and D. The materials include a spiral-bound set of reading passages for each form, the corresponding examiner's record booklets, and an examiner's manual. A stopwatch is also needed for administration.

The first passage of each form is introduced by a picture that provides the setting for the paragraph. Each of the 12 passages that follow is self-contained, so that the test may be started with any paragraph. The student reads aloud while the examiner marks errors in the examiner's record booklet and notes observations of the student's reading style and behavior on a checklist. Each passage is timed, and each is followed by four comprehension questions that are read to the student and answered orally. The passages within a form increase in difficulty in several ways: higher-level vocabulary, longer words, longer and more complex sentences, and higher-level concepts. The 13 paragraphs cover the range from preprimer to adult reading; 8 of the 13 paragraphs contain material at the elementary school level.

The student begins the test by reading a passage two years below grade level. If necessary, the examiner proceeds with easier paragraphs until the student reads one passage without error. Then the student progresses through more difficult paragraphs until seven or more errors are made on two successive paragraphs. The average student reads five or six paragraphs: two relatively easy, one or two at the achievement level, and two that are more difficult.

The Gray Oral tests are scored by combining the number of errors made in each paragraph with the time needed to read that paragraph. The resultant passage scores are then totaled to yield a test score that is converted into a grade equivalent. (The comprehension questions do not contribute to the grade-equivalent score.) Separate norms are provided for boys and girls.

STRENGTHS OF THE GRAY ORAL

• The Gray Oral is one of several good oral reading tests that all follow the same general format. Its wide age range and four equivalent forms make it an excellent tool for test-retest purposes. The unique feature of the Gray Oral is that speed of reading is an integral part of the grade score. In other oral reading tests, timing is optional, but in the Gray Oral, rate of reading is considered of equal importance to number of errors. Particularly with older students, combined assessment of accuracy and speed yields a grade-equivalent score that is more predictive of classroom performance.

• In addition to the scores, the Gray Oral tests yield a variety of diagnostic information. Oral reading errors are recorded and grouped into the following eight categories: (1) aid (examiner tells word after five-second hesitation),

(2) gross mispronunciation (*Ouropi* for *Europe*), (3) partial mispronunciation (*visit* for *visited*), (4) omission of word or phrase, (5) insertion of word or phrase, (6) substitution of one word for another, (7) repetition of one or more words, and (8) changes in word order. Analysis of these types of errors, together with observations of reading style noted on the checklist (lack of expression, loss of place, and so on), enables the examiner to plan an individualized reading program. In addition, the four comprehension questions that accompany each passage require only comprehension of literal meaning and immediate recall of facts, but they give some estimate of oral reading comprehension.

• The examiner's manual is clear and well organized. It presents many good suggestions for interpreting students' oral reading performance.

LIMITING FACTORS OF THE GRAY ORAL

• For students with reading disabilities, the timing aspect of the Gray Oral causes increased pressure. Because these are the students for whom the most accurate diagnostic data is needed, another test may need to be used with students whose performance is significantly affected by the stopwatch.

• It is questionable whether speed of reading is an important criterion for beginning readers. The beginning reader who reads slowly and cautiously but without errors is penalized by the Gray Oral scoring system. And for students with reading difficulties related to impulsiveness, reading speed may not be a desirable characteristic.

• While emphasizing reading speed, Gray has eliminated comprehension as a factor in determining grade scores. The test would be strengthened by the addition of other types of comprehension questions and of norms or guidelines for interpreting student performance in this area.

• The norms on the Gray Oral are described as "tentative" in the examiner's manual. Only about 40 students were tested at each grade level (20 boys and 20 girls). No efforts were made to obtain a balanced sample on such variables as race, IQ level, or socioeconomic class. All students with physical or emotional problems, with speech defects, or who had repeated or skipped a grade were eliminated from the sample. As a result, caution should be taken before applying the norms to groups of varying abilities and ethnic backgrounds. Local norms should be developed. Of particular interest are the different norms provided by the Gray Oral for boys and girls. Other achievement tests in reading have not found that sex difference requires different norms.

• Validity and reliability studies are notably lacking. The tests base their claim to validity on careful test construction, but research studies are needed.

Gilmore Oral Reading Test

John V. Gilmore and Eunice C. Gilmore
Harcourt Brace Jovanovich, Inc., 1963
757 Third Ave., New York, NY 10017

Purpose	To assess oral reading accuracy and comprehension skills
Major Areas Tested	Oral reading
Age or Grade Range	Grades 1–8
Usually Given By	Classroom teacher Special education teacher
Type of Test	Standardized Individual
Scores Obtained	Grade level Percentile Stanine Rating scale
Student Performance Timed?	Optional
Testing Time	15–25 minutes
Scoring/Interpretation Time	15 minutes
Normed On	Over 4,000 students from a wide range of socioeconomic levels in six school districts throughout the United States
Alternate Forms Available?	Yes

FORMAT

The materials for the Gilmore Oral Reading Test consist of a manual of directions, the booklet from which the student reads paragraphs, and the individual record blanks for recording the student's reading errors and answers to comprehension questions.

Two equivalent forms are available—Forms C and D (A and B are out of print). Each form consists of 10 paragraphs carefully constructed from graded vocabulary in basal readers. The paragraphs are graduated in length and difficulty from the primer through the eighth-grade level. The 10 paragraphs form a continuous story that is introduced with an illustration. Forms C and D are both printed in the same booklet, but separate record blanks are provided for each.

The examiner introduces the test through the illustration and selects a paragraph about two years below the student's expected reading level. The student reads the paragraph aloud, and the examiner times the reading with a stopwatch and marks any errors. The examiner reads the five comprehension questions following each paragraph, and the student answers orally. The testing stops when the student makes 10 or more errors in one paragraph.

Separate grade-equivalent, percentile, and stanine scores are obtained for accuracy, comprehension, and rate of reading. Performance ratings are also provided. Table 5 is an example of what a sixth grader's scores might look like.

Table 5. A Sixth Grader's Scores on the Gilmore Oral Reading Test

Score	Accuracy	Comprehension	Rate
Stanine	3	8	
Percentile band	11–22	89–95	
Grade equivalent	4.2	5.3	
Performance rating	Below average	Above average	Fast

STRENGTHS OF THE GILMORE ORAL READING TEST

• This is one of several good standardized oral reading tests. It provides a means of assessing a student's oral reading accuracy, comprehension, and rate. A system for analyzing the student's oral reading errors is built into the test format. Table 6 summarizes the types of errors that are possible.

• Careful analysis of the error pattern of an individual student can lead directly to planning a corrective program. For example, a student who waits for prompting from the

examiner needs to be taught how to use word analysis skills and needs to be encouraged to sound out new words; the student who makes frequent "substitutions" may need to learn to monitor oral reading with comprehension clues.

• The wide grade range of the Gilmore Oral Reading Test, together with its equivalent Forms C and D, make it a good instrument for measuring pupil progress through test-retest procedures. An added advantage of the test is that the timing is optional and separate from the scoring for accuracy and comprehension. The examiner may decide whether using the stopwatch will cause anxiety in a student that would significantly affect performance. Eliminating the timing simplifies test administration and does not affect the accuracy and comprehension scores.

LIMITING FACTORS OF THE GILMORE ORAL READING TEST

Users of this test should be aware of several factors that significantly affect interpretation of test results.

• The accuracy score is the only reliable and valid score on the test. The system for obtaining a comprehension score often results in a spuriously high score. This is because of a procedure that gives "bonus" points for paragraphs above the ceiling level. The authors make the assumption that, if a student could read the next paragraph after reaching the ceiling (that is, after making 10 errors), he or she would be able to answer almost the same number of questions as on the ceiling paragraph. The result of this assumption is the scoring system shown in Table 7.

Students frequently receive comprehension scores high above their accuracy scores, not because they answered the questions correctly, but simply because of the bonus system. Also, because the comprehension questions on the Gilmore Oral Reading Test require only recall of specific facts from the paragraph and no interpretation or abstract reasoning, comprehension scores rarely reflect the student's functioning level in classroom materials. It is safe to say that, if the student's comprehension score is higher than the accuracy score, it means little in terms of actual skills. However, if the student's comprehension score is lower than the accuracy score, beware! Given the types of questions and the bonus scoring system, a low comprehension score may reflect serious comprehension or memory problems that require further assessment.

• The vocabulary of the test is drawn from basal readers, which usually have a sight-word emphasis. Particularly at the lower levels, students who are being instructed in a phonic or linguistic approach are often unable to demonstrate their reading gains. For example, a student may have made great progress during the year in learning letter names, sounds, and phonically regular three- and four-letter words. These gains will not be seen on pre- and posttesting, because linguistically regular words are not featured. Parents

Table 6. Error Types on the Gilmore Oral Reading Test

Error Type	Definition	Example
Substitution	Real word is replaced by another	*Step* for *stop*; *father* for *farther*
Mispronunciation	Word produced is not a real word	*Frist* for *first*; *at'end* for *attend*
Lack of response	Student does not attempt word within five seconds	
Disregard of punctuation	Student does not pause for periods or commas	
Insertion	An extra word or words are added	*The boy and girl came home.* (the)
Hesitation	Student pauses at least two seconds before attempting word	
Repetition	A word, phrase, or sentence is repeated	
Omission	One or more words are omitted	*This is the best place to (have a) picnic.*

and teachers need to understand that the Gilmore Oral Reading Test will not reflect growth until the child also masters a basic sight-word vocabulary.

• The content of the upper-grade paragraphs of this test deals with the vocational aspirations of male and female students. Professionals today may find the orientation offensive (Dick prepares to be a doctor or scientist, but Mary considers secretarial work or nursing).

Table 7. Scoring System for the Comprehension Section of the Gilmore Oral Reading Test

Paragraph Number	Comprehension (number correct)	
1	5	Credited
2	5	
3	4	
4 Basal	3	Actually read
5	4	
6	3	
7 Ceiling	4	
8	3	"Bonus points"
9	2	
10	1	

Spache Diagnostic Reading Scales (Spache)

George D. Spache
CTB/McGraw-Hill Division, revised edition 1972
Del Monte Research Park, Monterey, CA 93940

Purpose	To evaluate reading skills, to assess supplementary phonics skills, and to determine instructional, independent, and potential reading levels
Major Areas Tested	Reading
Age or Grade Range	Grades 1–8; grades 9–12 (students with reading deficiencies)
Usually Given By	Special education teacher Diagnostician trained in reading assessment
Type of Test	Standardized Individual Criterion-referenced (supplementary phonics tests)
Scores Obtained	Grade level
Student Performance Timed?	Optional
Testing Time	30–45 minutes
Scoring/Interpretation Time	15 minutes
Normed On	Rural and urban students in southern and eastern United States
Alternate Forms Available?	Yes

FORMAT

The Spache Diagnostic Reading Scales (Spache) materials consist of an examiner's manual, an individual expendable record book for use by the examiner, and a reusable spiral-bound book for use by the students.

The battery includes three graded word recognition lists, two reading selections at each of 11 levels (ranging from grades 1.6 to 8.5 in difficulty), and eight supplementary phonics tests:

> Consonant Sounds
> Vowel Sounds
> Consonant Blends and Digraphs
> Common Syllables or Phonograms
> Blending
> Letter Sounds
> Initial Consonant Substitution
> Auditory Discrimination

The subtests are administered individually to a student in the order that follows. All but the first subtest consist of reading passages.

1. *Word Recognition Lists.* These graded word lists yield a tentative level of performance and are used to determine the level of the initial passage the student should be able to read orally in the next part of the test.

2. *Oral Reading (Instructional Level).* This level is determined by the highest-level passage a student can read with no more than the average number of errors and with 85 percent comprehension. (Each passage is followed by seven or eight short comprehension questions.) Oral reading errors include reversals, omissions, additions, substitutions or mispronunciations, repetitions of two or more words, and hesitations (after a five-second pause, the examiner aids the student).

3. *Silent Reading (Independent Level).* The passage selected for the silent reading test is at the level just above the student's *instructional level* (obtained from the oral reading test). The *independent reading level* is determined by the highest-level passage that the student reads with 60 percent comprehension. An estimate of reading speed (slow, average, or fast) can be obtained on the silent reading test.

4. *Auditory Comprehension (Potential Level).* The passage chosen by the examiner to be read aloud to the student is at the level just above the student's independent level (obtained from the silent reading test). The highest-level passage that the student listens to with 60 percent comprehension is estimated to be the *potential level*. The author believes that this measure represents the level to which a student's reading may be raised through special reading instruction.

5. *Supplementary Phonics Tests.* Any or all of the phonics tests (see the list above) may be administered to the student to obtain a detailed analysis of the student's word-attack skills and phonic knowledge. The phonics tests are essentially criterion-referenced rather than norm-referenced.

One set of passages (labeled A or C) is used for the initial testing. Parallel passages for retesting purposes are labeled B and D.

STRENGTHS OF THE SPACHE

• The Spache assesses word recognition and oral and silent reading in one battery. It is fairly easy to administer and takes relatively little time. The grade scores are made more useful by the informal information about a student's reading skills that can be obtained. For example, an analysis of specific errors gives clues to how the student attempts to read. Error analysis is as crucial for determining the instructional needs of a student as is the grade level achieved on the test. To facilitate analysis of types of errors, the student record book contains a Word Analysis Checklist and a Checklist of Reading Difficulties.

• The Supplementary Phonics Tests are helpful in revealing the nature of word analysis skills. They include tasks involving initial and final consonants, blends, vowels, and word endings. These criterion-referenced tests can identify specific skills that need to be mastered.

• The word lists used to evaluate the student's sight-word vocabulary are appropriately scaled, with the scores ranging in grade-level difficulty from first to sixth grade. Good estimates of reliability and predictive validity are given for the word lists.

• In addition to the standard test procedures, the manual contains useful suggestions for further informal analysis of reading difficulties. For example, the examiner may wish to present to the student words in isolation that were misread in context. Then the examiner can compare a student's success with words in context to success with them in isolation.

• Students failing in reading often feel threatened by a reading test. In the Spache, the passages that the student reads are not marked by grade level, an important and sensitive consideration.

• In summary, the Spache adequately assesses reading skills and difficulties. It appears most valid through the mid-elementary level, although its use extends to students with reading difficulties at higher grade levels.

LIMITING FACTORS OF THE SPACHE

• The Spache must be administered by a person with considerable clinical experience in reading diagnosis, because analysis of reading performance is often a subjective evaluation. Accurate recording of oral reading errors depends heavily on the judgment of the examiner.

• One caution is offered regarding the use of the Word Recognition Lists. The manual does not clearly state that only immediate responses are considered correct. Words pronounced accurately after a few seconds' delay are counted as mistakes, both in scoring and in determining the ceiling level. A useful provision would be separate norms for untimed recognition and timed recognition. Extending the word lists beyond the sixth-grade level would also be helpful.

• The comprehension questions at all levels are short-answer questions, the majority of which are straight recall of facts. For the student with a short-term memory problem, the comprehension score can be quite misleading. An alternative way of assessing comprehension that does not depend so heavily on immediate memory would add to the test's usefulness.

Adding other fundamental types of comprehension questions would be helpful at the upper grade levels. For example, the test does not cover such skills as the ability to grasp the main idea, the ability to weave together the ideas in a selection, or the ability to draw inferences from a short passage.

The short-answer comprehension questions pose some real concerns. Questions designed on the yes-or-no model are handicapped by a 50 percent probability of getting any question correct simply by guessing. This kind of question is all too prevalent at the upper-grade levels. For example, seventh-grade-level questions include ''Can we skim all kinds of reading?'' and ''Is marble always white?''

Answers to many other questions seem quite obvious, so that any student with sufficient experience and knowledge can derive the correct answer regardless of how well he or she read the passage. Typical questions are ''What color was his wagon?'' (second grade); ''How do birds help us?'' (fifth grade); ''What kind of flowers do poppies have?'' (fifth grade). The superficial understanding required by such comprehension questions is a serious drawback.

• The measurement of reading rate as fast, average, or slow similarly presents special concern. A student may have many reading rates, depending on such factors as the difficulty of the material, the content of the passage, and the purpose for which it is being read. In view of these factors, the silent reading rate on the Spache does not appear to be too meaningful.

• The examiner should keep in mind that performance on the Supplementary Phonics Tests can be directly related to the type of reading instruction a student receives. For instance, a student in a phonics-oriented program may perform much better on these tests than a student who is being taught by sight-word methods. As the manual states, the phonics tests do not possess any degree of reliability to justify grade norms. The Auditory Discrimination test has also not been found to be reliable for first-grade students and for students speaking a nonstandard dialect.

• An additional passage at each grade level (increasing the number to three) would be beneficial. In the current

design, if the examiner wishes to readminister a passage at the failed level, the B or D selections (which were designed for retest purposes) must be used. Administering the retest passages thus uses up the selections, so that they are not available for determining independent or potential levels.

• The assumption of the author that the potential level represents the level to which a student's reading may be raised through intensive instruction is not well founded. Studies show that most students in regular classrooms can comprehend material that is read to them approximately two grade levels above their grade placement. The assignment of a grade-level norm to the potential-level scale does not seem meaningful.

Another drawback of the potential level is that evaluation of comprehension is confounded by the memory factor inherent in the test. If a student fails a selection, the examiner needs to determine whether short-term memory is at fault or if a real comprehension problem exists.

• The content of the passages includes narrative, expository, and descriptive selections chosen from such sources as social studies, natural and physical sciences, and children's literature. Because of variation in content, scores beyond fourth grade may be affected to a significant degree by a student's past experiences and interests.

Durrell Analysis of Reading Difficulty
(Durrell Analysis)

Donald D. Durrell
Harcourt Brace Jovanovich, Inc., 1937; revised 1955
757 Third Ave., New York, NY 10017

Purpose	To measure various aspects of the reading process and to identify weaknesses in reading
Major Areas Tested	Oral and silent reading, listening comprehension, word analysis skills, spelling, and handwriting
Age or Grade Range	Grades 1–6
Usually Given By	Special education teacher
Type of Test	Standardized Individual
Scores Obtained	Grade level
Student Performance Timed?	Yes (some subtests)
Testing Time	30–90 minutes (depending on number of subtests given)
Scoring/Interpretation Time	15–30 minutes
Normed On	Not reported
Alternate Forms Available?	No

FORMAT

The materials for the Durrell Analysis of Reading Difficulty (Durrell Analysis) consist of the examiner's manual of directions, individual record booklets for recording each student's responses, a tachistoscope with word lists to accompany specific subtests, and a book containing the paragraphs for the Oral Reading, Silent Reading, and Listening Comprehension subtests.

The Durrell Analysis contains 14 subtests designed to assess a student's performance on various types of reading tasks. The subtests are described in Table 8. The examiner selects only those subtests appropriate for each student's reading level.

Following administration of each subtest, the examiner scores the test and calculates the grade-level score. These grade scores are rough approximations of instructional level; for example, on the Oral and Silent Reading subtests, which are based on time required to read the sixth paragraph, the student score is recorded as low, medium, or high fourth, fifth, or sixth grade. On several subtests, only middle-of-the-year grade norms are provided. Other subtests have no norms at all.

The individual record form contains checklists for recording observations of students' difficulties on each subtest. These checklists are more useful in planning a remedial program than the rough grade norms are. The results of the major subtests are plotted according to grade norms on the profile chart on the cover of the individual record booklet. This is intended to provide a graphic representation of the student's strengths and weaknesses in reading.

The manual provides directions for administering and scoring the tests, interpretation of the test results, and guidelines for planning a remedial program. No information on test construction or standardization is provided. Alternate forms for test-retest purposes are not available.

STRENGTHS OF THE DURRELL ANALYSIS

• The Durrell Analysis was developed to help reading teachers understand the reading process and plan individual reading programs. To reach this goal, a wide variety of subtests are included. When used wisely, they yield a wealth of information about a student. The Durrell Analysis is one of the few tests that allows assessment of oral and silent reading, listening comprehension, word analysis skills, and spelling all in the same battery. The variety of subtests allows for testing of nonreaders as well as readers with high-intermediate-grade skills.

• The manual is well organized and clearly written, and the checklists for recording reading difficulties are helpful in bridging the gap between test scores and daily performance.

• Several unique subtests are included. In particular, the Learning Rate subtest provides valuable information about a student's efficiency in learning a new reading task.

LIMITING FACTORS OF THE DURRELL ANALYSIS

• The Durrell Analysis should not really be considered a standardized test. No information on standardization is given, and no reliability or validity statistics are reported. Rather, the Durrell Analysis is an informal inventory providing a variety of tasks on which to assess reading skills. The approximations of grade scores should be ignored, as should the profile chart that is based on them.

• In considering the Durrell Analysis as an informal inventory, it is important to note which reading skills are poorly assessed or omitted. First, reading comprehension on both the Oral and Silent Reading subtests is limited to recall of specific facts. No interpretation or generalization is required. Second, tachistoscopic presentation, such as that used on the Word Recognition subtest, is often confusing for poor readers and gives inaccurate information regarding their word recognition skills. Word lists or flashcard procedures are often more accurate. Third, no subtests assessing discrimination or recognition of vowel sounds (long or short) are included. Fourth, no pure auditory tests of discrimination or blending are included. Finally, the Learning Rate subtest uses a sight-word presentation; no similar test using phonic presentation is included.

Table 8. Durrell Analysis Subtests

Subtest	Reading Grade Level	Task	Timed	Normed	Additional Information Gained
Oral Reading	1–6	Reading aloud a series of paragraphs graded for difficulty; answering comprehension questions	Yes	Yes	Error patterns in oral reading
Silent Reading	1–6	Reading silently a series of graded paragraphs; answering comprehension questions	Yes	Yes	Eye-movements per line, imagery, sequential recall
Listening Comprehension	1–6	Listening to graded paragraphs; answering comprehension questions	No	No	Comparison to silent reading
Word Recognition and Analysis	1–6	Reading word lists of graded difficulty, presented by tachistoscope; time for analysis given on words not recognized	Yes	Yes	Comparison of sight-word vocabulary and word analysis skills
Naming Letters	Nonreader–1	Naming capital and lower-case letters	No	No	Ability to identify letters named and/or to match letters
Visual Memory of Words	3 and below	Recalling words presented visually and locating them in a list of similar words	Yes	Yes	
Hearing Sounds in Words	3 and below	Listening to word pronounced by examiner and finding one that begins with the same sound from three printed choices	No	Yes	Ability to perceive beginning blends and ending sounds
Learning to Hear Sounds in Words	Students who cannot do Hearing Sounds in Words	Learning sounds of letters; identifying them in initial and final positions	No	No	Learning rate
Sounds of Letters	2 and below	Giving sounds for single consonants and blends	No	No	
Learning Rate	Nonreader–1	Learning five words through a sight-word presentation and being tested on them 20 minutes later	No	No	
Visual Memory of Words	4–6	Looking at a word for two to three seconds and then writing it from memory	No	Yes	Strategies for memory
Phonic Spelling	3–6	Writing dictated words exactly as they sound	No	Yes	Patterns of spelling errors
Spelling Test	2–6	Writing dictated spelling words correctly from a graded list	No	Yes	Comparison of phonic and sight spelling
Handwriting	2–6	Copying a sample in one minute	Yes	Yes	Letter formation, size, spacing

Gates-McKillop Reading Diagnostic Tests
(Gates-McKillop)

Arthur Gates and Anne McKillop
Teachers College Press, 1962
Teachers College, Columbia University, 1234 Amsterdam Ave., New York, NY 10027

Purpose	To assess a variety of skills related to reading
Major Areas Tested	Oral reading, word analysis skills, and related reading skills
Age or Grade Range	Grades 1–6
Usually Given By	Classroom teacher Special education teacher Diagnostician trained in reading disabilities
Type of Test	Standardized Individual
Scores Obtained	Grade level
Student Performance Timed?	No
Testing Time	30–40 minutes (depending on number of subtests given)
Scoring/Interpretation Time	15 minutes
Normed On	Not reported
Alternate Forms Available?	Yes

FORMAT

The Gates-McKillop Reading Diagnostic Tests (Gates-McKillop) are a battery of subtests designed to measure the subskills of reading. They are designed to be used with individual students in elementary school and include tasks from the readiness level through such advanced skills as syllabication. Subtests are selected based on the student's reading level and particular reading difficulties.

The materials consist of a reusable booklet that contains the materials to be read by the student; a booklet in which the student and the examiner record responses; and a manual that includes the rationale for the tests, directions for administering and scoring, grade-level scores, and interpretive ratings. The tests are available in two equivalent forms, I and II, for test-retest purposes.

The 17 subtests included in the Gates-McKillop are shown in Table 9. As the table shows, the tests yield two types of scores. Grade scores that may be converted into a rating of high, medium, low, or very low are given for the six gen-

Table 9. Gates–McKillop Subtests

Subtest	Task	Score Obtained
I. Oral Reading	Student reads orally seven paragraphs ranging in difficulty from grades 1 to 6. Errors recorded by the examiner and classified by type. No comprehension questions included.	Grade score
II. Words: Flash Presentation	Tachistoscope presents a graded list of words at half-second intervals. Tests sight recognition of single words.	Grade score
III. Words: Untimed	Presentation of same word list as above but student is given opportunity to use word analysis skills.	Grade score
IV. Phrases: Flash Presentation	Tachistoscope presents two-, three-, and four-word phrases to test sight recognition.	Grade score
V. Knowledge of Word Parts: Word Attack		
V-1. Recognizing and Blending Common Word Parts	Student reads a list of nonsense words made up of common word parts (*stade*, *shemp*, *whast*). If student is unable to read the whole word, the examiner may show how to break it into an initial blend and a common ending and then blend it back together (*wh-ast–whast*).	Interpretive rating
V-2. Letter Sounds	Student is shown printed letter and asked to give its sound.	Interpretive rating
V-3. Naming Capital Letters	Student is shown printed letter and asked to name it.	Interpretive rating
V-4. Naming Lower-Case Letters	Student is shown printed letter and asked to name it.	Interpretive rating
VI. Recognizing the Visual Form (Word Equivalents) of Sounds		
VI-1. Nonsense Words	Student is shown four nonsense words and asked to circle the one pronounced by examiner (*niting*, *temish*, *metisk*, *nettish*).	Interpretive rating
VI-2. Initial Letters	Student is shown five letters and asked to circle initial sound of word pronounced by examiner.	Interpretive rating
VI-3. Final Letters	Student is shown five letters and asked to circle final sound of word pronounced by examiner.	Interpretive rating

Table 9. —*Continued*

Subtest	Task	Score Obtained
VI-4. Vowels	Student is shown five vowels and asked to indicate which one is in a nonsense word pronounced by examiner (*vum, keb, hote, sate*).	Interpretive rating
VII. Auditory Blending	Student listens to word pronounced by examiner, with parts separated by quarter-second intervals; student pronounces whole word (*d-ar-k–dark*).	Interpretive rating
VIII. Supplementary Tests		
VIII-1. Spelling	Words from subtests II and III are presented to the student for oral spelling.	Grade score
VIII-2. Oral Vocabulary	Examiner reads the student a multiple-choice vocabulary question; the student responds orally ("To *flounder* means to: *giggle, fish, struggle, gloat*").	Grade score
VIII-3. Syllabication	Student is asked to read a list of nonsense words (*inmo, stadever, atelary*). The skill being measured is syllable blending.	Interpretive rating
VIII-4. Auditory Discrimination	Examiner pronounces pairs of words, and student identifies them as same or different (*dim-din, weather-wetter*).	Interpretive rating

eral ability tests that assess oral reading, word recognition, spelling, and oral vocabulary. These grade scores allow comparison of each student with others at the same grade level. On the diagnostic tests of specific skills, such as recognition of vowel sounds, interpretation tables facilitate the conversion of raw scores directly into ratings of normal, low, or very low. These ratings allow comparison of the specific subskill with the student's general reading ability, as measured by the Oral Reading subtest.

STRENGTHS OF THE GATES-McKILLOP

• The most obvious advantage of the Gates-McKillop battery is that many critical skills are included. Through thoughtful selection of subtests, the skilled examiner can develop a testing battery appropriate for a beginning reader or a struggling intermediate student. Careful selection of subtests allows every student some successful reading experiences during testing, while the examiner obtains maximum diagnostic information. The variety in the format and the informal tone of the procedures holds the interest of most students.

• Comparison of students' performances on various subtest pairs also yields invaluable diagnostic information. A few examples:

1. Subtests II (Words: Flash Presentation) and III (Words: Untimed) allow the examiner to compare sight-word vocabulary and word analysis skills on words of equivalent difficulty.

2. Subtests V-1 (Recognizing and Blending Common

Word Parts) and VI-1 (Nonsense Words) allow the examiner to compare a student's skills on a visual-to-auditory task with those on an auditory-to-visual task. This yields information on which form of presentation and instruction is more appropriate for the student.

3. Subtests VII (Auditory Blending) and V-1 (Recognizing and Blending Common Word Parts) offer another auditory-visual comparison. Subtest VII assesses the blending task with auditory stimuli, whereas V-1 assesses blending skills with printed words.

This type of diagnostic information can be obtained when the Gates-McKillop is used by a skilled examiner. Other features, such as the checklist of difficulties for the Oral Reading subtest and the discussion of interpretation of test results in the manual, are excellent.

LIMITING FACTORS OF THE GATES-McKILLOP

• No description of the norming sample is given, and no studies of reliability or validity are reported. The lack of these critical pieces of information strongly suggests that the Gates-McKillop should be used as an informal battery to obtain information about a student's skills in a variety of reading tasks. The information is excellent, but the grade scores are of little value.

• The Oral Reading passages are stilted in style and content. No measure of comprehension is included. The examiner should substitute another oral reading test (Gilmore Oral Reading Test, Gray Oral, Spache) or devise

Table 10. A Fifth-Grade Student's Subtest Ratings on the Gates-McKillop

Subtest	Grade Score	Rating
Oral Reading	3.3	Low
Words: Untimed	3.5	Low
Knowledge of Word Parts: Word Attack		
Recognizing and Blending Common Word Parts	3.3–3.6	Very low
Letter Sounds	4.3–4.6	Normal progress
Recognizing the Visual Form of Sounds		
Nonsense Words	4.7–4.9	Normal progress
Auditory Blending	4.0–4.2	Normal progress
Supplementary Tests		
Syllabication	3.0–3.3	Very low

comprehension questions for the Gates-McKillop in order to get some measure of oral reading comprehension.

• The practice of relating all diagnostic tests to the student's oral reading skill is an interesting concept. Table 10 is an example of one beginning fifth-grade student's subtest ratings. This student's scores indicate an oral reading performance one and a half years below grade level. In relation to third-grade oral reading, progress in auditory skills and matching visual forms to an auditory stimulus is normal. Progress on tasks requiring visual blending of letters and syllables, however, is very low, even for a third-grade reading level. Such skills would be the ones for remediation. Although a good concept, this process of comparing subskills with oral reading level is of little value, because the validity and the reliability of the oral reading measure has not been established.

Woodcock Reading Mastery Tests (Woodcock)

Richard W. Woodcock
American Guidance Service, Inc., 1973
Publishers' Bldg., Circle Pines, MN 55014

Purpose	To measure a wide range of reading skills and to provide new types of scores to allow more useful interpretations of a student's reading ability
Major Areas Tested	Reading
Age or Grade Range	Grades K–12
Usually Given By	Classroom teacher Special education teacher Psychologist Paraprofessional
Type of Test	Standardized Individual Criterion-referenced Norm-referenced
Scores Obtained	Grade level Achievement index Percentile Reading range Relative mastery
Student Performance Timed?	No
Testing Time	30–45 minutes
Scoring/Interpretation Time	20–30 minutes
Normed On	5,000 students from various racial and socioeconomic groups and geographical regions
Alternate Forms Available?	Yes

FORMAT

The Woodcock Reading Mastery Tests (Woodcock) are a battery of five individually administered reading subtests for use with students from kindergarten through twelfth grade. The materials include a test manual, an easel kit for presenting the test materials, and the response forms. On the examiner's side of the easel kit, the test items are presented with directions for administration. Simultaneously, the student sees the test items on the other side of the easel kit. The items require verbal responses to open-ended questions. Multiple-choice and yes-or-no items are not included.

The five subtests are:

1. *Letter Identification.* The 45 items of this subtest assess the student's ability to name letters of the alphabet. A variety of common letter forms in upper and lower case, manuscript and cursive, are presented.

2. *Word Identification.* The student reads aloud 150 words ranging in difficulty from preprimer to twelfth-grade level (for example, *the, go, and; facetious, beatitude, picayune*).

3. *Word Attack.* The 50 items included here assess the student's ability to pronounce nonsense words (like *dee, lat, idpan, depnonlel*) using phonic and structural-analysis skills.

4. *Word Comprehension.* The subtest contains 70 items that test knowledge of word meaning using an analogy format. The student reads three words silently and then tells the examiner a word to complete the analogy (for example, *bird-fly, fish-_____*).

5. *Passage Comprehension.* This subtest includes 85 items selected to assess reading comprehension using a cloze format. The student reads the one- or two-sentence passage and fills in the blank with an appropriate word. For example:

"Be sure to read all the signs. We don't want to _____ lost," said Mother.

Whizz! The ball slammed into the hornet's nest. Debby could _____ the wild angry buzzing.

The Woodcock is constructed so that students are tested only on those items within their operating range. The operating range is assumed to extend from a basal level marked by five consecutive correct responses to a ceiling level of five consecutive incorrect responses. On two subtests, Letter Identification and Word Attack, all students begin at the first item. For the other three subtests, a starting-point table based on estimated reading grade level is provided.

Forms A and B are equivalent and may be used for test-retest purposes. The manual suggests that both forms be given to the same student to obtain a more reliable score.

The Woodcock tests were designed as both criterion-referenced and norm-referenced tests. The tests yield a variety of scores, including relative mastery scores, grade-level scores, a reading range, an achievement index, and percentile ranks. The concept underlying the Woodcock's construction is the mastery score. Based on the equal-interval mastery scale, it allows the examiner to predict a student's performance on grade-level tasks. It makes possible such statements as "John can be expected to perform with 50 percent accuracy on word recognition tests performed with 90 percent accuracy by average students at his grade level." These relative mastery scores are then translated into percentile ranks, which are readily understandable by teachers and parents.

The Woodcock provides a mastery profile, on which the student's performance on each subtest is graphically displayed. An instructional range for each subtest is plotted. Figure 9 is an example of the interpretation page, completed for a seventh-grade boy.

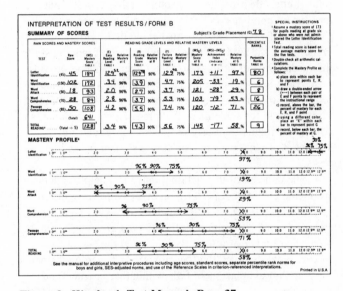

Figure 9. Woodcock Test Manual, Page 37

Modified norms are available for students performing above grade level 12.9 and below 1.0. Adjusted norms are also available for populations with differing socioeconomic status. Separate percentile ranks for boys and girls, means for converting mastery scores into age-equivalent scores, and procedures for converting percentile ranks into standard scores and stanines are available in the manual.

STRENGTHS OF THE WOODCOCK

• The Woodcock is a valuable addition to the field of individual oral reading tests. The five subtests present a wide variety of reading tasks over a wide age range. The easel kit format is easy to use and generally less formidable to the student. The suggested starting points, basal and ceiling procedures, and variety of tasks allow the examiner to move quickly and to hold the interest of the student.

• Test instructions are clear, and the test manual is unusually complete and well organized.

• Several of the subtests of the Woodcock are unique in the tasks they present. Letter Recognition provides a measure of form constancy, or the recognition of many types of print, which may provide some interesting information on beginning readers. The Word Comprehension subtest assesses verbal analogy skills in reading and gives the teacher an understanding of the language functioning of the student. The cloze procedure used on Passage Comprehension is a well-established technique for assessing comprehension of reading in the content areas, but before the Woodcock, it was available only on informal tests.

• The most important contribution of the Woodcock is its concept of relative mastery. Teachers have long recognized that different types of reading skills develop at different rates. Letter identification is acquired fairly rapidly, but passage comprehension begins later and develops gradually over several years. Teachers also know that, within a given grade level, the students have a wide range of reading skills; this wide range of skills is normal. Other tests that provide only grade-level scores may make a student's performance look very low or very high when actually it falls within the normal range for students of that grade level. Woodcock's concept of relative mastery provides a more realistic statement of what we can expect of a student in reading tasks.

• The concept of instructional range is a helpful one as well. Students do not perform on every word recognition task at a specific grade level, such as 3.2. They have a range of word recognition skills and on a given task may be somewhat higher or lower. By looking at the student's instructional range on the five subtests and seeing whether the actual grade placement falls within that instructional range, the examiner can make decisions about whether the student's reading program can be provided in the regular classroom.

• Extensive reliability data are included for each subtest and for the test as a whole. Split-half reliability and alternate form reliability, as well as standard error of measurement, are all provided. Several validity studies are also reported in the manual. For a relatively new test, the Woodcock has good reliability and validity data.

LIMITING FACTORS OF THE WOODCOCK

• The test construction and the concepts underlying the Woodcock are unfamiliar to most diagnosticians and teachers. Examiners need to administer the test to several students at various grade levels and to study the manual very carefully before they can feel confident about their interpretation of test scores.

• Because of the unique format of such subtests as Word Comprehension and Passage Comprehension, examiners must be cautious in generalizing scores on these subtests to all reading comprehension tasks. A student may have difficulty with the process of verbal analogies or the cloze procedure and not necessarily have difficulty with other kinds of reading comprehension. Supplementing the Woodcock with another reading comprehension test, such as the Gates-MacGinitie (p. 49) is advisable for students with low scores.

• The Word Comprehension and Passage Comprehension tasks are unusual in format and often difficult initially for students to understand. It is usually necessary to go back several items below the recommended starting point before a basal level is achieved. Because of the uniqueness of the tasks, students tend to read aloud, although the directions are to read silently. Although oral reading gives a great deal of diagnostic information about the student's performance, the student should be encouraged to read silently, because that is how the norms were obtained.

• The order of items in the Word Comprehension and Passage Comprehension subtests is questionable, because it seems difficult to obtain basal and ceiling levels.

Gates-MacGinitie Silent Reading Tests
(Gates-MacGinitie Tests)

Arthur Gates and Walter MacGinitie
Teachers College Press, first edition 1965
Teachers College, Columbia University, 1234 Amsterdam Ave., New York, NY 10027

The Riverside Publishing Co., second edition 1978
1919 S. Highland Ave., Lombard, IL 60148

Purpose	To measure silent reading skills
Major Areas Tested	Silent reading vocabulary and comprehension
Age or Grade Range	Grades 1–12
Usually Given By	Classroom teacher Special education teacher
Type of Test	Standardized Group
Scores Obtained	Grade level Standard Percentile
Student Performance Timed?	Yes
Testing Time	50–60 minutes
Scoring/Interpretation Time	15 minutes
Normed On	40,000 students of various educational and socioeconomic levels in 38 communities, varying in size and geographic location, throughout the United States
Alternate Forms Available?	Yes

FORMAT

The first edition of the Gates-MacGinitie Silent Reading Tests (Gates-MacGinitie Tests) is a series of multiple-choice, pencil-and-paper tests designed for group administration. Eight levels of tests are available, each with two or three forms for test-retest purposes. The available tests are:

1. *Readiness Skills*. Eight subtests for the end of kindergarten and beginning of grade 1.
2. *Primary A*. Vocabulary and Comprehension subtests for grade 1, Forms 1 and 2.
3. *Primary B*. Vocabulary and Comprehension subtests for grade 2, Forms 1 and 2.
4. *Primary C*. Vocabulary and Comprehension subtests for grade 3, Forms 1 and 2.
5. *Primary CS*. Speed and Accuracy subtests for grades 2 and 3, Forms 1, 2, and 3.
6. *Survey D*. Speed, Vocabulary, and Comprehension subtests for grades 4 through 6, Forms 1, 2, and 3 (Forms 1M, 2M, and 3M for machine scoring).
7. *Survey E*. Speed, Vocabulary, and Comprehension subtests for grades 7 through 9, Forms 1, 2, and 3 (Forms 1M, 2M, and 3M for machine scoring).
8. *Survey F*. Speed, Vocabulary, and Comprehension subtests for grades 10 through 12, Forms 1 and 2 (Forms 1M and 2M for machine scoring).

The test materials consist of a teacher's manual for each level of the test, separate test booklets for the students for each grade level and form, and three technical manuals: one for Readiness Skills, one for Primary A through Survey E, and one for Survey F. The teacher's manuals describe the tests and give directions for administration and scoring. Tables of standard scores, grade-level scores, and percentile scores are also in the teacher's manuals. More technical information about the construction and standardization of the tests, as well as interpretation, is available in the technical manuals.

Because of their different purpose and content, the Readiness Skills subtests are not reviewed here. The other levels of the Gates-MacGinitie Tests measure three basic silent reading skills: vocabulary, comprehension, and rate of reading. The Vocabulary subtests assess a student's ability to recognize and comprehend single words in isolation. At the primary levels, the student selects a word to match a picture (see Figure 10). In the Survey tests, the student selects one of five words that has the same meaning as the key word (see Figure 11). The Comprehension subtests assess the student's ability to read and understand complete sentences and short paragraphs (see Figures 12, 13, and 14). The Speed and Accuracy subtests are considered supplementary tests and should be given when more information on a student's rate of reading is desired. The students read short paragraphs of uniform difficulty, so that

speed of reading is the primary factor being measured. Time limits are imposed on the Vocabulary and Comprehension subtests for ease in group administration, but the limits are very liberal and present no serious constraints for most students.

Figure 10. Gates-MacGinitie Vocabulary, Primary A, Form 1

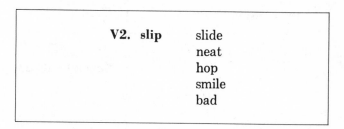

Figure 11. Gates-MacGinitie Vocabulary, Survey D, Form 1

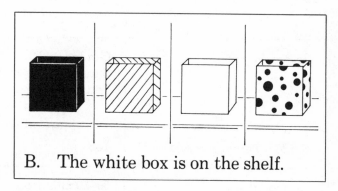

Figure 12. Gates-MacGinitie Comprehension, Primary A, Form 1

STRENGTHS OF THE GATES-MacGINITIE TESTS

• The Gates-MacGinitie Tests are well known and well normed. Because they are group tests, they are very appropriate for screening purposes, to determine which students are in need of more diagnostic testing.

• Their wide age range and alternate forms make the Gates-MacGinitie Tests excellent for test-retest procedures, to determine the progress an individual student has made in a remedial reading program. Many school districts use them routinely, fall and spring, to evaluate pupil progress in special and regular education programs. Each subtest is scored independently, so a student may be given one or all of the three test parts.

• The teachers' manuals and technical supplements are well prepared and easy to use.

Last year, for his seventh birthday, Eddie had a party at home. On his birthday this year, Eddie's father is taking him and his friend Bill to the circus.

A. Who will go with Eddie and his father?

his mother   Bill   Sally   an uncle

B. Eddie is going to the circus on

Friday   his vacation   his birthday   Hallowe'en

Figure 13. Gates-MacGinitie Comprehension, Primary C, Form 1

We have a playroom in our ___C1___. It is down in the basement, so we need to turn on an electric ___C2___ even on sunny days.

C1. stove   house   bed   car   lake

C2. storm   friend   ladder   room   light

Figure 14. Gates-MacGinitie Comprehension, Survey D, Form 1

LIMITING FACTORS OF THE GATES-MacGINITIE TESTS

• The Gates-MacGinitie Tests measure silent reading skills, a critical area of reading competence. In any silent reading test, analysis of errors is difficult. For example, in the Vocabulary subtest, the item shown in Figure 11 offers *slide, neat, hop, smile,* and *bad* as possible synonyms for *slip.* If the student marks *hop* as the word closest in meaning to *slip,* the examiner does not know which of the following occurred: (1) the student could not read the word *slip;* (2) the student could not read the word *slide;* (3) the student did not know the meaning of the word *slip;* or (4) the student did not know the meaning of the word *slide.* Because analysis of errors on group silent reading tests is difficult, low-scoring students should be administered individual tests such as the Spache (p. 36) or the Gates-McKillop (p. 42) to

determine more specifically the nature of their reading difficulties.

• The Comprehension sections of the Gates-MacGinitie Tests have two other important weaknesses. First, they rely on a student's vocabulary and general knowledge of facts not present in the paragraph itself. Second, they measure a very low level of comprehension. They do not assess the reader's ability to interrelate information and draw conclusions. Particularly in older students, the comprehension skills that are not measured may be crucial for classroom success.

• It is also important to remember that students being instructed in a specific phonic or linguistic reading program may not show significant gains on the Gates-MacGinitie Tests until they have mastered a basic sight-word vocabulary. Teachers of primary students need to be aware of this aspect of standardized testing and to develop supplementary informal tests on which their students can demonstrate their progress.

CHANGES IN THE SECOND EDITION

• Speed and accuracy tests are not included.

• Two tests levels are available for first grade.

• Norms are provided for students above and below test level; that is, norms for first and third graders taking the second-grade test.

• Careful attention has been given to content. Minority-, culturally-, and sex-biased items have been avoided.

• A Decoding Skills Analysis form has been included to improve the diagnostic use of the test.

Durrell Listening-Reading Series (DLRS)

Donald D. Durrell and Mary B. Brassard
Harcourt Brace Jovanovich, Inc., 1970
757 Third Ave., New York, NY 10017

Purpose	To compare an individual student's ability in listening comprehension and reading comprehension, to identify students with reading disability, and to measure the degree of difference between reading disability and listening disability
Major Areas Tested	Reading and listening comprehension
Age or Grade Range	Grades 1–9
Usually Given By	Classroom teacher Special education teacher
Type of Test	Standardized Group
Scores Obtained	Age level Grade level Percentile Stanine
Student Performance Timed?	Yes
Testing Time	1½ hours
Scoring/Interpretation Time	20–30 minutes
Normed On	22,247 students in 29 school districts throughout the United States; geographical region and socioeconomic status in proportion to the 1960 census figures
Alternate Forms Available?	Yes

FORMAT

The Durrell Listening-Reading Series (DLRS) consists of listening and reading tests at three levels: primary (grades 1 to 3.5), intermediate (grades 3.5 to 6), and advanced (grades 7 to 9). Alternate Forms DE and EF are available at each level. A machine-scorable edition can also be purchased. The materials consist of a manual and individual pupil booklets for each level, as well as scoring stencils for the hand-scorable editions and answer folders for the machine-scorable editions. The manuals contain detailed instructions for test administration and information on test design, statistical data, and interpretation of results.

The unique feature of the DLRS is the test design. At each level the test consists of parallel subtests of listening and reading comprehension. The four subtests are:

1. *Vocabulary Listening.* Students listen to a word pronounced by the examiner and assign it to a category previously introduced and illustrated at the top of the page. For example, students assign *canal* to one of three categories labeled *Water, From Trees,* or *Fanciful People* by marking a box under *Water* (a word and a picture). For *abundant,* students must select among *World, Thought, Enough,* and *Sad.* Three category choices are provided at the primary level, four at the intermediate level, and five at the advanced level.

2. *Vocabulary Reading.* This is a parallel test in which students read the words and assign them to the categories that are illustrated at the top of the page.

3. *Sentence or Paragraph Listening.* This subtest varies with the test level. At the primary level, the student listens to the sentence and assigns it to one of the three illustrated categories; that is, for *Winnie the weasel took out his gold watch,* the student marks the box under *Imaginary.* At the intermediate level, the student listens to a paragraph about two people, animals, or concepts—such as beavers and otters. Eight statements are then read to the student, who marks a box under *True Only Of* (otters), *True Only Of* (beavers), *True of Both,* or *Answer Not Given.* At the advanced level, the student listens to a paragraph and identifies the five statements as *True, False,* or *Not Given.* The sixth statement requires a multiple-choice answer, such as "According to this paragraph, *unicorn* is the name of a (a) decorative plant, (b) fabulous animal, (c) fragrant flower, (d) useless weed."

4. *Sentence or Paragraph Reading.* This is a parallel test in which students read the sentences or paragraphs and assign them to the categories.

Nine scores can be obtained on the DLRS, as shown in Table 11. Grade-equivalent scores are provided for potential, actual, and differential scores. Age-equivalent scores, stanines, and percentiles are provided for the potential and actual scores, in the appendix of the manual.

Table 11. DLRS Scores

1. Vocabulary Listening	
2. Sentence or Paragraph Listening	Potential Reading Scores
3. Total Listening (total of 1 and 2)	
4. Vocabulary Reading	
5. Sentence or Paragraph Reading	Actual Reading Scores
6. Total Reading (total of 3 and 4)	
7. Potential minus Actual Vocabulary (1 less 4)	
8. Potential minus Actual Sentences or Paragraphs (2 less 5)	Differential Scores
9. Potential minus Actual Total (3 less 6)	

The DLRS is designed as a group test and can be administered to class-sized groups. Time limits are provided to facilitate group administration, but they are generous and do not serve as constraints for most students. The authors recommend that the vocabulary and sentence subtests be given in separate testing sessions (on the same day, if necessary) and that a time interval of two to seven days be allowed between the listening and reading sections.

STRENGTHS OF THE DLRS

• The unique format of the DLRS, with its parallel subtests, allows a direct comparison of listening and reading comprehension within an individual student on a raw score or grade-equivalent basis. This is important diagnostic information for planning programs for students with reading disabilities, suspected or known language deficits, bilingualism, or cultural differences. For example, if a student reading three years below grade level can demonstrate average listening comprehension skills, placing him or her in a regular classroom for discussion subjects becomes a possibility.

• The manual is clearly written, with explicit directions for administration and scoring.

• The content of the listening and reading tests was carefully selected to be representative of the categories in *Roget's Thesaurus* as well as to reflect the frequency counts of words used in instructional materials at each grade level. Therefore, the tests reflect the language used in classroom instruction.

• Extensive reliability and validity data is reported in the manual. The broad standardization sample, the careful item selection, and adequate reliability data make the DLRS one of the more thoughtfully constructed tests available in the language arts. Standard errors of measurement are provided for the potential and actual scores but not for the differential scores.

LIMITING FACTORS OF THE DLRS

• Interpretation of scores on the DLRS is very confusing, for two reasons. First, the DLRS authors have based their test design on the assumption that listening comprehension is the best single predictor of reading potential. This assumption is open to question; clearly, in students with significant language disorders such as aphasia, reading skills often surpass listening skills at an early age. The same discrepancy is frequently found in students with auditory learning disorders. In the authors' own research, reported in the manual, the sentence and paragraph reading skills of regular classroom students reached the level of their listening skills by sixth grade and surpassed them by ninth grade. This demonstrates that listening skills are not a measure of reading potential at the upper levels of the DLRS. Faced with the fact that actual reading scores were higher than potential reading scores, the authors redefined *potential,* stating that ''Potential Reading Grade Equivalent indicates the reading level at which a child can understand spoken language—it does *not* represent the level at which a pupil *should be* reading, nor does it set an upper limit for reading ability'' (Primary Manual, p. 16). This gives a very different meaning to the term *potential* and makes interpretation of scores confusing. The real meaning of the differential score is unclear.

Second, the DLRS is a well-researched series of tests with a good-sized standardization population. Because the reading and listening tests are equal in statistical difficulty and content, the potential reading grade-equivalent score is the reading score students would obtain if they could read as well as they can listen. It does not represent their grade-equivalent scores on the listening test alone; that information is available in the appendix of the manual. Although this point is made clearly in the manual, it is very easy to become confused and to interpret scores on the Vocabulary Listening and Sentence or Paragraph Listening subtests as listening comprehension scores. This can be done only by using the supplementary tables in the manual's appendix.

• A minor but interesting point is that the score box does not provide a place for recording the differential score. The whole purpose of the DLRS is to allow a comparison between listening and reading, so the differential score would seem critical. It is also important to note that, although standard errors of measurement are provided for the potential and actual scores, none are provided for the differential scores. This is another reason for interpreting differential scores with great caution.

• The construct validity of the DLRS is very good. However, concurrent validity through correlations with other tests is weak. In particular, the concept of potential reading ability as measured by listening skills needs verification.

• The type of response used on the DLRS may affect some students' listening comprehension scores. The student is asked to listen to a series of words or statements and assign them to the correct category. At the primary and intermediate levels, the categories are illustrated to help the student with reading disability. Some of these categories are easily illustrated:

Category	Illustration
Buildings	Picture of house (Primary, Vocabulary G)
In space	Earth and planet (Primary, Sentence A)

Other illustrations, however, can be very ambiguous for the student who cannot read the category name:

Category	Illustration
Changes	Butterfly (Primary, Sentence C)
Tell	Radio announcer (Intermediate, Vocabulary IV)
Soften	Melting butter (Intermediate, Vocabulary VIII)

By the intermediate level, when a student must recall 4 category names to classify 12 vocabulary words, these ambiguous illustrations can create a problem. If the student fails to understand even one response category, because it is used several times, his or her score will be affected.

In contrast to the problem of ambiguous pictures, on the intermediate paragraph listening test and both listening tests at the advanced level, no illustrations of category headings are provided. This means that a seventh-grade student with poor reading skills must be able to recall the category names *Before, Rest, Complete, Cunning,* and *Sway* to classify 20 vocabulary items, whereas the good reader can refer back to the printed word. This is a serious problem if the listening comprehension score is to be used as an estimate of reading potential. Interestingly, the authors stress in the primary manual that the examiner should make sure the category headings are understood. These directions are omitted from the intermediate and advanced manuals.

• At the intermediate and advanced levels, the DLRS requires several types of comprehension: simple factual recall, categorization, inference, and other types of interpretation. The test would be strengthened if the authors had provided a scoring key that analyzed the student's responses to each type of comprehension question.

Spelling and Written Language Tests

Larsen-Hammill Test of Written Spelling (TWS)

Stephen Larsen and Donald Hammill
Academic Therapy Publications, 1976
1539 Fourth St., San Rafael, CA 94901

Purpose	To provide an adequately standardized, reliable, and valid measure of written spelling
Major Areas Tested	Written spelling
Age or Grade Range	5–15 years
Usually Given By	Classroom teacher Special education teacher
Type of Test	Standardized Individual Group
Scores Obtained	Age level Grade level Spelling quotient
Student Performance Timed?	No
Testing Time	15–20 minutes
Scoring/Interpretation Time	10 minutes
Normed On	A random sample of 4,544 children in 22 states
Alternate Forms Available?	No

FORMAT

The Larsen-Hammill Test of Written Spelling (TWS) materials consists of a teacher's manual and a set of individual forms on which the students write the dictated words. The student forms are not necessary; ordinary notebook paper may be used.

The TWS includes two subtests or lists of spelling words. The first list includes 35 Predictable Words—words that follow basic spelling rules; the second list contains 25 Unpredictable Words—words that essentially have to be memorized. For example:

Predictable Words	Unpredictable Words
dog	music
trip	sure
spend	fountain
hardly	awful
tardy	collar
district	campaign

The examiner pronounces each word, uses it in a sentence, and pronounces it again. The student writes each word.

The same word lists are used with students at all grade levels. All students begin with the first word, and the testing is discontinued when the student misspells five consecutive words on each of the two word lists.

In addition to raw scores, the TWS yields three scores on each subtest. The spelling age score allows a comparison with other students of the same age; the grade-equivalent score allows a comparison with other students of the same grade. The spelling quotient is calculated by the following formula:

$$\text{Spelling quotient (SQ)} = \frac{\text{Spelling age (SA)} \times 100}{\text{Chronological age (CA)}}$$

STRENGTHS OF THE TWS

- The TWS is a well-constructed, well-normed test.

Good reliability and validity studies are reported. Information on item validity and percentage of difficulty for each of the 60 spelling words is presented.

- Dividing the words into two types allows the classroom teacher to plan an appropriate individualized spelling program. For example, two beginning fourth-grade students might receive the scores shown in Table 12. As the table shows, Student A has significantly more difficulty with unpredictable words than with predictable words and needs a spelling program that focuses on techniques for memorizing sight words. Student B is having difficulty with rule-based words as well and needs a systematic approach to this type of spelling.

- The teacher's manual contains clearly written instructions for administration and scoring and a description of the theoretical basis for the test. Reliability and validity data and some guidelines for interpretation are also included.

- The first 10 or 12 words on the Predictable Word list are generally familiar to all students past the first grade and allow even the very weak speller to experience success.

LIMITING FACTORS OF THE TWS

- The first few words on the Unpredictable Word list are much more difficult than those on the Predictable Word list, not only because they are not rule-based, but also because they are less familiar. For example:

Predictable Words	Unpredictable Words
up	myself
that	people
it	knew
bed	uncle
dog	music

If the authors wished to provide a comparison of the student's skills on predictable versus unpredictable words,

Table 12. Two Fourth Graders' Scores on the TWS

	Predictable Words	Unpredictable Words	Total Test
Student A			
Age score	10.1	8.7	9.4
Grade score	4.6	3.3	3.9
Spelling quotient	98.0	83.0	91.0
Student B			
Age score	8.11	8.1	8.8
Grade score	3.3	2.7	3.2
Spelling quotient	87.0	79.0	84.0

they should have selected words of equal familiarity.

• The Unpredictable Word list is too difficult for first-, second-, and third-grade students. Because the unique feature of this test is a comparison of the student's skills with both types of words, the test is most effectively used with fourth-grade or older students.

• The spelling quotient score has little meaning. The spelling age and grade-equivalent scores allow a comparison between each student and others of the same age and grade. Deriving a spelling quotient (similar to an intelligence quotient) adds little information.

Diagnostic Word Patterns (Buckley Tests)

Evelyn Buckley
Educators Publishing Service, Inc., 1978
75 Moulton St., Cambridge, MA 02138

Purpose	To provide a quick assessment of basic sound-symbol associations in spelling and reading, to identify students in need of further testing, and to lead directly to planning remedial programs
Major Areas Tested	Written spelling and word recognition
Age or Grade Range	Grade 2–college
Usually Given By	Classroom teacher Special education teacher Paraprofessional
Type of Test	Informal Individual Group Criterion-referenced
Scores Obtained	None (guidelines for evaluating test performance)
Student Performance Timed?	No
Testing Time	15–20 minutes
Scoring/Interpretation Time	15–20 minutes
Normed On	Not normed
Alternate Forms Available?	No

FORMAT

The Diagnostic Word Patterns (Buckley Tests) contain three spelling tests of 100 words each. Each test can be given as a spelling or oral word recognition test. The materials consist of a teacher's manual, individual student charts for each test, and cards for the word recognition tests. The manual contains detailed instructions for administration and scoring as well as the word lists for each test.

Each of the three spelling tests includes 100 words, 10 words from each of 10 common spelling patterns. The three reading tests use the same word lists.

Spelling Test 1 includes the following patterns and examples:

Short vowels: cvc pattern (consonant, vowel, consonant)—*pat*
cvcc—*tint*
ccvc—*prod*
ccvcc—*stunt*
k and *ck* endings—*risk, dock*
sh, ch, wh, th—*shed, check, whip, thug*
Adding *ed*—*lasted*
ch and *tch* endings—*pinch, notch*
ng and *nk* endings—*flung, rink*
Nonphonetic words—*are, gone, said*

Spelling Test 2 includes the following patterns and examples:

Long vowels: vce pattern (vowel, consonant, *e*)—*tile, stone*
ai and *ay*—*clay, faint*
oa and *ow*—*roast, blow*
ee and *ea*—*beach, speed*
ie and *igh*—*died, tight*
ou and *ow*—*trout, growl*
aw and *au*—*straw, fault*
er, ir, ur—*stern, swirl, church*

$\overline{oo}$ and $\breve{oo}$—*shoot, brook*
Nonphonetic words—*again, only, goes*

Spelling Test 3 includes the following patterns and examples:

e and *ea*—*etch, head*
oy and *oi*—*toy, coil*
Suffixes—*sadly, helpless*
Double consonant before suffix—*winner, wedding*
ar and *or*—*carbon, sport*
tion and *sion*—*tension, invention*
Silent *e* plus ending—*famous, smiling*
Compound words—*backlog, flagship*
Two-syllable words—*transcript, kindling*
Nonphonetic words—*enough, laugh*

The teacher dictates the first spelling list to an individual student or group of students. Usually only 20 or 30 of the words are dictated, because an error pattern quickly emerges. The teacher then records the student's errors on an individual chart (see Figure 15).

By studying the individual error pattern, gaps in knowledge of sound-symbol association can easily be determined. Students who know most or all of the spelling patterns in Test 1 are given Test 2, and so on.

The three word recognition tests are administered by having the individual student read aloud each word as the examiner records errors on the student's chart. The same word list is used as in the three spelling tests. The author recommends that the word recognition tests be given to students with serious spelling problems; that is, to those who misspell 40 to 50 percent of the words. In this way a comparison can be made between the student's visual (reading) and auditory (spelling) skills.

In addition to the instructions for administration and scoring, the manual provides an evaluation procedure and samples of test evaluations.

Individual Student Chart
Diagnostic Word Patterns Test 1

Name _____ Date _____ School _____ Grade _____

Categories

1. v —	mat	peg *pig*	but *bute*	tip *tipe*	bog
2. v — —	sent	damp	must *mast*	lost	lint

Figure 15. Buckley Tests, Individual Student Chart

STRENGTHS OF THE BUCKLEY TESTS

• The Buckley Tests are very new. They provide a means for quickly assessing a student's or classroom group's knowledge of sound-symbol associations. Although the selected spelling patterns follow the sequence outlined by Orton (1937) and Gillingham and Stillman (1965), they are common patterns that apply to many reading methods and materials. The organization of the individual student chart simplifies the analysis of errors and leads the teacher directly toward planning individualized spelling and reading programs for single students or small groups.

• The tests are quick, inexpensive, and easily administered by teachers or paraprofessionals. The individual student charts provide an easy and effective means of determining instructional objectives and charting pupil progress. The first 50 words of each test can be given as a diagnostic test, and the second 50 words as a posttest.

• In addition to targeting skills that an individual student needs to be taught, the test can serve as a screening instrument. Students who do very poorly on both the spelling and reading tests should be given further educational assessment.

LIMITING FACTORS OF THE BUCKLEY TESTS

• The Buckley Tests are criterion-referenced and survey the sequence of skills taught in the Orton-Gillingham curriculum. For students taught reading by other methods, the progression from Test 1 to Test 2 to Test 3 may not be accurate. For example, long vowels (Test 2) may be taught before blends and endings (Test 1), or compound words (Test 3) before vowel digraphs (Test 2). However, because the Buckley Tests are informal, the teacher may simply administer all three tests or reorder the items according to curriculum needs. Suggestions for doing this are given in the manual.

• The nonphonetic or sight-word sections of the spelling tests are a minimal measure of visual recall for spelling. The 10 words on each test serve to indicate which students have good phonics skills and poor sight recall but are not extensive enough to lead to instructional programs in that area.

• The Buckley Tests are so new to the field that it is not possible to determine whether they will be useful with students of wide age ranges and educational experience. But as a criterion-referenced measure of sequential phonic skills in spelling, they look promising.

Myklebust Picture Story Language Test (PSLT)

Helmer R. Myklebust
Grune & Stratton, Inc., 1965
111 Fifth Ave., New York, NY 10003

Purpose	To assess various written language skills
Major Areas Tested	Written language
Age or Grade Range	7–17 years
Usually Given By	Special education teacher Speech/language clinician
Type of Test	Standardized Individual Group
Scores Obtained	Age level Percentile Stanine
Student Performance Timed?	No
Testing Time	20–30 minutes
Scoring/Interpretation Time	20–30 minutes
Normed On	Metropolitan, rural, and suburban school populations in one midwestern state
Alternate Forms Available?	No

FORMAT

The Myklebust Picture Story Language Test (PSLT) is a test of written language most often administered individually, but it can be given to groups ranging in size from 8 to 10 students. More than 10 students may be tested simultaneously if additional test pictures are available. The test picture is a black-and-white photograph, 10½ by 13½ inches, that shows a young boy playing with dollhouse figures (see photo).

Other materials needed to administer the PSLT include the test manual and the printed record forms used for scoring. The manual is a clothbound book *(Development and Disorders of Written Language, Volume One)* containing administration and scoring procedures, as well as chapters discussing the author's ideas about the development of written language skills.

The examiner must supply the type of writing paper and pencils that the students are familiar with. Standard-sized writing paper is suggested, because it affords the same potential story length for all students.

Administration of the PSLT requires simple oral directions. The examiner holds up the picture so that all can see and says, ''Look at this picture carefully.'' The examiner waits 20 seconds and says, ''You are to write a story about it. You may look at it as much and as often as you care to. Be sure to write the best story you can. Begin writing whenever you are ready.''

The picture is then placed in a central position, where it can be viewed by all students. It is permissible for a student to pick up the picture for close inspection. It should be replaced in a central position after the student finishes examining it.

Questions are answered neutrally. For example, a student might ask, ''Should I write about how the boy is dressed?'' A typical reply would be, ''If you want to. Write the story the way you think is best.'' The examiner may encourage

PSLT Stimulus Picture

students to write something if they are having difficulty thinking of a story but must refrain from offering any suggestions that might influence the content of the story.

The PSLT is not timed; the students continue to write until they have completed their story. Alternate, equivalent forms for test-retest purposes are not available.

STRENGTHS OF THE PSLT

• Tests measuring written expression are virtually nonexistent. The PSLT then, being the first of its kind, is a landmark test.

• The PSLT is easy to administer and requires no special training. The wide age range makes it a particularly good instrument for measuring the progress of a student's writing skills in relation to age. Separate norms are provided for boys and girls, reflecting sex differences in the development of written language at different age levels. Provision has been made for converting the raw scores into age and percentile equivalents and stanine ranks.

• Three attributes of language usage are evaluated by the PSLT. Scores are provided for the following scales: *Productivity* measures the length of the expression and includes counts of total words, total sentences, and words per sentence; *Syntax* measures the correctness of what is expressed and includes accuracy of word usage, of word endings, and of punctuation (errors of additions, omissions, substitutions, and word order are counted); *Abstract-Concrete* measures the meaning of the ideas being expressed on a continuum ranging from concrete to abstract. Norms for each of these measures were established developmentally for both boys and girls.

• The three aspects of language that are measured are useful because they make it possible to obtain a profile of a student's strengths and weaknesses in written language. For example, one student may write a story deficient in syntax but highly imaginative and abstract. Another student may write a syntactically correct story that is limited in ideation, tending toward the concrete. In planning a writing program, the teacher would study the student's performance on each of the three scales.

• Another diagnostic use of the PSLT is to compare the student's facility with the spoken and the written word. Initially the test may be administered by having the student tell a story about the picture. The next day the student is asked to write a story. Although the PSLT has not been standardized for spoken language, the findings from an oral test may be significant for remediation.

• The manual includes scored stories (illustrating normal and handicapped children), which are particularly helpful for the examiner who is learning how to score and interpret the PSLT. It will often be necessary to refer to these sample stories for comparison.

• The PSLT answers a critical need for a test of written language. In addition, volume 2 of *Development and Disorders of Written Language: Studies of Normal and Exceptional Children* (Myklebust, 1973) includes further analyses of the PSLT results for normal students and comparative findings for exceptional students—learning disabled, mentally retarded, socially and/or emotionally disturbed, speech handicapped, and reading disabled.

LIMITING FACTORS OF THE PSLT

• The norming procedures described in the test manual are inadequate. The sample came from only one midwestern state, and as yet there is no information available on geographic differences in written language development.

The author claims that a wide range of socioeconomic levels and cultural backgrounds were included in the standardization sample. However, data regarding the racial breakdown or number of minority students included in the study are lacking. Caution should be the rule when using the PSLT norms with students from different cultural backgrounds.

• Another consideration concerning standardization is that only odd ages from 7 to 17 were sampled. The author interpolates scores for ages not tested. This is a questionable practice, especially because the standard deviations for the sampled ages are quite large.

• The author makes the statement that the PSLT appears to be a valid test but offers no evidence to support this assumption. No attempt was made to evaluate the face validity of the test. How motivating, for example, is the test picture in comparison with other pictures that might have been used?

• The author states that the test-retest reliability coefficients were statistically significant but does not report the data. The coefficients for the syntax scale seem to indicate that there is not sufficient interscorer reliability, especially with untrained examiners. This should be noted in the information on test administration.

• Scoring the PSLT is a time-consuming, tedious job that requires a highly skilled clinician. Training in the use of the syntax scale is essential for its correct use. Scoring is also not entirely objective. Judgment of the level of abstraction of the stories in relation to criteria given in the manual is very subjective. Even after carefully studying each criterion and the illustrative examples, it is still difficult in many cases to determine the appropriate level.

• Principles for scoring the syntax scale pose some concern. The scale was designed to measure accuracy of usage only. Thus the student who writes productively or who attempts to use more complex sentence constructions has a higher probability of making more errors and receiving a lower syntax score than the student who writes simply

(subject-verb sentences), using a limited range of
punctuation marks. Consider the samples below, both
written by 8-year-old boys.

Story A: *This is a picture of a boy playing with dollhouse
people. He is having fun.*

Story B: *A young boy Jimmy is playing with some dolls
his brother in law gave him. He said, "I like my new toys."
After an hour or so he went to lunch and said to his brother,
what a fun day this is.*

Story A contains no errors of syntax and would receive a
high score. Story B has several scorable errors (comma,
hyphen, and quotation mark omissions) and would receive
a lower syntax score. This seems misleading. The second
student tried to use a variety of punctuation marks, mastery
of which he has not yet achieved. Hence the scoring procedures actually penalize, unfairly, the student who attempts to write complex structures requiring a wider range
of punctuation marks. Perhaps criterion-referenced evaluation, designed to discriminate between mastery and
nonmastery of specific objectives, would be more meaningful than the traditional norm-referenced evaluation in
the assessment of written language skills.

Mathematics Test

KeyMath Diagnostic Arithmetic Test   68

KeyMath Diagnostic Arithmetic Test (KeyMath)

Austin J. Connolly, William Nachtman, and E. Milo Pritchett
American Guidance Service, Inc., 1971
Publishers' Bldg., Circle Pines, MN 55014

Purpose	To assess mathematic skills
Major Areas Tested	Mathematics
Age or Grade Range	Preschool–grade 6
Usually Given By	Classroom teacher Special education teacher Psychologist Paraprofessional
Type of Test	Standardized Individual Criterion-referenced
Scores Obtained	Grade level
Student Performance Timed?	No
Testing Time	30–45 minutes
Scoring/Interpretation Time	10–15 minutes
Normed On	Children from urban, suburban, and rural areas of the West, Midwest, and East with wide range of racial representation, based on the 1970 census
Alternate Forms Available?	No

FORMAT

The KeyMath Diagnostic Arithmetic Test (KeyMath) materials include a test manual, an easel kit, and individual diagnostic record forms on which the examiner records the students' responses. Stimulus materials and directions for administering each item are sequentially displayed to the examiner in the easel kit. Most subtests require verbal responses to open-ended questions that are presented orally in conjunction with colorful pictorial materials. The easel kit is durable and has a convenient flip-page arrangement for presentation.

The KeyMath is an individually administered test consisting of 14 untimed subtests grouped into three major areas: Content, Operations, and Applications. Following is a description of the three areas, along with a listing of their respective subtests.

The subtests in the Content area investigate basic mathematics concepts and knowledge essential to an understanding and practical application of the number system. The subtests are:

A. Numeration
B. Fractions
C. Geometry and Symbols

The subtests in Operations include the basic computational processes. Some problems are of a pencil-and-paper variety. These problems are presented on the back of the diagnostic record form. Other subtests in Operations evaluate the ability to perform more than one computational process. The subtests in the Operations are:

D. Addition
E. Subtraction
F. Multiplication
G. Division
H. Mental Computation
I. Numerical Reasoning

The subtests in Applications focus on the functional use of mathematics. The content is designed to evaluate school arithmetic skills necessary and relevant in daily life. The subtests are:

J. Word Problems
K. Missing Elements
L. Money
M. Measurement (assesses standard weights and measures of the United States; a recently developed Metric Supplement is now available)
N. Time

For all of the subtests on the KeyMath, students complete only those items appropriate to their range of ability. This range extends from a basal level established by three consecutive correct responses to a ceiling level marked by three consecutive errors. Alternate, equivalent forms of the KeyMath are not available for test-retest purposes.

STRENGTHS OF THE KEYMATH

• The KeyMath has many excellent features. It is a criterion-referenced instrument based on the developmental sequence of skill acquisition and logical thinking. Extensive clinical training and experience in test administration are not required for the KeyMath, making it a helpful screening and diagnostic tool.

• Responses are easily recorded during administration on the record form (see Figure 16). A general pattern is identified according to student performance in the three major areas—Content, Operations, and Applications. The record form also graphically profiles a student's strengths and weaknesses in the 14 subtest areas. In addition, the examiner is provided with a comprehensive evaluation of the student's performance on individual items. A description of each item, stated as a behavioral objective, can be found in the appendix of the manual. For example, the objective for the Measurement subtest (item 8) reads: "Given the concept of a dozen, [the student] indicates the number of its elements." The objective for item 15 of the same subtest reads: "Given a common object, [the student] estimates its weight." Thus the teacher can quickly determine whether the student has or has not mastered a certain objective. This knowledge helps the teacher establish with certainty where instruction in the different areas should begin.

• Another level of information provided by the KeyMath is a grade-equivalent score, ranging from preschool to grade 6, based on total test performance. Separate grade scores for each of the 14 subtests are not provided. Scoring the test is simple and objective, taking approximately 10 minutes.

• The KeyMath is a highly motivating test for students because of the broad range and diversity of item content and the colorful and stimulating materials. The pictures that it uses are very much in the realm of experience of today's students (for example, illustrations of Raisin Bran cereal and Campbell's soup). Contemporary pictures contribute greatly to student interest in the test.

• Because of its diagnostic structure and almost total lack of reading and writing requirements, the test is particularly useful for students with a wide range of intellectual abilities and those who are learning disabled.

• In addition to measuring the usual math skills, the KeyMath also includes some unique subtests, one of which is Missing Elements. The word problems in this subtest are novel in that some missing information impedes their solution. For example: "Susan is 4 feet tall. She is how much taller than her brother?" The student must specify the missing information, which emphasizes the application of logical thinking and directly taps the student's ability to analyze and understand the structure of a verbal problem.

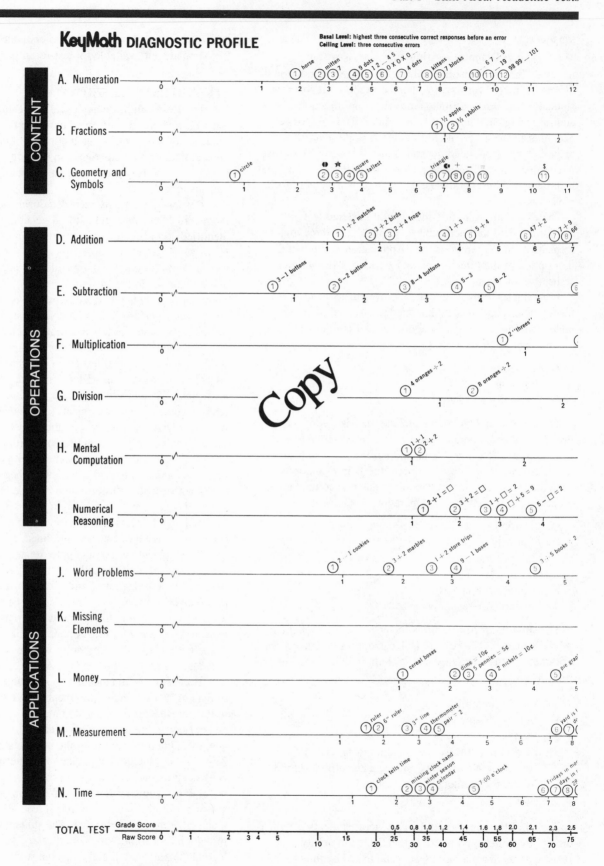

Figure 16. KeyMath Diagnostic Profile

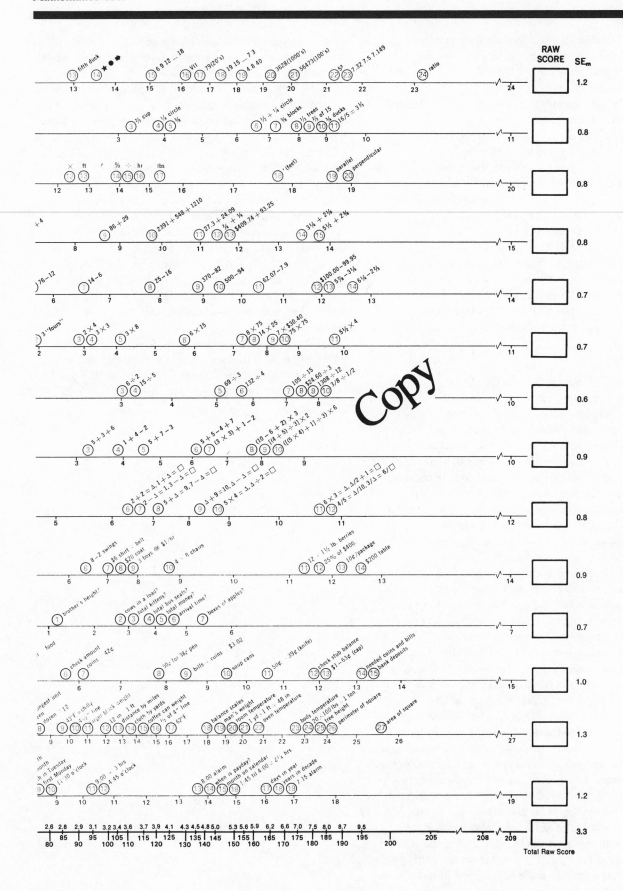

RAW
SCORE   SE_m

1.2

0.8

0.8

0.8

0.7

0.7

0.6

0.9

0.8

0.9

0.7

1.0

1.3

1.2

3.3

Total Raw Score

This is a skill generally not included in other math tests.

- In terms of standardization, the KeyMath sample contained a wide range of geographic and racial types. The sample was weighted on the demographic variables of race and community size to conform to the proportions obtained in the 1970 U.S. census.

- Reliability coefficients for total test performance are consistently high across grade levels. Moderate subtest reliabilities are reported in the manual. The manual also lists the standard errors of measurement for the total test and for each of its subtests, as well as for each grade level. These indices provide the range within which the student's performance may be expected to vary.

- As an extension of the test, the authors of KeyMath are currently developing an instructional program in mathematics. KeyMath Instruction (KMI) is based on the theoretical work of Piaget, Bruner, Dienes, Benoit, Guilford, and Gagné. The KMI instructional program promises to offer an innovative approach to the teaching of mathematics.

LIMITING FACTORS OF THE KEYMATH

- Although the primary value of the KeyMath is its use as a criterion-referenced instrument, grade norms for the total score are provided. However, the grade scores tend to be inflated and often do not correspond accurately to the student's day-to-day classwork in mathematics. The discrepancy between KeyMath scores and daily classroom functioning may reflect the nature of the test itself. Many different areas of mathematics performance are measured by the KeyMath, in addition to written computation. In contrast, a student's level of math performance in school is frequently a measure solely of mastery of written computational skills in the basic operations.

There is a tendency to report grade level scores on KeyMath subtests by using the graph at the bottom of the record form. This should not be done; the grade score norms were obtained by using total test scores only.

A further caution concerns the use of KeyMath grade scores alone to determine a student's eligibility for special instruction in mathematics (as is the case in some school systems). As with any test, scores alone are of little value. The degree of subtest variability as seen on the diagnostic profile is a very important factor, because it demonstrates the variability in a student's math skills. Some students have superior abilities in math concepts and specific disabilities in computation, whereas for others the reverse is true.

- The norms for the KeyMath extend to the 8.8 grade level. But the number of students in the standardization sample at the junior high level is insufficient to warrant the test's use with regular seventh- and eighth-grade students. As stated in the manual, the test is intended for use from preschool through grade 6. Inclusion of test

items appropriate for older students and extension of the standardization sample to include upper grade levels would greatly increase the test's usefulness.

- The KeyMath provides basal and ceiling levels, which are convenient testing features that allow the examiner to administer less than the entire test. Some subtests, however, have fewer numbers of items than others, so that significant gaps occur at different points on the grade-level continuum for those particular subtests. For example, in the Fractions subtest, item 2 has a relative grade-level difficulty of 1.3. Item 3 corresponds to a relative grade-level difficulty of 3.6, a jump of over two years from the previous item. If the ceiling level procedure of three consecutive errors is followed, a kindergarten student might have to be administered item 3 (which is beyond his or her ability range) to reach the described ceiling. More items are needed in some subtests to cover the grade-level gaps so that the examiner does not have to administer superfluous items that are too difficult.

- Finally, as with any new instrument, more research efforts are needed to demonstrate the reliability and validity of the test. Thus far the data on concurrent validity that have been collected have involved earlier forms of KeyMath.

Perception and Memory Tests

Despite controversy over their concurrent and predictive validity, tests of perception and memory are routinely used in assessing students' academic skills. Although their relationship to academic skills may require further definition, perception and memory are clearly processes required for learning. As mentioned in the Introduction, if these process tests are used in conjunction with tests that assess basic academic skills, they can provide information that is useful in planning a student's instructional program.

This chapter begins with reviews of three comprehensive tests. The Detroit Tests of Learning Aptitude are an extensive battery of subtests containing measures of language, verbal comprehension and reasoning, fine motor coordination, spatial perception, and number skills. It has been placed in this chapter because several of its subtests assess visual and auditory perception and memory. A unique series of tests, the Slingerland Screening Tests for Identifying Children with Specific Language Disability, measure visual and auditory perception and memory, as well as kinesthetic memory skills. The Malcomesius Specific Language Disability Test, for students in grades 6 through 8, has the same format and content as the Slingerland Tests.

Following these comprehensive tests, three tests of auditory perception are reviewed. The Wepman Auditory Discrimination Test was one of the first diagnostic tests of auditory skills, whereas the Goldman-Fristoe-Woodcock Test of Auditory Discrimination is a more recent addition to the field. The Lindamood Auditory Conceptualization Test expands the range of auditory processes assessed to include not only discrimination, but sequencing and syllable analysis as well.

The last section of this chapter includes four tests in the area of visual perception. The first two tests—the Marianne Frostig Developmental Test of Visual Perception, a forerunner in the field of perceptual assessment, and the Motor-Free Visual Perception Test—assess a wide range of visual perception processes. In contrast, the Bender Visual Motor Gestalt Test and the Beery-Buktenica Developmental Test of Visual-Motor Integration focus on the assessment of eye-hand coordination through design-copying tasks.

In addition to these 10 tests, other tests containing subtests that assess perception and memory are reviewed in the remaining chapters. These tests are found in Chapter Four: Gross Motor Tests, Part II: Preschool and Kindergarten Tests, and Part III: General Intelligence Tests and Developmental Scales. Readers who are specifically interested in this area are referred to these sections.

Comprehensive Tests

Detroit Tests of Learning Aptitude (Detroit)

Harry J. Baker and Bernice Leland
Bobbs-Merrill Company, Inc., 1935; Examiner's Handbook revised 1967
4300 W. 62nd St., Indianapolis, IN 46206

Purpose	To assess a wide range of intellectual functioning, including reasoning and comprehension, practical judgment, verbal ability, time and space relationships, number ability, auditory and visual attention, and motor ability
Major Areas Tested	General intelligence functions
Age or Grade Range	3–19 years
Usually Given By	Special education teacher Psychologist Speech/language clinician
Type of Test	Standardized Individual
Scores Obtained	Mental age IQ
Student Performance Timed?	Yes (some subtests)
Testing Time	60–75 minutes (9–13 subtests)
Scoring/Interpretation Time	20–30 minutes
Normed On	600 public school children in Detroit, Michigan
Alternate Forms Available?	No

FORMAT

Test materials for the Detroit Tests of Learning Aptitude (Detroit) include the examiner's handbook, the student's record booklet, and a reusable spiral-bound book containing pictorial material.

The Detroit contains 19 tests measuring various aspects of intellectual functioning. No student is given all 19; only those tests that tap the particular range of abilities and that focus on the skills of particular interest should be given. The authors recommend that from 9 to 13 tests be administered individually and that they include one or more for each of the specific faculties (see Figure 17). A general idea of the nature of each test is given in Table 13. Detailed directions for scoring each test are given in the examiner's handbook. The raw score for each test is converted to a mental-age score. To obtain a total test score, the mental-age scores from all the tests are put in rank order to find the midpoint. This midpoint is the median mental-age score. The individual test results are also plotted on a profile to give a graphic representation of the student's strengths and weaknesses.

STRENGTHS OF THE DETROIT

- The Detroit provides a broad sampling of a student's mental processes and specific intellectual, perceptual, and cognitive functions.

- The provision for separate mental-age scores for each test increases the flexibility of the scale, because it allows for specific analysis of a student's strengths and weaknesses. An individual profile may be obtained, outlining a student's abilities and disabilities in a way that teachers and parents can readily understand. For example: "Sally is good at dealing with language and auditory tasks, as reflected by her strong performance on tests 2, 4, and 6, but she has difficulty when she must process, interpret, and remember information presented visually, as seen by her poor performance on tests 9 and 16."

- The profile of abilities and disabilities is much more useful diagnostically than the overall median mental age, and accordingly, less emphasis should be placed on the tests as an entity. Instead, the astute clinician will analyze performances on the various tests that together use many different combinations of modalities in order to determine which combinations facilitate or hinder the learning process. For example, when assessing auditory memory, the examiner might compare performance on Oral Directions (test 18) with performances on Auditory Attention Span for Unrelated Words (test 6) and Auditory Attention Span for Related Syllables (test 13). Questions might include, Is memory better when a motor response is required and input is visual as well as auditory (test 18)? Or is it better when response is oral and no visual material is viewed (tests 6 and 13)? What strategies does the student employ to aid recall? Verbal rehearsal? Shutting eyes to block out distracting

THE TESTS AND SPECIFIC MENTAL FACULTIES

Test	Reasoning and Comprehension	Practical Judgment	Verbal Ability	Time and Space Relationships	Number Ability	Auditory Attentive Ability	Visual Attentive Ability	Motor Ability
1. Pictorial Absurdities	X						X	
2. Verbal Absurdities	X		X					
3. Pictorial Opposites							X	
4. Verbal Opposites			X					
5. Motor Speed and Precision		X						X
6. Auditory Attention Span for Unrelated Words						X		
7. Oral Commissions		X			X	X		X
8. Social Adjustment A	X							
9. Visual Attention Span for Objects							X	
10. Orientation	X	X		X				
11. Free Association			X					
12. Memory for Designs				X			X	X
13. Auditory Attention Span for Related Syllables						X		
14. Number Ability					X			
15. Social Adjustment B	X							
16. Visual Attention Span for Letters							X	
17. Disarranged Pictures	X			X			X	
18. Oral Directions		X				X	X	X
19. Likenesses and Differences			X					

Figure 17. Detroit Tests

Figure 18. Detroit Pictorial Absurdities, Test 1

Table 13. Subtests of the Detroit

Test	Age Range	Presentation	Response	Task Description	Timed
1. Pictorial Absurdities	3.0–10.0	Visual	Oral	Student must detect absurdities in pictures (see Figure 18 on p. 76)	No
2. Verbal Absurdities	5.3–16.6	Oral	Oral	Student must listen to statement and identify the illogical or erroneous cause-effect relationship (*I knew my father had walked all the way from Europe because his shoes were covered with mud.*)	No
3. Pictorial Opposites	3.0–9.3	Visual	Pointing	Student must examine sample picture and select from two choices the picture that shows the opposite relationship (see Figure 19 on p. 78)	No
4. Verbal Opposites	5.3–19.0	Oral	Oral	Student must name antonyms for sample words that gradually increase in difficulty (*deep-shallow*)	No
5. Motor Speed and Precision	4.6–18.6	Visual	Visual-motor	Student must make Xs in circles gradually decreasing in size (see Figure 20 on p. 79)	Yes
6. Auditory Attention Span for Unrelated Words	3.0–19.0	Oral	Oral	Student must remember and repeat series of unrelated words that increase in number from two to eight per span, after the examiner says them (*man-horse-song*)	No
7. Oral Commissions	3.0–8.3	Oral	Performance of task	Student must perform series of commissions, the units increasing in number from one to four (*Show me the window.*)	No
8. Social Adjustment A	3.6–13.6	Oral	Oral	Student must answer questions reflecting an ability to make judgments about social situations (*What is the thing to do if you break a school window?*)	No
9. Visual Attention Span for Objects	3.0–18.9	Visual	Oral	After viewing cards briefly, student must remember and recall sets of pictures on cards, the pictures increasing in number from two to eight per card (see Figure 21 on p. 80)	Yes
10. Orientation	3.0–13.6	Oral	Oral or performance of task	Student must answer questions and perform tasks reflecting temporal-sequential and spatial concepts (*What year is it now? Put your left foot behind you.*)	No
11. Free Association	5.3–19.0	Oral	Oral	Student must show verbal fluency by saying as many words as possible in a specified time period (*book, paper, pencil*)	Yes
12. Memory for Designs	3.0–15.9	Visual	Visual-motor	Student must either copy geometric forms from a model or reproduce them from memory after viewing them for a few seconds (see Figure 22 on p. 81)	Yes

Table 13. *—Continued*

Test	Age Range	Presentation	Response	Task Description	Timed
13. Auditory Attention Span for Related Syllables	3.0–19.0	Oral	Oral	Student must repeat sentences of increasing length and complexity, after the examiner says them (*We will go for a walk.*)	No
14. Number Ability	3.0–11.0	Oral	Visual-motor tor or oral	Student must answer questions reflecting knowledge of arithmetic (*Count by 5s.*)	No
15. Social Adjustment B	3.0–17.9	Oral	Oral	Student must answer questions about civic affairs and common objects (*What is a jail?*)	No
16. Visual Attention Span for Letters	5.9–15.9	Visual	Oral	After viewing cards briefly, student must remember and recall sets of letters on cards, the letters increasing in number from two to seven (see Figure 23 on p. 82)	Yes
17. Disarranged Pictures	5.6–17.6	Visual	Visual-motor	Student must mentally rearrange pictures that are broken into sections and mark the correct answer in the test booklet (see Figure 24 on p. 82)	Yes
18. Oral Directions	6.3–19.0	Oral and visual	Visual-motor	Student must remember sets of oral directions, the units increasing in number from 2 to 5, and then carry out the directions by marking in the test booklet (see Figure 25 on p. 83)	Yes
19. Likenesses and Differences	6.9–19.0	Oral	Oral	Student must express similarities and differences between pairs of terms that gradually become more abstract (*sofa-bed, effort-achievement*)	No

Figure 19. Detroit Pictorial Opposites, Test 3

5. Motor Speed and Precision
(See pages 29-32 of Handbook)

Score ....

☐ Right or ☐ Left

Figure 20. Detroit Motor Speed and Precision, Test 5

visual stimuli? Grouping the information by intonation or stress? In this example, the examiner will gain some information about whether auditory or visual approaches will enhance or inhibit learning.

• Another advantage of the Detroit is the wide age range it covers—from 3 to 19 years. Although many tests reach their ceiling before age 19, most of the memory and language tests span the upper age levels. Few instruments are currently available that assess these skills in older students. Overall, however, the test is most appropriate for the elementary school student.

• In summary, the Detroit is a flexible scale with easily added or substituted tests. The tests require few materials, tasks begin at an easy level so that initial success is usually guaranteed, and examiners generally find the tests easy to administer.

Figure 21. Detroit Visual Attention Span for Objects, Test 9

LIMITING FACTORS OF THE DETROIT
• A very serious defect of the Detroit is the inadequate and haphazard standardization. The tests were standardized on 50 average children at each grade level. The sample apparently came from only one city—Detroit. A breakdown of the sample's socioeconomic background and sex is not reported. The norms, reported in units of three months, are misleading, inasmuch as only 50 cases were used in each *year* group. Preferably, scores should be established in less-frequent age intervals, with means and standard deviations given, to make interpretation more meaningful. It is impossible to tell from the examiner's handbook the exact

number of students on which any one test item was standardized.

There is also a lack of statistical reliability and validity in the Detroit. Reliability information was published for only one test of the battery. In general, the test authors draw many conclusions about its soundness but fail to provide supporting data. In particular, the concept of "specific mental faculties" is not backed by any evidence.

• Some of the administration procedures for the tests are ambiguous and need to be made more explicit. For example, on Likenesses and Differences (test 19), the handbook states that testing should "continue through three or four zero scores in succession." On Verbal Opposites (test 4), the handbook states that testing for older students should "begin at a point at which all items are completed successfully." No basal levels are provided; such specific starting points would greatly improve the tests.

The lack of a ceiling on some memory tests is still another procedural drawback. A test must be administered in its entirety, even though the student is obviously failing and becoming frustrated. This is particularly difficult for the young or very disabled student to endure.

• Poor range of item difficulty on some tests is also a concern. For example, on Verbal Opposites (test 4), the relatively easy word *begin* is preceded by more difficult words, such as *public* and *cruel*. Therefore, the assignment of credit for items below the starting point may be misleading; it cannot be assumed that earlier items have been successively easier.

• Because the Detroit was published in 1935 and has never been revised, many of the test materials are very dated. Questions like "What is the board of health?" are not in the realm of experience of today's students. Pictures that show potatoes sold by the bushel and a quill pen are anachronisms.

• In conclusion, although the Detroit is poorly standardized, it can be a useful test in the hands of a highly skilled examiner. Age scores from the normative tables may not be valid and should probably be used only as a ranking device. IQ scores and median mental-age scores calculated from the Detroit are meaningless. Tests should be examined for their content and not taken at face value. Comparison of these test scores with other test scores should be done with caution.

12. Memory for Designs
(See pages 58-68 of Handbook)
GROUP A

Score A............ ....
B............ ....
C............ ....
Total   ....

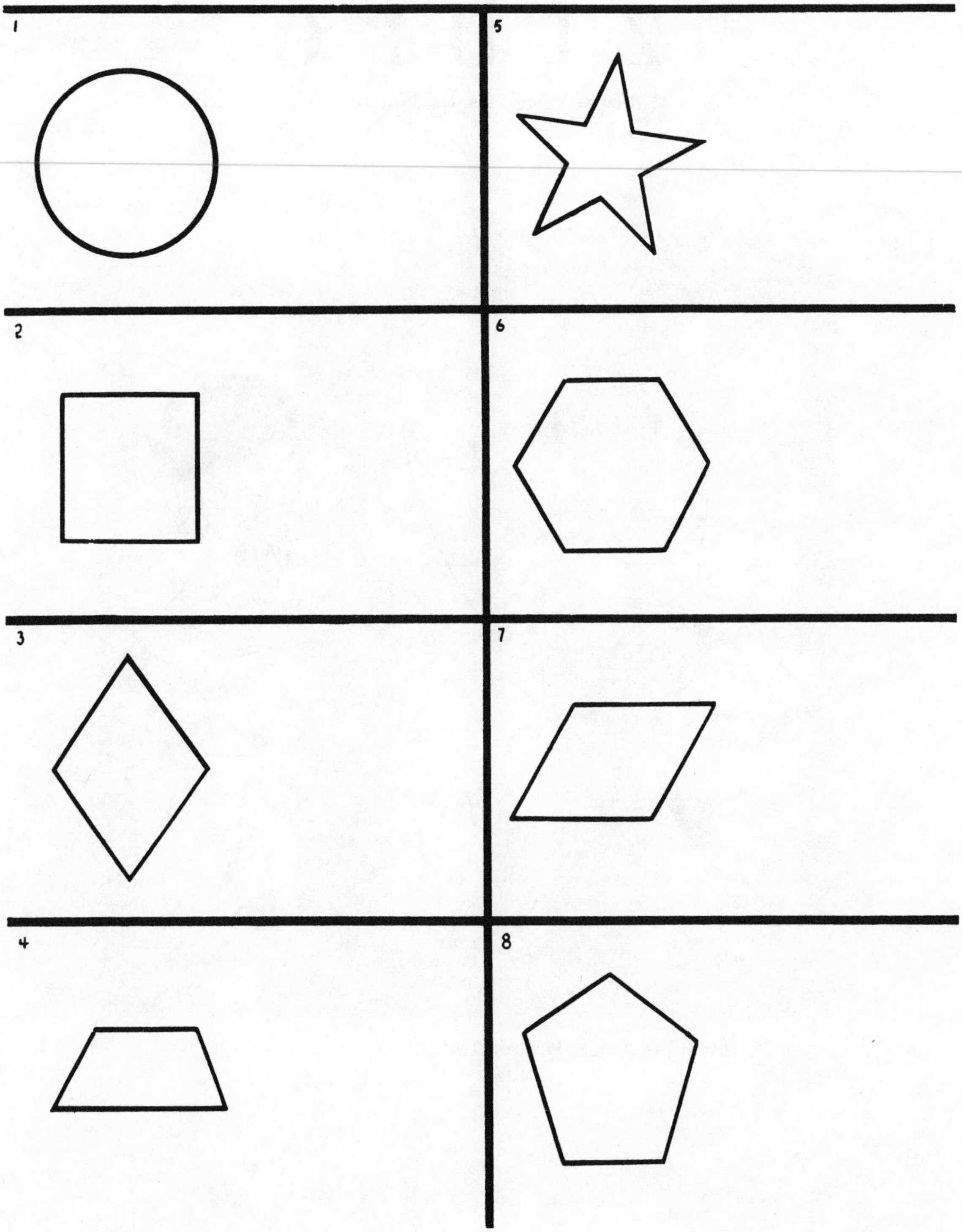

Figure 22. Detroit Memory for Designs, Test 12

z t b r c

Figure 23. Detroit Visual Attention Span for Letters, Test 16

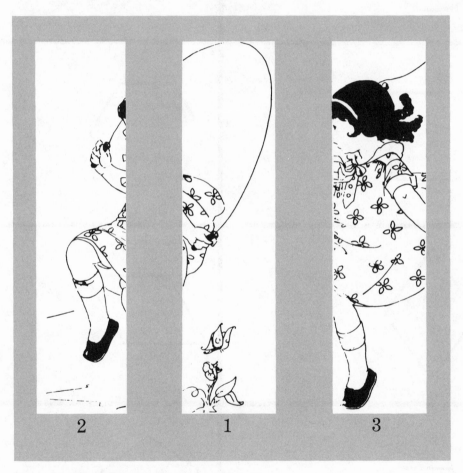

Figure 24. Detroit Disarranged Pictures, Test 17

18. Oral Directions
(See pages 87-91 of Handbook)

Score........................

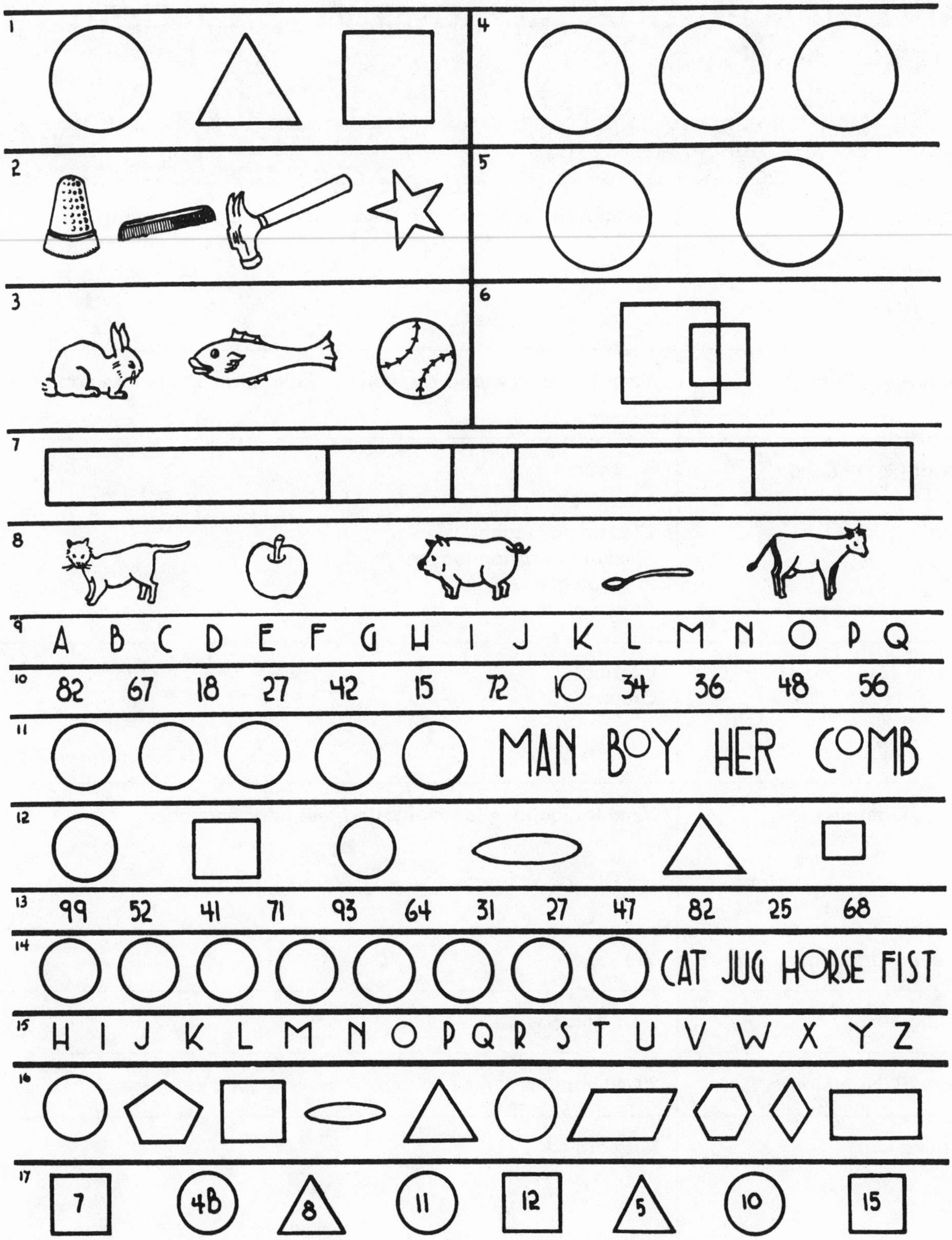

Figure 25. Detroit Oral Directions, Test 18

Slingerland Screening Tests for Identifying Children with Specific Language Disability
(Slingerland Tests)

Beth Slingerland
Educators Publishing Service, Inc., Forms A, B, C, 1962; revised 1970; Form D, 1974
75 Moulton St., Cambridge, MA 02188

Purpose	To identify students with a specific language disability
Major Areas Tested	Visual, auditory, and kinesthetic skills related to reading and spelling
Age or Grade Range	6–12 years
Usually Given By	Classroom teacher Special education teacher Psychologist Administrator
Type of Test	Informal Group
Scores Obtained	None (guidelines for evaluating test performance)
Student Performance Timed?	Yes
Testing Time	1–1½ hours
Scoring/Interpretation Time	30–40 minutes
Normed On	Not normed
Alternate Forms Available?	No

FORMAT

The Slingerland Screening Tests for Identifying Children with Specific Language Disability (Slingerland Tests) are a series of pencil-and-paper tests published in five forms for various grade levels.

Form	Grade Level
Pre-Reading	End of kindergarten to beginning of first grade
A	End of first grade to beginning of second grade
B	End of second grade to beginning of third grade
C	End of third grade to beginning of fourth grade
D	Fifth and sixth grades

The materials for each form include the students' booklets, in which they write their answers, and a set of cards and charts for the examiner. Although the Slingerland Tests are not normed and therefore provide no age- or grade-level scores, standardized administration procedures are described in the examiner's manuals. One manual is provided for the Pre-Reading Test; a second includes the instructions for Forms A, B, and C; and a third is available for Form D. Directions for scoring and guidelines for evaluating test performance are also included in the manuals.

The Slingerland Tests (and the teaching method) are based on Orton-Gillingham techniques for teaching reading and spelling through a multisensory approach. The linkages among auditory, visual, and kinesthetic modalities are the essence of the model. The tests are designed to assess these linkages.

Forms A, B, C, and D of the Slingerland Tests include the same eight group subtests. Form D includes an additional group subtest. Forms A, B, C, and D also include a series of auditory subtests to be given individually at the conclusion of the group subtests. The eight basic subtests and the individual auditory tests are described in Table 14. Although the number and difficulty of the items within each subtest vary, the skill being measured remains the same. This format allows assessment of student progress on the same series of tasks in grades 1 through 6.

Because of their different format, the Slingerland Pre-Reading Screening Procedures are reviewed separately in Part II (see p. 221).

STRENGTHS OF THE SLINGERLAND TESTS

• Beth Slingerland, the author of the tests, is an experienced teacher of students with specific language disability. She developed the tests for use in public schools, and they reflect her knowledge of teaching. The subtests measure skills that are directly related to classroom performance.

• Students with specific language disability have deficits in auditory, visual, and kinesthetic skills and the integration of these three systems, or modalities. Through careful analysis of a student's errors on the Slingerland Tests, a teacher can determine which modalities are the weakest and plan a remedial program accordingly. In contrast to the Illinois Test of Psycholinguistic Abilities (p. 141), the Slingerland subtests measure the modalities with regular academic tasks, which makes them much more usable for the classroom teacher.

• The Slingerland Tests were designed as screening instruments. They can be administered by classroom teachers to total classroom groups. They are an economical way to identify students with difficulties in visual, auditory, or kinesthetic skills. Although no norms are available, there is increasing research data to support the tests' validity as useful predictive instruments.

• As in all test batteries, some subtests are better than others. The three subtests measuring visual processing are particularly useful in determining the level of a visual perception problem. For example, the following performance on these three tests is very typical of students who have difficulty reading:

Visual Perception Memory (test 3): 80 percent correct
Visual Discrimination (test 4): 100 percent correct
Visual Kinesthetic Memory (test 5): 50 percent correct

These scores are interpreted to mean that, as the visual process becomes more complex, and when memory and a written response are required, the student's performance is poorer. In contrast is this typical performance of another student with reading difficulty:

Visual Perception Memory (test 3): 50 percent correct
Visual Discrimination (test 4): 70 percent correct
Visual Kinesthetic Memory (test 5): 95 percent correct

In this case, the kinesthetic (written) response seems to increase the efficiency of the visual processes.

LIMITING FACTORS OF THE SLINGERLAND TESTS

• At the present time, the Slingerland Tests must be viewed as informal tests. Although very specific directions for administration are given and complex scoring procedures are presented, no norms are provided. Thus, judgments about an individual student's performance are very subjective, depending on the sophistication of the examiner. The author stresses the need to develop local norms, which is probably true but not very realistic. Reliability and validity data are limited to unpublished manuscripts that have little value for the classroom teacher or school psychologist.

Table 14. Slingerland Subtests

Subtest	Description	Modality	Relationship to Classroom Skills
1. Far-Point Copying	Student copies paragraph from a chart on the wall	Visual, kinesthetic	Assesses visual-motor skills related to handwriting
2. Near-Point Copying	Student copies single words printed at top of page on lines at bottom	Visual, kinesthetic	Assesses visual-motor skills related to handwriting
3. Visual Perception Memory	Student is shown a word card for 10 seconds and then asked to find the word in a group of four visually similar words (*mnoey, mouey, woney, money*)	Visual	Assesses visual memory skills related to reading and spelling
4. Visual Discrimination	Student is asked to match words containing many easily confused letters (*lady, daly, laby, baby, lady*)	Visual	Assesses basic visual discrimination without memory component or written response
5. Visual Kinesthetic Memory	Student is shown word or design card for 10 seconds and then asked to write or draw the word or design	Visual, kinesthetic	Assesses the combination of visual memory and written response, which is necessary for written spelling
6. Auditory Kinesthetic Memory	Examiner dictates sequences of letters, numbers, and words, and then the student writes what the examiner dictated	Auditory, visual, kinesthetic	Combines auditory perception and memory with written response, skills necessary for dictation lessons
7. Initial and Final Sounds (Level D includes vowel sounds)	Examiner pronounces a word, and the student writes the initial or final sound (*shimmer—sh; clasp—p*)	Auditory, visual, kinesthetic	Assesses auditory discrimination and sequencing related to basic phonics with a written response
8. Auditory-Visual Integration	Examiner pronounces a word, and the student selects it from a group of four visually similar words (*baddy, babby, dabby, daddy*)	Auditory, visual	Assesses visual discrimination related to word recognition
9. Following Directions (Form D only)	Examiner gives a series of directions requiring a written response (*Write the alphabet. Do not use capital letters. Put a comma after each letter.*)	Auditory, kinesthetic	Assesses auditory memory and attention with a written response
Individual Auditory Tests (Forms A, B, C, and D)			
Echolalia	Examiner pronounces a word or phrase and the student repeats it four or five times aloud (*animal-animal-animal-animal*)	Auditory, kinesthetic	Assesses auditory-kinesthetic confusion related to pronunciation
Word Finding	Examiner reads a sentence with a missing word, and the student fills in the missing word (*A long yellow fruit is called a _____ .*)	Auditory	Assesses comprehension and the ability to produce a specific word on demand; word-finding problems often identify children with specific language disability
Story Telling	Examiner reads a story aloud, and the student retells it	Auditory	Assesses auditory memory and verbal expression of content material

• One advantage of the Slingerland Tests is the fact that they use skills related to classroom tasks. But precisely because they measure classroom tasks, the tests are long and difficult for many students to take. Several subtests require extensive writing, and many students become discouraged. Because the items were selected to produce the visual and auditory sequencing and discrimination errors characteristic of students with specific language disability, many students become frustrated and require a great deal of emotional support to complete the test.

• There seems to be no rationale for the number or order of items within a subtest. There is no systematic increase in the difficulty of items, other than increasing vocabulary difficulty from Form A through Form D.

• Administration procedures are complex and difficult: scoring procedures are long and also difficult, especially in view of the fact that the tests are not normed. The tests require considerable study before they can be used successfully.

• The terminology of the Slingerland Tests is very confusing. The term *specific language disability* requires explanation because it is often confused with oral language problems of other types. The titles of the subtests have no meaning to teachers or parents who have not seen the subtest items. School districts that choose to use this test need to devise a system of scoring, reporting scores, and describing results that is easily understood.

• Of great concern is the fact that the Slingerland Tests are frequently used as the only instrument to diagnose a student as having specific language disability. Such a practice is highly questionable for any single test and particularly for a nonstandardized, nonnormed instrument.

Malcomesius Specific Language Disability Test (Malcomesius Test)

Neva Malcomesius
Educators Publishing Service, Inc., 1967
75 Moulton St., Cambridge, MA 02188

Purpose	To identify students with a specific language disability
Major Areas Tested	Auditory, visual, and kinesthetic skills related to reading, writing, and spelling
Age or Grade Range	Grades 6–8
Usually Given By	Classroom teacher Special education teacher
Type of Test	Informal Group
Scores Obtained	None (guidelines for evaluating test performance)
Student Performance Timed?	Yes
Testing Time	1½ hours
Scoring/Interpretation Time	20–30 minutes
Normed On	Not normed
Alternate Forms Available?	No

FORMAT

The materials for the Malcomesius Specific Language Disability Test (Malcomesius Test) consist of a teacher's manual, test booklets for the students, and a set of cards and charts used in administering the test.

Because the Malcomesius Test was designed as an upward extension of the Slingerland Tests (junior high school level), the 10 subtests are almost identical to those in the Slingerland Tests, Forms A to D. The tests are also designed for group administration. Table 15 compares the Malcomesius subtests to those of the Slingerland. (Refer also to Table 14, page 86.) It is interesting that, in the Spelling—Auditory to Motor subtest (subtest 10), the focus is on sound-symbol association rather than correct spelling. Thus the following words would all be considered correct: *dubious-doobious; exceed-excead.*

The Malcomesius Test does not include any of the individual auditory tests that are found in the lower levels of the Slingerland Tests.

STRENGTHS OF THE MALCOMESIUS TEST

- As in the Slingerland Tests, the Malcomesius Test battery includes a series of school-related tests to aid the classroom teacher in identifying students with specific language disability. There are few tests designed for adolescents, and the Malcomesius Test provides a means of assessing the auditory, visual, and kinesthetic skills of this age group on tasks related to classroom performance.

LIMITING FACTORS OF THE MALCOMESIUS TEST

- The Malcomesius Test is subject to the same limiting factors as the Slingerland Tests, the most serious of which is the lack of norms. No reliability or validity studies are reported. In addition, the author seems to assume that the only difference between beginning readers and more mature readers is the length of the words they can process and the speed with which they can process them. This is shown by the fact that the items for sixth, seventh, and eighth graders

Table 15. Comparison of the Malcomesius and Slingerland Subtests

Malcomesius Subtests	Description	Corresponding Slingerland Subtest
1	Paragraph Copying from a wall chart	1
2	Near-Point Copying of a list of words	2
3	Visual Discrimination, requires matching visually similar words (*innuendo, inunendo, innuendo, inuennbo, innuenbo*)	4
4	Visual Perception and Recall, requires identifying correct words and number sequences presented visually (*barbraian, barbarian, bardarian, darbraian*)	3
5	Visual Kinesthetic Recall, requires writing phrases after a visual presentation (*Keep quite quiet.*)	5
6	Auditory Discrimination, requires discrimination of words that sound very much alike (*trick, trek*)	None
7	Auditory Kinesthetic Memory, requires writing phrases from dictation (*parents of the girl*)	6
8	Auditory-Visual Integration, requires listening to a word or sequence of numbers and selecting it from four similar choices presented visually (*9,586; 6,589; 9,856; 9,589*)	8
9	Comprehension, requires listening to a paragraph and writing it	None
10	Spelling—Auditory to Motor, requires writing a list of 20 dictated words. The focus is on sound-symbol association, *not* correct spelling (*dubious-doobious, exceed-excead*)	None

are all the same; only time limits differentiate them. It may well be that an entirely different set of tasks should be used to identify these older disabled readers, rather than those used with the elementary students assessed by the Slingerland Tests.

• Subtests 9 and 10 are particularly poorly labeled. Subtest 9 is much more a measure of written language skills and sequential memory than it is of comprehension, and subtest 10 cannot be called spelling when the scoring directions specifically say, ''Do not count spelling.''

• The teacher's manual includes a page of ''General Directions for Evaluating the Tests.'' This page contains a number of statements about specific language disability that are presented as fact when they really represent the author's opinion. The person using the Malcomesius Test needs to be alert to these statements and to avoid conclusions about a student's learning disability based on performance on this test alone.

Auditory Tests

Wepman Auditory Discrimination Test

Joseph M. Wepman
Language Research Associates, 1958; revised 1978
950 E. 59th St., Chicago, IL 60621

Purpose	To evaluate the student's ability to recognize fine differences that exist between phonemes in English speech
Major Areas Tested	Auditory discrimination
Age or Grade Range	5–8 years
Usually Given By	Special education teacher Speech/language clinician
Type of Test	Standardized Individual
Scores Obtained	Rating scale
Student Performance Timed?	No
Testing Time	10–15 minutes
Scoring/Interpretation Time	5–10 minutes
Normed On	Children from urban and nonurban communities
Alternate Forms Available?	Yes

FORMAT

The materials for the Wepman Auditory Discrimination Test include a brief manual and forms for recording individual responses. The manual contains some information on test development, directions for administration, and guidance in the interpretation of test results.

The test consists of 40 pairs of monosyllabic meaningful words. The words were selected from the *Lorge-Thorndike Teacher's Word Book of 30,000 Words* (1944). Of the 40 word pairs, 30 differ by only one sound: *muss-mush*. The 10 word pairs that do not differ are included as false choices and aid in the judgment of test validity.

The words in each pair are of equal length. Comparisons are made between 13 initial consonants, 13 final consonants, and 4 medial vowels. Consonants chosen for contrast are within the same phonetic category—for example, the stops /p/, /t/, and /k/. Vowel comparisons are based on such criteria as (1) the part of the tongue that is raised, (2) the height of the tongue, and (3) the position of the lips.

The word pairs are read by the examiner. The student indicates whether the words pronounced were the same or different. No pictures are used, and the examiner prounounces the words with lips covered. Thus visual skills are not involved. A rating scale is used to interpret a student's performance. The scale provides descriptions of ability ranging from ''very good development'' to ''below the level of the threshold of adequacy'' for the ages 5 to 8 years.

STRENGTHS OF THE WEPMAN AUDITORY DISCRIMINATION TEST

• This test is a brief, inexpensive, and relatively simple tool for assessing auditory discrimination ability. The test is carefully constructed. Word length and complexity of test items are controlled.

• Test-retest reliability is high. The existence of equivalent forms provides the examiner with a good reevaluation procedure.

LIMITING FACTORS OF THE WEPMAN AUDITORY DISCRIMINATION TEST

• Some young handicapped children may have difficulty understanding the concept of *same/different*. A low score may represent difficulty in grasping that concept or in sustaining attention for the task, rather than auditory discrimination difficulty. This problem was found in clinical practice and was verified by Blank (1968) in her research.

• This test provides a measure of auditory discrimination of isolated word pairs. Additional testing or observation is necessary to assess discrimination skills of other types and in other situations, such as conversational speech and discrimination of sound against a background of noise.

• Although many phonemic contrasts are presented, others are missing. For instance, the sounds /ng/, /l/, /r/, /j/, and /ch/ are not included in the discrimination tasks. In addition, the contrast of voiced/voiceless consonants (for example, *bad-bat*) is not included. Also, only a limited number of vowel discriminations are assessed.

• Some of the contrasts presented in the test are not commonly made in nonstandard English—for example, ĕ/ĭ and *v*/*th*(voiced). Consequently, a low score by a student speaking nonstandard English may not indicate an auditory discrimination problem. Interpretation of the performance of this group of students, as well as students from bilingual backgrounds, should be made with caution, because no information on the norming population is available.

NOTES

In addition to the Auditory Discrimination Test, Joseph Wepman and his associates have since published two additional tests of auditory processing. The Auditory Memory Span Test (Wepman and Morency 1973*a*) requires the student to repeat a series of unrelated words pronounced by the examiner. Series of two, three, four, five, and six words are presented, three trials on each. The series does not have to be recalled in sequence. The student's raw score consists of the number of words recalled; performance is interpreted through the use of the rating scale, as on the Auditory Discrimination Test.

The Auditory Sequential Memory Test (Wepman and Morency 1973*b*) requires the student to repeat a series of digits pronounced by the examiner. The number of digits in each series increases from two to eight, and the series must be repeated in sequence. Two trials are given for each series length. Here, again, raw scores are interpreted through the use of the rating scale.

The three tests—Auditory Discrimination, Auditory Memory Span, and Auditory Sequential Memory Span—can be used together as a quick screening of auditory processes to identify students who need further assessment of their auditory skills.

Goldman-Fristoe-Woodcock Test of Auditory Discrimination (GFW)

R. Goldman, M. Fristoe, and R. Woodcock
American Guidance Service, Inc., 1970
Publishers' Bldg., Circle Pines, MN 55014

Purpose	To identify individuals who have difficulty discriminating speech sounds and to provide a measure of discrimination under ideal listening conditions and in the presence of controlled background noise
Major Areas Tested	Speech-sound discrimination
Age or Grade Range	4–70 years and over
Usually Given By	Special education teacher Speech/language clinician
Type of Test	Standardized Individual
Scores Obtained	Standard Percentile
Student Performance Timed?	No
Testing Time	20–25 minutes
Scoring/Interpretation Time	10–15 minutes
Normed On	745 subjects from an eastern, a midwestern, and a southern state
Alternate Forms Available?	No

FORMAT

Materials for the Goldman-Fristoe-Woodcock Test of Auditory Discrimination (GFW) consist of a manual, response forms, a spiral-bound book of pictures, a prerecorded test tape, and a set of 61 large training plates. The manual contains information on test development, directions for administering and scoring the test, and technical data on validity and reliability. Appendixes include suggestions for teaching the vocabulary, a description of the distinctive-feature classification used in constructing the GFW, and the norms.

The response form provides a place to record performance on the three parts of the test: the training procedure and two subtests, one with and one without background noise. An error-analysis matrix on the response form aids in the analysis of errors according to distinctive features.

The test book contains 60 test plates (30 each for the quiet and noise subtests) and 16 training plates. There are four black-and-white line drawings on each page. The book can be set up as an easel during administration. Instructions and directions for the subtests are contained on the prerecorded tape. The training procedure, which ensures familiarity with the vocabulary, is administered orally by the examiner. Large training plates are available for training students with inadequately developed vocabulary. Each plate is a simple enlarged picture from the test.

On each of the test's training plates, four monosyllabic words having little phonemic similarity (for example, *lake, nail, pear,* and *tea*) are pictured. On the test plates, either all initial or all final consonants differ (for example, *night, bite, write,* and *light*; or *core, coal, comb,* and *cone*). Sounds for contrast were selected on the basis of the distinctive-feature analysis of consonants. The stimulus word differs from the foils by only one or two features, including voicing, nasality, and manner of production (such as plosive). These are summarized in the manual. The voiced and voiceless /th/ contrast and vowel discrimination are not included.

Background noise on the noise subtest consists of typical cafeteria sounds. Three training stimuli are presented, with the noise intensity gradually increased to the point where it remains throughout the administration of that subtest.

A pointing response is used. The student points to the picture denoting the stimulus word on the tape. Headphones are suggested for student and examiner; normative data was obtained using headphones. Standard scores and percentiles are provided for each subtest for 32 age groups, from 3 years to over 70.

STRENGTHS OF THE GFW

• The authors have attempted to limit the variables involved in assessing auditory discrimination skills. As much time as needed may be allotted to training the vocabulary. Brief directions and the use of a pointing response simplify the task. Control of the examiner's voice is accomplished by the use of a prerecorded taped presentation.

• The GFW is applicable to a wide age range and is useful in a variety of settings (clinical, educational, and industrial). It is easy to administer. The manual provides clear instructions for administering the test and information that is helpful in understanding the results. In addition to the normative data on the standard population, selected data on clinical populations is also given. Data is available on limited numbers of hard-of-hearing, culturally disadvantaged, retarded, and learning-disabled children, and on children with speech and language problems.

• Test construction is well thought out. Most of the vocabulary that is used is familiar to young children. Words are all monosyllabic, and only one label is applied to each picture. The application of distinctive-feature theory is well described in the manual.

• Extensive information on reliability and validity has been compiled and is discussed in the manual.

LIMITING FACTORS OF THE GFW

• To keep pace with the taped presentation, the examiner must be familiar with the material. For some students, the pace of presentation may be too rapid. The examiner may momentarily stop the tape, but the stimulus should not be repeated.

• Some of the vocabulary included on the test requires flexible thinking. For instance, *Jack* is pictured as a jack-in-the-box and *we* as two friends. Younger children and those with significant conceptual delays may be slow to grasp such concepts, in spite of the training procedure.

• Although error analysis by distinctive features is included on the response form, it lacks satisfactory reliability and should be used only for clinical exploration and research.

Lindamood Auditory Conceptualization Test (LAC)

Charles Lindamood and Patricia Lindamood
Teaching Resources Corporation, 1971
100 Boylston St., Boston, MA 02116

Purpose	To measure auditory discrimination and the ability to identify the number and order of sounds in a sequence
Major Areas Tested	Auditory preception
Age or Grade Range	Preschool–adult
Usually Given By	Special education teacher Speech/language clinician Remedial reading teacher Paraprofessional
Type of Test	Standardized Individual
Scores Obtained	Grade level
Student Performance Timed?	No
Testing Time	10–15 minutes
Scoring/Interpretation Time	10–15 minutes
Normed On	660 students in grades K-12 from a range of socioeconomic and ethnic backgrounds in a California school district
Alternate Forms Available?	Yes

FORMAT

The materials for administering the Lindamood Auditory Conceptualization Test (LAC) include a manual, individual record sheets, and a set of 18 half-inch colored cubes (three each of red, yellow, blue, green, white, and black). The manual contains directions for administration and scoring, information on test construction, and suggestions for interpreting results. A record is provided for the examiner to use as a guide for the pronunciation of individual sounds and syllable patterns.

The LAC Test consists of four parts:

1. *The Precheck*. This part contains five items designed to determine whether the student can demonstrate knowledge of the following concepts: same/different, numbers to 4, left-to-right order, and first/last.

2. *Category I, Part A*. The student must identify the number of isolated sounds heard from a list of 10 items, and decided whether they are the same or different.

3. *Category I, Part B*. The student is given six items and asked to identify not only the number of isolated sounds heard and their sameness or difference, but also their order.

4. *Category II*. From a list of 12 items, the student must determine the number of sounds in a syllable and changes in the sound pattern when sounds are added, omitted, substituted, shifted, or repeated.

The Precheck is given to determine that the student understands the basic concepts necessary to obtain a valid test score. If knowledge of the Precheck concepts is not demonstrated, the test is discontinued. Categories I and II are each preceded by demonstration procedures.

In the LAC, the student manipulates colored blocks to indicate understanding of sound patterns. Each block represents a sound. There is no constant relationship between a specific color and a specific sound, so the student may select any colors. Different sounds within a pattern are represented by different colors. Table 16 illustrates the test format.

As the examiner pronounces each sound pattern, the student may use visual cues (the examiner's lip movements) to aid discrimination; the examiner notes this diagnostic information. Patterns may not be repeated unless an environmental noise interferes with the student's hearing. Testing is discontinued after five consecutive errors in Category I. In Category II, the student is given an opportunity to do another similar pattern after an error. Testing is discontinued after five errors in Category II.

Points are given for each correct block pattern, and on that basis a raw score is obtained. The raw score is converted to a weighted score (one point for each correct response in Category I, Part A; three in Category I, Part B; and six in Category II). A single weighted score is obtained for the total test; no subtest scores are provided. The examiner then compares the weighted score with a table that provides recommended minimum scores for each grade level. These minimum scores should be considered predictive of success in reading or spelling at or above that grade level.

Two equivalent forms, A and B, are available for reevaluation purposes.

STRENGTHS OF THE LAC

• The LAC provides a means of evaluating auditory perception skills related to reading and spelling without using written symbols. The student need not have knowledge of sound-symbol associations to demonstrate auditory perception skills. This makes the LAC a valuable tool for assessing auditory perception in beginning or remedial readers.

• Many tests are available for assessing auditory

Table 16. LAC Test Format

	Examiner Pronounces	Student's Block Pattern
Category I, Part A	Three same sounds (/b/, /b/, /b/)	Three same colors
	Two different sounds (/t/, /m/)	Two different colors
Category I, Part B	Two same sounds followed by one different sound (/s/, /s/, /p/)	Two same colors followed by one different color
Category II	Two different sounds in a syllable (/al/)	Two different colors
	New sound added at beginning of a syllable (/pal/)	New color added at beginning
	Change in last sound of a syllable (/pab/)	Change in last color

discrimination of whole words (including the Wepman Auditory Discrimination Test, p. 92, and the Goldman-Fristoe-Woodcock Test of Auditory Discrimination, p. 94). Other tests assess sound blending or auditory synthesis (see the Illinois Test of Psycholinguistic Abilities, p. 141). The LAC, however, assesses analysis of the number and order of sounds as well as discrimination. These skills are crucial in reading and spelling.

• The Precheck section of the LAC is excellent. It allows the examiner to assess quickly the student's knowledge of the basic concepts necessary to take the test. Once it is determined that the student understands these basic concepts, errors on the test can more accurately be related to skill deficiencies in auditory perception.

• The manual provides an excellent discussion of the relationship among auditory perception, reading, and spelling. Teachers and clinicians will find the discussion of follow-up remediation techniques helpful, as well as the authors' interpretation of test performance.

• The LAC can be used with a wide age range of students. The alternate test forms make it a usable tool for evaluating progress in a remediation program.

• The norming sample, although small, was reportedly carefully selected to include various socioeconomic groups and ethnic backgrounds. Reliability and validity studies are reported in the manual.

LIMITING FACTORS OF THE LAC

• The LAC is not an easy test to administer, and extensive practice is recommended before using it with students suspected of auditory disorders. Although the administration manual is clearly written, the process of using colored blocks to illustrate sound patterns is a difficult one. Category II, in particular, requires extensive verbal explanation, and many students become confused if the examiner is not quite skilled in test administration. The order of items in Category II is particularly difficult to administer.

• Students with intellectual deficits or delays in concept development have difficulty learning the relationship between the colors and the sounds. They may continue to believe that there is a direct relationship between color and sound, such as red always equals /p/. This confusion is seen in such statements as "There aren't enough colors." Such students may actually be able to spell the syllables in Category II (illustrating good auditory analysis) without being able to do the block patterns.

• The LAC authors have chosen to allow students to use visual cues (lip movements) to aid their auditory discrimination. It is true that visual cues are usually available in natural conversations. However, it is important for the examiner to note carefully whether or not the student uses visual cues. If the student does not, teaching him or her

to do so is a good first step in remediation. If they are used extensively, it is important for the teacher to realize that, in activities where the student does not have direct contact with the speaker, auditory perception may be quite poor.

• The score obtained on the LAC is difficult to interpret. For example, suppose a third-grade student obtains a total test score of 60. According to the minimum scores table in the manual, a score of 60 is the minimum score predicting high probability of successful reading and spelling performance in high-first-grade material. Does this mean that the third-grade student's auditory perception skills are at a first-grade level? Or that the student should be instructed in first-grade material? The interpretation becomes even more confusing with an older student. A score of 93 is the minimal score for predicting reading and spelling success for the second half of fourth and fifth grades, but 94 is the minimum recommended score for sixth through twelfth grades. The lack of clarity in test score interpretation suggests that the LAC is better used as an informal test—a task-analysis approach to auditory perception, rather than a standardized test yielding grade-level scores.

• Throughout the manual, reading and spelling are treated as identical tasks requiring the same auditory perception skills. Validity studies should be done to separate these two processes. Although the authors feel that the reading method the student has been taught does not affect performance on the LAC, this seems questionable. Students with phonics training have clearly had more practice with auditory analysis than sight-word readers.

Visual and Visual-Motor Tests

Marianne Frostig Developmental Test of Visual Perception (DTVP)

Marianne Frostig, in collaboration with Welty Lefever and John R. B. Whittlessey
Consulting Psychologists Press, Inc., 1961; Manual revised 1966
577 College Ave., Palo Alto, CA 94306

Purpose	To measure certain visual perceptual abilities and to detect difficulties in visual perception at an early age
Major Areas Tested	Visual perception
Age or Grade Range	3–8 years
Usually Given By	Special education teacher Occupational therapist Psychologist
Type of Test	Standardized Individual Group
Scores Obtained	Age level Scale Perceptual Quotient (PQ)
Student Performance Timed?	No
Testing Time	30–45 minutes (individual administration); 40–60 minutes (group administration)
Scoring/Interpretation Time	10–15 minutes
Normed On	2,116 white, middle-class students from Southern California
Alternate Forms Available?	No

FORMAT

The Marianne Frostig Developmental Test of Visual Perception (DTVP) is a paper-and-pencil test. The test materials consist of an examiner's manual and monograph, expendable test booklets for the students, demonstration cards, and plastic scoring keys. The examiner must also supply four colored pencils or crayons (red, blue, green, and brown) and a pencil without an eraser for each student. For group administration, access to a blackboard is necessary, for demonstration purposes.

During the testing session, the student completes tasks arranged in order of increasing difficulty in five areas of visual perception. The subtests and selected items from each are described below.

1. *Eye-Motor Coordination* (16 items). The student must draw continuous straight, curved, or angled lines between increasingly narrow boundaries or draw straight lines to a target (see Figure 26).

2. *Figure-Ground* (8 items). The student must distinguish between intersecting shapes and find embedded figures (see Figure 27). The student must outline the hidden geometric forms with a colored pencil or crayon.

3. *Constancy of Shape* (17 items). The student must

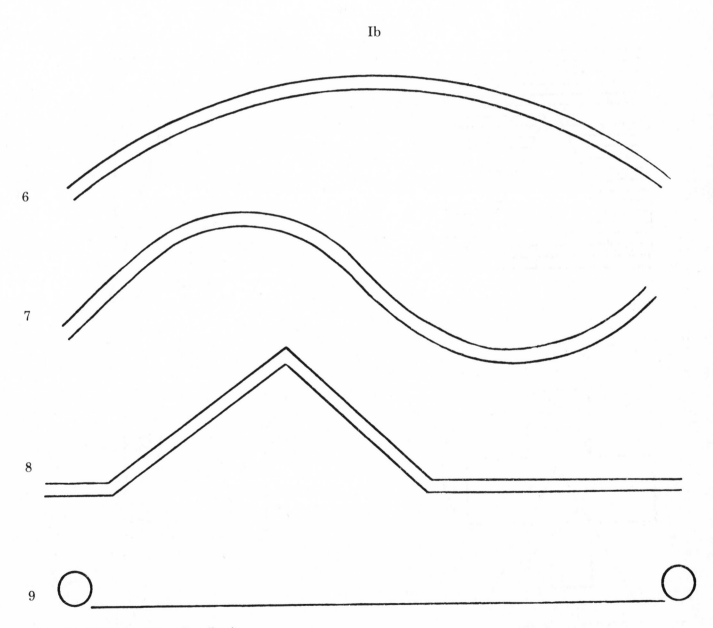

Figure 26. DTVP Eye-Motor Coordination

discriminate common geometric shapes (circles and squares), presented in different sizes, shadings, textures, and positions, from other similar shapes (see Figure 28). The student must outline the recognized figures with a colored pencil or crayon.

4. *Position in Space* (8 items). The student must distinguish between figures in an identical position and those in a reversed or rotated position (see Figure 29), marking the different figure.

5. *Spatial Relations* (8 items). The student must copy simple forms and patterns by joining dots (see Figure 30).

The DTVP may be administered individually or in groups. The optimum number of students in a group depends on the age of the students. For example, a group of 8 to 10 is appropriate for kindergarten students, whereas 10 to 20 second graders may be tested simultaneously. Large groups require paraprofessionals who can circulate among the students to help monitor the test.

Instructions for the test are verbal, but there is an adaptation of the manual for hard-of-hearing, deaf, and non-English-speaking students. Additional examples and gestures are used.

IIa

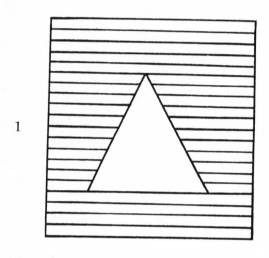

1

2

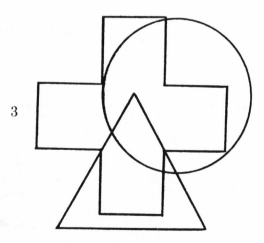

3

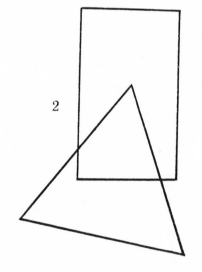

4

Figure 27. DTVP Figure Ground

Although the items are presented in one test booklet, parts of the test are omitted for nursery school and kindergarten students. The student may not erase, make corrections, or turn the test booklet. The test is not timed. Alternate, equivalent forms of the DTVP are not available.

Raw scores on each subtest are converted to age scores and scaled scores. The scaled scores on the five subtests are added to obtain a total test score; when divided by a student's age, the total score yields a perceptual quotient. Subtest scaled scores range from 0 to 20, with 10 as average and 8 or below indicating need for remediation. A perceptual quotient of 90 is suggested as the cut-off for children entering first grade; lower scores indicate the need for perceptual training.

STRENGTHS OF THE DTVP

• The DTVP is a well-known test, a forerunner in the field. It evaluates both visual perception and eye-hand coordination in young students. No expensive equipment is required. In addition to individual testing, the DTVP is useful as a screening instrument with groups of students. The test can also be used by the experienced clinician to

IIIa

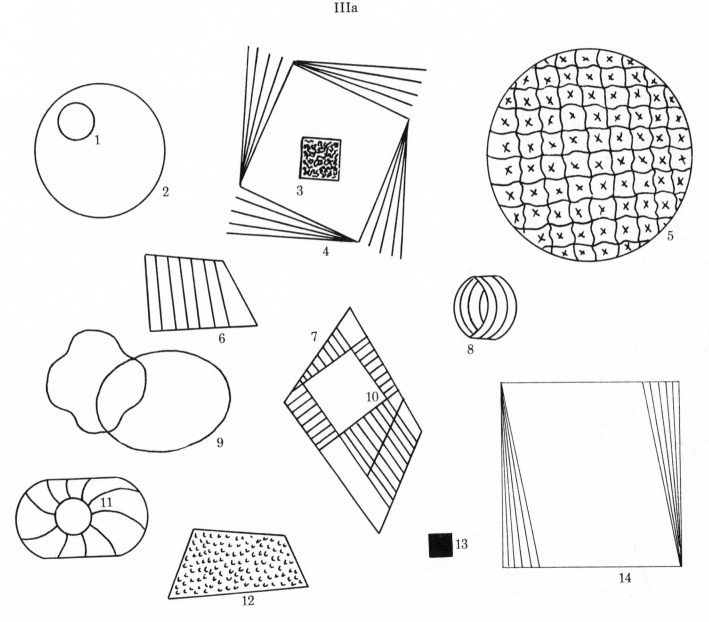

Figure 28. DTVP Constancy of Shape

gain diagnostic information on older students who have learning problems.

• The particular tasks on the DTVP are simple in design and arranged in order of increasing difficulty. The subtests can generally be performed quickly. For the most part, the directions for administering the test are clear. Examiner demonstration of each subtest, either on the blackboard or with demonstration materials, is especially helpful for the young student.

• The instructions for scoring the DTVP are fairly explicit. Examples are given that illustrate criteria for scoring each item. Scoring stencils provided for some items further increase objectivity. Time required for scoring is relatively short—approximately 10 minutes.

• The test-retest reliability coefficient for the whole

DTVP is adequate. In studies of predictive validity, the test scores have been found to discriminate poor readers from good readers at the first-grade level with modest correlations.

• A particular advantage of the test is the accompanying training program for remediation of perceptual difficulties. This program is directly related to a student's performance on the DTVP and includes motor and worksheet activities for each subtest. For example, if a student scores low on the Position in Space subtest, he or she is provided with activities to improve that skill (training in body image, body schema, and body concept). Thus the DTVP and the corresponding training materials are of value to experienced teachers; when used wisely, they provide good supplementary curricular activities.

IVa

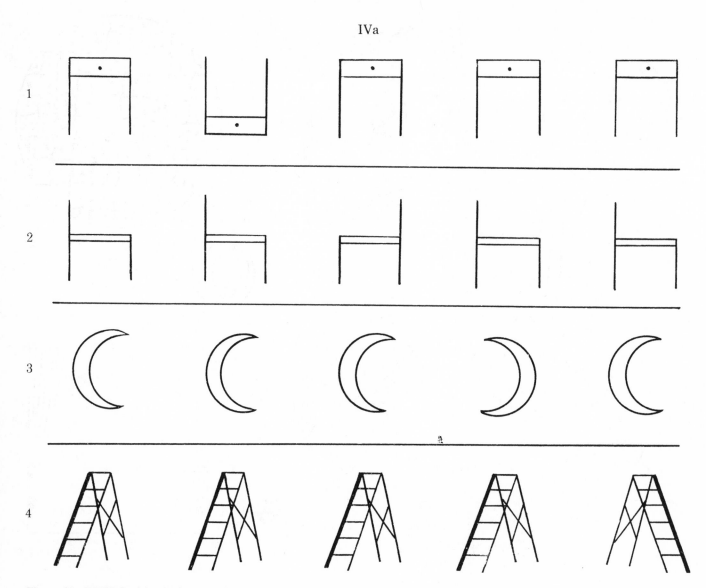

Figure 29. DTVP Position in Space

LIMITING FACTORS OF THE DTVP

• The DTVP purports to measure five distinct aspects of visual perception. Frostig's correlation studies indicate independence of the subtests. However, contradictory evidence has been found in several other investigations. Such studies show that the DTVP subtests do not measure five different and relatively independent visual perceptual abilities. More research seems warranted to evaluate with certainty the independence of the subtests. The degree to which the subtests measure one or more general visual perceptual factors also needs to be established (Hammill and Weiderholt 1972).

• The process of transforming raw scores to scaled scores is very confusing. For example, in students over 8 years of age, someone who receives a perfect score on a subtest receives a scaled score of only 10, whereas younger students can make errors and get a higher score. Salvia and Ysseldyke (1978, p. 311) state, "The transformed scores for the DTVP are not only confusing; they are questionably derived and therefore absolutely must not be used in making diagnostic decisions."

• The test items on the DTVP consist only of geometric forms and shapes; no letters or numbers are used. Although students may be able to distinguish a particular form from

Vc

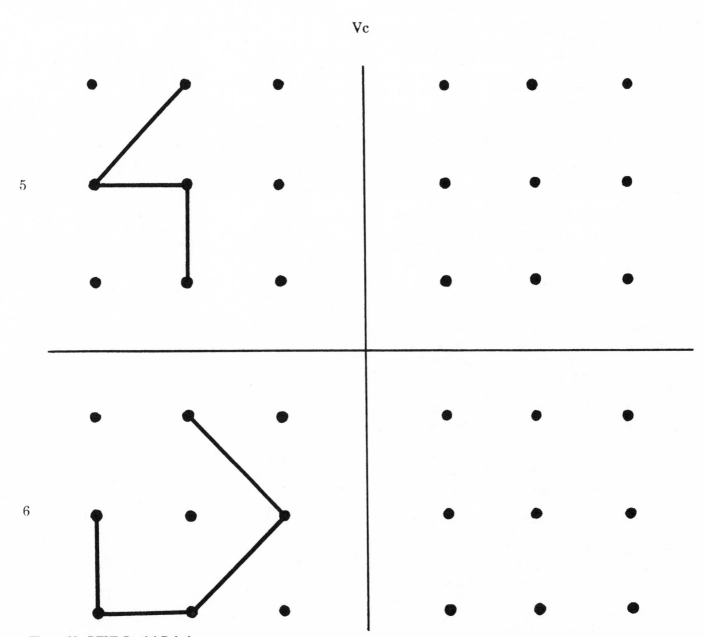

Figure 30. DTVP Spatial Relations

other figures presented in an identical, rotated, or reversed position, they still may not be able to differentiate letters having the same form but different positions (for example, *b* and *d*). The examiner should not conclude that a student's good performance on the DTVP automatically rules out difficulties in perceiving the symbols for language.

• Another difficulty with the DTVP is that visual perceptual skills are not measured apart from motor skills. The added motor component (tracing with a pencil), especially on the Figure-Ground subtest, contaminates the purity of the visual perceptual process. Visual perceptual abilities and motor skills should be measured as separate entities as well as integrative functions.

• Reliability results on the subtests range from .29 to .68, too low to be used in differential diagnosis. No reliability studies are given for students below age 5. Reliability on other tests is often low at this age level. This means that the results of a single administration to a preschooler should not be considered definitive of impairments in visual perception and eye-motor coordination.

• Validity studies reported in the manual were poorly designed and controlled (Salvia and Ysseldyke 1978, pp. 314–316).

• As with most tests, only trained persons should administer the DTVP. Explicit standards for trained examiners are provided in the manual. The authors urge that the regular classroom teacher not administer the test without extensive experience in testing procedures.

• Some of the administration procedures are in need of revision. For example, if a student spends too much time on an item, it is unclear what the procedure should be. During group administration, the manual states, ''If one child takes longer than the rest of the group, stop him and continue the test.'' This instruction may penalize the slower-working or cautious student. The administration time for the entire test may be excessive for preschoolers and needs to be broken down into two or three testing sessions.

• Vocabulary items used in the test directions may be unfamiliar to the students and pose some difficulty. For example, the word *outline* is often new to many students. Several vocabulary words in the directions stand for concepts that have a spatial reference (*right side up, middle, upside down*). The concept of not lifting the pencil from the paper is also frequently hard for young students to understand.

• The DTVP taps visual perception and eye-motor coordination exclusively. As part of a comprehensive test battery, it should be used with other measures assessing strengths and weaknesses in all developmental areas (sensorimotor, language, higher thought processes, social-emotional adjustment, and others). The DTVP should not be used alone to diagnose learning disabilities, just as no single test should be used in this way.

Motor-Free Visual Perception Test (MVPT)

Ronald P. Colarusso and Donald D. Hammill
Academic Therapy Publications, 1972
1539 Fourth St., San Rafael, CA 94901

Purpose	To measure overall visual perceptual processing ability
Major Areas Tested	Visual perception
Age or Grade Range	4–9 years
Usually Given By	Classroom teacher Special education teacher Occupational therapist
Type of Test	Standardized Individual
Scores Obtained	Age level Perceptual Quotient (PQ)
Student Performance Timed?	No
Testing Time	10–15 minutes
Scoring/Interpretation Time	15–20 minutes
Normed On	881 urban, suburban, and rural children from all races and economic levels in 22 states
Alternate Forms Available?	No

FORMAT

The materials required for administering the Motor-Free Visual Perception Test (MVPT) are the test manual, the book of test plates, and an individual scoring sheet. The test consists of 36 items arranged into five sections, each section with its own demonstration item and instructions.

Section 1. From an array of four drawings, the student selects a drawing of a geometric form that matches a stimulus drawing. The first three items in this section require matching by spatial orientation; the remaining five items require recognizing the correct form in a rival background, as shown in Figure 31.

Section 2. The student selects the geometric form that is the same shape as the model but is rotated, darker, or a different size. On some items in this section, the correct figure must also be distinguished from a rival background, as shown in Figure 32.

Section 3. The student is first shown a stimulus drawing and then is asked to choose it from memory from an array of four similar drawings (see Figure 33).

Section 4. The student selects, from an array of incomplete drawings, the drawing that would, if completed, match the model (see Figure 34).

Section 5. The student selects from four drawings the one that is different. The difference involves a change in spatial orientation of the drawing or a part of the drawing (see Figure 35).

The examiner tallies the number of correct responses in all five sections to determine the raw score. This score can then be converted to an age equivalent, a perceptual quotient, and with some computation, a standard score. Each of these scores represents the student's performance on the total test; separate scores are not given for each section.

STRENGTHS OF THE MVPT

• The motor-free aspect of this test makes it a useful diagnostic tool, because it helps to detect which component of visual-motor integration activities may be causing an individual student's difficulty. When used as part of a test battery that includes tests of visual-motor integration and various aspects of coordination, it can make an important contribution to delineating the specific problem area and setting up an appropriate intervention program.

• The MVPT is easy to administer, and although it must be given individually, it is not excessively time consuming. The scoring procedure is simple and objective. Admin-

A   B   C   D

Figure 31. MVPT, Section 1, Item 6

istering the test requires no disposable materials, except for the one-page scoring sheet, making it a relatively inexpensive test to give.

• The method of reporting scores is quite useful; the availability of age scores, perceptual quotients, and standard scores makes it easy to compare a student's performance on this test to performance on other tests. In addition, the availability of scores in several forms serves as a system of checks and balances against the pitfalls of the individual scoring systems.

• The authors' use of the standard error of measurement in reporting age-equivalent scores is useful because it requires the examiner to view the student's score as a range within which the "true" score is likely to fall. The examiner is also cautioned to take into account the standard error of measurement when interpreting perceptual quotients, although this is not "built into" the reporting of these scores (unlike the age-equivalent scores).

• The test directions are, for the most part, clear and simple. However, language-impaired students sometimes have difficulty understanding what is expected on the visual closure items, and the standard procedure outlined in the manual does not permit much additional explanation.

• The MVPT's reliability is acceptable for students aged

5 years to 8 years, 11 months but is borderline for 4-year-olds. Construct validity is acceptable for students aged 5 years to 7 years, 11 months.

LIMITING FACTORS OF THE MVPT

• The authors caution that guessing, random answering, and perseveration are factors that must be considered in interpreting scores on this and most other tests. A raw score of less than 10 indicates less than chance performance and cannot be interpreted with confidence.

• No information is given about the selection of the normative sample nor about the proportions of subgroups included in the sample.

• The sample populations for students aged 4 years through 4 years, 11 months and for students aged 8 years, 6 months through 8 years, 11 months were too small to allow confident test interpretation for students in these age groups.

• The high success rate on each item for 7-year-olds makes the MVPT nondiscriminatory at the upper age limits.

• The content validity of the test is open to question. The authors state that the test assesses five areas of visual perception: spatial relationships, visual discrimination, figure-ground perception, visual closure, and visual mem-

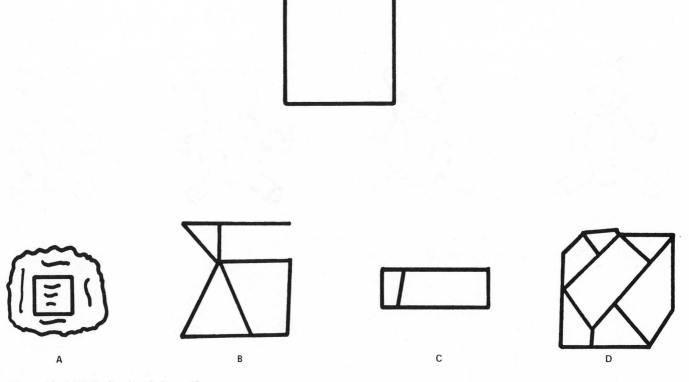

A   B   C   D

Figure 32. MVPT, Section 2, Item 12

ory. For each of the five types, other researchers are cited who have measured similar aspects of visual perception. However, the authors do not establish adequately that these five areas are mutually exclusive nor that they represent all aspects of visual perception.

- Some of the definitions of perceptual categories are vague and confusing. This is complicated by the division of the test into five unlabeled sections that do not seem to correspond in all cases with the perceptual categories the authors have defined. Section 1, for example, includes five figure-ground items, as well as three items that the authors would, it seems, include in their definition of spatial relations.

- The number of items in each perceptual category ranges from 5 to 11. Because the test provides only a total score, the larger percentage of items on visual closure, for example, means that a student with this difficulty may achieve an unrealistically low score.

- No information is provided about the test's construct validity for 4-year-olds and 8-year-olds.

- In studying the MVPT's criterion-related validity, the authors did not correlate MVPT scores exclusively with other motor-free tests, thus introducing too many variables for accurate interpretation. This problem was further complicated by using a homogeneous sample for the intertest correlations.

A   B   C   D

Figure 33. MVPT, Section 3, Item 15a, Item 15b

Figure 34. MVPT, Section 4, Item 29

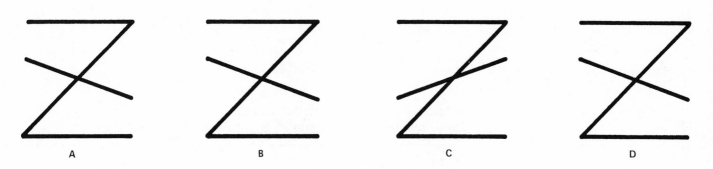

Figure 35. MVPT, Section 5, Item 34

The Bender Visual Motor Gestalt Test (Bender)

Lauretta Bender
The American Orthopsychiatric Association, Inc., 1938; Koppitz Developmental Scoring
System, 1963; Pascal and Suttell Scoring System, 1951
1775 Broadway, New York, NY 10019

Purpose	To assess level of maturity in visual-motor perception and to detect emotional disturbances
Major Areas Tested	Visual-motor integration and emotional adjustment
Age or Grade Range	5–11 years (Koppitz Scoring System) 15–50 years (Pascal and Suttell Scoring System)
Usually Given By	Psychologist
Type of Test	Standardized Individual Group
Scores Obtained	Age level Percentile
Student Performance Timed?	No
Testing Time	10 minutes (individual administration) 15–25 minutes (group administration)
Scoring/Interpretation Time	10–20 minutes
Normed On	1,100 students from the Midwest and East, including public school children in rural, small town, suburban, and urban areas; 1974 sample included Blacks, Orientals, Mexican-Americans, and Puerto Ricans (norms refer to Koppitz standardization)
Alternate Forms Available?	No

FORMAT

The Bender Visual Motor Gestalt Test (Bender) is a series of nine abstract designs to be copied in pencil by the student (see Figure 36). The figures illustrate certain principles of Gestalt psychology. The designs, printed on four-inch by six-inch cards, are presented one at a time. The student copies each design, with the sample before him or her. When the student finishes drawing a figure, the card is removed, and the next card is placed at the top of the paper. A modification of the test requires the student to recall the designs from memory after initial performance.

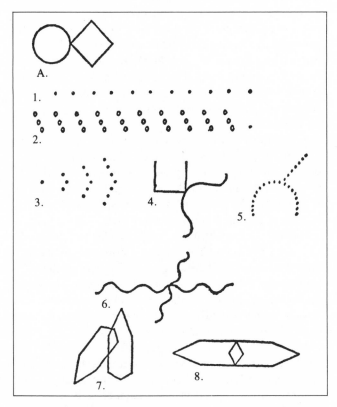

Figure 36. Bender, Plate I

The Bender is usually administered individually but can be given to a group of students. As a group test, different techniques have been devised for administration: projecting the designs onto a screen or wall, using enlarged stimulus cards, using individual decks of cards for each student, or using special copying booklets.

The standard individual administration of the Bender permits the student to erase and rework the reproductions. More than one sheet of paper may be used, and although there is no time limit on this test, data presented by Koppitz (1964) shows the average time required to complete the test along with the critical time limits. Timing the test, then, can be useful. Manipulation of the stimulus cards is allowed, but

they must be replaced in the original position before the student begins copying. If the student rotates the paper while copying a design, it should be returned to its original position before the next figure is presented.

There is no basal or ceiling level on the Bender. The student copies all nine designs, which are presented in a specified order. Alternate, equivalent forms for test-retest purposes are not available.

The original Bender did not include any formal scoring system. However, as the test became more popular in clinics and schools, several scoring systems were developed. One of the most frequently used was devised by Elizabeth Koppitz, a clinical psychologist who used the test extensively with children with learning and emotional disorders. Koppitz's book, *The Bender-Gestalt Test for Young Children* (1964), describes a scoring system, age norms for children between the ages of 5 and 11 years, and reliability and validity data. Volume 2 of the same book (Koppitz 1975) presents a revised scoring system, a norming population expanded to include minority groups, and a compilation of the research available on the test. These two books are essential for scoring and interpreting test performance.

In the Koppitz scoring system (described in detail in her books), errors are counted for distorting the shape of the design, perseverating, falsely integrating two forms, and rotating forms. The student's total error score is converted to a developmental-age score. Volume 2 provides tables for converting the total number of errors to both age-equivalent and percentile scores. Examples of error types are found in Figure 37. Koppitz reports that these types of errors are most indicative of minimal brain dysfunction.

STRENGTHS OF THE BENDER

• The Bender is a quick, reliable, easy-to-administer test that is generally nonthreatening and appealing to students. It is popular with psychologists and a widely used clinical instrument. The test is inexpensive and requires few materials.

• The Bender provides developmental data about a student's maturity in visual-motor integration. Of equal value is the important clinical information that can be obtained by observing a student's behavior while taking the test. For example, the experienced examiner notes such behaviors as excessive erasing and reworking of the designs, rotation of the drawing paper, time needed to complete the test, the spatial organization of the designs on the paper, and the student's attitude during testing. Two students may achieve the same score on the Bender, even producing similar-looking finished protocols, but the clinical observations of the two students may be very different. The behaviors observed during testing provide valuable diagnostic insight.

• Research has also supported the use of the Bender to detect emotional problems. Koppitz (1975) has developed two new emotional indicators (Box around Design and Spontaneous Elaboration, or Addition to Design) to add to her previous list of 10 (Confused Order, Wavy Line, Dashes Substituted for Circles, Increasing Size, Large Size, Small Size, Fine Line, Careless Overwork or Heavily Reinforced Lines, Second Attempt, and Expansion). She reports that the presence of three or more emotional indicators on a student's final product suggests the need for further psychological evaluation.

• The group adaptation of the Bender is particularly economical in terms of time. Combined with other brief tests, it is moderately effective as a screening instrument, to identify high-risk students in need of further evaluation. Used in a pretest-posttest manner, the Bender can also be used as a means of evaluating the effectiveness of perceptual-motor training programs.

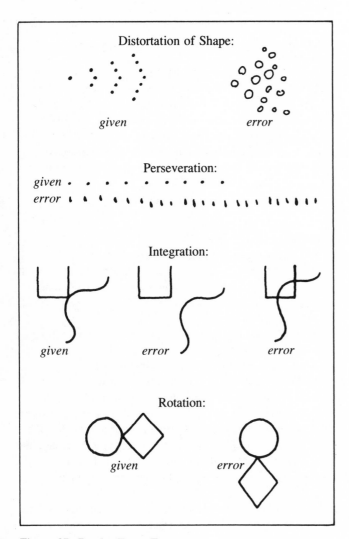

Figure 37. Bender Error Types

• The development of various scoring systems to meaningfully quantify a student's performance on the Bender has increased the test's utility. In addition to the Koppitz system for children, the Pascal and Suttel Scoring System has proven useful for adult protocols.

LIMITING FACTORS OF THE BENDER

• The Bender can be interpreted both intuitively and objectively. In either case, the examiner must be highly trained and experienced to effectively analyze the test protocols and to observe and evaluate the student's behavior while taking the test. For example, difficulties in copying the designs may result from immaturity in visual perception, motor coordination, or the integration of perceptual and motor skills. Less experienced examiners should definitely be cautioned against interpreting the Bender through subjective, intuitive procedures; use of an objective scoring system is more appropriate. Considerable experience is also necessary to achieve a high degree of score reliability with the Bender.

• In spite of recent improvements in the Koppitz Scoring System, the procedures still contain a high degree of subjectivity. The examiner must compare the student's reproductions with the model according to specific criteria. Scoring a Bender protocol can take considerable time because of the careful inspection required.

• Koppitz reports that the Bender can be used as a measure for detecting neurological impairment (minimal brain dysfunction). The Bender may be helpful in this regard when used in conjunction with other tests and with intellectual evaluation, medical evaluation, and social history. Such a diagnosis should *never* be made on the basis of Bender performance alone.

• Projective interpretations of the Bender should be employed with caution. The emotional indicators can discriminate between well-adjusted and emotionally disturbed groups of students but cannot be used for a definitive diagnosis of an individual child. The 12 indicators can differentiate neurotic, psychotic, and brain-damaged students only when accompanied by other tests and background data.

• The Bender is limited by age because of its developmental ceiling. The test distinguishes between students with outstanding or average visual-motor perception and those with immature perception only for students between the ages of 5 and 8. Most normal 10-year-old students can copy the Bender designs without any difficulty. Scores are meaningful for older students only if their perceptual-motor development is below the 9-year-old level.

• Only one set of norms is provided for both boys and girls (Koppitz standardization). This is in contrast to the separate age norms provided for boys and girls on the

Beery-Buktenica Developmental Test of Visual-Motor Integration (p. 116). Koppitz maintains, however, that various research studies have shown no statistically significant differences between the Bender scores for boys and girls from the end of kindergarten through the fifth grade.

• As a group test, the Bender has certain drawbacks. The examiner cannot observe and supervise each student individually; therefore some of the clinical value of the test is lost through group administration. For very immature and hyperactive students who cannot work independently, individual administration is more appropriate.

• A last consideration is the use of the Bender in research studies. The reported findings on using the test as a means of predicting academic achievement have often been contradictory. Further investigation might clarify these discrepant findings. More research is also needed to determine what the recall method of the Bender measures and what diagnostic implications this procedural variation holds. Another area that needs to be more fully explored and substantiated concerns the recent finding that the rate of development in visual-motor perceptual skills differs among students of various ethnic groups.

• Given the conflicting results of research using the Bender, it is best to think of this test as a measure of visual-motor integration through design copying, rather than as a test of intelligence, emotional disturbance, or minimal brain damage.

Beery-Buktenica Developmental Test of Visual-Motor Integration (VMI)

Keith E. Beery and Norman Buktenica
Follett Publishing Company, 1967
1010 W. Washington Blvd., Chicago, IL 60607

Purpose	To assess visual-perception and fine-motor coordination
Major Areas Tested	Visual-motor integration
Age or Grade Range	2–15 years
Usually Given By	Classroom teacher Special education teacher Occupational therapist Psychologist
Type of Test	Standardized Individual Group
Scores Obtained	Age level
Student Performance Timed?	No
Testing Time	10–15 minutes
Scoring/Interpretation Time	10 minutes
Normed On	1,039 urban, suburban, and rural children in regular classrooms in the Midwest
Alternate Forms Available?	No

FORMAT

The materials for the Beery-Buktenica Developmental Test of Visual-Motor Integration (VMI) consist of the manual and individual test booklets. The VMI is a pencil-and-paper test. It may be presented to groups of students but is more often used individually. The test booklet presents 24 geometric forms for the student to copy. The forms are printed in heavy black outlines and arranged three to a page, with a space below each one for the student to copy the form. The format is clear and uncluttered, and the forms are arranged from the simplest to the most complex (see Figures 38a, b, and c). The student copies the forms and may not erase or rotate the book. The test is not timed, and the student continues working until three consecutive errors are made. Although the same booklet is used for students of a wide age range, the student only copies forms within his or her ability. The raw score consists of the total number of forms copied correctly before reaching the ceiling; this score is converted to an age score using the tables in the manual.

The VMI is published in two forms. The Long Form contains all 24 geometric forms and covers the age range of 2 to 15 years. The Short Form is somewhat less expensive, contains only the first 15 geometric forms, and is recommended for students between 2 and 8 years of age. Alternate, equivalent forms for test-retest purposes are not available.

STRENGTHS OF THE VMI

• The VMI is a well-constructed test. The 24 geometric forms were chosen over letter forms because they were equally familiar to children of varying backgrounds. The forms are developmentally sequenced, with careful thought to increasing task complexity. The wide age range makes the VMI a good instrument for screening purposes as well as measurement of student progress. Separate age norms are provided for boys and girls, reflecting the sex differences that occur in visual-motor integration at different age levels.

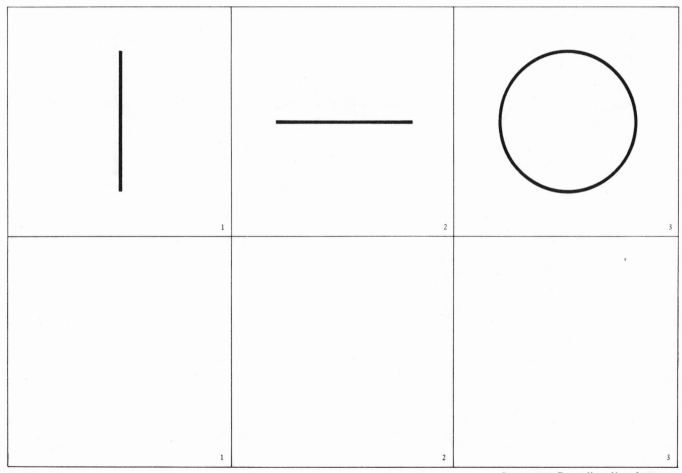

DEVELOPMENTAL TEST OF VISUAL-MOTOR INTEGRATION
Copyright © 1967 by Keith E. Beery and Norman A. Buktenica

Figure 38a. VMI, Items 1, 2, 3

• The VMI is an enjoyable test for most students. The directions are clear and easy to understand. The beginning forms allow even young or seriously impaired students to experience success, whereas the more complex forms present a challenge for the adolescent student.

• The VMI has clear directions for administration and is a good instrument for the classroom teacher to use with small groups of students. The global score is readily understood by parents. The provision of age norms for each item provides the teacher with a basis for understanding which types of geometric forms can be expected to be mastered next. That is, if a student can complete the right oblique line (/) and the left oblique line (\ ) successfully, we can expect that next the student will probably learn to reproduce the oblique cross (×).

• The VMI manual is particularly helpful in describing the process of visual-motor integration and outlining a sequence of visual-motor training activities.

LIMITING FACTORS OF THE VMI

• The VMI measures visual-motor integration. As in all tests of this type, it is often difficult to determine whether the student's difficulty lies only in the visual perception process, only in the motor response, or in both. Low scores on the VMI suggest that further testing or diagnostic teaching procedures be used to separate the two processes. One clue is often the student's frustration level on the test. If the student becomes very frustrated when he or she recognizes that the reproduction does not match the stimulus form, the student is probably perceiving it correctly but having difficulty with the motor response. Another student may not see that the reproduction and the stimuli are different, indicating that visual perception may also be impaired.

• Although the VMI has age norms for students up to 15 years old, it seems most useful with preschool and primary-age students. It can be used as either an individual

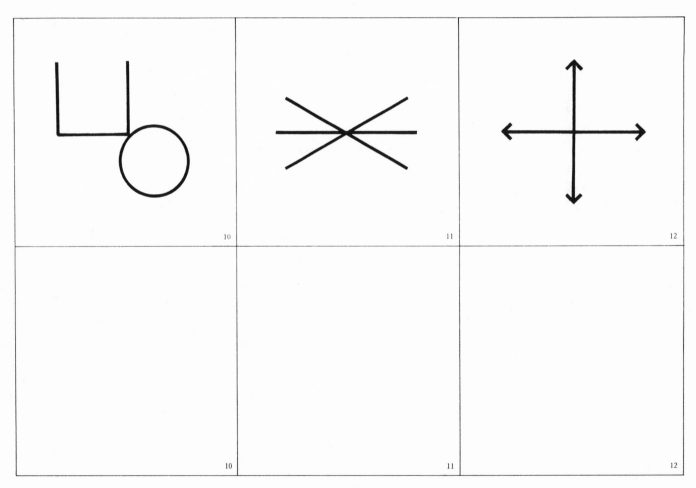

Figure 38b. VMI, Items 10, 11, 12

or group test with one set of age norms. If used as a group test, monitors should be provided to keep students from rotating the book or skipping forms.

• The scoring procedures for the VMI are somewhat inconsistent. On some items, great precision is required, and the examiner must use a protractor to score the item; on others, scoring is very subjective. It is important that the examiner emphasize to students that they do their best. Some students view the test as "so easy" that they work carelessly and then are penalized by the precise scoring system. In some places in the scoring system, the student who gets one more form correct gets a significantly higher age score. For example, a girl who obtains a raw score of 17 will receive an age-equivalent score of 9.4, although a raw score of 18 (one more form copied correctly) lifts her to an age score of 10.2—a 10-month gain.

• The VMI does not measure spatial organizational skills. Each form is copied in the space provided. A student may

have much more difficulty on a test like the Bender Visual Motor Gestalt Test, where nine forms are copied on a blank piece of paper. A very low score on the VMI often reflects an impulsive, careless approach to the test, and this must be sorted out from true deficits in visual-motor integration.

• The information on the validity and reliability of the VMI is not systematically reported. New data is currently being gathered by the authors. The size and composition of the standardization sample indicates that the norms are most adequate for the 5- to 13-year age range.

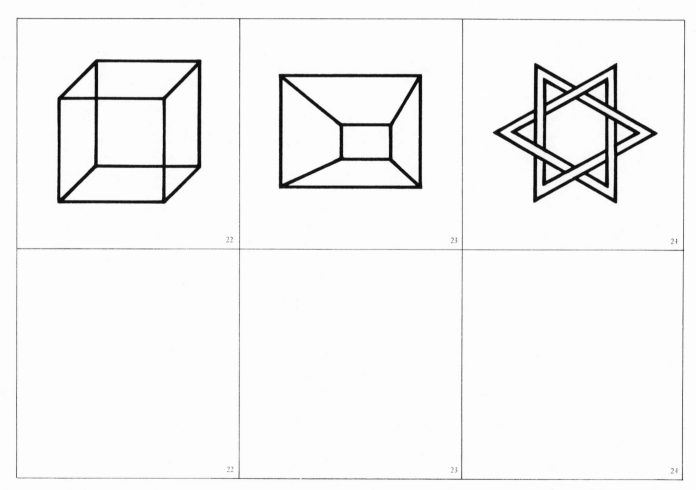

Figure 38c. VMI, Items 22, 23, 24

Speech and Language Tests

The primary, first-learned language system is oral. Long before children come to school, they develop skills of listening and speaking that enable them to communicate with others. The secondary language system, written language, is learned in school. Difficulties in the acquisition of reading and writing often have their basis in the student's oral language skills. This chapter deals with the assessment of oral language—its reception and expression. The 13 tests reviewed here are usually given by speech and language therapists or clinicians.

A complete speech and language evaluation includes assessment in the four major components of language:

1. *Phonology.* This is the sound system that constitutes spoken language. Phonemes such as /k/ and /f/ have no meaning in isolation, but their combination in specific sequences creates words.

2. *Morphology.* Morphemes are the smallest meaningful units of language. They are usually words like *picnic, work,* or *slow,* but they may also be grammatical markers signifying specific concepts, such as plurality (picnic*s*), tense (work*ed*), or shifts from adjective to adverb (slow*ly*).

3. *Syntax.* This is the grammatical aspect of spoken language, the system for ordering words into meaningful sequences. Grammatical structure plays an important role in the comprehension and production of spoken language.

4. *Semantics.* This includes the meaning of words, sentences, and paragraphs. Vocabulary is a basic part of semantics.

A speech and language clinician assesses both the receptive and expressive processes of each of these four components. For example, in the area of syntax:

- *Receptive.* Can the student comprehend past tense?
- *Expressive.* Can the student express ideas in past tense?

In the area of semantics:

- *Receptive.* What is the level of the student's listening vocabulary?
- *Expressive.* What is the level of the student's spoken vocabulary?

The tests reviewed in this chapter include measures of receptive and expressive skills in the four components of language. The chapter is divided into two sections. The first section includes four tests of articulation, or speech production. The Fisher-Logemann Test of Articulation Competence, the Goldman-Fristoe Test of Articulation, the Templin-Darley Tests of Articulation, and the Compton-Hutton Phonological Assessment all measure the phonological system in a variety of contexts. In addition to the individual reviews, a comparison of these four tests is presented in chart form in Appendix E.

The second section includes nine language tests, beginning with the most comprehensive measure, the Illinois Tests of Psycholinguistic Abilities (ITPA). The ITPA contains a variety of subtests that assess perception, memory, and language skills in both reception and expression. Some critics feel that it probably should not be called a language test; however, it does measure aspects of phonology, morphology, syntax, and semantics and is routinely given by speech and language clinicians. Therefore, it is reviewed in this chapter.

Following the ITPA are four measures of receptive language. The Peabody Picture Vocabulary Test assesses single-word receptive vocabulary; the Assessment of

Children's Language Comprehension and the Test for Auditory Comprehension of Language include not only reception of single words but phrases, sentences, and grammatical markers. The Boehm Test of Basic Concepts assesses knowledge of familiar concepts.

Two tests, the Northwestern Syntax Screening Test and the Sequenced Inventory of Communication Development (SICD) include measures of both receptive and expressive skills. The SICD is a developmental test containing both verbal and nonverbal communication tasks.

The language section concludes with two measures for assessing spontaneous speech. Developmental Sentence Scoring and Language Sampling, Analysis, and Training are not tests but rather procedures for gathering and assessing spontaneous samples of children's language. Relatively new, they are important contributions to the field of language assessment.

Each of the 13 tests reviewed in this chapter was designed for use with preschool children, attesting to the importance of the speech and language area in the assessment of very young children. The tests reviewed in Part II: Preschool and Kindergarten Tests all include significant language components. Those who are interested in the language assessment of young children are referred to that material.

Many of the tests reviewed in this chapter lack validity for students from bilingual backgrounds. Those who are interested in the assessment of Spanish-speaking children are referred to the extensive material in Appendix F.

Articulation Tests

The Fisher-Logemann Test of Articulation Competence (Fisher-Logemann)

Hilda B. Fisher and Jerilyn A. Logemann
Houghton Mifflin Company, 1971
Test Department, Box 1970, Iowa City, IA 52240

Purpose	To examine a student's phonological system in an orderly framework and to facilitate the recording and analysis of phonetic notations of articulation and the comprehensive and accurate analysis and categorization of articulation errors
Major Areas Tested	Articulation
Age or Grade Range	3 years–adult (Picture Test) 9 years–adult (Sentence Articulation Test)
Usually Given By	Speech/language clinician
Type of Test	Individual Criterion-referenced
Scores Obtained	None
Student Performance Timed?	No
Testing Time	10 minutes (screening test); 25 minutes (complete test)
Scoring/Interpretation Time	15–20 minutes (complete test)
Normed On	Not reported
Alternate Forms Available?	Yes

FORMAT

The Fisher-Logemann Test of Articulation Competence (Fisher-Logemann) is made up of two parts, the Picture Test and the Sentence Articulation Test. The materials consist of 109 picture stimuli on 35 hardboard cards in an 8½- by 11-inch folio, two sets of 8½-by-11-inch record forms, and a test manual. The manual contains detailed instructions for administering each part of the test, as well as directions for recording responses and distinctive-feature analysis of the misarticulations.

The Picture Test uses spontaneous identification of colorful picture stimuli to assess the production of 25 single-consonant phonemes, 23 consonant blends, 12 single vowels, and 4 diphthongs. Single-consonant productions are evaluated in each of the syllabic positions in which they occur in the English language. This test uses only words that have the test consonant phoneme next to a vowel. Therefore, consonants may occur in "prevocalic" (*d*og), "intervocalic" (le*tt*er), and "postvocalic" (do*g*) positions. Test words were chosen on the basis of familiarity and frequency of occurrence in the vocabulary of young children.

The picture folio can be converted easily into a convenient easel for presentation of the picture stimuli. The stimulus word, test phoneme, and item number corresponding to the record form are printed on the back of each card, which faces the examiner. A suggested "prompting phrase" is printed under the test word for use if a verbal prompt is necessary to elicit the response.

The two sets of record forms provide an abundance of useful information for the examiner. Transcriptions for the Picture Test are made on both sides of a single sheet. Productions of consonant phonemes are recorded on the front of the sheet, and articulation of consonant blends and vowel phonemes are transcribed on the back. The front of the sheet is organized into a chart that highlights the nature of the articulation deficit by distinctive-feature analysis (see Figure 39). The distinctive-feature analysis includes place of articulation, voicing, and manner of formation. Some unique features of this recording sheet include:

• A description of each single-consonant phoneme in terms of its distinctive features. For example, the *t* sound is listed as a voiceless, tip-alveolar phoneme produced as a stop consonant.

• Space for recording the specific types of misarticulation patterns, which are discussed and listed in the Phonetic Notation section of the test manual.

• International Phonetic Alphabet (IPA) symbols for each sound.

• Common spelling of each phoneme.

• The developmental age for each sound. This is the age at which 90 percent of the children are expected to have achieved mastery of the sound in all syllabic positions

(Hejna 1959). As an example, the chart indicates that 90 percent of all 7-year-olds should be able to articulate correctly the /s/ phoneme.

On the reverse of this recording form, productions of consonant blends using the phonemes /s/, /r/, and /l/ are transcribed (see Figure 40). Spaces are provided for noting the phonemic contexts discovered to be least and most conducive to adequate production of each. Vowel productions are also recorded on this side of the sheet and are organized in terms of place of articulation (front, central, back) and degree of constriction (high, mid, low).

The Fisher-Logemann also contains a rapid screening form of the Picture Test. This short form comprises 11 selected cards with marginal tabs for easy location. Productions of phonemes thought to be most commonly misarticulated are assessed (/θ/, /ð/, /l/, /s/, /z/, /ʃ/, /ʒ/, /tʃ/, /dʒ/, /j/, /r/).

The Sentence Articulation Test consists of a single card on which there are 15 sentences to be read by the student. The test evaluates production of every single-consonant sound in all three syllabic positions as well as all vowel phonemes in English. The sentences require third-grade or higher reading level. Each cognate pair of consonants (phonemes with the same place of articulation and manner of formation) is assessed in the same sentence, but consonant sounds with no cognates are grouped by similarity in the manner of production—for example, the nasal phonemes /m/ and /n/. The test phonemes are indicated by IPA symbols before each sentence, and the letters corresponding to the sounds are underlined within the utterances (for example, /tʃ, dʒ/ *George is at the church watching a magic show*). Spaces for recording misarticulations are provided above each test sound.

A summary of the student's sentence misarticulations may be recorded on the back of the record form. Each manner of formation and place of articulation is listed, followed by the sentence number in which the phonemes of that specific type are assessed.

STRENGTHS OF THE FISHER-LOGEMANN

• The Fisher-Logemann is available in a convenient test folio that converts easily into an easel for displaying the stimulus pictures. Its compact size makes it portable and easy to store.

• The test manual is well organized and concisely written. Detailed information on test development and administration and on recording and analyzing responses is supplemented by sample test protocols and a listing of common dialectal variations.

• This instrument is a comprehensive diagnostic tool. Articulation is assessed in both single-word productions and connected speech. Vowel sounds as well as single consonants and blends are included. Many conventional

THE FISHER-LOGEMANN TEST OF ARTICULATION COMPETENCE

Screening ☐ Complete ☐

Record Form for the Picture Test

Name____________ Date________ Examiner____________

Age______ Grade (or Occupation)__________ School (or Employer)__________

Birthdate__________ Home Address________________

Native Dialect__________ Foreign Language in home____________

CONSONANT PHONEMES

Place of Articulation

Card #	IPA Phoneme	Common Spelling	Dev. Age	Place of Articulation	Voicing	Stop Pre.	Stop Inter.	Stop Post.	Fricative Pre.	Fricative Inter.	Fricative Post.	Affricate Pre.	Affricate Inter.	Affricate Post.	Glide Pre.	Glide Inter.	Glide Post.	Lateral Pre.	Lateral Inter.	Lateral Post.	Nasal Pre.	Nasal Inter.	Nasal Post.
1 2 3 4 5	p b ʍ w m	p b wh w m	3 5 3 3	Bilabial	V̶	/p	/p	/p	/ʍ[1]														
					V	/b	/b	/b							/w	/w					/m	/m	/m
6 7	f v	f v	4 7	Labio-dental	V̶				/f	/f	/f												
					V				/v	/v	/v												
8 9	θ ð	th th	7 8	Tip-dental	V̶				/θ	/θ	/θ												
					V				/ð	/ð	/ð												
10 11 12 13	t d l n	t d l n	6 5 6 3	Tip-alveolar	V̶	/t	/t[2]	/t															
					V	/d	/d	/d										/l	/l	/l	/n	/n	/n
14 15	s z	s z	7 7	Blade-alveolar	V̶				/s	/s	/s												
					V				/z	/z	/z												
16 17 18 19	ʃ ʒ tʃ dʒ	sh zh ch j	6 7 6 7	Blade-prepalatal	V̶				/ʃ	/ʃ	/ʃ	/tʃ	/tʃ	/tʃ									
					V					/ʒ	/ʒ[3]	/dʒ	/dʒ	/dʒ									
20	j	y	5	Front-palatal	V̶																		
					V										/j	/j							
21	r	r	6	Central-palatal	V̶																		
					V										/r	/r	/r[4]						
22 23 24	k g ŋ	k g ng	4 4 5	Back-velar	V̶	/k	/k	/k															
					V	/g	/g	/g														/ŋ	/ŋ
25	h	h	3	Glottal	V̶				/h	/h													

SUMMARY OF MISARTICULATION PATTERNS:

MANNER OF FORMATION ERRORS:

PLACE OF ARTICULATION ERRORS:

VOICING ERRORS:

Notes: (These and additional notes are discussed in the Manual under "Dialectal Variations")

1. Either /ʍ/ or /w/
2. Either /t/ or /d/
3. Either /ʒ/ or /dʒ/.
4. Either /r/ or /ɚ/ or lengthening of the preceding vowel.

Figure 39. Fisher-Logemann Record Form

CONSONANT BLENDS

CARD & ITEM #	/s/ + CONSONANT	CARD' & ITEM #	CONSONANT + /r/	CARD & ITEM #	CONSONANT + /l/
26–1	_____/s _spoon	28–1	_____/r present	30–1	_____/l sled
26–2	_____/s star	28–2	_____/r bread	30–2	_____/l blue
26–3	_____/s slide	28–3	_____/r fruit	30–3	_____/l plane
		28–4	_____/r frying pan		
26–4	_____/s snake	28–5	_____/r three	30–4	_____/l flag
27–1	_____/s skate	29–1	_____/r tree	31–1	_____/l clown
27–2	_____/s swing	29–2	_____/r dress	31–2	_____/l glass
27–3	_____/s smoke	29–3	_____/r cry	31–3	_____/l bottle
		29–4	_____/r green		
Best Context: _____		Best Context: _____		Best Context: _____	
Worst Context: _____		Worst Context: _____		Worst Context: _____	

VOWEL PHONEMES

	FRONT	CENTRAL	BACK
HIGH	32–1. _____/i key 32–2. _____/ɪ mitten		34–4. _____/u two 34–3. _____/ʊ foot
MID	32–3. _____/e table 32–4. _____/ɛ bell	33–4. _____/ɚ shirt 33–3. _____/ə cup	34–2. _____/o phone
LOW	33–1. _____/æ hat		34–1. _____/ɔ ball 33–2. _____/ɑ sock

PHONEMIC DIPHTHONGS: 35–1. _____/aɪ eye   35–3. _____/ɔɪ boy

35–2. _____/aʊ house   35–4. _____/ju U

ANALYSIS OF VOWEL MISARTICULATIONS:

Figure 40. Fisher-Logemann Consonant Blends and Vowel Phonemes

articulation tests do not contain stimulus items that specifically evaluate vowel production. Consequently, the articulation of these sounds must be assessed independently by the examiner.

• The further value of the Fisher-Logemann as a diagnostic tool lies in its adaptability to either comprehensive assessment of articulation or quick screening. It is therefore appropriate for use in public school systems where rapid measures of articulation must be made or as part of lengthier diagnostic evaluations that require in-depth testing. Because a single record form is used for both the screening and complete versions of the word test, it is possible to switch easily to the in-depth form if multiple articulation problems are revealed by the screening.

• The stimulus pictures are interesting and colorful and therefore elicit the stimulus words easily in most testing situations. Alternate pictures have been provided for students who might be affected by geographical differences in pronunciation and by dialect factors. Care was also taken to choose items for the Picture Test with which students are known to have maximum familiarity: 90 percent of the selected words are included in the Kindergarten Union Word List, a study of preschool vocabulary, and 74 percent are found in the Horn Word List of the most frequently used vocabulary items of children through age 6. The same criterion of familiarity was used in choosing the reading vocabulary for the Sentence Articulation Test.

• An excellent feature of the Fisher-Logemann is its information about the phonological variations that should be expected for several dialect groups. Common variations among standard and class dialects in different regions of the United States are presented in footnotes on both record forms. Dialect notes in the test manual list phonemic substitutions for several native dialects (general American, Eastern, New York City and environs, Southern, and Black) and describe foreign dialect influences from Spanish, Italian, French, German, and Russian and the Scandinavian, Oriental, and Eastern European languages. Such vital information broadens the use of this tool and aids the clinician in making an appropriate diagnosis of either an articulation deficit or a dialect variation.

• Perhaps the most innovative facet of the Fisher-Logemann is the organization of its record forms. They are easy to use, yet they allow the examiner to note an abundance of useful information. Particularly useful are the guidelines for distinctive-feature analysis, which describes phonemes according to the factors that govern their discrete production. The result, therefore, is not only knowledge of the phonemes a student has misarticulated, but also the specific rules of sound production that have been violated. For example, if a student consistently substitutes /p/ for /f/ and /b/ for /v/, examination of the record form immediately reveals difficulties with manner of formation and place of

articulation—although the concept of voicing is intact. Furthermore, the examiner can determine that bilabial stop phonemes are being substituted for labiodental fricatives. Immediate access to such information aids greatly in planning appropriate therapy.

• Many conventional articulation tests assess the production of phonemes in initial, medial, and final positions within a word. But this type of analysis does not allow for assimilation effects. Stimulus words are not selected with careful attention to the influence of surrounding phonemes on pronunciation of the test phonemes; they may be preceded or followed by either consonant or vowel sounds. But the Fisher-Logemann uses prevocalic, intervocalic, and postvocalic positioning to account for these assimilation factors. The coarticulation effects of dissimilarly produced consonant sounds are eliminated. This method of organization enables the clinician to evaluate sound production within a systematized phonology rather than as isolated occurrences.

• The judgment of whether stimulus items provide a representative sample of a student's phoneme production is essential in determining the content validity of an articulation test. The Fisher-Logemann demonstrates content validity by assessing all the consonant and vowel sounds in the English language. Furthermore, stimulus words were chosen on the basis of their frequency in the vocabulary of young children.

LIMITING FACTORS OF THE FISHER-LOGEMANN

• Inherent in the organization of a formal articulation test like the Fisher-Logemann is a limitation imposed by the environment in which articulation skill is assessed. Conversational usage of speech sounds is not evaluated. Experienced clinicians are aware that students can often produce a sound correctly in single words while making errors in less restrained conversation. The Sentence Articulation Test does provide some assessment of articulation in connected speech, but this cannot be considered a measure of spontaneous production. Furthermore, because the Sentence Articulation Test can only be used with students at a third-grade reading level, evaluation of connected speech cannot be completed with younger students, beginning readers, or students with reading disability; yet these are the groups of students who are most likely to display articulation errors.

• The developers of the Fisher-Logemann do not provide any information in the manual about the reliability of their assessment instrument. It appears that studies to determine test-retest reliability as well as inter- and intra-rater reliability have not been performed.

The Goldman-Fristoe Test of Articulation
(Goldman-Fristoe)

Ronald Goldman and Macalyne Fristoe
American Guidance Service, Inc., 1969; revised 1972
Publishers' Bldg., Circle Pines, MN 55014

Purpose	To provide systematic assessment of articulation of the consonant sounds in English
Major Areas Tested	Articulation
Age or Grade Range	3–16 years
Usually Given By	Speech/language clinician
Type of Test	Individual Criterion-referenced
Scores Obtained	Percentile
Student Performance Timed?	No
Testing Time	20 minutes
Scoring/Interpretation Time	15–20 minutes
Normed On	38,884 students in grades 1–12 throughout the United States
Alternate Forms Available?	No

FORMAT

All materials for administering the Goldman-Fristoe Test of Articulation (Goldman-Fristoe) are contained in the easel kit—a compact device for displaying and storing the test. These materials include 35 large and colorful picture stimuli and response forms. A manual contains information about test construction and gives concise instructions for administering the test and recording responses.

The three subtest assessment procedures provided by this tool include the following:

1. *Sounds-in-Words*. Productions of all single-consonant sounds (except /ʒ/) and of 11 common consonant blends are elicited by the identification of pictures illustrating common objects and activities. The examiner asks, "What is it?" to elicit the test phoneme and then may pose additional relevant questions to produce the desired response. Consonant phonemes are classified as occurring in initial, medial, and final positions of the stimulus words. Medial position, according to the authors, does not necessarily refer to the middle consonant in a word but rather to some internal position within a polysyllable. Not all of the consonant phonemes are evaluated in each of three positions; omitted because of the rarity of their occurrence in the English phonological system are /h/ (medial), /w/ (medial), /hw/ (medial), /j/ (medial), and /ð/ (final).

The stimulus words are printed on the back of the picture, facing the examiner, with the letters representing the test phonemes set off in bold type and with extra spacing around them. The numbers corresponding to the record sheet are indicated above the test phonemes. For example, the test item shown in Figure 41 evaluates production of the consonant sounds /t/ and /f/.

2. *Sounds-in-Sentences*. The examiner reads two short stories aloud to the student while showing a corresponding

What is this?

13   9

t ele **ph** one

Figure 41. Goldman-Fristoe Sounds-in-Words, Plate 2

set of pictures. In presenting each story, the examiner emphasizes the ''key words'' that appear in bold type on the examiner's side of the easel kit. These words contain the phonemes being evaluated in the subtest, those sounds considered by the authors most likely to be misarticulated by children. The student is then asked to retell the story in his or her own words, using the illustrations as a memory aid. These pictures help provide some control over the content of the speech sample. The examiner is encouraged to prompt the student to produce any key words not elicited by the pictures.

3. *Stimulation*. This subtest evaluates the student's ability to produce previously incorrect phonemes correctly, in the context of syllables, words, and sentences, with stimulation by the examiner. The student is instructed to watch the examiner closely and to try to repeat the sound heard. Only phonemes that were misarticulated in the Sounds-in-Words subtest are evaluated and only in the word position (initial, medial, final) where the errors originally occurred. Stimulation pictures in this subtest list specific syllables, words, and sentences for testing stimulability for each phoneme. If the student is unable to imitate a sound accurately in any of three contexts, ''multiple stimulation'' is used, whereby the examiner repeats the phoneme three times before the student is asked to reproduce it again. Whenever a student is unable to articulate a phoneme correctly with multiple stimulation, testing for that sound should be discontinued. The Stimulation subtest provides valuable information concerning the sounds that may most readily be remediated by speech therapy.

The test phonemes on the response form are coded by color to designate the word positions being evaluated and also by number to designate the location of the sound on the response matrix. Blue always indicates the initial position within a word, yellow the medial position, and green the final position. Responses from the Sounds-in-Words and Stimulation subtests are recorded on one side of the form, and the responses from the Sounds-in-Sentences subtest are recorded on the other side. Side-by-side comparison of behavior on all three subtests is possible by folding over the Sounds-in-Sentences response matrix.

Misarticulations for the Sounds-in-Words and Sounds-in-Sentences subtests may be recorded with a simple X or with notations that describe the specific type of error. The manual reviews the standard notations for indicating phoneme substitutions, omissions, distortions, and additions, as well as the markings for making more detailed transcriptions about such problems as dentalizations and nasalizing. On the Stimulation subtest the examiner notes whether the student is able to imitate a specific phoneme correctly by making a checkmark for correct production and marking an X for failure.

STRENGTHS OF THE GOLDMAN-FRISTOE

• The Goldman-Fristoe uses large and colorful pictures that are highly interesting for most students, making it relatively easy to elicit the stimulus word under usual circumstances. This helps to make the time required to administer the test reasonable for diagnostic purposes. The ''condensed'' method of testing, which assesses more than one sound per stimulus word, also allows for fairly rapid administration of this tool.

• The easel kit designed by the authors proves to be a convenient method for displaying the stimulus pictures as well as for storing the materials. It is compact, light, and easily portable. The manual provides clear and concise information on test rationale and construction as well as detailed instructions for administering the test and for recording responses. The authors state that teachers with only a minimum of training in articulation and phonetic theory should be able to administer the test after a careful study of the manual.

• The unique value of the Goldman-Fristoe is the variety of contexts in which phonemic production is evaluated. Not only is articulation performance in single-word production evaluated, but also articulation in a controlled connected speech sample. This tool therefore provides more useful and complete data about a student's articulation skills than many other conventional tests. The Sounds-in-Sentences subtest may be of further diagnostic value in generating a speech sample for an informal analysis of expressive language. Inclusion of this subtest, which uses imitation, helps the speech and language clinician to identify the phonemes that respond most readily to stimulation and to develop appropriate therapy goals.

• Although the Goldman-Fristoe is designed for analysis of consonant production, articulation of vowels may also be judged. All the vowel sounds of English are present in the Sounds-in-Words subtest, and an alert examiner may obtain information on the student's production of these phonemes.

• The most useful information an articulation test can provide is the particular sounds that a student misarticulates and the types of misproductions that occur. The Goldman-Fristoe, however, also contains normative data for examiners who wish to supplement the diagnostic interpretation. Tables in the manual, provided by the National Speech and Hearing Survey, can be used to compare a student's articulation performance (judged by the number of errors) with national findings. This data was based on the articulation of 38,884 children in grades 1 to 12 (6 years to 16+ years) throughout the country. Percentile rankings have been computed, with separate tables for boys and girls (significant differences in performance were found between sexes at many age levels). The authors caution that these norms should not be used for labeling the severity of an articulation disorder as mild, moderate, or severe but for obtaining more descriptive information.

• An innovative item available at additional cost is a filmstrip depicting each of the stimulus pictures. This tool may help to hold the attention of immature or easily distracted students who do not respond readily to the easel kit.

LIMITING FACTORS OF THE GOLDMAN-FRISTOE

• A major weakness of the Goldman-Fristoe is the complicated format for recording responses. Although the form is color-coded to indicate sounds occurring in initial, medial, and final positions within the words, it is often difficult to locate these phonemes rapidly on the response matrix. Even highly trained diagnosticians may have difficulty evaluating several phoneme productions within a single word and then recording these judgments in various places on the response matrix—while maintaining the attention of the student. If an examiner attempts to record all the responses while administering the test, a more definitive judgment than "acceptable" or "unacceptable" production is difficult to make. In order to use this tool to make an accurate assessment of articulation, it is frequently necessary to tape record the session and to transcribe errors at a later time. This obviously extends the time needed to complete the evaluation.

• The Goldman-Fristoe is not available in a screening form and therefore may be too lengthy for use in public school screenings. Administration of the entire test is quite time-consuming (approximately 20 minutes), and the examiner may have difficulty maintaining the attention of young students or students who exhibit multiple articulation errors.

• Although the test manual does provide detailed information about interpreting students' responses, no consideration for dialect variations has been included. Frequently the speech and language clinician may be asked to evaluate the articulation of a nonnative English speaker or an individual from a different section of the United States. Some basic information on expected articulation variations for major dialect groups—such as Americans residing in the southern, northeastern, or midwestern United States or Mexican-American students—would certainly enhance the value of this tool.

• In the organization of this test, attention was not given to using the rules that govern production of specific speech sounds. The test provides information on which phonemes are misarticulated by the student, but it does not give information about what kind of errors occurred in terms of manner of formation or place of articulation. Distinctive-feature theory, which describes phonemes on the basis of common factors essential to their discrete production (such as voicing, continuity, and stridency), has been ignored. Therefore, the speech clinician needs to determine the pattern of a student's misarticulations independently in order to plan appropriate therapy goals.

• The assessment of phoneme production in terms of initial, medial, or final occurrence within a word does not account for coarticulation factors. *Coarticulation* refers to the influence of preceding or subsequent phonemes on the production of any specific sound in connected speech. Research has shown that these factors affect the articulation of phonemes significantly. Certainly one might expect that production of the medial /t/ phoneme in the stimulus word *bathtub* would be influenced by the preceding /th/ sound and may differ substantially from articulation of /t/ in the intervocalic position in the word *letter*. The authors provide little information about the criteria used to select specific stimulus words for this test.

• An important consideration in the selection of phonemes for testing purposes is the general age at which one would expect them to be a stable part of a student's sound repertoire. Consequently, a clinician would not attempt to correct a 5-year-old's articulation of the /th/ sound, because this phoneme's developmental age is generally considered to be 7 or 8 years. It would have been quite helpful if the developers of the Goldman-Fristoe had included developmental ages for phoneme acquisition on their response form. Although the sounds are arranged on the response matrix in roughly developmental sequence, more specific information on phoneme acquisition would be invaluable for interpreting test results and planning therapy.

• The reliability of this articulation test may be judged by the consistency with which the same response is recorded for each phoneme in initial, medial, and final positions within the stimulus words. Test-retest reliability was obtained for the Sounds-in-Words and Sounds-in-Sentences subtests only. Measures of interrater and intrarater reliability were obtained only for the Sounds-in-Words subtest. The lack of research to determine interreliability and intra-reliability for the Sounds-in-Sentences and Stimulation subtests is clearly a weakness of this tool.

• The content validity of a measure of articulation skill must involve stimulus items that provide a representative sample of a student's phoneme production. The developers of this test do not provide substantial information concerning the choice of the stimulus words, nor do they discuss the influence on articulation of such variables as word frequency and the grammatical function of a specific sound. Some measure of content validity, however, is assured by the fact that all but one of the consonants contained in the English language are assessed in the Sounds-in-Words subtest.

The Templin-Darley Tests of Articulation
(Templin-Darley)

Mildred C. Templin and Frederic L. Darley
The University of Iowa, 1960; revised 1969
Bureau of Educational Research and Service, The University of Iowa, Iowa City, IA 52240

Purpose	To assess general accuracy of articulation (Screening Test); to assess production of a wide range of speech sounds in a variety of word positions and phonetic contexts (Diagnostic Test); to evaluate consistency of production of various types of speech elements (Iowa Pressure Articulation Test)
Major Areas Tested	Articulation
Age or Grade Range	3 years–adult
Usually Given By	Speech/language clinician
Type of Test	Individual
Scores Obtained	Age level
Student Performance Timed?	No
Testing Time	15 minutes (Screening Test); 25–30 minutes (Diagnostic and Iowa Pressure Articulation Test)
Scoring/Interpretation Time	10 minutes (Screening Test); 15–20 minutes (Diagnostic and Iowa Pressure Articulation Test)
Normed On	480 white, monolingual public school children aged 3–8 years in Minneapolis and St. Paul, Minnesota; children of normal intelligence with no gross evidence of hearing loss
Alternate Forms Available?	No

FORMAT

The Templin-Darley Tests of Articulation (Templin-Darley) make up a compact diagnostic instrument comprising three separate tests: (1) the Screening Test, (2) the Diagnostic Test, and (3) the Iowa Pressure Articulation Test. A manual contains detailed information on test administration, the stimulus words and pictures, the normative data, and a general discussion of diagnostic procedures and research in the field of articulation. Record forms must be ordered from the publisher separately.

The total test contains 141 sound elements, many of which occur in more than one test. These stimulus elements can be organized into several different diagnostic units by using the record form overlays provided. Any combination of these diagnostic units may be administered, depending on specific diagnostic needs.

1. *Screening Test.* This test consists of the first 50 pictures in the manual, which are used to elicit the sounds found to be good predictors of articulation problems in preschool and kindergarten students. Cut-off scores have been provided for ages 3 to 8, at six-month intervals, based on the number of sounds correctly articulated. The authors state that these scores should be used to separate a student with adequate articulation from those requiring more in-depth articulation testing.

2. *Diagnostic Test.* This 42-item grouping of single consonants contains 22 stimulus sounds assessed in the initial position of words and 20 consonant phonemes in the final position. Use of the appropriate record form overlay identifies the items to be evaluated in this section. The mean number of consonant sounds correctly produced by children aged 3 to 8 years is provided at one-year intervals for comparison purposes.

3. *Iowa Pressure Articulation Test.* This test contains 43 items selected to assess the adequacy of a student's intraoral pressure for phoneme productions. This subtest, then, can be used to evaluate velopharyngeal closure and nasality. The stimulus consonants consist of fricative, plosive, and affricate sounds that have been found to require greater intraoral breath pressure than other phoneme types.

4. *Additional consonant cluster groupings.* These may be used to determine the phonetic contexts in which the student produces specific consonants adequately. It evaluates production of /r/, /ð/, /l/, /l/, and /s/ clusters, among others.

5. *Groupings of vowels and diphthongs.* This test assesses production of 11 vowel sounds, 5 diphthongs, and 1 consonant-vowel combination. Mean scores at one-year intervals for students 3 to 8 years old are provided for vowel and diphthong groups.

For young students, the examiner displays each picture and elicits the stimulus word by asking "What is this?" or

by using the questions and statements printed on the back of each card (such as "What's pouring out of the chiminey?"). The phonetic symbols are also printed on the back of the cards, with the item numbers corresponding to the record form. The examiner is encouraged to have the student imitate the stimulus word if the student does not produce it spontaneously with only the pictures as motivation.

There are 141 stimulus sentences (in addition to the 141 sound elements) for assessing the articulation of older students who are able to read and for whom the use of picture stimuli seems inappropriate. The phonemes tested in the sentence format correspond to those evaluated by the picture stimuli. Two test words containing the stimulus sound are included in each sentence.

The Templin-Darley record form lists each test phoneme, provides space for recording articulation performance, gives an outline for analyzing the test results, and allows for further comments. Sections are included for listing phonemes that are consistently misarticulated throughout the testing and for recording error sounds noted in the student's conversational speech. The authors suggest using standard phonetic notations to indicate correct sound productions (√), substitutions (enter phoneme uttered), omissions (−), distortions (X), nasal emissions (ne), and no response (nr).

After the student's responses have been recorded, the examiner should test the stimulability of the misarticulated sounds. The student should be asked to imitate each error phoneme in isolation, in a syllable, in a word, and in a sound cluster within a word. Space is provided on the record form for recording the student's imitative performance.

STRENGTHS OF THE TEMPLIN-DARLEY

• The Templin-Darley is perhaps the most comprehensive and versatile set of articulation tests available, and it can be used for testing the articulation of both adults and children. It is applicable for screening large groups in a public school setting, for obtaining a detailed analysis of articulation skill in order to determine the need for therapy, and for describing a pattern of misarticulations to aid in planning remediation goals. It is a practical investment for those on a limited budget, because it is a single instrument that can serve several diagnostic purposes.

• In addition to detailed information on administration and interpretation of the test, the manual includes a lengthy discussion about articulation testing and research. It is an excellent resource tool for speech pathology students and for clinicians who do not have extensive diagnostic experience.

• A unique feature of the Templin-Darley is the Iowa Pressure Articulation Test, which provides for quick screening of a student's velopharyngeal competency. However, normative data was obtained for presumably normal students and consequently does not relate specifically to those with cleft palates or velopharyngeal incompetency.

• The ability of a student to imitate a particular phoneme is an important consideration in the choice of a sound for remediation. This factor is often omitted in the format of articulation tests. The Templin-Darley, however, includes evaluations of the stimulability of error sounds in several phonemic contexts (in isolation, in a syllable, in a word, and in a sound cluster).

• The Templin-Darley in its entirety evaluates the production of 141 sound elements, including single consonants, vowels, diphthongs, and sound clusters. It is extremely useful as an instrument because it assesses a wider range of articulation performance than any other commercially available articulation test.

• The authors established the validity of this diagnostic instrument by conducting a study of the articulation performance of 150 children, aged 5 to 10 years. The children's performances on selected test items were found to be significantly related to a trained judge's ratings of the students' articulation in connected speech samples.

LIMITING FACTORS OF THE TEMPLIN-DARLEY

• The Templin-Darley assesses phoneme production in initial, medial, and final positions within stimulus words. This method of evaluation does not account for the influence of preceding and subsequent phonemes on the articulation of the stimulus sound. For example, production of /dʒ/ and /g/ in the word *engine* may be influenced by the preceding /n/ sound.

Moreover, in the Diagnostic Test, consonant singles (stimulus sounds and consonant phonemes) are assessed only in the initial and final positions. The authors defend the omission of medial consonants by questioning their validity—on the grounds that all consonants are either syllable-releasing or syllable-arresting in ongoing speech. This premise is shaky. All other commonly used articulation tests evaluate consonants in this position, and it is important to remediate error productions within a word to improve phonemic sequencing skills.

• Judgments of misarticulation on the Templin-Darley are based on general American dialect. No information is given about the effect of geographical variations and foreign dialects on articulation. Provision should have been made for considering such influences when scoring sound errors, because these are important considerations for clinicians who are planning appropriate remediation goals.

• The product of the Templin-Darley is knowledge of the specific sounds that a student misarticulates. However, interpretation of these errors in terms of such factors as voicing, manner of formation, and place of articulation must be made independently by the clinician. Information on the distinctive-feature analysis of sound productions and the developmental sequence of phonemic acquisition would have been valuable for interpreting test results and planning therapy.

• Comparison of an articulation performance with the norms presented for a specific subtest will indicate whether the student's sound development is above, equal to, or below that of peers. But to use the normative data provided by the authors, sound productions must be scored as ''right'' or ''wrong.'' This scoring system fails to account for the severity or specific type of misarticulations exhibited by the student. Placing an equivalent point value on all phonemes does not take into consideration the frequency of a particular sound in the English language. Certainly a student who consistently misarticulates the /s/ and /r/ phonomes is more unintelligible than one who has difficulty with /h/ and /v/.

• The authors report reliability data for only the 50-item Screening Test. Test-retest reliability coefficients ranging from .93 to .99 were obtained for the picture test and from .97 to .99 for the sentence test. Further research appears to be warranted to establish the reliability of the other tests.

• The rapid administration of a picture articulation test depends greatly on the student's recognition of and familiarity with the stimulus items. All but four of the stimulus words in the Templin-Darley appear on the Rinsland Basic Vocabulary list, developed in 1945. (We, the authors, have found that several of the stimulus words are difficult to elicit.) Apparently such an outdated word list includes items no longer relevant to the daily experiences of students. Items like *possum, shredded wheat, sharp, large,* and *help* are particularly difficult for many students to recognize and often can be assessed only on an imitative basis.

• The manual provides a great deal of information that is interesting but not essential for experienced diagnosticians. Instructions for administering the instrument are scattered through the descriptive material and are difficult to follow. In addition, a great deal of practice is required to be able to easily manipulate the record form overlays.

Compton-Hutton Phonological Assessment
(Compton-Hutton)

Arthur J. Compton and J. Stanley Hutton
Carousel House, 1978
P.O. Box 4480, San Francisco, CA 94101

Purpose	To provide a structured, step-by-step approach to the linguistic analysis of misarticulations
Major Areas Tested	Articulation
Age or Grade Range	Preschool–adult
Usually Given By	Speech/language clinician
Type of Test	Individual Criterion-referenced
Scores Obtained	None
Student Performance Timed?	No
Testing Time	20–25 minutes
Scoring/Interpretation Time	30–40 minutes
Normed On	200 children aged 3–10 years from diverse ethnic backgrounds
Alternate Forms Available?	No

FORMAT

The Compton-Hutton Phonological Assessment (Compton-Hutton) is based on the understanding that misarticulations are systematic in nature and that articulation therapy should consequently take into account each student's patterns of misarticulation. The materials consist of the manual, the stimulus pictures (conveniently bound together), and individual response-analysis forms. The manual explains the rationale underlying the Compton-Hutton, gives instructions for administration and analysis, provides notes on phonetic transcription, and suggests some therapy planning based on the assessment. The 50 stimulus pictures are clear and easy-to-recognize line drawings. The word list was carefully selected to assess the maximum number of sounds with a minimum number of words.

During the administration of the Compton-Hutton, the student looks at each picture and names it. The student is asked to say each word twice. The clinician listens for the initial and final consonant production of each word. These productions are noted in phonetic transcription in appropriate spaces on the response-analysis form.

The response-analysis forms are in three parts. Part I contains the word list, the sounds to be tested, and the spaces to record the student's production in the manner mentioned above. Part II contains the pattern analysis. Here, the sounds of English are grouped into meaningful patterns, such as stops, frictions, and r-blends. The responses recorded in Part I are transferred to the appropriate sections in Part II. Error responses are recorded in red, and correct responses in black. On completion, the patterns of misarticulation become evident. Part III contains a list of phonological rules, which the authors believe will describe 80 percent of the misarticulations observed in children. This is an optional section and is used by comparing the pattern analysis to the rules and circling those that are applicable. These phonological rules allow the clinician to characterize more precisely the patterns of misarticulations. Figure 42 is an example of a completed response-analysis form.

No scores are provided by the Compton-Hutton. Its purpose is to analyze a student's articulation errors according to phonological rules in order to plan an appropriate individual therapy program.

STRENGTHS OF THE COMPTON-HUTTON

- The Compton-Hutton is a criterion-referenced instrument that brings techniques of linguistic analysis to clinical speech pathologists in a fairly simple and easy-to-use manner. The manual and response-analysis forms are well designed and are of high-quality material. The pattern analysis helps to show the systematic nature of misarticulations, because the student's productions are summarized on a single page in an organized manner. The instrument can be used with a wide age range of students and enables the therapist to plan appropriate remediation programs.

LIMITING FACTORS OF THE COMPTON-HUTTON

- The purpose of the Compton-Hutton is to help provide an individualized remediation program in the area of articulation. It does not provide any information for comparing a student's performance with others of the same age or grade.

- Some clinicians may hesitate to use this assessment because it requires close phonetic transcription of consonant productions. The authors suggest tape recording some evaluations in the beginning in order to check on-the-spot transcriptions against the tape. The reliability of the transcription is crucial to the overall reliability of the assessment procedure.

- The authors state that their procedure has been used with 200 children, ages 3 to 10 years, over the past eight years. The rules relating to commonly occurring deviant phonological productions, contained in Part III of the response-analysis forms, are derived from approximately 100 children, ages 3 to 10, from a wide variety of ethnic backgrounds. These rules cover 80 percent of the misarticulations observed only in this small sample group of students, and their ethnic backgrounds are not described.

The validity of the procedure has been established in the literature; however, the authors state that more data may be needed to establish patterns in individual cases, particularly if the student has a severe articulation problem.

III. PHONOLOGICAL RULE ANALYSIS

(Circle all rules or those parts of rules which apply)

COMMON DEVIANT PHONOLOGICAL RULES

INITIAL CONSONANTS AND BLENDS

Liquids (Non-blends)

1.  $\begin{bmatrix} l \\ r \end{bmatrix} \longrightarrow [w]$

2. $[l] \longrightarrow \phi$

3. $[l] \longrightarrow [j]$

Glides

4. $[j] \longrightarrow [l]$

Liquids (Blends)

5. $\begin{bmatrix} l \\ r \end{bmatrix} \longrightarrow \phi$

6. $\begin{bmatrix} l \\ r \end{bmatrix} \longrightarrow [w]$

Stops (Blends and Non-blends)

7. $\begin{bmatrix} p \\ t \\ k \end{bmatrix} \longrightarrow \begin{bmatrix} p=\sim b \\ t=\sim d \\ k=\sim g \end{bmatrix}$ B (Blend)   NB (Non-blend)

8. $\begin{bmatrix} k \\ g \end{bmatrix} \longrightarrow \begin{bmatrix} t \\ d \end{bmatrix}$ B   NB

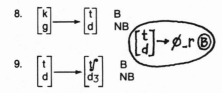

9. $\begin{bmatrix} t \\ d \end{bmatrix} \longrightarrow \begin{bmatrix} tʃ \\ dʒ \end{bmatrix}$ B   NB

Frictions (Blends and Non-blends)

10. 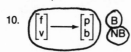 $\begin{bmatrix} f \\ v \end{bmatrix} \longrightarrow \begin{bmatrix} p \\ b \end{bmatrix}$ B NB

11. 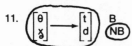 $\begin{bmatrix} θ \\ x \end{bmatrix} \longrightarrow \begin{bmatrix} t \\ d \end{bmatrix}$ B NB

12. $[θ] \longrightarrow [f]$ B NB

Frictions (Non-blends)

13. $\begin{bmatrix} s \\ z \end{bmatrix} \longrightarrow \begin{bmatrix} t \\ d \end{bmatrix}$

14. $[z] \longrightarrow [s]$

15. $[z] \longrightarrow [dʒ]$

16. 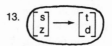 $[ʃ] \longrightarrow [t]$

17. $[ʃ] \longrightarrow [s]$

18. $[ʃ] \longrightarrow [tʃ]$

Affricates

19. $\begin{bmatrix} tʃ \\ dʒ \end{bmatrix} \longrightarrow \begin{bmatrix} t \\ d \end{bmatrix}$

20. $[tʃ] \longrightarrow [ʃ]$

S-Blends

21a. 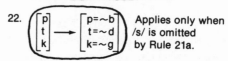 $[s] \longrightarrow \phi \; / \; \underline{\quad} \begin{bmatrix} p \\ t \\ k \end{bmatrix}$

21b. $[s] \longrightarrow \phi \; / \; \underline{\quad} \begin{bmatrix} m \\ n \end{bmatrix}$

22. 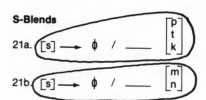 $\begin{bmatrix} p \\ t \\ k \end{bmatrix} \longrightarrow \begin{bmatrix} p=\sim b \\ t=\sim d \\ k=\sim g \end{bmatrix}$ Applies only when /s/ is omitted by Rule 21a.

23. $[s] \longrightarrow [ʃ] \; / \; \underline{\quad} [l]$

24. 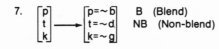 $[s] \longrightarrow [f] \; / \; \underline{\quad} [w]$

Figure 42. Compton-Hutton Response-Analysis Form

III. PHONOLOGICAL RULE ANALYSIS (cont.)

FINAL CONSONANTS

Stops

25. $\begin{bmatrix} b \\ d \\ g \end{bmatrix} \longrightarrow \begin{bmatrix} p \\ t \\ k \end{bmatrix}$

26a. $\begin{bmatrix} p \\ t \\ k \end{bmatrix} \longrightarrow \begin{bmatrix} p^7 \\ t^7 \\ k^7 \end{bmatrix}$

26b. $\begin{bmatrix} b \\ d \\ g \end{bmatrix} \longrightarrow \begin{bmatrix} b^7 \\ d^7 \\ g^7 \end{bmatrix}$

27a. $\begin{bmatrix} p \\ t \\ k \end{bmatrix} \longrightarrow \phi$

27b. $\begin{bmatrix} b \\ d \\ g \end{bmatrix} \longrightarrow \phi$

Nasals

28. $[n] \longrightarrow \phi$

29. $[\eta] \longrightarrow [n]$

Frictions

30a. $\begin{bmatrix} \theta \\ s \\ \int \end{bmatrix} \longrightarrow [t]$

30b. $\begin{bmatrix} \chi \\ \eth \\ z \\ 3 \end{bmatrix} \longrightarrow [d]$

31. $\begin{bmatrix} f \\ v \end{bmatrix} \longrightarrow \begin{bmatrix} p \\ b \end{bmatrix}$

32. $\begin{bmatrix} \theta \\ \chi \\ \eth \end{bmatrix} \longrightarrow \begin{bmatrix} f \\ v \end{bmatrix}$

33. $[z] \longrightarrow [s]$

34. $\begin{bmatrix} \int \\ 3 \end{bmatrix} \longrightarrow \begin{bmatrix} s \\ z \end{bmatrix}$

35a. $\begin{bmatrix} f \\ \theta \\ s \\ \int \end{bmatrix} \longrightarrow \phi$ (circled)

35b. $\begin{bmatrix} v \\ \chi \\ \eth \\ z \\ 3 \end{bmatrix} \longrightarrow \phi$ (circled)

Affricates

36a. $\begin{bmatrix} t\int \\ d3 \end{bmatrix} \longrightarrow \begin{bmatrix} \int \\ 3 \end{bmatrix}$

36b. $\begin{bmatrix} t\int \\ d3 \end{bmatrix} \longrightarrow \begin{bmatrix} s \\ z \end{bmatrix}$

37. $\begin{bmatrix} t\int \\ d3 \end{bmatrix} \longrightarrow \begin{bmatrix} t \\ d \end{bmatrix}$ (circled)

38. $\begin{bmatrix} t\int \\ d3 \end{bmatrix} \longrightarrow \phi$

Vocalics /l/ and /ə/

39. $[l] \longrightarrow \phi$ (circled)

40. $[a] \longrightarrow [ə]$ (circled) opt.

Additional Comments:

Language Tests

Illinois Test of Psycholinguistic Abilities (ITPA)

S. A. Kirk, J. J. McCarthy, and W. D. Kirk
University of Illinois Press, 1961; revised 1968
Urbana, IL 61801

Purpose	To assess how a child communicates with and receives communication from the environment and to provide a framework for planning remediation and developing instructional programs
Major Areas Tested	Visual-motor and auditory-vocal skills
Age or Grade Range	2–10 years
Usually Given By	Psychologist Speech/languge clinician
Type of Test	Standardized Individual
Scores Obtained	Age level Scale
Student Performance Timed?	Yes (some subtests)
Testing Time	1½ hours
Scoring/Interpretation Time	30–40 minutes
Normed On	962 average children from medium-sized towns and cities in the Midwest; 4 percent Black students
Alternate Forms Available?	No

FORMAT

The Illinois Test of Psycholinguistic Abilities (ITPA) materials consist of a manual, two books of test pictures, objects for description, visual-closure picture strips, and individual student record forms, all packaged in a carrying case.

The ITPA is based on Osgood's model of communication (Osgood 1957), which postulates three dimensions to cognitive abilities: *channels* (auditory, visual, vocal, motor), *processes* (reception, association, expression), and *levels* (automatic, representational). The subtests of the ITPA represent these dimensions. There are ten basic subtests and two other supplementary tests. The summary sheet (see Figure 43) shows how the ITPA is organized.

The two levels postulated by Osgood are the representational and the automatic. At the *representational level* (or meaningful level), the processes of *reception, association,* and *expression* are assessed in the two major channels, auditory and visual. Functioning at the *automatic level* is assessed in the two major channels in terms of closure and sequential memory skills. The two supplementary tests provide additional information about automatic functioning in the auditory channel. The supplementary scores are not included when deriving the total or mean scores for the test.

Precise directions for administrating and scoring each subtest are contained in the manual. Raw scores are converted to age scores and scaled scores and recorded on the summary sheet. Scaled scores are plotted on the profile sheet to provide a graphic representation of a student's performance (see Figure 44).

An individual's test performance may be viewed in several ways. The total of the raw scores from the ten basic

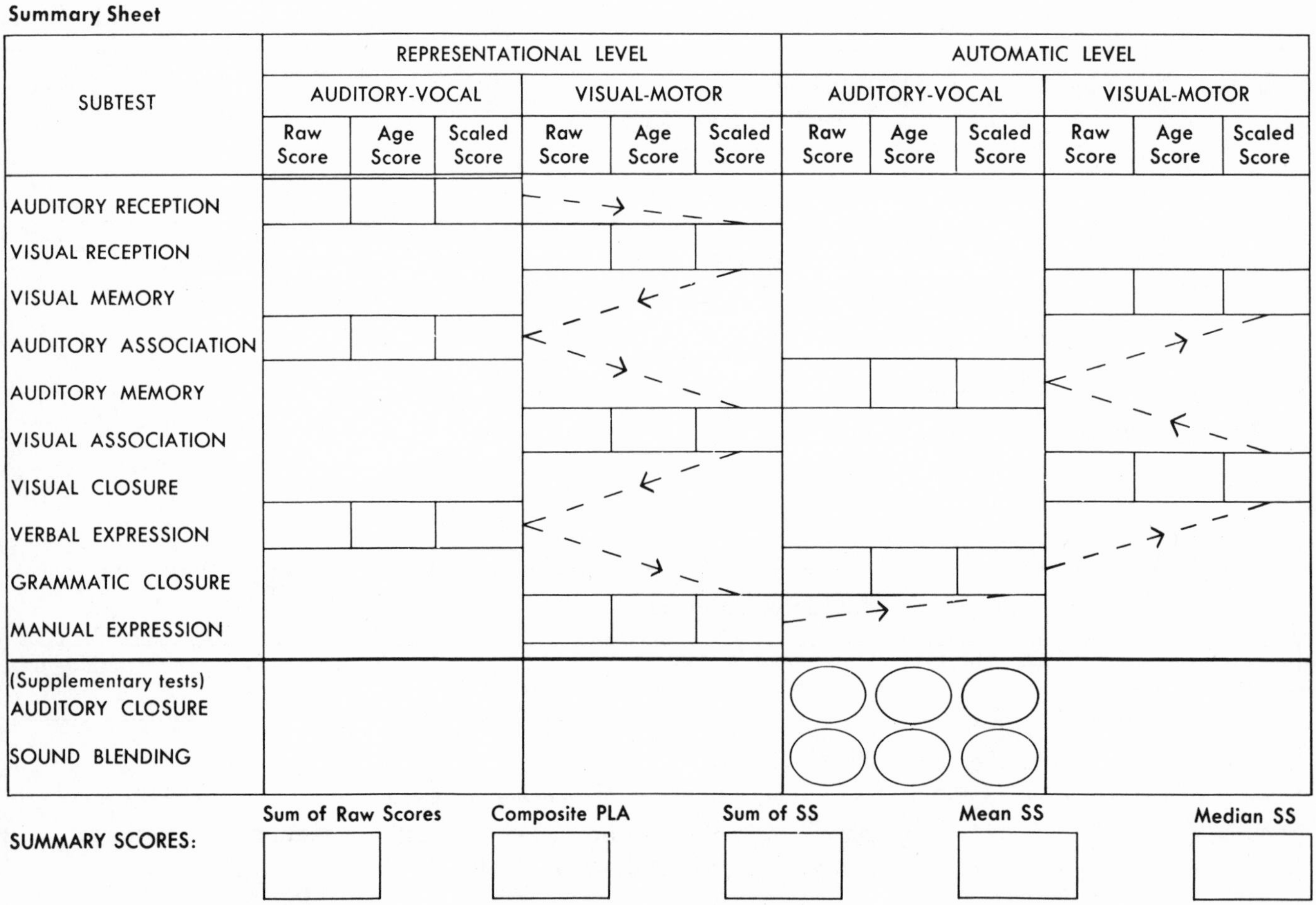

Summary Sheet

SUBTEST	REPRESENTATIONAL LEVEL						AUTOMATIC LEVEL					
	AUDITORY-VOCAL			VISUAL-MOTOR			AUDITORY-VOCAL			VISUAL-MOTOR		
	Raw Score	Age Score	Scaled Score	Raw Score	Age Score	Scaled Score	Raw Score	Age Score	Scaled Score	Raw Score	Age Score	Scaled Score
AUDITORY RECEPTION												
VISUAL RECEPTION												
VISUAL MEMORY												
AUDITORY ASSOCIATION												
AUDITORY MEMORY												
VISUAL ASSOCIATION												
VISUAL CLOSURE												
VERBAL EXPRESSION												
GRAMMATIC CLOSURE												
MANUAL EXPRESSION												
(Supplementary tests) AUDITORY CLOSURE												
SOUND BLENDING												

SUMMARY SCORES: Sum of Raw Scores | Composite PLA | Sum of SS | Mean SS | Median SS

Figure 43. ITPA Summary Sheet

subtests is converted into a "psycholinguistic age," which provides an overall index of the student's level of psycholinguistic development. The raw scores are also translated individually into scaled scores. The mean scaled score for the normative population is 36, with a standard deviation of plus or minus 6. The student's own mean is derived by averaging the scaled scores of the ten basic subtests. Discrepancies of plus or minus 10 from the student's own mean or the median scaled score are considered substantial. Using the student's mean or median scaled score as a reference point assists the examiner in viewing strengths and weaknesses.

In addition, patterns of performance may be found by analyzing the results further. Several ways of doing this are described by Kirk and Kirk in *Psycholinguistic Learning Disabilities* (1971). For example:

1. *Comparison of levels of organization.* The representational-level score is obtained by averaging age scores and scaled scores of tests at the representational level. The automatic-level score is obtained by averaging age scores and scaled scores of tests at the automatic level.

2. *Comparison of channels.* The auditory-vocal score is obtained by averaging age scores and scaled scores from auditory and verbal subtests. The visual-motor score is obtained by averaging age scores and scaled scores from visual and motor subtests.

3. *Comparison of psycholinguistic processes.* Scores for reception, association, and expression are obtained by averaging scaled scores for each process.

Table 17 describes and comments on the individual subtests.

PROFILE OF ABILITIES

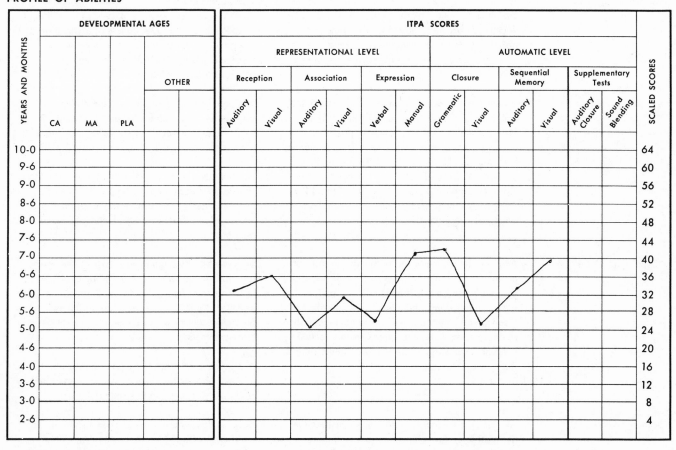

Figure 44. ITPA Profile Sheet

Table 17. ITPA Subtests

Subtest	Description	Comments
Auditory Reception	Assesses the student's ability to derive meaning from verbally presented material. Questions of controlled length and structure are presented by the examiner. Vocabulary increases in difficulty. A simple yes or no response is required of the student. (*Do dogs eat? Do cosmetics celebrate?*)	The examiner is cautioned not to influence the student's response by inflection or facial expression. The simple response that is required makes it possible to test nonverbal children. However, some students may be tempted to give minimal involvement to the task and thereby respond in random fashion.
Visual Reception	Assesses the student's ability to match concepts presented visually. After brief exposure to a single stimulus picture, the student selects the correct match from four choices on the following page. Objects and situations conceptually similar to the stimulus are to be chosen (see Figure 45 on p. 147).	Mild and moderate visual handicaps do not appear to affect performance on this subtest. It appears to measure central rather than peripheral processes (Bateman 1963).
Auditory Association	Assesses the student's ability to complete verbal analogies presented by the examiner. The vocabulary becomes more difficult as the task progresses. (*I sit on a chair; I sleep on a _____ . Years have seasons; dollars have _____ .*)	The student needs to grasp the analogy and to select the correct word that expresses it. Although included as a test of the process of association, the receptive and expressive processes are also involved. Careful analysis of a student's performance is needed to sort out the processes.
Visual Association	Assesses the student's ability to relate associated concepts, such as sock/shoe and hammer/nail. Stimulus and response pictures are presented on one page. At the lower level, the stimulus picture is surrounded by four choices (see Figure 46a on p. 148). At the higher level, analogous relationships are employed (see Figure 46b on p. 149). They follow the format "If this goes with this, then what goes with this?"	The process of selecting one of the pictures surrounding the stimulus picture is difficult for some children to understand. Some may imitate the examiner's model, pointing to all the pictures. At the higher level, it is possible for a student to choose the correct item without following the two-part analogy. Success at this level does not necessarily indicate an understanding of analogous relationships.
Verbal Expression	Assesses the student's ability to express concepts pertaining to familiar objects. The student is presented four objects individually—a ball, a block, an envelope, and a button—then asked to "Tell me all about this." The score is the number of discrete, relevant, and approximately factual concepts expressed. There is a one-minute time limit for each object.	This subtest, although labeled *Expression,* gives little information about the linguistic development of the student. Sentence use and grammar are not assessed. Rather, it is a test of cognitive awareness regarding objects and of the ability to express those concepts. A calm state, alertness to detail, and the ability to free associate and to respond within a time limit are basic to success on this subtest.
Manual Expression	Assesses the student's ability to demonstrate the use of objects through pantomime. A stimulus picture is presented, accompanied by the verbal request to "Show me what you do with a _____ ." The student's movements are recorded on a checklist of behaviors. Objects pictured include a guitar and binoculars.	Because this subtest assesses observation of and familiarity with objects in the environment, some students may be penalized by lack of exposure to such items as guitars and binoculars. Students respond best to this task when relaxed and uninhibited.

Table 17. —*Continued*

Subtest	Description	Comments
Manual Expression—*continued*		A study by McCarthy, reported in Kirk and Kirk (1971), found Down's Syndrome children to be superior in this area to other retarded children, and in relation to their other abilities. Many children with severe verbal language deficits do well on this measure of gestural language.
Grammatic Closure	Assesses the student's ability to complete verbal statements presented by the examiner. Each item consists of a complete statement followed by one to be completed with the correct word or grammatical inflection. Pictures serve as stimuli. (*Here is a boy. Here are two _____ . Each child has a ball. This is hers and this is _____ .*)	The ITPA was standardized on a basically Caucasian population. Standard American dialect was predominant. Therefore, responses of students from other populations may be informative, but they should not be scored. Students with speech defects were found to be deficient on this subtest in studies done by Ferrier (1966) and Foster (1963). This subtest does not provide complete analysis of grammatical form. Language sampling should be employed for more complete information.
Visual Closure	Assesses the student's ability to recognize a pictured object (or objects) when partially obscured in a scene. The task requires visual closure and figure-ground discrimination. Items to be recognized in the scene shown in Figure 47 (see p. 148) are dogs. A pointing response is used. There is a 30-second time limit.	Scanning ability and a reasonable searching procedure assist the student on this task. Also, an ability to function under time pressure is involved, although not explicitly stated.
Auditory Memory	Assesses the student's short-term memory for digits presented at the rate of two per second. Two trials are allowed. The digit series increase in length from two to eight numbers.	This subtest assesses immediate recall of unstructured, nonsyntactic material. Performance may be unrelated to short-term memory for other material, such as sentences. Because it requires verbal output, it may also be unrelated to tests of short-term retention of directions that are acted out rather than spoken. Performance on this subtest requires attention, a calm state, and retention of sequential material.
Visual Memory	Assesses the student's ability to reproduce sequences of nonmeaningful figures from memory. A pictured sequence is shown for five seconds; then the student places corresponding tiles in the same order. Two trials are allowed. Sequences increase in length from two to eight designs and include such patterns as those shown in Figure 48 (see p. 150)	This subtest requires a minimum of accumulated knowledge. Performance may be influenced by the ability to focus attention, function within a time limit, and retain sequential patterns. Patience and tolerance for a frustrating task are an aid. Some students are assisted by their verbal description of the designs. This helps the examiner understand a student's strategy but diminishes the test's value as a discrete measure of visual memory. This subtest only assesses memory of nonmeaningful pictorial material.

Table 17. —*Continued*

Subtest	Description	Comments
Auditory Closure (Supplementary)	Assesses the student's ability to supply mentally, then verbally, the sounds omitted in word(s) presented by the examiner. A progression from easier to more difficult vocabulary is used. Stimuli include ''airpla/'' (*airplane*) and ''auto/o/ile'' (*automobile*).	The student needs adequate hearing, good vocabulary, and attentive behavior to accomplish this task.
Sound Blending (Supplementary)	Assesses the student's ability to blend sounds spoken by the examiner at half-second intervals into words. At the lower end of the test, pictures are employed. The test progresses through synthesis of words with no picture clue (*f-i-s-h*) to nonsense words (*t-e-k-o*).	The upper limit for this subtest is below that for the test as a whole, specifically 8 years, 7 months. Adequate hearing, auditory discrimination, and retention of sounds in sequence are required for adequate performance. Performance may also reflect training approaches. For instance, students in the primary grades who have been instructed in a phonic approach often do not reach a ceiling. A recording is provided to ensure correct presentation.

Figure 45. ITPA Visual Reception

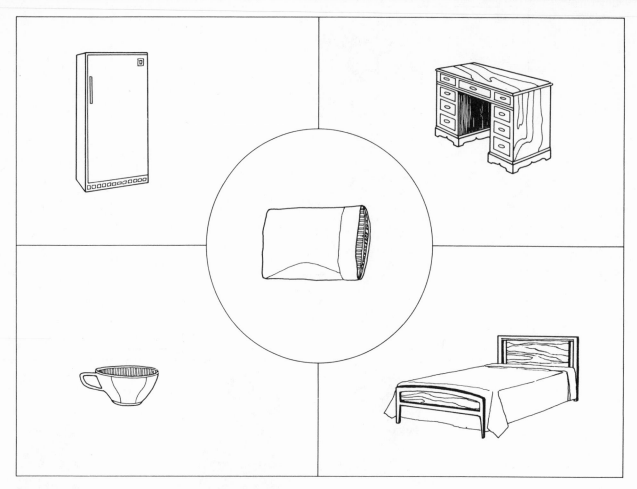

Figure 46a. ITPA Visual Association, Lower Level

Figure 47. ITPA Visual Closure

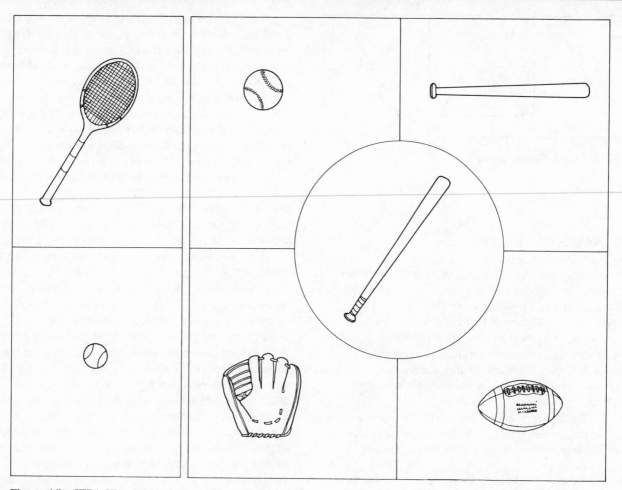

Figure 46b. ITPA Visual Association, Higher Level

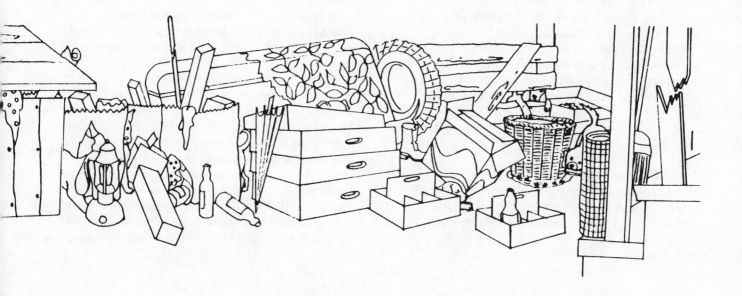

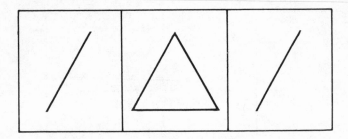

Figure 48. ITPA Visual Memory

STRENGTHS OF THE ITPA

• The ITPA is widely used and highly respected. It has been carefully constructed, its organization derived from the Osgood and Sebeok (1965) model of communication. This model makes it possible to view an individual's strengths and weaknesses in terms of channels, levels of organization, and processes. The ITPA provides a basis for making observations about an individual's pattern of performance. Supplemented by other diagnostic measures, it assists in accurate diagnosis of learning and language problems.

• Directions for presenting and scoring the ITPA are well stated in the manual. The examiner will find the profile sheet useful in viewing an individual's strengths and weaknesses.

• The variety of tasks included in the test enables the examiner to alter task presentation to meet the needs of the student. Tasks requiring the greatest concentration can be presented when attention and interest are adequate. The visual tests provide a means for evaluating children with poor language skills and give them the opportunity to demonstrate normal functioning.

• The ITPA has been widely studied. Many publications are available to increase the examiner's understanding of the test. Courses are taught on its construction and administration, and a film is available to help prepare examiners.

LIMITING FACTORS OF THE ITPA

• The term *psycholinguistic abilities* used in the title of this test is misleading. The ITPA samples cognitive functioning in verbal and nonverbal areas through different processes, but it does not analyze a student's psycholinguistic abilities.

• The ITPA purports to measure "discrete" functions. However, it is difficult to define, and to develop, tests that measure "discrete" functions. Subtests that are designed to assess nonlanguage functioning, such as Visual Memory, may still involve the use of vocabulary. Some students use labeling to retain the visual patterns.

• The ITPA was standardized on a limited sample of the population, drawn from medium-sized towns and cities in the Midwest. Rural and metropolitan areas were not represented. Only 4 percent of the population was Black, and the number of Spanish-Americans is not even reported. Thus the usefulness of the ITPA for minority populations is extremely limited. The results must be interpreted with caution when used with minorities or students from lower socioeconomic classes. Reference to research on the use of the ITPA with these groups is included in Kirk and Kirk's book (1971).

• Caution is also advised in the interpretation of scores. Within the age range of 2 to 10 years, scores should be compared to the student's scaled score. To do this, all ten subtests must be given. Age scores should not be compared at these ages. Interpretation of scores is difficult at both the lower and upper ends of the age range. Many of the ITPA subtests do not provide a high enough ceiling. Above age 10, language-age scores, rather than scaled scores, should be used to describe performance.

• Accurate administration and meaningful interpretation of the ITPA require good preparation and experience. Its use by untrained and inexperienced people is fraught with danger, much as the use of IQ tests is. Its administration is also more time-consuming than the manual would suggest. Usually an hour and a half are required for its presentation, and another hour for scoring and interpretation.

• The ITPA does not, and should not, stand alone as a diagnostic tool. The examiner needs to know how to interpret the results and to supplement the testing to obtain needed information, whether academic, cognitive, or linguistic.

• Studies on the validity of the ITPA are limited. Factor-analytic studies of the ITPA have neither proven nor disproven the construct validity of the test, according to the authors (Kirk and Kirk 1978, p. 64). A study by Elkins (1972) analyzed construct validity and found that the process and channel dimensions were verified but that the representational and automatic levels were not clear. Evidence of predictive validity is not presented. Although Paraskevopoulos and Kirk (1969) state that scores deviating from the child's mean make it more likely that the child will have learning disabilities, no data is provided to support this conclusion.

- Reliability data is summarized by Salvia and Ysseldyke in their book on assessment (1978, p. 357). Internal consistency is generally high in the ITPA, but particular caution should be taken in interpreting the Visual Closure and Auditory Closure subtests. Test-retest reliability is significantly lower than internal-consistency reliability. Salvia and Ysseldyke (1978) provide a summary of the reliability data.

Peabody Picture Vocabulary Test (PPVT)

Lloyd M. Dunn
American Guidance Service, Inc., 1959; revised 1965
Publishers' Bldg., Circle Pines, MN 55014

Purpose	To assess a student's hearing vocabulary and to provide an estimate of verbal intelligence
Major Areas Tested	Receptive single-word vocabulary
Age or Grade Range	2–18 years
Usually Given By	Special education teacher Psychologist Speech/language clinician
Type of Test	Standardized Individual
Scores Obtained	Mental age IQ Percentile
Student Performance Timed?	No
Testing Time	10–15 minutes
Scoring/Interpretation Time	10–15 minutes
Normed On	More than 4,000 white Southern urban students
Alternate Forms Available?	Yes

FORMAT

The materials for the Peabody Picture Vocabulary Test (PPVT) consist of a book of line drawings printed four on a page, individual record forms, and an examiner's manual. To administer the test, the examiner pronounces a word, and the student selects the corresponding picture ("Show me *meringue.*"). No verbal response is needed because the student can simply point to the correct picture. The vocabulary words gradually increase in difficulty, from such items as *wagon, tumble,* and *freckle* through *appliance* and *hassock* to *sibling* and *emaciated.*

Although all the items are together in one picture book, the student is tested on only the vocabulary appropriate for his or her age and language development. There are no subtests. Equivalent Forms A and B are provided; both may be given in alternate sessions to increase the reliability of the score, or they may be used as pre- and posttests for evaluting a student's progress. The manual includes detailed directions for administering and scoring as well as tables for converting raw scores to mental-age scores, IQs, and percentiles.

STRENGTHS OF THE PPVT

• The PPVT is well designed and well normed for a white middle-class population. The format of presenting a picture to elicit a pointing response makes it a nonthreatening test that even the young or seriously impaired student can take successfully. It is frequently used as the first in a battery of tests, because its easy format makes it a good warm-up for more difficult material. The wide age range covered by the PPVT and its alternate forms make it a good instrument for test-retest purposes; it can be administered every year to assess a student's progress in specific language therapy or in language development generally. The PPVT is relatively quick to administer and interpret. Although it is usually used as a global measure of receptive vocabulary, analysis of a student's errors can reveal information about the specific nature of a vocabulary deficit. For example, the student who makes errors on such items as *erecting, assaulting,* and *welding* would seem to be having difficulty with verbs.

LIMITING FACTORS OF THE PPVT

• The PPVT is a test of single-word vocabulary only. The comprehension of spoken language in context is a different skill, and the examiner must not assume that a student's receptive language is adequate simply because he or she obtains a high PPVT score. Knowing the meaning of *group* when it is pronounced clearly and represented by a picture of four kittens is quite different from understanding the word when the teacher says, "First do the group of subtraction problems on page 10, and then do the group on page 14, starting with line 3." In addition, the PPVT

assesses only receptive vocabulary. A high PPVT score may not predict high verbal performance in the classroom. Understanding a word and using it correctly in spoken language are two different skills.

• The PPVT does not assess all parts of speech. Only nouns, verbs, and adjectives are included. The understanding of prepositions, a critical skill, is not included.

• Although the PPVT yields an IQ score and has a high correlation with several individual IQ tests, it is not a comprehensive measure of intellectual ability and should not be used as such. Its use should be limited to measuring receptive vocabulary only.

• The PPVT was normed on a white Southern urban population. Caution must therefore be used when applying norms to another group. Cultural background may affect scores, because students from disadvantaged homes may not have had experience with the pictured items. In a student from a middle-class home and community, a low score may reflect a true deficit in ability to comprehend spoken language, but in a student from a culturally different or disadvantaged background, a low score may reflect lack of language stimulation or experience. The program for developing language skills in these two students would be quite different.

• As in all tests, the student's attention span is a big factor in performance. Low scores on the PPVT may be related to impulsive responses caused by an inability to scan four pictures. Or they may result from perseveration—continued pointing to the same position on the page. Such behavior is not unusual in low-functioning children with physical or emotional attention problems. A low PPVT score therefore may not reflect low vocabulary development but rather an inability to scan and select visual material.

• In the PPVT, hearing vocabulary is measured through picture stimuli. Clearly, two processes are involved in doing this: the understanding of the spoken word and the understanding of the line drawings. A low score may not necessarily reflect a problem in receptive vocabulary but possibly a problem in comprehending pictures. For example, a student may know the meaning of the word *descending* but not be able to tell which man pictured on the escalator is going down. Other measures of receptive vocabulary and picture comprehension are needed to confirm the results of the PPVT if a specific definition of the disability is needed.

Assessment of Children's Language Comprehension (ACLC)

R. Foster, J. Gidden, and J. Stark
Consulting Psychologists Press, Inc., 1973
577 College Ave., Palo Alto, CA 94306

Purpose	To define receptive language problems in young children using single-word vocabulary and phrases
Major Areas Tested	Receptive language
Age or Grade Range	3–7 years
Usually Given By	Speech/language clinician
Type of Test	Standardized Individual Group
Scores Obtained	Ratio Percentage
Student Performance Timed?	No
Testing Time	15–20 minutes
Scoring/Interpretation Time	5 minutes
Normed On	A small sample of normal nursery school and kindergarten children from diverse socioeconomic levels and ethnic groups in Florida and California
Alternate Forms Available?	No

FORMAT

The Assessment of Children's Language Comprehension (ACLC) materials consist of a spiral-bound book of silhouette and line drawings, a teacher's manual, and record sheets. The test has four sections. Part A assesses the student's comprehension of a core vocabulary of 50 single words (nouns, verbs, prepositions, and modifiers). The examiner pronounces the words one at a time, and the student responds by pointing to the correct drawing from a group of five. Testing is terminated if it becomes apparent that the student does not know the core vocabulary.

Parts B, C, and D each consist of 10 items using the core vocabulary in phrases of two, three, and four critical elements. For example: *horse standing, broken cup* (two critical elements); *chicken in the basket, happy lady sleeping* (three critical elements); *happy little girl jumping, cat standing under the bed* (four critical elements). The examiner pronounces the phrase, and the student points to the correct drawing. A record sheet for each student is used to note the error patterns.

A group form of the ACLC also exists, composed of 17 plates from the complete version. This is used as a screening test for groups. Each student receives a booklet and marks the appropriate pictures in response to the words and phrases given by the teacher.

STRENGTHS OF THE ACLC

• The ACLC is an inexpensive test and is easy to give and score. Very young and nonverbal children can be assessed with this measure, because it requires no verbal responses. The pictures are generally clear and unconfusing. Simple directions, easy responses, and a relatively fast pace hold the attention of most young children.

• The analysis of error patterns yields good information for planning therapy and for communicating information to parents. For instance, knowing that their young child cannot retain more than two critical elements (for example, *broken cup*) helps parents understand why the child cannot retain and comprehend longer utterances and directions. If analysis of error patterns indicates difficulty primarily in a certain area, such as verbs in isolation and in phrases, a remediation program is suggested. Such information is clearly observable on the well-organized score sheet.

• The manual presents an overview of language development and impairment as well as information on the design of the ACLC. Guidelines are given for language training based on expansion of critical elements.

LIMITING FACTORS OF THE ACLC

• Normative data are considered tentative and are based on an earlier form, but new and more complete norms are being collected. The numbers tested at certain age levels are very small: 16 children at 3 years to 3 years, 5 months. Data comparing performance on the group screening test with performance on the complete, individually administered scale are not yet available.

• Interpretation of the results is easiest for students with significant language problems. Only percentage scores are given; without the aid of standard deviations, it is difficult to interpret borderline performance accurately.

• Young children with visual scanning problems may have difficulty attending to all the pictures prior to selecting the appropriate one. They need to be taught how to look at all the pictures on a page before their responses can be considered valid.

Test for Auditory Comprehension of Language (TACL)

Elizabeth Carrow
Learning Concepts, 1973; revised 1977
2501 N. Lamar Blvd., Austin, TX 78705

Purpose	To measure auditory comprehension of vocabulary and structure (syntax and grammar) in English- and Spanish-speaking students
Major Areas Tested	Receptive language
Age or Grade Range	3–7 years
Usually Given By	Speech/language clinician
Type of Test	Standardized Individual Group (Screening Test)
Scores Obtained	Age level Percentile
Student Performance Timed?	No
Testing Time	20–30 minutes
Scoring/Interpretation Time	10–15 minutes
Normed On	200 middle-class Black, Caucasian, and Mexican-American children
Alternate Forms Available?	No

FORMAT

The materials for the Test for Auditory Comprehension of Language (TACL) consist of the test manual and response sheets. In the manual are directions for administration and interpretation, information on test development, and 101 plates of test pictures. The pictures, arranged three per page, are black-and-white line drawings (see Figures 49a and 49b).

With Figure 49a, the examiner says, "His puppy is black and white" or "El perrito de él es blanco y negro." With Figure 49b, the examiner says, "Second" or "Segundo." The student responds by pointing to the picture representing the vocabulary or structure given. No oral response is required. Responses are recorded on a form that includes information on the ages at which 75 percent and 90 percent of the normative sample passed each item. An analysis section organizes recorded errors under the headings Vocabulary, Morphology, and Syntax. Raw scores for the total test are converted to age-equivalent scores and percentiles.

A screening version of the TACL is also available, with 25 items from the longer version. It can be given to small groups of students. The author recommends that a student who scores below the tenth percentile for his or her age on the screening test be given the full test.

STRENGTHS OF THE TACL

• The TACL is relatively easy to administer and score. Directions for presentation are clear. Tables for the interpretation of scores are well organized and easy to use.

• Diagnostic information provided on the response sheet can be useful in planning remediation. Specific areas of need, such as pronouns, may emerge in the analysis of performance. However, further assessment would be necessary to determine thoroughly the deficits in such an area, because only a few items are provided in each category.

• The TACL demonstrates high test-retest reliability, according to several studies reported in the manual, and is valuable in showing a developmental progression in the comprehension of language. Scores increase with both age and subsequent language development.

• Words used to test linguistic structures have first been tested in their basic form. For instance, *tall* is tested prior to *taller*. Thus there is some control in assessing acquisition of morphological features.

• The nonverbal response mode makes the test useful with young or nonverbal students.

LIMITING FACTORS OF THE TACL

• The entire test must be presented in order to make use

Figure 49a. TACL, Item 28

of the normative data, but its length—101 plates—makes it tedious for young and immature students. Even normally developing children of lower age levels may miss half the items presented. The amount of failure and the resulting confusion may make this an inefficient means of assessing the language comprehension of young children delayed in development.

• The pictured stimuli make the TACL a test of visual processing as well as language processing. The student's ability to concentrate on, scan, and interpret the pictures should be noted in addition to performance on the test.

• Although mean scores and standard deviations are provided for six-month age intervals, they are not very discriminating. For example, a raw score of 58 is within normal limits for both a child of 3 years and a child of 4 years, 5 months. A raw score of 80 is within normal limits for children from 4 years to 6 years, 5 months. This means that only students with serious language problems can be identified with the TACL. Although a screening test of 25 items is available, it is of questionable value when the complete test is so imprecise and nondiscriminating. The long version of the TACL would more appropriately be thought of as a screening test except for its lengthy administration time.

• In the analysis section of the response sheet, the as-signment of certain structure errors to Morphology is not clear. For instance, errors in prepositions would seem to be listed more correctly under Vocabulary than under Morphology. And errors in answering questions beginning with *who, what,* and *when* reflect problems in the comprehension of syntactic transformations rather than in morphology.

• The Spanish version of the TACL is a translation of the English test. This is a questionable procedure for obtaining information about a student's auditory understanding of Spanish. Differences in Spanish grammar, structure, and regional vocabulary may result in errors that do not reflect comprehension level. In addition, no norms are available for the Spanish version, making it interesting but of little diagnostic value. See Appendix F for more information on this test.

Figure 49b. TACL, Item 63

Boehm Test of Basic Concepts (Boehm)

Ann E. Boehm
The Psychological Corporation, 1967; Form A, 1969; Form B, 1971
757 Third Ave., New York, NY 10017

Purpose	To assess knowledge of concepts basic to early academic success and to identify students with low-level concept mastery
Major Areas Tested	Comprehension of space, quantity, and time concepts
Age or Grade Range	Grades K–2
Usually Given By	Classroom teacher Special education teacher Speech/language clinician
Type of Test	Standardized Individual Group (Screening Test)
Scores Obtained	Percentile
Student Performance Timed?	No
Testing Time	30–40 minutes
Scoring/Interpretation Time	10 minutes
Normed On	More than 12,000 urban children from grades K–2 throughout the United States
Alternate Forms Available?	Yes

FORMAT

The Boehm Test of Basic Concepts (Boehm) materials include the manual, test booklets, and class record forms. The manual provides directions for administering, scoring, and interpreting the test and gives some information on test development and standardization.

Alternate test Forms A and B are available; each comprises Booklets I and II, containing 25 items each. Concepts of space, quantity, and time are assessed in approximate order of difficulty. For example, the concept *next to* occurs near the beginning of the test, and *half* is the last concept in Booklet I.

The test may be given either individually or to a small group. The teacher reads the directions for each item from the manual. In the test booklets, the students mark the picture or aspect of the picture that correctly portrays the concept presented. For example, in using the item shown in Figure 50, the examiner would say, "Look at the toys. Mark the toy that is *next to* the truck. Mark the toy that is *next to* the truck."

The number of correct responses is tallied, and the total is converted to a percentile score related to age, grade placement, and socioeconomic class.

On the class record form, space is provided for recording the success or failure of 30 students on each item. Such information leads directly to group language lessons.

STRENGTHS OF THE BOEHM

• The Boehm is an inexpensive way to assess the understanding of space, quantity, and time concepts in young school-aged students. Most young children find it interesting. The illustrations are clear, and the format is well organized. A gross marking response is adequate. A pointing response may also be used if the student is unable to handle a pencil or crayon and if the test is being individually administered.

• The manual is also well organized, and it is informative, providing extensive information on test development, analysis of results, normative data, and remediation approaches. Performance information on students from different socioeconomic levels is included from kindergarten to grade 2. Also included is information on students' performance at the beginning and middle of the year. The manual lists concepts known by most students of the ages tested and therefore not included on the test. These concepts include *bottom*, *flat*, *straight*, and *fast/slow*, and they should be assessed informally in students who have great difficulty with the Boehm material.

• The mechanics of presentation and scoring are simple. Thoughtfully employed, the test results can be useful to teachers in identifying the needs of individual students and planning remediation.

LIMITING FACTORS OF THE BOEHM

• The concepts were initially chosen through a review of curriculum materials in reading, math, and science. But the criteria for selection, described in the manual, are subjective and not well defined. They include (1) concepts occurring frequently in curriculum materials, (2) concepts not usually defined in curriculum materials, and (3) concepts representing relatively abstract basic ideas. The meanings of *frequently* and *relatively abstract* are not clarified.

• It is claimed that the concepts in the Boehm are basic to academic success in the early years of school. However, no documentation of this is given. Both a review of the literature and validity data are missing.

• The Boehm is described as useful for kindergarten through grade 2. However, analysis of typical performances

Figure 50. Boehm Test, Form A, Item 4

indicates that the test may be too easy to be of value for first graders from middle and upper socioeconomic levels and for second graders from all socioeconomic levels. For instance, at the second-grade level, all but two items from Booklet I were passed by 90 percent of the students.

• Knowledge of a concept in one context does not insure familiarity with it in another context. For example, a child may be able to identify *nearest* and *farthest* with objects but not recognize the concepts in pictured form. Furthermore, the concept may be understood, but the specific label called for in the test may not be known. For example, a student may understand the concept *same,* but when the direction labels it as *alike,* the student may not be able to equate that label with the concept he or she understands.

• Although this is a test of concept understanding, it presumes a certain level of language comprehension. The directions include complex language, such as, ''Look at the pictures of the house and the boy. Mark the house with the boy *inside* it.'' It is possible for a student to fail to understand these directions but demonstrate comprehension of the concept *inside* in another context. The test manual does caution about the interpretation of errors.

• Individual and group presentations are described in the manual. However, individual administration is recommended for children suspected of having difficulty in this area. Analysis of the student's performance during testing will enable the examiner to interpret performance more accurately.

Northwestern Syntax Screening Test (NSST)

Laura Lee
Northwestern University Press, 1969; revised 1971
1735 Benson Ave., Evanston, IL 60201

Purpose	To provide a quick estimate of a student's syntactic development and to identify those students requiring more thorough language evaluation
Major Areas Tested	Receptive and expressive language
Age or Grade Range	3–7 years
Usually Given By	Speech/language clinician
Type of Test	Standardized Individual
Scores Obtained	Age level Percentile
Student Performance Timed?	No
Testing Time	15–25 minutes
Scoring/Interpretation Time	15 minutes
Normed On	344 children from the middle and upper-middle classes in suburban Chicago, Illinois
Alternate Forms Available?	No

FORMAT

The materials for the Northwestern Syntax Screening Test (NSST) include a spiral-bound book of test pictures, an examiner's manual, and individual record forms. The test consists of 40 items—20 receptive and 20 expressive. In the receptive section, four black-and-white line drawings are displayed on each page, and in the expressive section, two drawings are displayed on each page. A demonstration item precedes each section. The norms and the instructions for presentation, interpretation, and scoring are all included in the manual. The individual record forms provide for scoring of individual responses.

Sentence pairs are arranged in the order in which the normative population accomplished the tasks. Consequently, identical structures are presented in a somewhat different sequence in the two sections. Among the structures assessed are prepositional phrases, negation, and subject-verb agreement. Vocabulary and structure are controlled; only the structure being assessed varies.

In administering the receptive portion, the examiner verbally presents the two statements or question forms given on the record form. These are given without the use of stress or intonation. Each statement or question is then regiven individually, and the student indicates the picture best described by it. For example, the statements accompanying Figure 51 are "The cat is behind the chair" and "The cat is under the chair."

For the expressive section, the examiner verbally presents the key statements pertaining to the two pictures. The student is then asked to repeat the appropriate statement or question as the examiner points to each picture. For example, the statements accompanying Figure 52 are "The cat is behind the desk" and "The cat is under the desk."

STRENGTHS OF THE NSST

• The NSST provides a quick and relatively easy means of screening the receptive and expressive language abilities of 3- to 8-year-old middle- and upper-middle-class white children.

• A study by Ratusnik and Koenigsknecht (1975) has demonstrated the value of the NSST for differentiating among normal language development, severely delayed expressive language, and retarded language development. Internal consistency of the NSST was demonstrated in their findings.

• A student's performance on the NSST often provides the examiner with hints as to what area needs further evaluation. For example, a student who fails to discriminate between *the shelf* and *himself* may need in-depth assessment of auditory discrimination skills.

• The NSST may be useful in evaluating a student's progress in therapy. Comparison with the student's own past performances may reveal progress in the comprehension and expression of specific structures.

• A short method for screening large numbers of children is described in the introduction to the NSST (revised 1971).

LIMITING FACTORS OF THE NSST

• The NSST was standardized on a limited socio-economic population (middle- and upper-middle classes) from a single geographical area. Applicability of the norms to other populations is questionable, and the author has expressed the need for those using the test to develop local norms.

• A narrow range of performance is noted at the 7- to 8-year-old age level, with only a four-point difference between those scoring at the tenth and the ninetieth percentiles. The author of the test states that these scores were included so that examiners would note the cutoff at age 8.

• The norms were derived from a limited sampling. At three of the five given age levels, fewer than 50 subjects were included.

• The NSST is designed as a screening instrument only. More thorough investigation of structures, pronouns, and prepositions is necessary before making definitive diagnostic statements or planning remediation.

• Only limited information regarding test development, reliability, and validity has been published.

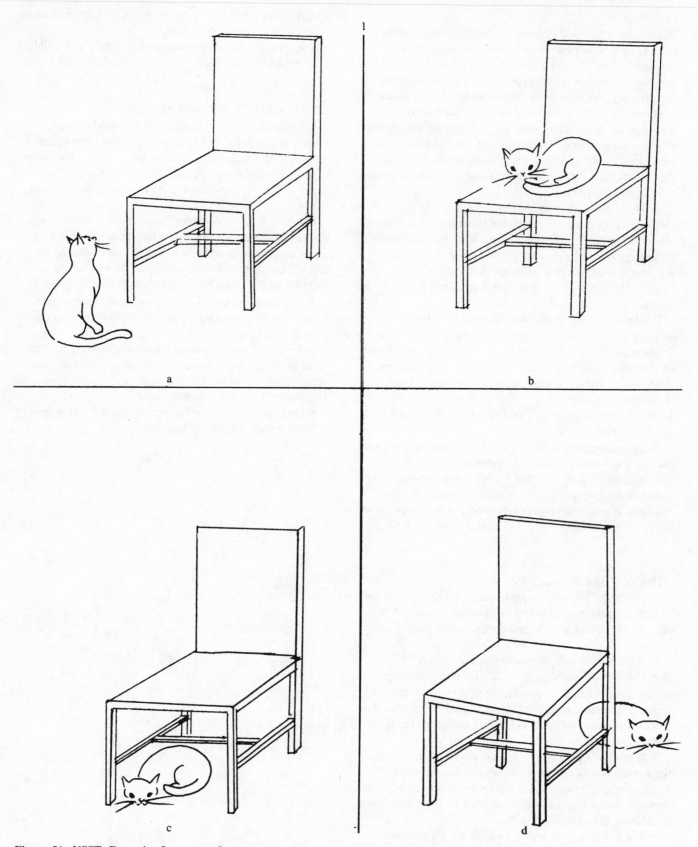

Figure 51. NSST, Receptive Language, Item 1

4

a

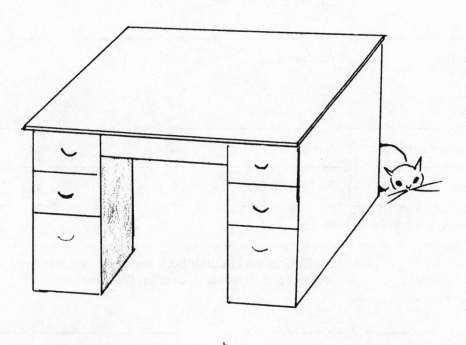

b

Figure 52. NSST, Expressive Language, Item 4

Sequenced Inventory of Communication Development (SICD)

E. Prather Hedrick and A. Tobin
University of Washington Press, 1975
4045 Brooklyn N.E., Seattle, WA 98105

Purpose	To evaluate development of verbal and nonverbal communication in very young children and to estimate levels of receptive and expressive language functioning
Major Areas Tested	Receptive and expressive communication
Age or Grade Range	4 months–4 years
Usually Given By	Special education teacher Speech/language clinician
Type of Test	Standardized Individual Criterion-referenced
Scores Obtained	Age level
Student Performance Timed?	No
Testing Time	30–75 minutes
Scoring/Interpretation Time	30 minutes
Normed On	252 Caucasian children from the upper, middle, and lower socioeconomic levels in Seattle, Washington
Alternate Forms Available?	No

FORMAT

The materials for the Sequenced Inventory of Communication Development (SICD) consist of a kit of objects used in administering the test, an examiner's manual, and two test booklets (receptive and expressive scales) for each student. The manual includes information on test development, directions for administration and scoring, and tables to aid in test interpretation. The "receptive" and "expressive" test booklets each include a profile sheet for recording responses and for viewing patterns of success and failure systematically.

The SICD is based on a model of early communication patterns and the interaction of behaviors. Many of these behaviors are not linguistic in nature but represent ways that a young child relates to the environment. Some test items have been adapted from well-established sources, such as the Denver Development Scale (p. 201) and the Illinois Test of Psycholinguistic Abilities (p. 141).

Factors included on the receptive scale are awareness, discrimination, and understanding. Skills are documented by observation of motor responses to sound or speech clues and by parental reports of the child's responses to sounds and speech at home. Examples of the skills evaluated in each area follow. These tasks are passed by 75 percent of the children at the given age levels.

Awareness
Sound: Baby turns to sound of rattle and cellophane (8 months).
Speech: Baby looks up or smiles in response to "Hi there" (8 months).

Discrimination
Sound: Baby responds to environmental sounds at home, such as phone ringing (16 months).
Speech: Child discriminates between words such as *socks* and *box, tree* and *key,* and *bear* and *chair* by pointing to objects (24 to 28 months).

Understanding
Words plus situational cues: Child responds to command "Give it to me" (28 months).
Words: Child indicates correct blocks as examiner names colors (36 to 44 months).

Communicative behaviors analyzed on the expressive scale are imitation, initiation, and response. Parental report of behaviors is also included on this scale. Examples of the skills evaluated in each area follow.

Imitation
Motor: Child imitates examiner, placing blocks in box (16 months).
Vocal: Child imitates intonation patterns heard at home (20 months).
Verbal: Child imitates common words on request (28 months).

Initiation
Motor: Child uses gestures to elicit labeling response from parent (24 months).
Vocal: Child uses questioning inflection (16 months).

Verbal: Child asks "Why?" at home (40 months).

Response
Vocal: Child responds vocally to parents' verbalizing (4 months).
Verbal: Child names objects such as car, spoon, and shoe (36 months).

Verbal output and articulation may be analyzed as expressive behaviors, but they are not included in the scoring of the expressive scale. An articulation profile sheet is included with each expressive scale test booklet. The language sample is obtained following the methods outlined by Johnson, Darley, and Spriestersbach (1963). A mean length response and a structural complexity score can be derived. A description of the child's language structure may also be recorded on the record form by indicating the structures observed—for example, use of adverbs (36 months).

STRENGTHS OF THE SICD

- The SICD provides a means of assessing the language skills of very young children through parent report and observation. The inclusion of nonverbal tasks that are precursors to later language development is what makes this test valuable with the very young, as well as with very impaired children.

- Interexaminer and test-retest reliability are high. A high correlation between the receptive communication age and expressive communication age would be expected and is reported in the manual. The mean scores obtained by normal subjects closely resemble chronological age.

- The manual is very thorough. Specific directions for administering and scoring are presented, and several tables help in understanding test construction and student performance. Mean scores and standard deviations assist the examiner in interpreting performance accurately.

- By incorporating supplemental information from articulation testing, language sampling, and other assessment tools with the SICD, a total communication diagnosis can be established. If the child's errors are viewed in terms of consistency and with reference to developmental stages and overall level of functioning, goals for remediation can be selected.

- With experience, the examiner will find the test flexible to administer. Receptive and expressive tasks can be interspersed, depending on the child's interest. The use of objects, as well as pictures, to elicit language appeals to young children.

LIMITING FACTORS OF THE SICD

- Practice is required to become comfortable with test administration. Tasks vary, and the manipulation of the objects can be confusing for the examiner and distracting for the child.

- As the authors of the test point out, caution should be

used in interpreting the results. Results should be integrated with performance on other assessment tools to provide a thorough picture of an individual child's functioning. The authors stress that differences between the receptive communication age and expressive communication age of one age level (4 months) are not significant diagnostically.

• The SICD was normed on white children from the Northwest, and caution must be used when interpreting the results of other racial and geographical groups.

Developmental Sentence Scoring (DSS)

Laura Lee and R. A. Koenigsknecht
Northwestern University Press, 1974
1735 Benson Ave., Evanston, IL 60201

Purpose	To provide a systematic procedure for analyzing a student's grammatical structure and for estimating the extent to which the student has learned generalized grammatical rules enough to use them in conversation
Major Areas Tested	Grammatical structure of spoken language
Age or Grade Range	2–7 years
Usually Given By	Speech/language clinician
Type of Test	Individual
Scores Obtained	Percentile
Student Performance Timed?	No
Testing Time	30–60 minutes
Scoring/Interpretation Time	2 hours
Normed On	200 white monolingual children between ages 2 and 7 years, from middle-income homes where standard American English was spoken
Alternate Forms Available?	No

FORMAT

Developmental Sentence Scoring (DSS) involves obtaining a conversational language sample by using stimulus materials that the student is interested in, such as toys or pictures provided by the clinician. A corpus of 50 different, consecutive, intelligible, nonecholalic, complete (subject and verb) sentences is used for analysis. The authors state that this procedure, therefore, is appropriate only for students who use complete sentence structures at least 50 percent of the time. Fragmentary utterances are discarded from the sample. Detailed information about elicitation of the sample and the acceptability of various utterances in the language corpus is provided by the authors in the book containing the test (Lee and Koenigsknecht 1974).

The utterances are evaluated in terms of eight grammatical features that psycholinguistic research has found to be early components of language. Research has also provided information about their developmental progression. These features are based on transformational generative grammar (Chomsky 1957, 1965) and case grammar (Brown 1973; Fillmore 1968). The grammatical criteria includes the following:

1. Indefinite pronouns and/or noun modifiers
2. Personal pronouns
3. Main verbs
4. Secondary verbs
5. Negatives
6. Conjunctions
7. Interrogative reversals
8. *Wh-* question words

Each grammatical form present in a sample utterance is independently assigned a score from 1 to 8 points according to a weighted scoring system. The weighted scores indicate a developmental sequence of grammatical growth within each category. Furthermore, an additional sentence point may be added if the entire utterance is correct in all aspects—syntactically as well as semantically. This sentence point is designed, in part, to account for other grammatical features not individually scored, such as plurals, possessive markers, word order, and prepositions.

Comprehensive scoring guidelines are provided by the authors in both tabular and narrative form. Emerging structures may be indicated by inserting attempt marks (–) under the appropriate categories. A model chart format for listing and scoring the transcribed sentences appears in the authors' book (Lee and Koenigsknecht 1974), but practical tables must be made by the clinician. The DSS scoring procedure is illustrated in Table 18.

Scores for the 50-sentence utterance sample are totaled; then the mean score per sentence is computed. This is the Developmental Sentence Score (DSS), which is compared with the normative data available for the student's chron-

ological age. Percentile values have been computed for the ninetieth, seventy-fifth, fiftieth, twenty-fifth, and tenth percentile ranks at six-month intervals for ages 2 to 7. An estimate of the student's expressive language level can be obtained by finding the age range where the DSS is approximately equivalent to the fiftieth-percentile score.

The authors suggest, in addition, that students scoring close to the tenth percentile for their age receive further speech and language evaluation and be considered potential candidates for therapy. When the DSS is used to measure progress, the authors state that students might be dismissed from therapy when their scores approximate the lower limits of the normal range for their age group. However, other important factors, such as conceptual development and auditory skills, must be taken into consideration.

STRENGTHS OF DSS

• DSS is an inexpensive language assessment procedure, with an authors' book that provides all the information necessary for administration and interpretation. Transcription forms are not provided, but they can easily be designed by the clinician.

• Because DSS is a detailed, painstaking procedure, a thorough reading of the author's book is necessary. Comprehensive information about various utterance types in the language corpus is included. Numerous examples illustrate the method of developmental scoring. The convenient chart provided by the authors usually contains enough specific scoring information to meet the requirements of typical language samples. Background psycholinguistic research and essential language-sampling techniques are also concisely presented.

• It is felt that 50 spontaneous and complete sentences is a reasonable number to use in assessing language-impaired children. There is no sufficient evidence that supports the collection of larger samples for analysis purposes. In fact, established criteria do not yet exist for determining adequate sample size for linguistic analysis.

• A significant amount of diagnostic information can be obtained by examining the scatter of scores on DSS charts, because consistent error categories and stereotyped structures are indicated in repetitive scoring patterns. The chart makes it especially easy to see what structures are missing and what forms the child is consistently substituting for others.

• Many psycholinguistic researchers and therapists of language-disordered students have espoused language-sampling measures such as DSS over traditional tests of morphological and syntactic competency. They feel that conversational speech places a ''grammatical load'' on the student because it requires the student to combine several transformations into single sentences. As a student gains linguistic competence with age, one can expect progressive

Table 18. DSS Scoring Procedure*

Sentence	Indefinite Pronoun/ Noun Modifier	Personal Pronoun	Primary Verb	Secondary Verb	Negative	Conjunction	Inter-rogative Reversal	Wh-Question Word	Sentence Point	Total
I want to eat.		1 I	1 want	2 to eat					1	5
What you doing?		1 you	– are (omitted)					2 what	0	3
The dog won't go in the house.			4 won't go		5 won't				1	10
She's trying to take it off.	1 it	2 she	1 is trying	5 to take					1	10
He drinked all the milk.	3 all	2 he	– drinked/ drank						0	5
Look at me!		1 me	1 look						1	3
He said, "Where's my house?"		2, 1 he, my	2, 1 said, is				1 where is my house?	2 where	1	10

*Numbers in columns indicate points assigned to each element.

growth in the grammatical load of his or her utterances. This increasing load results from mastery of new, higher-level morphological forms and syntactic structures, as well as growth in the number of forms and structures that the student can incorporate into a single utterance. DSS assesses the impact of both these developmental aspects. In addition, rule consistency and frequency of usage can also be assessed more accurately in conversational speech than under rigid testing conditions.

• The validity of a test of conversational language behavior is difficult to assess directly because adequate and appropriate external criteria are lacking. Therefore, determining the internal consistency of DSS and the consistency of repeated applications with different clinicians and different stimulus materials becomes more significant.

Validity of the DSS construct was established when the test was normed on 200 children from middle-income homes. Validity was indicated by the significant differences between age groups in the overall scoring procedure, as well as by all the component grammatical categories. Further validity was obtained through verification of the grammatical hierarchies in a reciprocal averaging procedure that resulted in a minor revision of the original weighted scoring system of DSS, presented in 1971.

High reliability coefficients obtained by DSS lend major support to the scoring procedure. The overall internal consistency was .71 (estimated by coefficient Alpha), and the reliability coefficient for the overall DSS was .73.

LIMITING FACTORS OF DSS

• DSS is a highly time-consuming procedure as compared with other conventional language-assessment techniques. Inherent in it are great opportunities for errors in transcribing and scoring the language samples. To minimize such errors, it is recommended that clinicians transcribe and score their own samples, using the authors' book to clarify the scoring procedure when necessary.

• Caution should be exercised in comparing a student's DSS with the percentile scores presented by the authors. The sample used to obtain normative data for each six-month age period was small (20 individuals). Furthermore, criteria used to determine the ''normalcy'' of these subjects' language appears to have been inadequate. The only objective, standardized measure of adequate language skill was a score within one standard deviation of the mean for age on the Peabody Picture Vocabulary Test (p. 152). Other criteria included normal developmental histories without reports of overt hearing problems, severe misarticulations, or discernible behavioral problems. More intensive evaluation of language skills with other standardized measures should have been undertaken.

• The usefulness of DSS is limited by the fact that the end product is a score rather than a descriptive, composite picture of the student's linguistic performance. Errors merely reduce a student's overall score without specifying the incorrect generalizations he or she may be using. A score may be spuriously high simply because the student uses many words.

• The authors have stated that an essential purpose of DSS is the planning of remediation goals. However, the absence of a descriptive summary sheet that examines performance on individual grammatical criteria tends to defeat this purpose. In addition to the lengthy assessment process, the clinician must also summarize the student's linguistic performance by reviewing individual sentence errors. Moreover, appropriate goals for language therapy cannot be developed solely from examination of DSS error patterns but require more detailed knowledge found through other language measures.

• The DSS procedure is appropriate only for students who can produce 50 complete sentences within a reasonable time. Clinicians should be aware that Lee and Koenigsknecht (1974) have developed an alternate method of language-sampling analysis for students exhibiting lower-level language development.

• The DSS was designed solely to assess the linguistic performance of students who have learned standard American English. Further research is needed to systematize analysis of other dialects of English as well as other languages. Allen Toronto (1972) has developed a scoring system similar to DSS for the Spanish language (see Appendix F). It is not a translation of DSS but a developmental scale of Spanish grammatical forms, and it can help clinicians differentiate between bilingual interference with language development and a disability in the student's native language.

• DSS uses a limited number of discrete grammatical

criteria. Although there is little doubt that these are essential components of language development, such basic grammatical criteria as plurals, possessive markers, adverbs, and prepositions, have been omitted.

• The authors claim that DSS is a useful tool for evaluating progress during therapy, but it should be limited to the assessment of longitudinal changes and not applied to short-term changes. Research has shown that a significant practice effect can be produced when the DSS is repeated over a short time (four applications over two weeks). Furthermore, when DSS is used as an objective measure of grammatical growth during an interim and posttherapy assessment procedure, it is essential that the same stimulus materials be used to minimize test variables as much as possible.

Language Sampling, Analysis, and Training
(Tyack and Gottsleben)

Dorothy Tyack and Robert Gottsleben
Consulting Psychologists Press, 1974
577 College Ave., Palo Alto, CA 94306

Purpose	To provide a grammatical analysis of a student's expressive language and, through a "resample" procedure, to provide a measure of carryover of these grammatical rules following speech and language training
Major Areas Tested	Grammatical structure of oral language
Age or Grade Range	Not given (most effective with 2–7 years)
Usually Given By	Speech/language clinician
Type of Test	Individual
Scores Obtained	None
Student Performance Timed?	No
Testing Time	60 minutes
Scoring/Interpretation Time	2 hours
Normed On	Not reported
Alternate Forms Available?	No

FORMAT

All the instructions for completing the Language Sampling, Analysis, and Training (Tyack and Gottsleben) are described in the handbook. A set of four analysis forms and information about ordering more are also included.

The initial step in this assessment procedure is to obtain a language sample of approximately 100 sentences. The authors suggest eliciting these utterances through a discussion of a set of pictures taken from *People in Action* (Shaftel and Shaftel 1970), during which the examiner gives open-ended verbal prompts. They define a sentence as "any utterance which contains at least two structurally related morphemes."

The authors have designed a transcription sheet for transcribing the utterances. It provides spaces for recording direct questions asked by the clinician, expanded forms of the utterances if appropriate, and helpful contextual

information. A transcription sheet is shown in Figure 53a.

Analysis of the language sample involves the following set of procedures:

1. Counting words and morphemes in each sentence. Detailed instructions and illustrative examples for obtaining these word and morpheme counts are provided in the handbook. The counts for the utterances shown in Figure 53a are listed below:

	Words	Morphemes
She sleep on the couch.	5	5
Her won't eat candy.	4	4
He eating her hamburger.	4	5
(Oops), I dropped them.	3	4
Another picture?	2	2
Who's running?	2	4

Language Sampling, Analysis, and Training: Transcription Sheets
D. Tyack and R. Gottsleben

Child_____ Examiner_____ Date_____

#1   #

| She sleep on the couch. |
| *is   ing* |

#2   #

| Her won't eat candy. |
| *She* |

#3 What's he eating?   #

| He eating her hamburger. |
| *is   his* |

#4 (drops one piece of candy)   #

| Oops, I dropped them. |
| *it* |

#5   #

| Another picture? |
| *That is another picture?* |

#6   #

| Who's running? |
| |

Figure 53a. Tyack and Gottsleben Transcription Sheet, Utterances Noted

2. Calculating the "word-morpheme index." Add the mean number of words per sentence to the mean number of morphemes per sentence. Then divide the sum by two. The word-morpheme index for the utterances shown in Figure 53a is four.

3. Assigning the sample to a linguistic level based on the word-morpheme index:

Level I: 2.0–2.5
Level II: 2.5–3.0
Level III: 3.0–4.0
Level IV: 4.0–5.0
Level V: 5.0–6.0

The authors state that these are arbitrary levels to be used only for organizing the progression of syntatic development and that they do not represent cognitive differences.

4. Identifying the forms and construction types in the sample sentences and sorting them into the categories listed on the sequence of language acquisition sheet. On the transcription sheet, all forms present in the utterances (or forms substituted) are circled, and the form omissions are checked. This procedure is illustrated in Figure 53b. Each sentence is then assigned a construction type based on the theory of transformational grammar. The classifications are listed below:

She sleep on the couch:	Noun + Verb + Noun
Her won't eat candy:	Negative—Noun + Modal + Verb + Noun
He eating her hamburger:	Noun + Verb + Noun
(Oops), I dropped them:	Noun + Verb + Noun
Another picture?:	Question—Quantifier + Noun
Who's running?:	Question—Noun + Verb

Language Sampling, Analysis, and Training: Transcription Sheets
D. Tyack and R. Gottsleben

Child_____ Examiner_____ Date_____

1
5-5 (She) sleep on (the) couch.
         is   ing

2
4-4 (Her) (won't) eat candy.
     She

3 What's he eating?
4-5 (He) eating (her) hamburger.
       is   his

4 (drops one piece of candy)
3-4 Oops, (I) dropped (them)
                         it

5
2-2 Another picture?
     That is another picture?

6
2-4 Who(s) running?

Figure 53b. Tyack and Gottsleben Transcription Sheet, Forms Noted

The construction types are written above the sample sentences, as illustrated in figure 53c.

The sequence of language acquisition sheet (not shown) illustrates graphically the developmental progression of various grammatical forms and constructions. Based on Morehead and Ingram's research (1973), the grammatical criteria (forms and simple sentence constructions) have been assigned linguistic levels of acquisition. Specific lexical categories in this analysis include:

Pronouns	Modals
Prepositions	Copula verb
Demonstratives	Present progressive tense
Articles	Present tense (third-person singular form)
Plurals	Verb particles
Locatives	Past-tense verbs
Conjunctions	

Negative and question constructions are listed in order of acquisition, although specific levels have not been assigned to them. Because of the inconclusive research cited by the authors, the order of acquisition of complex sentence structures is not known at present.

The number of sample utterances containing a listed form or construction is entered on the sequence of language acquisition sheet. Columns are provided to indicate where a form has occurred correctly (+), where a form was missing when obligatory by standards of adult English (−), and where one form was substituted for another (X).

5. Entering data on the baseline and goal analysis sheets. These are the final forms in the Tyack and Gottsleben analysis procedure. The baseline analysis lists the forms and constructions used correctly by the student, and the goal analysis lists those needed to bring the student to his or her assigned linguistic level (see Figures 54 and 55).

Language Sampling, Analysis, and Training: Transcription Sheets

D. Tyack and R. Gottsleben

Child_____ Examiner_____ Date_____

5-5 # 1 N+V+N   #
She sleep on the couch.
    is   ing

4-4 # 2 Neg N+modal+V+N   #
Her won't eat candy.
She

4-5 # 3 N+V+N   #
He eating her hamburger.
    is   his

3-4 # 4 N+V+N   #
Oops, I dropped them.
            it

2-2 # 5 Q quan.+N   #
Another picture?
That is another picture?

2-4 # 6 Q N+V   #
Who's running?

Figure 53c. Tyack and Gottsleben Transcription Sheet, Construction Types Noted

Language Sampling, Analysis, and Training: Goal Analysis
D. Tyack and R. Gottsleben

Child _____ Age _____ Sex   M   F   Sample Date _____

Referral Source _____ Clinician _____ | Level: ____ |

Reasons for Referral:

Background Information:

Data for items A through F on this form are obtained from the Sequence of Language Acquisition form. With the child's Level as a reference point, list below forms and constructions mastered; list on the reverse side, forms and constructions which appear inconsistently or not at all in his language sample. In planning for training on Negatives, Questions, and Complex Sentences, refer directly to the SLA form since these categories are not summarized on this form.

BASELINE DATA

A. Forms and constructions mastered* *at and below* assigned level:

Forms			Constructions	
A. Pronouns	B. Prepositions	E. Modals	Noun Phrase	NP+VP+(NP)
I	on	could	N	N+V
me	C. Demonstratives	F. Particles	Dem+N	N+V+N
my	that	up	Adj+N	N+V+N+N
it	this	down		N+Modal+V+N
you	D. Locatives	at	VP+NP	
she	here	on	V+N	NP+Copula+N/Adj.
them	there	out	V+Modal+N	N+ +N/adj.
he	over there	off		N+'is'+N/adj.
they	inside	G. Pres.Prog.Tense		
		am		

B. Forms and constructions mastered* *above* assigned level:

Forms	
A. Pronouns	E. Modals
her	don't
one	would
B. Prepositions	
down	
inside	

C. Unclassifiable forms and constructions:

*Mastery is defined as correct occurrence of the structure 90% or more in obligatory contexts.

© Copyright, 1974, by Consulting Psychologists Press, Inc.

Figure 54. Tyack and Gottsleben Baseline Analysis, Correct Forms and Constructions Noted

Language Sampling, Analysis, and Training: Goal Analysis
D. Tyack and R. Gottsleben

GOAL DATA

D. Forms and constructions *at or below* the assigned level which *do not appear*:

MISSING–OBLIGATED

MISSING–NOT OBLIGATED

MISSING–OBLIGATED	MISSING–NOT OBLIGATED			
<u>Modals</u>	<u>Forms</u>			<u>Constructions</u>
will	<u>Pronouns</u>	<u>Demonstratives</u>	<u>Copula</u>	N+'are'/'am'+N/adj.
can	your	these	are, 're	
	his	those	am, 'm	
<u>Pres.Prog.Tense</u>	him	<u>Plurals</u>		
are	we	-ez		
	us	<u>Modals</u>		
<u>Pres.Tense</u> (3 p.sing.)	<u>Prepositions</u>	want, wanna		
-ez	with	hafta, gonna, shall		
	up			

E. Forms and constructions *at or below* assigned level which appear *inconsistently* (i.e., less than 90% in obligatory contexts). Show these as fractions with no. of correct responses over no. of obligatory contexts.

<u>Forms</u>			<u>Constructions</u>
<u>Pronouns</u>	<u>Articles</u>	<u>Pres.Prog.Tense</u>	N+V (5/8)
1+(2/3)	a, the (36/47)	-ing (5/10)	N+'is'+N/adj. (2/6)
<u>Prepositions</u>	<u>Plurals</u>	is (5/7)	
in (4/7)	-s, 2 (5/6)	<u>Pres.Tense</u> (3 p.sing.)	
on (5/6)	<u>Conjunctions</u>	-s, 2 (3/5)	
to (1/2)	and (1/2)		
at (2/4)	<u>Copula</u>		
<u>Possessive Marker</u>	is, 's (19/26)		
's(z) (6/9)			

F. Forms and constructions *above* the assigned level which appear inconsistently:

Other factors relevant to training program:

Figure 55. Tyack and Gottsleben Goal Analysis, Incorrect Forms and Constructions Noted

STRENGTHS OF THE TYACK AND GOTTSLEBEN

• The Tyack and Gottsleben language-sampling procedure provides an extremely thorough assessment of a student's morphological and syntactic competence. It considers a wider range of forms and constructions than most conventional tests of grammar or such language-sampling techniques as Development Sentence Scoring (Lee and Koenigsknecht 1974). A great deal of useful developmental information can be procured by examining the analysis sheets. Because spaces are provided for recording contextual information, some knowledge of the student's semantic competency can also be obtained.

• The authors' handbook is clearly written and relatively inexpensive, and it supplies numerous details and examples of all phases of their method. Unanalyzed language samples are also included for practice purposes. The series of analysis forms provide a concise and graphic method of presenting baseline language behavior and goals for training. The authors have increased the usefulness of their handbook by including information about structuring language remediation programs and choosing appropriate therapy goals. Data-taking procedures are also discussed.

• The Tyack and Gottsleben method of language analysis is based on the premise that language-deviant students acquire morphological and syntactic rules in the same sequence as normal students. There are no age norms included, and appropriate remediation goals are based not on chronological age but on the linguistic capabilities and needs of the student. In support of this, research has shown that mean morpheme measure is a more reliable indicator of linguistic development than chronological age is (Menyuk 1969; Bloom 1970; Brown 1973).

• The definition of a sentence as "at least two structurally related morphemes" makes this procedure an effective assessment tool with students who exhibit only low-level language structures. Developmental Sentence Types, described by Lee and Koenigsknecht in Developmental Sentence Analysis (1974), is the only other systematic measure of such immature linguistic forms that is available to speech and language clinicians. However, it does not provide detailed information on choosing appropriate remediation goals.

LIMITING FACTORS OF THE TYACK AND GOTTSLEBEN

• The Tyack and Gottsleben language-assessment procedure is complicated, tedious, and extremely time consuming. Although the handbook presents detailed instructions, many opportunities arise for errors in transcription and analysis of the language samples. A clinician who attempts to minimize such errors by transcribing and analyzing his or her own samples may find the time involved to be unrealistic. Furthermore, collecting the 100

utterances suggested by the authors may require several sessions with a severely language-handicapped student. Although this procedure produces a great deal of information about the student's language behavior, time constraints may make it impractical.

• This procedure for acquiring and analyzing a language sampling is quite difficult to learn solely from reading the authors' handbook. The analysis forms can be confusing and awkward to handle. A solid background in psycholinguistic theory is necessary for classifying utterances into the forms and constructions listed on the analysis sheet. Thus, if one plans to use this procedure efficiently, attending a language-sampling workshop given by the authors is tremendously helpful.

• The purpose of the Tyack and Gottsleben is to provide data for planning an individualized remediation program, and it should not be considered a diagnostic tool. It does not provide information for comparing one student's performance with others of the same age or grade level. No validity or reliability studies have been conducted, although the basic premises on which the program is based come from years of linguistic and behavioral research.

• The grammatical criteria are based on standard American English. The authors do not provide any information about assessment of nonstandard dialects or other languages. Clinicians are encouraged to explore the current research on dialectical variations if warranted by their therapy caseloads.

• The speech and language clinician may frequently be asked to evaluate a student whose word-morpheme mean exceeds the limits of Level V. Because the alternate method of language-sampling analysis, Laura Lee's Developmental Sentence Scoring (p. 169) also has a ceiling at the 8-year-old level, no adequate tool for assessing the older child's conversational language is available at present. This is an area warranting further research.

Gross Motor Tests

Relatively few standardized tests of gross motor skills are available. More often, informal rating scales are devised by the special education teacher interested in perceptual motor training. In addition to the usual skills emphasized in physical education—running, catching, throwing, and total body coordination—basic skills such as balance and posture have often been found to be underdeveloped in children with learning and language disabilities. Special education theorists such as Newell Kephart (1960) and A. Jean Ayres (1973) have hypothesized that adequate motor development is prerequisite to developing higher-level perceptual and cognitive skills. Although recent research (Hallahan and Cruickshank 1973; Cratty 1970) has shown no direct connection between motor skills and academic performance, no one disputes the fact that many special education students have delayed motor skills for which they need specific teaching. Although training in balance, posture, rhythm, and ball skills may not improve spelling, it often leads to improvement in the equally important areas of playground activities and social skills.

For this reason it is important to be familiar with some tests of gross motor ability. In this chapter four test batteries are reviewed. The Purdue Perceptual-Motor Survey is the oldest and one of the best-known assessment tools. The Bruininks-Oseretsky Test of Motor Proficiency is a recent modification of the earlier Oseretsky scales familiar to many special education teachers. The Frostig Movement Skills Test Battery is another new test of motor skills, still in an experimental version. The Southern California Sensory Integration Tests is a highly technical battery administered by occupational and physical therapists to assess not only gross motor skills but also tactile and kinesthetic perception systems. All four of the tests reviewed here include both gross and fine motor skills, attesting to the close relationship between the two areas. In addition to the individual reviews, a comparison of the features of these four tests in chart form is found in Appendix G.

Developmental delays in motor skills and coordination are often one of the first signs of possible learning disorders. As a result, many of the tests for preschool children include assessments of gross motor skills. In Part II: Preschool and Kindergarten Tests, four of the six tests reviewed have sections on gross motor skills. Readers interested in the assessment of motor skills in very young children are referred to this section.

Purdue Perceptual-Motor Survey (Survey)

Eugene G. Roach and Newell C. Kephart
Charles E. Merrill Publishing Company, 1966
1300 Alum Creek Dr., Columbus, OH 43216

Purpose	To assess perceptual-motor abilities, including both gross and fine motor skills
Major Areas Tested	Laterality, directionality, and perceptual-motor skills
Age or Grade Range	6–10 years
Usually Given By	Classroom teacher Physical education teacher Special education teacher Motor therapist Occupational therapist
Type of Test	Informal Individual Criterion-referenced
Scores Obtained	None (Profile only)
Student Performance Timed?	No
Testing Time	30–40 minutes
Scoring/Interpretation Time	10–15 minutes
Normed On	200 urban and rural elementary school students in Indiana, from grades 1–4 and from all socioeconomic levels; students with known achievement or motor problems excluded; 97 nonachievers of the same age and school used in a validation study
Alternate Forms Available?	No

FORMAT

The Purdue Perceptual-Motor Survey (Survey) is not a test but a series of tasks designed to provide the examiner with a structure for observing a student's motor skills. The materials consist of an examiner's manual and individual student record forms. Materials required are those usually found in a school setting—walking board, broom handle, small pillow, mat or rug, chalk and chalkboard, penlight. The manual includes information on the rationale and development of the test, directions for administering and scoring, and a set of cards for the form-copying task.

The Survey is composed of 11 subtests organized into 5 major skill areas, and it provides 22 item scores. The organization of the Survey and descriptions of the subtests are presented in Table 19.

In order to secure the student's best performance, each subtest has four possible levels of administration:

1. *Unstructured Instruction.* The student is given general verbal directions for the task, and the examiner then observes how the student performs. For example, on the Walking Board subtest, the student would be told simply, "Walk to the other end."

2. *Verbal Directions.* If the student cannot perform the task at the unstructured instruction level, the examiner gives more explicit verbal directions, such as, "Step up on the board here and walk forward slowly to the other end."

3. *Demonstration.* At this level, the examiner helps the student by saying, "Do it like this" and then demonstrating the task for the student to imitate.

Table 19. Survey Subtests

Skill Area	Subtest
Balance and Posture	1. *Walking Board.* Student is asked to walk on a walking board four inches wide and six inches off the ground, to obtain a measure of dynamic balance. Three scores are obtained: forward, backward, and sidewise.
	2. *Jumping.* Student is asked to jump and hop on each foot and both feet in a series of eight tasks designed to measure laterality and rhythm.
Body Image	3. *Identification of Body Parts.* Student is asked to point to nine common body parts.
	4. *Imitation of Movements.* Student is asked to imitate a series of 17 arm positions to measure the ability to translate visual information into a motor act.
	5. *Obstacle Course.* Student is asked to step over, step around, and duck under a broom handle to assess spatial orientation.
	6. *Kraus-Weber Test of Physical Fitness.* Student is asked to raise upper body and legs from a prone position, to test physical strength and muscular fitness.
	7. *Angels in the Snow.* Student is asked to perform a series of tasks requiring moving specific limbs individually and in pairs.
Perceptual-Motor Match	8. *Chalkboard.* Student is asked to perform a series of four chalkboard tasks assessing visual-motor coordination, with particular emphasis on directionality and midline problems.
	9. *Rhythmic Writing.* Student is asked to reproduce a series of eight continuous writing motifs (⌐_⌐_ , *pbpbpb*). Rhythm, accuracy, and orientation on the blackboard are observed and scored.
Ocular Control	10. *Ocular Pursuits.* Student is asked to perform a series of four visual-tracking exercises.
Form Perception	11. *Developmental Drawings.* Student is asked to copy seven geometric forms to assess visual-motor coordination.

4. *Guided Movements*. If the student cannot imitate the task, the examiner physically guides his or her movements.

The level of structure that the student requires for each task is noted, together with other observations of performance, on the individual record forms. Each item is rated on a four-point scale following the guidelines in the examiner's manual. All scores are recorded on the record forms. Because the survey is not intended as a test but as a structured observation, the rating scores are not translated into age scores or percentiles but are simply used as a guide to adequate or inadequate performance.

STRENGTHS OF THE SURVEY

• The Purdue Perceptual-Motor Survey provides a structure for assessing a variety of gross and fine motor tasks in elementary school students. The manual is clearly written, and directions for administration and scoring are easy to follow. Little equipment is necessary, so the Survey is an inexpensive way to assess motor skills. The Survey is intended to be used as a structured observation. The increasing assistance provided for the student in the four levels of task administration is very helpful in determining the type of instruction each student will need, and the profile of strengths and weaknesses helps the teacher plan appropriate perceptual-motor activities.

• The Survey was developed from the theoretical framework described by Kephart (1960) in *The Slow Learner in the Classroom*. This book is very helpful to the teacher who is planning a perceptual-motor program. Also helpful are the checklists of motor performance provided by Chaney and Kephart (1968) in *Motoric Aids to Perceptual Training*.

LIMITING FACTORS OF THE SURVEY

• The Survey should be used as it was intended—as an informal assessment procedure. Normative data was gathered on a limited sample of students. Although the test-retest reliability was high in one study reported in the manual, the four-point rating scale for each item clearly leads to subjective scoring decisions. The five skill areas are general categories rather than discrete motor functions. There is much overlapping, and a differential diagnosis of motor disabilities should not be attempted from this informal scale.

• Validity studies, which were carried out with a very small sample, demonstrated that students who are low achievers academically performed more poorly on the Survey than high-achieving students. Even in the authors' studies, performance of the motor tasks did not improve with age or socioeconomic class. There is not sufficient evidence to document the authors' claim that performance of these tasks is "necessary for acquiring academic skills by usual instructional methods" (Examiner's Manual, p. iii).

• Although the Survey is an informal test, it requires a skilled examiner. Many of the tests are difficult to administer, and the observations of student performance take the eye of a person trained and experienced in motor skills.

• The manual does not provide any guidelines for interpreting the profiles or subtest patterns. Such information would be very helpful to the teacher who is inexperienced in the area of motor development.

Bruininks-Oseretsky Test of Motor Proficiency
(Bruininks-Oseretsky Test)

Robert H. Bruininks
American Guidance Service, 1978
Publishers' Bldg., Circle Pines, MN 55014

Purpose	To assess motor skills, to develop and evaluate motor-training programs, and to assess serious motor dysfunctions and developmental delays in children
Major Areas Tested	Motor proficiency and gross and fine motor skills
Age or Grade Range	4½–14½ years
Usually Given By	Special education teacher Occupational therapist Physical education teacher Motor therapist
Type of Test	Standardized Individual
Scores Obtained	Age level Standard Percentile Stanine
Student Performance Timed?	Yes (some subtests)
Testing Time	45–60 minutes (complete battery); 15–20 minutes (short form)
Scoring/Interpretation Time	15–20 minutes
Normed On	765 students from north central, southern, and western states and Canada, balanced for age, sex, race, and community size according to the 1970 census
Alternate Forms Available?	No

FORMAT

The materials for the Bruininks-Oseretsky Test of Motor Proficiency (Bruininks-Oseretsky Test) consist of the examiner's manual, individual record forms for recording responses and scores, student booklets that include materials for pencil-and-paper and cutting tasks, and a variety of manipulative materials for use with the various subtests. All of the materials are packaged in a specially designed metal carrying case.

The test is designed to yield three estimates of motor proficiency: a gross motor score, a fine motor score, and a battery composite score. The 46 items are divided into 8 subtests:

Gross Motor Skills

1. *Running Speed and Agility* (1 item). Running speed during a shuttle run is measured.

2. *Balance* (8 items). Static balance and walking balance on a taped line and a balance beam are assessed.

3. *Bilateral Coordination* (8 items). Simultaneous coordination of upper and lower limbs is measured by asking the student to reproduce such rhythmic patterns as tapping alternate feet and hands or jumping and clapping hands.

4. *Strength* (3 items). Shoulder and arm, abdominal, and leg strength are measured by tasks that include the broad jump, situps, and pushups.

Gross and Fine Motor Skills

5. *Upper-Limb Coordination* (9 items). Coordination of visual tracking with arm and hand movements and precise movements of the arms and hands is assessed by throwing and catching a ball, fingers-to-nose and thumb touching, and others.

Fine Motor Skills

6. *Response Speed* (1 item). Quick response to a moving visual target is measured by catching a sliding stick on the wall.

7. *Visual-Motor Control* (8 items). Coordination of precise visual and hand movements is assessed by such tasks as cutting, copying designs, and following mazes.

8. *Upper-Limb Speed and Dexterity* (8 items). Hand and finger dexterity and hand and arm speed are assessed by such tasks as placing pennies in a box, stringing beads, and rapidly drawing lines and dots.

Raw scores for individual items are converted to a point score using the conversion tables printed directly below each item on the individual record form. Item scores are totaled to obtain subtest scores, which are in turn totaled to make the three composite scores:

1. Gross motor composite score (total of subtests 1 to 4)

2. Fine motor composite score (total of subtests 6 to 8)

3. Total battery composite score (total of subtests 1 to 8)

The three composite scores are converted to normalized standard scores with a mean of 50 and a standard deviation of 10. Percentile ranks and stanines are provided for the composite scores; age-equivalent scores are available for each subtest. Standard error of measurement is provided for the three composite scores.

A short form of the Bruininks-Oseretsky Test is also described in the manual. Fourteen items have been selected from the 46 items comprising the total test. Each of the 14 items was selected because of its high correlation with the subtest and total test scores, the range of ages for which it was useful, the short amount of time needed to administer the item, and the ease of scoring. The short-form items are clearly marked in the manual and on the individual record form. A standard score, percentile, stanine, and standard error of measurement are provided for the short form.

STRENGTHS OF THE BRUININKS-OSERETSKY TEST

• The Bruininks-Oseretsky Test is a modification of the Oseretsky motor tests developed in Russia in the 1920s. The most-used form of the Oseretsky tests for children was the Lincoln-Oseretsky Development Scale. Bruininks's carefully constructed test reflects advances in content and technical quality. Extensive efforts were made to secure a balanced norming sample, and validity figures indicate that the test provides a good estimate of developmental changes in motor proficiency.

• The wide variety of items included in the eight subtests, together with well-designed manipulative materials, makes the test interesting and challenging for students with a wide range of ages and abilities.

• The administration procedures include several good features: a pretest for determining the preferred hand and leg, more than one trial on most subtests, and demonstration of items by the examiner.

• The short form of the test is particularly helpful when large numbers of students need to be screened. Because the short form is embedded in the full test, the short form items can be used for reevaluation purposes.

• The manual is clearly written and gives not only directions for administration and scoring but also information on test construction, norming, reliability, and validity.

LIMITING FACTORS FOR THE BRUININKS-OSERETSKY TEST

• The Bruininks-Oseretsky Test requires a skilled examiner. Many items require setting up equipment in a specific manner and timing the student's responses precisely. Several items need to be demonstrated to the student, so the examiner must also be coordinated. This test is difficult to administer and score. Inexperienced persons should not administer it without careful study of the manual and several practice tests.

• The Bruininks-Oseretsky Test requires space. A running area of 15 meters is necessary, so a playground or multipurpose room will be needed. If many students are to be tested, it is most convenient to set up the physical equipment and leave it in place for the duration of the testing.

• The scoring system for the test is complex. Each item has very specific and different scoring techniques—some record time, others number of correct responses, others pass-fail. Once each item receives a point score, the translation into standard scores, percentiles, stanines, and age-equivalent scores is a many-stepped process. The examiner is urged to doublecheck all scoring for accuracy.

• Test-retest reliability on the individual subtests is somewhat low and makes interpretation of results somewhat questionable. Professionals using this test should be aware of the low reliability factor and not use the test alone to diagnose motor problems.

• Although the author claims that the test can be used to determine ''whether a student should enter school early'' or be placed in a higher grade, such usage of a motor test is highly questionable. Although some research studies using mentally retarded and learning-disabled students are reported in the manual, it reports little data on the relationship between the disabilities and the lack of motor proficiency.

• The manual does not present any information on how to use the Bruininks-Oseretsky Test results to plan individual or small-group motor programs. Presumably the eight subtests would serve as guidelines for the components of a motor training program; more information in this area would be helpful to the user.

Frostig Movement Skills Test Battery

R.E. Orpet
Consulting Psychologists Press, experimental edition, 1972
577 College Ave., Palo Alto, CA 94306

Purpose	To assess strengths and weaknesses in sensory-motor development
Major Areas Tested	Gross and fine motor coordination, balance, strength, and flexibility
Age or Grade Range	6–12 years
Usually Given By	Classroom teacher Physical education teacher Special education teacher Motor therapist Occupational therapist
Type of Test	Standardized Individual Group
Scores Obtained	Age level Standard Scaled score
Student Performance Timed?	Yes
Testing Time	20–25 minutes (individual administration); 45 minutes (group administration)
Scoring/Interpretation Time	15–20 minutes
Normed On	744 Caucasian children from grades K–6 in a Southern California school district
Alternate Forms Available?	No

FORMAT

The Frostig Movement Skills Test Battery consists of 12 subtests designed to measure a variety of sensorimotor skills. The materials for the battery consist of the examiner's manual, profile of abilities forms for recording each student's performance, and a variety of equipment including such things as wooden beads, wooden blocks, a metric ruler, a stopwatch, exercise mats, and a balance beam. The equipment kit (excluding the stopwatch and the balance beam) may be purchased from the publisher or assembled by the examiner. The manual includes a description of and dimensions for each piece of equipment, for those who wish to assemble their own.

The 12 subtests in the battery were designed to measure five areas of motor skills: coordination, agility, balance, flexibility, and strength. Each subtest is timed, and they are administered in the order shown in Table 20.

The tests are usually administered individually to each student; however, three or four students can be tested in a group. In the group administration, the examiner explains and demonstrates each subtest; then each student performs the task alone.

Raw scores on each subtest are converted into scaled scores with a mean of 10 and a standard deviation of 3. Separate scaled-score tables are provided for each year from ages 6 through 12. Separate norms are provided for boys and girls.

Five factors emerged from factor-analytic studies of the 12 subtests. The five factors and the related subtests are grouped as shown on the top of page 190.

Table 20. Subtests of the Frostig Movement Skills Test Battery

Subtest	Ability Assessed	Task
1. Bead Stringing	Bilateral eye-hand coordination, dexterity	Stringing half-inch-square beads in 30 seconds
2. Fist/Edge/Palm	Unilateral coordination, motor sequencing	Placing hand on table in sequence of three positions
3. Block Transfer	Eye-hand coordination, crossing the midline	Moving one-inch blocks from one side of a board across midline of body to other side
4. Beanbag Throw	Visual-motor coordination, aiming, accuracy	Tossing beanbags at a paper wall target
5. Sitting/Bending/Reaching	Flexibility of trunk and hip	Sitting on the floor with knees straight, bending forward, and reaching with hands
6. Standing Broad Jump	Leg strength	Standing broad jump
7. Shuttle Run	Running speed; ability to make quick stops, changes of direction, and body position	Moving beanbags one at a time from one circle to another as quickly as possible (circles 20 feet apart)
8. Changing Body Position	Speed and agility in changing body position	Changing as rapidly as possible from a prone to a standing position and back again
9. Sit-ups	Abdominal muscle strength	Sit-ups with knees bent, hands behind head
10. Walking Board	Maintaining dynamic balance	Walking heel-to-toe on a wide (four-inch) and narrow (two-inch) walking board four inches above floor
11. One-Foot Balance	Static balance	Balancing on either foot with hands on hips, with eyes both open and closed
12. Chair Push-ups	Arm and shoulder girdle strength	Push-ups with hands gripping chair seat, body prone position, feet on floor

Factor	Subtests
Hand-eye coordination	Bead Stringing Fist / Edge / Palm Block Transfer
Strength	Standing Broad Jump Shuttle Run Changing Body Position Sit-ups Chair Push-ups
Balance	Walking Board One-Foot Balance
Visually guided movement	Bean Bag Throw
Flexibility	Sitting / Bending / Reaching

Mean scaled scores are computed for each factor on the profile of abilities as well as for the total test. Test results can then be interpreted on three levels: (1) total test score, (2) five factor scores, and (3) individual subtest scores. Such analysis can form the basis of an individualized movement skills remediation program.

STRENGTHS OF THE FROSTIG MOVEMENT SKILLS TEST BATTERY

• The test battery is easy to administer and score, particularly for someone experienced in motor skill training. The manual is well written, and administration procedures are clear. The battery includes a broad sampling of specific motor skills and yields information on the global question of whether or not a student's motor performance is at age level.

LIMITING FACTORS OF THE FROSTIG MOVEMENT SKILLS TEST BATTERY

• The Frostig Movement Skills Test Battery is currently in an experimental edition. Norms are based on a homogeneous sample of white students from one Southern California school district. The norming population obviously needs to be expanded and more studies of reliability and validity carried out. In the author's reported factor-analytic study, reliability coefficients are low for most subtests at several age levels.

• No validation studies correlating the Frostig Movement Skills Test Battery and existing tests were carried out, because the author felt no adequate criterion measure existed. This may be true for the total test, but other tests do measure some of the major factors, specifically eye-motor coordination and balance. Validation studies are needed to support or refute the author's factor-analysis study.

• On several subtests, at some age levels, the standard

deviation is very large, suggesting that parts of the test battery are not very discriminating and should be viewed more as screening tests. It would be helpful if the standard error of measurement were provided for each age on each subtest.

• The labeling of factors is not well documented in the manual. For example, the factor common to Bead Stringing, Fist/Edge/Palm, and Block Transfer could be motor planning as well as eye-hand coordination.

• Other subtests to measure flexibility and visually guided movement should be added to the battery so that scores in these factors are not based on a single subtest.

• No interpretation of the individual scores or subtest patterns is discussed. This is a serious omission because the examiner, at the completion of the scoring procedures, is given no guidelines for their interpretation.

Southern California Sensory Integration Tests (SCSIT)

A. Jean Ayres
Western Psychological Services, 1972
12031 Wilshire Blvd., Los Angeles, CA 90025

Purpose	To assess sensory integrative functioning
Major Areas Tested	Visual, tactile, kinesthetic, and vestibular functioning; motor planning ability; postural mechanisms; bilateral integration; and coordination of gross and fine motor skills
Age or Grade Range	4–9 years
Usually Given By	Occupational therapist Physical therapist
Type of Test	Standardized Individual
Scores Obtained	Standard
Student Performance Timed?	Yes (some subtests)
Testing Time	1½ hours
Scoring/Interpretation Time	1 hour
Normed On	Heterogeneous population of children from public and private schools, organizations, and children's centers from metropolitan Los Angeles, California and surrounding areas
Alternate Forms Available?	No

FORMAT

The Southern California Sensory Integration Tests (SCSIT) consist of 18 standardized tests and a series of informal clinical observations. The format of each of the standardized tests is described in Table 21. The clinical observation items include a variety of motor tasks designed to provide supplementary information about postural mechanisms, praxis, bilateral integration, muscle tone, and other aspects of motor functioning.

The materials consist of a test manual, an interpretation manual, scoring forms, profile sheets, and picture and manipulative materials for the 18 tests. The materials for the total SCSIT can be purchased in one kit; most of the test materials can also be purchased separately.

STRENGTHS OF THE SCSIT

• The SCSIT is designed to assess the student's ability to interpret and use meaningfully certain kinds of sensory information from the environment and from the student's own body. Visual, tactile, kinesthetic, and vestibular functioning are assessed, as well as motor planning skill (praxis), postural mechanisms, bilateral integration, and coordination for basic gross and fine motor skills. The skills assessed are automatic rather than cognitive functions.

• The SCSIT is, therefore, a comprehensive battery of tests that provides information about a broad range of motor functioning. Through the use of 18 short tests, a balance is achieved between the need to maintain student interest and the need to include sufficient numbers of test items to gain meaningful information.

• The test battery is useful not only in determining which students are experiencing difficulty in the sensorimotor areas, but also in defining the nature of those difficulties. Through the use of factor-analytic studies, several areas of sensory integrative functioning have been identified, and the SCSIT provides information necessary for this differential diagnosis. For example, an apraxic student may score poorly in the tactile tests and on the motor-involved tests but may achieve average or above-average scores on tests of form and space perception, which do not require precise motor responses. In this example, the SCSIT not only would indicate that this student is experiencing difficulties in the sensorimotor areas but would also identify the area of dysfunction, providing information necessary for planning an appropriate intervention program.

• The SCSIT is a useful tool for evaluating sensorimotor development in language-impaired students. Expressive language requirements are minimal. The student is required to respond orally (one-word answers are sufficient) on two items on Right-Left Discrimination; no other tests in the battery require oral responses. The understanding of language required of the student is somewhat more demanding. However, directions are simple, they can be

repeated and reexplained on most tests, and all tests include trial items with additional explanations as indicated. In addition, a great deal of imitation is used in the administration of the tests.

• Although most of the tests in the battery cannot be used in isolation, the tests of Motor Accuracy and Design Copying have adequate reliability to be used independently. These two tests may provide useful information regarding a child's progress in fine motor coordination and visual-motor integration skills. The Motor Accuracy test is particularly sensitive for measuring small skill changes in younger students.

• The student's scores are presented on a profile that graphically illustrates how his or her scores compare to those of the normative population, as well as how scores in one area of functioning compare to scores in another area (see Figure 56). This profile is a clear and accurate means of reporting scores to parents and other professionals.

• The test manual provides, for the most part, thorough statistical information, including coefficients of test-retest reliability, standard errors of measurement, size and sex distribution of the normative sample, means, standard deviations, and standard scores for each age group on each test. With the exception of Motor Accuracy, the size of the standardization sample was adequate for each age group, ranging from 60 to 125 students. The manual also provides basic information about test interpretation and validity studies, including analyses of the relationship between SCSIT scores and other established measures of perceptual-motor skills, as well as the relationship between SCSIT scores and various aspects of sensory integrative functioning. The author cautions, quite appropriately, that meaningful interpretations of the SCSIT are still in the early stages.

LIMITING FACTORS OF THE SCSIT

• The SCSIT is a complex battery to administer and interpret, and it requires a highly trained examiner. A workable system exists for training and certifying professionals (usually occupational and physical therapists), but there is no requirement that an individual be certified before purchasing and administering the tests. The subtleties of administration and interpretation leave the SCSIT highly vulnerable to misuse by untrained examiners.

• The tests are time consuming to administer, score, and interpret.

• With the exception of the Motor Accuracy and Design Copying tests, meaningful use of the SCSIT requires administration of the whole battery. Many of the tests have poor test-retest reliability, and an isolated score on one of these tests has little significance. The author suggests that the standard error of measurement, which is a function of both reliability and standard deviation, be used as one of the more important guides to the tests' usefulness. The use of scores from several tests in one area of functioning (tactile perception, for example) provides greatly increased reliability.

- The test scores are sometimes used to hypothesize about suspected areas of brain dysfunction (right or left cortical hemisphere, brainstem). This interpretation is highly controversial.

- Owing to the nature of the tasks, it is often difficult to determine the student's degree of attentiveness. This is particularly true of the tactile tests.

- The tests were designed to assess automatic rather than highly cognitive functions, but a bright, motivated student may be able to respond adequately on some tests through cognitive skills, thus obscuring some deficits in automatic functioning. A trained examiner is alert to this possibility, but observation of it is subjective at best.

- It is likely that many of the functions assessed, particularly on the visual tests, are related to intelligence. There is no information regarding intelligence distribution in the standardization population.

- The author states that "the geographic and socioeconomic levels of metropolitan Los Angeles and the surrounding areas were represented." This does not provide adequate information about the socioeconomic level of the normative sample. The description of the process of selecting a random sample is also sketchy.

- The classroom teacher may gather some information from these tests results that is useful in determining appropriate classroom activities for a particular student. However, the therapy that is often recommended for a child who had difficulty with these tests must be individually tailored by a therapist with a medical background and, in most cases, cannot realistically be implemented by a teacher in a regular classroom program.

- With the exception of Motor Accuracy and Design Copying, the tests have very limited use for measuring progress. They are primarily a diagnostic tool.

Table 21. SCSIT Tests

Test	Task	Functions
Space Visualization	The student is given a simple formboard (one shape), with a peg in it, and two blocks, each with a hole. Without manipulating the blocks, the student must select the block that fits onto the formboard with the hole correctly aligned over the peg. He or she then indicates the choice by placing one block onto the formboard. The item is scored for time and accuracy from the moment the student first moves (or points to) a block. Early items require only discrimination by shape, but more complex, later items require mental manipulation of the blocks.	Visual perception
Figure-Ground Perception	The student is shown a test plate of several superimposed figures and a response plate of six separate figures. The student must select the three figures embedded in the test plate. Figure-ground discrimination is required. Both common objects and geometric forms are used.	Visual perception
Position in Space	This test is in three parts. For parts 1 and 2, the student is shown a stimulus figure (a geometric form or a sequence of forms) and two to four response figures from which to choose a match. This may require discriminating among reversed or rotated forms or matching sequences of forms. A complex procedure minimizes the effect of chance, and considerable instruction is permitted. For part 3, the stimulus is removed, requiring the student to rely on visual memory.	Visual perception, visual memory
Design Copying	The student copies patterns on dot grids. The responses are scored according to the aaility to connect the correct dots and the precision with which the lines are drawn.	Visual perception, visual motor integration, fine motor coordination
Motor Accuracy	With one hand, then the other, the student traces a curved line about 51 inches long, printed on paper 17 by 11 inches. This requires fine finger movements, as well as shoulder girdle and elbow adjustments on a horizontal surface. In scoring, the examiner measures the length of the line the student traced inaccurately and the distance strayed from the correct line. The scores achieved with the more and the less accurate hands are compared to the more and the less accurate hands of the normative sample.	Praxis, other aspects of upper-extremity coordination
Kinesthesia	A shield occludes the student's vision throughout. The examiner places the student's index finger at a spot on the kinesthesia chart, then says that it is the student's ''pretend house,'' from which he or she will visit a ''pretend friend's house.'' The examiner moves the student's finger to a second spot (''Bob's house''), then back to the original spot. The student attempts to return to ''Bob's house'' without guidance, and the examiner measures the distance from it to the student's finger. The process is repeated for each ''friend's house.''	Perception of joint position and movement
Manual Form Perception	With a shield occluding the student's vision, the examiner places a geometric form in the student's hand. The student feels the form then points to the picture that he or she thinks shows that form.	Tactile discrimination, form and space perception
Finger Identification	With a shield occluding the student's vision, the examiner touches one or two of the student's fingers, and the student attempts to point to the designated finger(s) on a paper chart.	Tactile discrimination

Mode of Presentation	Mode of Response	Significant Motor Component?	Timed?	Notes
Visual, three-dimensional	Pointing to and/or moving blocks	No	Yes—separate accuracy scores, timed and untimed	The test discriminates well in younger age groups. It is less effective in discriminating between average and above-average performance in older age groups. The large chance factor in selecting answers requires cautious interpretation of scores.
Visual, two-dimensional	Pointing to figures in a plate (multiple choice)	No	Not precisely—a time limit is set for each item	Test performance is particularly vulnerable to anxiety. The large chance factor in selecting answers requires cautious interpretation of scores.
Visual, two-dimensional	Pointing or saying yes/no to figures (multiple choice)	No	Part 2 only	This test does not discriminate well among 4-year-olds with severe perceptual handicaps.
Visual, two-dimensional	Dot-to-dot drawing with pencil	Yes	No	Students experienced in exercises of this kind may achieve unrealistically high scores. The test does not discriminate well among 4-year-olds with perceptual deficits.
Visual	Tracing with pencil	Yes	Yes—separate accuracy scores, timed and untimed	The test does not discriminate well among well-coordinated 8-year-olds. It does provide a precise tool for measuring subtle changes in accuracy with a pencil in younger children, particularly poorly coordinated ones.
Kinesthetic, vision occluded (examiner moves student's arm)	Moving arm, vision occluded	Yes	No	The test provides the opportunity to observe automatic postural adjustments.
Tactile, vision occluded	Pointing to pictures, vision permitted	No	Yes	These five tactile discrimination tests must be given in one sitting and in the correct order. The scores must also be viewed as a constellation if interpretation is to be accurate. A score on any one of the tests should not be taken in
Tactile, vision occluded	Pointing to fingers, vision permitted	No	No	

Table 21. —*Continued*

Test	Task	Functions
Graphesthesia	With a shield occluding the student's vision, the examiner traces a simple design with a pencil eraser on the back of the student's hand. The examiner then removes the shield, and the student attempts to retrace the design with a fingertip on his or her own hand.	Tactile discrimination, form and space perception, fine motor coordination
Localization of Tactile Stimuli	A shield occludes the student's vision throughout the test. First, the examiner touches a spot on the student's hand or arm with the tip of a pen; then the student attempts to touch the spot with a fingertip. The examiner measures the distance from the spot to the student's finger.	Tactile discrimination
Double Tactile Stimuli Perception	Standing behind the student, the examiner uses two pencil erasers simultaneously to touch the student's hands, cheeks, or one hand and one cheek. The student then attempts to point to the places where he or she felt the erasers. The response that is scored is touching the correct cheek or hand.	Tactile discrimination
Imitation of Postures	The examiner quickly assumes positions requiring precise placement of hands and arms and, on some items, of trunk and/or legs. The student then attempts to copy these postures.	Praxis, postural mechanisms, bilateral integration
Crossing the Midline of the Body	The examiner points to his or her ear or eye, and the student copies in mirror image. Explicit instructions and trial items establish whether the student understands the concept of mirror image. The examiner scores according to whether the student crosses the body midline in responding. For example, does the student consistently use the right hand to point to the right ear or eye, even when the correct imitation requires using the left hand?	Bilateral integration, praxis
Bilateral Motor Coordination	The examiner demonstrates a rhythmic pattern of light slaps against his or her thighs, and the student imitates in mirror image. The student's ability to coordinate arm movements enters into the scoring.	Bilateral integration, praxis
Right-Left Discrimination	The examiner asks the student to indicate the right, or left hand, foot, ear, and so on. Two items also require the student to distinguish between right and left on the examiner.	Bilateral integration
Standing Balance, Eyes Open	With eyes open, the student folds his or her arms and balances as long as possible first on the right foot, then on the left foot.	Postural mechanisms
Standing Balance, Eyes Closed	With eyes closed, the student repeats the procedure above.	Postural mechanisms
Postrotary Nystagmus	The student sits on a PNT board (a board that rotates on ball bearings) and is turned in the same direction 10 times in 20 seconds. The student then stares at a blank wall, and the examiner observes his or her eyes for nystagmus. The examiner also watches for postural changes and dizziness. This procedure is repeated with turns in the opposite direction.	One component of vestibular function, namely selected aspects of response to rotation

Mode of Presentation	Mode of Response	Significant Motor Component?	Timed?	Notes
				isolation, because each is highly subject to testing error. These tests also provide an opportunity to observe the presence or lack of tactile defensiveness.
Tactile, vision occluded	Retracing designs with a fingertip, vision permitted	Yes	No	
Tactile, vision occluded	Touching designated spots on hands and arms, vision occluded	No	No	
Tactile, vision occluded	Pointing to hands and cheeks	No	No	
Visual	Motor—whole body	Yes	Not precisely—a time limit is set on each item for full and partial credit	This and the five tests that follow must be administered in one sitting and in the correct sequence.
Visual	Pointing to ears and eyes	Yes, although precise movements are not required	No	
Visual	Motor—hands and arms used in clapping pattern	Yes	No	Scoring coordination on this test is more subjective than on the other tests in the battery.
Oral	Pointing to body parts and saying "right" and "left"	No	Not precisely—a time limit is set on each item for full credit	This test includes the only two items in the battery that require oral responses.
Oral	Motor	Yes	Yes	
Oral	Motor	Yes	Yes	
Vestibular input	No voluntary response required	No	Yes	This test is discontinued if the student becomes fearful, excessively dizzy, or uncomfortable in any way. It may be contraindicated for seizure-prone children.

Southern California Sensory Integration Tests

Profile of Standard Scores
by A. Jean Ayres, Ph.D.

Published by

WPS WESTERN PSYCHOLOGICAL SERVICES
PUBLISHERS AND DISTRIBUTORS
12031 WILSHIRE BOULEVARD
LOS ANGELES, CALIFORNIA 90025

A DIVISION OF MANSON WESTERN CORPORATION

Name _____   **Test Date**   Yr. _____ Mo. _____ Dy. _____

Examiner _____   **Birth Date**   Yr. _____ Mo. _____ Dy. _____

Preferred Hand: L Ⓡ ; **Preferred Eye:** L Ⓡ _____   **Chron. Age**   Yr. _7_ Mo. _5_ Dy. _3_

Double Tactile Stimuli Perception −2.4

Localization of Tactile Stimuli −1.9

Motor Accuracy, Right Hand −1.8 (raw score 443)

Standing Balance, Eyes Open −1.7

Motor Accuracy, Left Hand −1.6 (raw score 420)

Graphesthesia −1.5

Standing Balance, Eyes Closed −1.4

Manual Form Perception −1.3

Crossing the Midline of the Body −1.3

Imitation of Postures −1.1

Kinesthesia −1.0

Bilateral Motor Coordination −1.0

Design Copying −0.5

Postrotary Nystagmus −0.2

Space Visualization 0.0

Finger Identification +0.2

Right-Left Discrimination +0.4

Position in Space +0.5

Figure-Ground Perception +1.3

−4.0   −3.0   −2.0   −1.0   0.0   +1.0   +2.0   +3.0   +4.0

Figure 56. SCSIT Profile

PART II

Preschool and Kindergarten Tests

Early identification of children with learning disabilities has been a major topic of discussion in special education for the past 15 years. The early detection of any type of handicap receives wide support from the fields of medicine, psychology, and education; the recognition and diagnosis of a specific condition leads directly to treatment.

The process becomes a little less clear, however, when the condition being identified is predicted rather than currently present. In other words, assessing preschool children's performance on test items believed to be related to academic success may result in a prediction of academic failure when the actual academic failure has not occurred—and may not occur. It is one thing to assess learning disabilities in the third grader who has not learned to read; it is another to assess potential learning disabilities in a 5-year-old. Everyone agrees that the earlier a child gets help, the better. But many professionals are afraid that the identification of potential problems may create in parents and teachers an expectation set that will increase the likelihood that the problem will occur.

The concerns regarding early identification procedures are well outlined by Keogh and Becker (1973, pp. 5–11). They divide the problems of early identification into three main areas: (1) the predictive validity of the tests, (2) the implications of the diagnostic information for placement and remediation, and (3) the weighing of the benefits of early detection with the possible negative effects of such recognition.

In order to validate early identification measures, the students tested during their preschool and kindergarten years must be followed to determine their actual academic success in the primary and intermediate years. Longitudinal research

can help to show whether the predictive tool did, in fact, predict academic success or failure with a high degree of accuracy. The best-known longitudinal research was reported by de Hirsch, Jansky, and Langford (1966) in *Predicting Reading Failure*. A wide variety of standardized and informal tests were administered to over 400 kindergarten students, who were then followed for two years. This study resulted in a predictive index of five tests that could be administered in 15 to 20 minutes. The predictive index identified three out of four students with reading failure in second grade. Longitudinal research is currently in progress using other instruments and student populations (Satz *et al.* 1975; Morrissey 1979). Because the decisions about placement and program that result from early identification procedures are crucial, the use of assessment measures with high predictive validity is imperative.

Preschool and kindergarten tests can be classified in various ways: group versus individual, single content area versus multiple areas, standardized versus informal, and screening instruments versus diagnostic tools. The seven tests reviewed in Part II are arranged in order from the general to the specific: The first four assess developmental delays in young children; the last three assess delays in specific content areas (language, mathematics, and reading) and are used with older children.

The first test reviewed, the Denver Developmental Screening Test, has been widely used in medical and educational settings for several years as a quick individual screening test to identify high-risk infants and preschool children. The Brigance Diagnostic Inventory of Early Development is a very new and comprehensive assessment

199

instrument. It lowers the age range of the criterion-referenced format of the Brigance Diagnostic Inventory of Basic Skills (reviewed in Chapter One) from kindergarten to birth. Developmental Indicators for the Assessment of Learning is a unique instrument for screening individual children between 3 and 5 years of age within a group setting, and the Meeting Street School Screening Test is a carefully prepared individual screening battery for 5- to 7-year-olds.

Of the tests measuring a single content area, the Compton Speech and Language Screening Evaluation is a quick, efficient method of screening 3- to 6-year-olds for language problems. The Kraner Preschool Math Inventory assesses math skills at the readiness level and also provides an assessment of language in the areas of spatial and quantitative concepts. The Slingerland Pre-Reading Screening Procedures is the kindergarten-level test of the Slingerland Screening Tests for Identifying Children with Specific Language Disability, reviewed in Chapter Two. It is designed to identify children who are at high risk for reading failure.

Many tests reviewed in other chapters of this book are appropriate for preschool and kindergarten children. Appendix H lists these tests.

Denver Developmental Screening Test (DDST)

William Frankenburg and Josiah Dodds
Ladoca Project and Publishing Foundation, Inc., 1970
East 51st Ave. and Lincoln St., Denver, CO 80216

Purpose	To detect developmental delays
Major Areas Tested	Social, fine motor, gross motor, and language skills
Age or Grade Range	Birth–6 years
Usually Given By	Special education teacher Speech/language clinician Occupational therapist Doctor/nurse Psychologist
Type of Test	Standardized Individual
Scores Obtained	Age level
Student Performance Timed?	No
Testing Time	20 minutes
Scoring/Interpretation Time	10 minutes
Normed On	1,000 children from Denver, Colorado, with race, ethnic, and occupational group characteristics of the 1960 Denver census; children with atypical birth histories or known handicaps excluded
Alternate Forms Available?	No

FORMAT

The Denver Developmental Screening Test (DDST) consists of an examiner's manual and individual scoring sheets. A few simple materials, such as red wool, one-inch colored blocks, and a tennis ball, are included in the kit. The 105 test items are arranged in four sections as shown in Table 22.

The individual scoring sheets are arranged with age scales across the top and bottom, as shown in Figure 57. Ages are given in monthly intervals from 1 to 24 months and in three-month intervals from 2 to 6 years. Each of the 105 items is represented on the form by a bar that indicates at what age 25, 50, 75, and 90 percent of the children in the

standardization sample passed the item. A vertical line is drawn on the scoring sheet to represent the child's chronological age.

Every effort is made to make the young child comfortable with the testing situation. A parent or other familiar person is always present, and the infant or young child often sits on that person's lap. Items in the Personal-Social sector are administered first, because many of the items can be passed by parent report. In other sectors, the examiner begins with items slightly below the child's chronological age and continues downward until three items are passed; then the examiner proceeds to items at the child's age level or above until three items are failed. Items are scored Pass, Fail,

Table 22. DDST Sectors

Sector	Description of Tasks	Age	Sample Tasks	
			Task Name	Task
Personal-Social	Tasks that indicate the child's ability to get along with people and to take care of himself or herself	5½ mo.	Resists Toy Pull	Resists having toy taken away
		2½ yr.	Dresses with Supervision	Puts on any article of own clothing
Fine Motor-Adaptive	Tasks that indicate the child's ability to see, to use hands to pick up objects, and to draw	3½ mo.	Reaches for Object	Reaches for toy placed in front of him or her
		2 yr.	Tower of Eight Cubes	Balances eight cubes on top of each other
Language	Tasks that indicate the child's ability to hear, to carry out commands, and to speak	1 yr.	Three Words Other Than Ma-ma, Da-da	Uses at least three specific words for three objects
		4½ yr.	Defines Words	Defines six out of nine words by use, shape, composition, or category (words are *ball, lake, desk, house, banana, curtain, ceiling, hedge, pavement.*)
Gross Motor	Tasks that indicate the child's ability to sit, walk, and jump	11 mo.	Stoops and Recovers	Bends over, picks up a toy, and stands up again without holding on or touching the floor
		2½ yr.	Broad Jump	Jumps with both feet together over an 8½-inch paper placed flat on the floor

Refusal, or No Opportunity. If a child refuses to try an item, the examiner instructs the parent on how to administer it. All items are allowed three trials before being scored as failed.

The DDST attempts to discover delays in development. A *delay* is defined as any failed item that is completely below the chronological age line; that is, the child fails an item that 90 percent of the children pass at a younger age. Test results are determined *abnormal* when (1) two sectors have two or more delays or (2) one sector has two delays and another sector has one delay and no passes at age level. Test results are determined *questionable* when (1) one sector has two delays or (2) one sector has one delay and no passes at age level. Children whose tests are determined abnormal or questionable should be retested in two or three weeks. If test

results are still abnormal, the child should be referred to a doctor.

STRENGTHS OF THE DDST

• The Denver Developmental Screening Test is clearly a screening test, designed to give quick but reliable and valid information on children's performance in the major areas of early development. Designed to be administered by persons unfamiliar with psychological testing, it is concise, clear, and relatively simple to administer and interpret.

• The manual is well written and gives explicit directions for each test item, as well as for such basic procedures as what to tell parents and how to calculate chronological age.

• The scoring sheet is well designed, and the scoring procedures are as explicit as possible. Although the

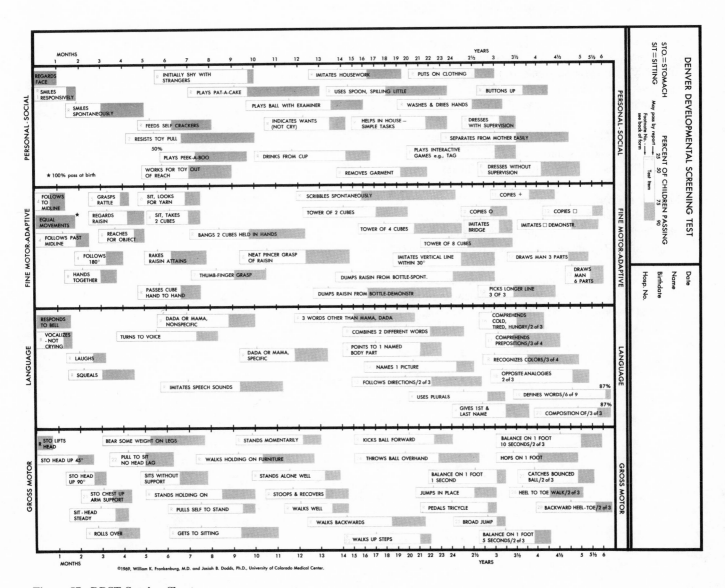

Figure 57. DDST Scoring Sheet

standardization sample was limited in size and region and included few minority-group children, the DDST has been used successfully in medical and psychological research and seems to hold up well as a tool for the early detection of developmental problems (Wallace and Larsen 1978, p. 165).

LIMITING FACTORS OF THE DDST

• The DDST was developed primarily by doctors for use in medical settings. The examples given in the manual reflect this orientation, suggesting physical causes for developmental delays. The term *abnormal* applied to test results also reflects the medical model. However, as a screening tool the DDST is useful in both infant and preschool educational programs.

• Although the examiner's manual states that the test may be given by persons unfamiliar with psychological testing, the authors strongly recommend that the test be administered only by those trained in its use.

• The child can pass many of the items by the parent's report. For example, 17 of the 23 Personal-Social items and 12 of the 20 Language items may be passed by the parent's report. Parents vary greatly in their reliability as reporters. The examiner needs to be aware of this even on a screening test.

• The DDST manual reports a validity study that obtained high correlations among the DDST, the Stanford-Binet Intelligence Scale, and the Revised Bayley Infant Scales (Bayley 1969). A more recent study of 236 children (Moriarity 1972, p. 733) reports that the DDST identified significantly fewer abnormal children than the Bayley Scales. Validity was questionable for infants under 30 months and for 3-year-olds. It was best for children ranging in age from 4 to 4½ years.

• The assessment of infants is a very specialized field, and the DDST is often used by examiners untrained in testing and assessment. The authors of the DDST stress that it is a quick screening test; all who use it should keep that in mind.

Brigance Diagnostic Inventory of Early Development

Albert H. Brigance
Curriculum Associates, Inc., 1978
6 Henshaw St., Woburn, MA 01801

Purpose	To assess developmental or performance levels in children, to identify appropriate instructional objectives, and to provide a systematic record-keeping tool
Major Areas Tested	Psychomotor, self-help, speech and language, general comprehension, and preacademic skills
Age or Grade Range	Birth–6 years
Usually Given By	Classroom teacher Administrator Special education teacher Paraprofessional Psychologist
Type of Test	Informal Individual Criterion-referenced
Scores Obtained	Age level
Student Performance Timed?	No
Testing Time	30–60 minutes (depending on purpose of testing)
Scoring/Interpretation Time	15–30 minutes
Normed On	Literature review; field-tested in a wide variety of programs in 16 states
Alternate Forms Available?	No

FORMAT

The Brigance Diagnostic Inventory of Early Development consists of 98 subtests (skill sequences) organized into the following categories:

A. Pre-Ambulatory Motor Skills and Behaviors (4 subtests, including sitting, standing)

B. Gross Motor Skills and Behaviors (13 subtests, including running, hopping, balance, wheel toys)

C. Fine Motor Skills and Behaviors (9 subtests, including blocks, puzzles, clay)

D. Self-Help Skills (11 subtests, including eating, dressing, household chores)

E. Pre-Speech (3 subtests, including receptive language, gestures, vocalization)

F. Speech and Language Skills (10 subtests, including syntax, vocabulary, articulation)

G. General Knowledge and Comprehension (13 subtests, including body parts, colors, weather)

H. Readiness (5 subtests, including visual discrimination, letter recognition)

I. Basic Reading Skills (11 subtests, including auditory discrimination, initial sounds, beginning reading)

J. Manuscript Writing (7 subtests, including printing from copying and dictation)

K. Math (12 subtests, including rote counting, ordering numerals, beginning computation)

The materials consist of the examiner's notebook and individual developmental record books. The examiner's notebook opens flat between the examiner and the child. The examiner's page includes a statement of the skill being assessed, directions for administration and scoring, and instructional objectives for each skill. The child's page includes the test items. The author gives permission for the child's pages to be reproduced. Some pages have been designed to be cut apart so that items can be presented separately as in Figure 58. (In this example, the bottom row of geometric shapes is cut out, and the child is asked to match them with the appropriate shapes above.)

A variety of assessment procedures can be used, specifically, parent interview, observation of the infant or child, and the child's performance on structured tasks. If using the test as an informal inventory, the examiner is

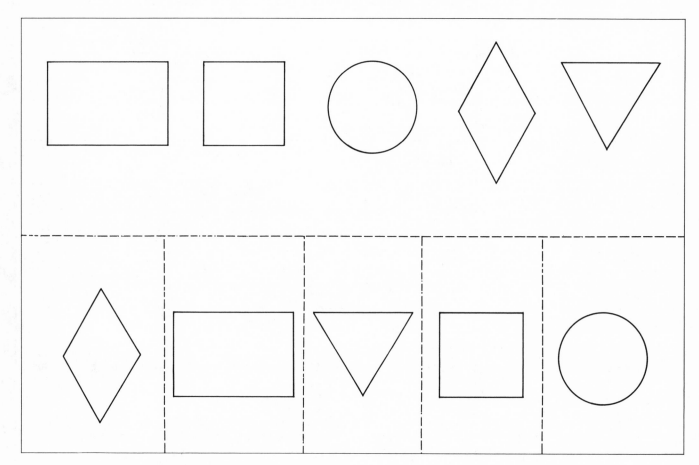

Figure 58. Brigance Diagnostic Inventory of Early Development

encouraged to modify the material to give the child the best opportunity to demonstrate his or her skill. Some tasks require verbal responses, others require pointing, and still others are pencil-and-paper tasks. The child's performance, observation report, or parent interview information is recorded in the individual developmental record book. Different colored pens are used to record the data each time the test is administered, to provide an ongoing record of progress. Each skill the child has achieved is circled; some items have an optional bar graph that can be colored to denote developmental level. A group developmental record book is also available.

The Brigance Diagnostic Inventory of Early Development is an informal assessment tool. It covers a wide age range, so no child would be assessed in all of the 98 skill sequences. The examiner selects only those skills that are appropriate for each child, depending on age and purpose of the testing. Because each skill sequence covers several years, the examiner also selects an approximate developmental level to begin the assessment. Developmental levels are printed on both the examiner's page and the developmental record book (see Figure 59).

The examiner's notebook also includes references to the literature that was used to validate the skill sequences and developmental ages, as well as information on field testing of the test.

STRENGTHS OF THE BRIGANCE DIAGNOSTIC INVENTORY OF EARLY DEVELOPMENT

- The Brigance Diagnostic Inventory of Early Development is a comprehensive instrument assessing a wide range of skills over the critical infant and preschool period. Although it is primarily a criterion-referenced tool, developmental ages are also provided for key skills. Many skills not usually assessed are included, such as use of wheel toys, brush painting, and knowledge of weather and

Developmental Record Book

B. GROSS MOTOR

Test Page	
B-1 24-26	**STANDING:** 1-0 1. *Standing with broad stance. 2. Standing with normal stance. 1-6 3. Standing on one foot with one hand held. 4. Standing on either foot with one hand held. 5. *Squats to pick up object from floor and re-erects. 6. Standing with heels together. 2-0 7. Standing on tiptoes momentarily—1 second. 2-6 8. Bends at waist to pick up object from floor. 9. Attempts to stand on 1 foot—no assistance. 3-0 10. Stands on 1 foot momentarily—1 second. 11. Stands on either foot momentarily—1 second. 4-0 12. Stands on one foot 5 seconds. 13. Stands on either foot 5 seconds. 5-0 14. Stands on one foot 10 seconds. 15. Stands on either foot 10 seconds. 6-0 16. Stands on one foot momentarily with eyes closed. 17. Stands on either foot momentarily with eyes closed. 18. Stands heel and toe 5 seconds. 7-0 *1 year 2 3 4 5 6 7*
	NOTES:
B-2 28-30	**WALKING:** 1-0 1. *Walks with broad stance. 2. *Walks with knees slightly bent and shoulders slightly hunched. 3. *Walks holding hands out for balance rather than at side. 4. Walks with hands swinging at side. 5. Walks sideways. 1-6 6. Walks well and rarely falls. 7. Walks fast. 8. Walks stepping over 2"x4" (5 cm x10cm) board without difficulty. 2-0 9. Walks backwards three steps. 10. Walks backward distance of 6'8" (2 m). 11. Walks on tiptoes 3 steps. 3-0 12. Walks forward heel and toe three steps. 13. Walks on tip toes a distance of 6'8" (2 m). 14. Walks on straight line. 4-0 15. Walks circular 1" (25 mm) line. 16. Walks forward on line heel and toe a distance of 6'8" (2 m). 17. Walks scissor steps across 1" (25 mm) wide line a distance of 6'8" (2 m). 5-0 18. Walks backward toe and heel six steps. 19. Walks backward toe and heel a distance of 6'8" (2 m). 7-0 *1 year 2 3 4 5 6 7*
	NOTES:
B-3 30-31	**STAIRS AND CLIMBING:** 1-0 1. Creeps up stairs. 2. Creeps down stairs backward. 3. Climbs on/in low furniture such as a low couch. 4. Climbs in and out of adult chair. 1-6 5. Walks up stairs with one hand held. 6. Walks down stairs with one hand held. 7. Walks up stairs alone holding rail. 2-0 8. Walks down stairs alone holding rail. 9. Walks up stairs using alternate feet with one hand held. 3-0 10. Walks down stairs using alternate feet with one hand held. 11. Climbs ladder of low play equipment. 12. Walks up stairs using alternate feet, holding rail. 4-0 13. Walks down stairs using alternate feet, holding rail. 14. Walks up stairs carrying object in one hand, not holding rail. 15. Walks down stairs carrying object and not holding rail. 5-6 16. Walks up and down stairs carrying object(s) with both hands. 7-0 *1 year 2 3 4 5 6 7*
	NOTES:

Figure 59. Brigance Diagnostic Inventory of Early Development, Developmental Record Book

time concepts. Because these skills represent curriculum areas common in many preschool programs, they are useful for many teachers. The inclusion of instructional objectives also increases the usefulness of the instrument for teachers who need to plan individual educational programs. The built-in record-keeping system is also very helpful.

• The Brigance Diagnostic Inventory of Early Development is easy to administer and can be used by well-trained paraprofessionals. The materials are compact, well organized, and reasonably priced.

• The nature of the tool allows such variety in assessment procedures that it can be used with older low-functioning children.

LIMITING FACTORS OF THE BRIGANCE DIAGNOSTIC INVENTORY OF EARLY DEVELOPMENT

• The Brigance Diagnostic Inventory of Early Development is very new to the market. Although the test has had extensive field testing, no validity or reliability data is available at this time. Studies comparing this instrument with other preschool screening devices, such as the Denver Developmental Screening Test, are needed, as are test-retest reliability data.

• The grouping of the 98 skill sequences into 11 categories is somewhat haphazard. For example, colors and body parts are grouped under General Knowledge and Comprehension; most tests describe them as readiness skills. Readiness, in this inventory, includes only five subtests, four of which deal with the alphabet; these subtests would seem more appropriately placed under Basic Reading Skills. Examiners should study all the subtests carefully, rather than relying on category headings, to ensure that all areas appropriate for the child are included in the assessment.

• The examiner's page includes so much information in addition to the directions for administration that the examiner needs to become quite familiar with the instrument before using it with infants and young children. The developmental record books are also quite complex in format—they include extensive information all on one page. If they are to be used effectively as a communication tool with parents, the examiner will need a good deal of practice in explaining the record form. It may well be necessary to transfer the assessment information to a summary sheet for parents.

• The inventory uses parent report as the data for tasks that are not easily observed during a school program. As with all assessments using parent reports to determine the skill levels of a child, the examiner needs to help parents become reliable reporters. When in doubt about a parent's accuracy, tasks and situations should be established at school to observe the child's performance.

Developmental Indicators for the Assessment of Learning (DIAL)

Carol Mardell and Dorothea Goldenberg
DIAL, Inc., 1972; revised 1975
1233 Lincoln Ave. South, Highland Park, IL 60035

Purpose	To identify children with potential learning disabilities
Major Areas Tested	Gross motor, fine motor, concepts, and communication skills
Age or Grade Range	3–5 years
Usually Given By	Special education teacher Paraprofessional
Type of Test	Standardized Individual Group
Scores Obtained	Age level
Student Performance Timed?	No
Testing Time	25–30 minutes
Scoring/Interpretation Time	15–20 minutes
Normed On	4,356 rural and urban children in the Chicago, Illinois area, balanced for sex, demographic setting, race, and socioeconomic status
Alternate Forms Available?	No

FORMAT

The Developmental Indicators for the Assessment of
Learning (DIAL) screening procedure is designed to permit
the assessment of small groups of preschool children in
four basic skill areas: gross motor, fine motor, concepts,
and communication. Groups of four to eight children are
screened in the four skill areas using a "station" organization; that is, each child rotates to each station, where he
or she is given a series of individual tasks in that skill
area (see Figure 60).

STATION PLAN

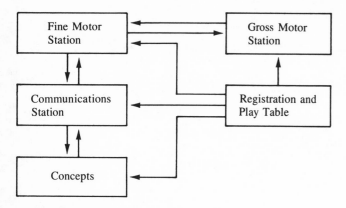

Figure 60. DIAL Station Plan

The DIAL kit contains a manual, an individual score
sheet for each child, and a set of manipulative materials for
each station. The following personnel are suggested for
screening several groups of children: one professional
coordinator, who handles the administrative responsibilities
and the training of paraprofessionals; four paraprofessionals,
one to administer the task at each station; and two or three
volunteers to play with the children between stations and
facilitate the organization. The tasks presented at each
station are shown in Table 23.

The individual score sheet accompanies the child from
station to station, and the paraprofessional records the
child's scores. Raw scores are converted to scale scores; a
score of 21 is possible at each station. This consistency
allows the examiner to plot a profile of the child's performance in each area.

Cutoff points have been established at two-month
intervals from ages 2 years, 6 months to 5 years, 5 months.
Separate norms are established for girls and boys, reflecting
sex differences. For example, a boy between the ages of 3.9
and 3.11 should receive a scaled score of 11 in each skill
area to "pass" the screening. Scaled score totals below the

Table 23. DIAL Tasks

Skill Area	Tasks
Gross motor	Throwing
	Catching
	Jumping
	Hopping
	Skipping
	Standing still
	Balancing
Fine motor	Visual matching
	Block building
	Cutting
	Copying shapes
	Using small muscles
	Imitating clapped patterns
Concepts	Sorting by color
	Naming colors
	Counting
	Using prepositions
	Following directions
	Recognizing polar concepts (fast/slow, hot/cold)
	Identifying body parts
Communications	Articulation
	Using short-term memory
	Picture naming
	Problem solving
	Naming self, age, sex
	Classifying
	Telling a story

cutoff points place the child in the lowest 10 percent of the
children tested in that skill area. Children whose scores fall
below the critical cutoff point are described as "seriously
delayed" and "needing follow-up," and further observation
and testing is recommended. If a child needs follow-up at
one station only, suggestions of activities may be given to
the parent. If the child's score falls into the follow-up range
in two areas, Re-DIALing (administering the tests again) is
suggested. If the child is below the criterion point in three or
four stations, or below the criterion point in Communica-
tions, complete diagnostic evaluation is suggested. The
cutoff points are conveniently printed at the bottom of the
individual score sheets to facilitate scoring.

In addition to the scores, each paraprofessional records
the child's behavior at that station. These subjective
impressions of a child's behavior in key areas should also be
considered when a diagnostic evaluation is recommended.

The following are examples of the behaviors recorded: separation problems, clumsiness, hyperactivity, impulsivity, unusual passivity.

The DIAL manual includes explicit directions for organizing the screening program, setting up the room, making the materials needed, and administering and scoring the tasks. The rationale for test construction and reliability and validity data are included. Suggestions are given on how to present information to parents and what tests to use when further evaluation is indicated.

STRENGTHS OF THE DIAL

• The DIAL process is carefully constructed for screening preschool children on a variety of developmental tasks. The manual includes extensive information on test construction, including the theoretical model, task analysis of each activity, and standardization procedures.

• Serious efforts were made by the authors to balance their standardization sample for sex, urban and rural locations, race, and socioeconomic level, making DIAL an appropriate instrument for use with mixed racial groups of preschool children. Extensive reliability and validity data are presented in the manual.

• The station format is an excellent one. It allows each child to be tested individually while providing the examiners with some observations of the child's group behavior. The station format allows for movement about the room, and the 5 to 10 minutes needed for each child at each station is appropriate for the attention span of preschool children.

• The tasks selected for each skill area are based on the authors' knowledge of developmental tasks appropriate for preschool children. They are designed to be interesting to the child and are easily administered and scored by a trained paraprofessional.

• The use of paraprofessionals is a good method for reducing the cost of expensive preschool screening programs. College students and community people can be trained to administer and score the tasks. This provides experience for the paraprofessionals and frees the professional to communicate with the parents and focus on those children who need follow-up.

LIMITING FACTORS OF THE DIAL

• Training of paraprofessionals to administer the DIAL tests must be carefully done. All of the reliability and validity data is based on administration by carefully trained and monitored paraprofessionals. Results can be easily affected by variations in test administration and scoring.

• DIAL is intended for screening groups of children in preschool programs to identify those with serious delays in need of further assessment. The cutoff points are set to identify the lowest 10 percent. Middle-class children or

other groups with extensive nursery school experience rarely fall below the cutoff point, but they may well have significant learning disabilities that will show up in an academically oriented kindergarten. DIAL should be considered a gross screening instrument—not one that will identify the child with marginal disabilities.

The Meeting Street School Screening Test (MSSST)

Peter K. Hainsworth and Marian L. Siqueland
Crippled Children and Adults of Rhode Island, Inc., 1969
Meeting Street School, 333 Grotto Ave., Providence, RI 02906

Purpose	To identify children with potential learning disabilities
Major Areas Tested	Gross motor skills, fine motor skills, visual perception, and language
Age or Grade Range	5—7½ years
Usually Given By	Classroom teacher Special education teacher Psychologist Paraprofessional
Type of Test	Standardized Individual Norm-referenced
Scores Obtained	Age level Standard
Student Performance Timed?	No
Testing Time	15–20 minutes
Scoring/Interpretation Time	15 minutes
Normed On	500 students, including 50 girls and 50 boys at each 6-month age interval
Alternate Forms Available?	No

FORMAT

The materials for the Meeting Street School Screening Test (MSSST) consist of a record form for each student and the manual which includes nine test administration cards. The manual is contained within a monograph, *Early Identification of Children with Learning Disabilities: The Meeting Street School Screening Test*. In addition to administration and scoring procedures and statistical information related to the MSSST, the monograph includes extensive information on screening programs for young and high-risk children and a discussion of the information-processing model on which this test is theoretically based.

The MSSST is composed of three subtests, each covering a skill area and comprising several tasks. The organization of the test is shown in Table 24.

Scores are recorded on the record form as the tasks are performed, according to the scoring directions in the manual. Four raw score totals are obtained: motor patterning, visual-perceptual-motor, language, and MSSST total.

For kindergarten children, a MSSST total raw score of 39 points or below indicates that the child is at high risk for learning disabilities. For first-grade children, a raw score of 55 points or below is the cutoff score. These scores were selected for children tested about four months into the school year.

The raw scores are converted to scale scores using a table that corresponds to the student's chronological age. The scaled scores are then plotted on the profile of scores on the record form. This gives a graphic summary of the child's strengths and weaknesses.

The record form also provides a behavior rating scale that rates each child on the following dimensions:

Test cooperation
Attention
Concentration
Use of feedback
Motor Control
Pencil skills
Eye control
Speech
Language
Overall efficiency

These dimensions were selected because they have been found to be important indicators of learning disabilities. Each of the dimensions is discussed in depth in the manual.

STRENGTHS OF THE MSSST

• The MSSST is a well-designed, theoretically based screening instrument for kindergarten and first-grade children. The Meeting Street School in Providence, Rhode Island has long been known for its diagnosis and treatment of children with cerebral palsy. The multidisciplinary staff turned to the evaluation of children with learning dis-

abilities, and the MSSST is the result of their expertise. The manual (p. 49) defines the "learning disability child" as one "whose information processing inefficiencies in the language, visual-perceptual-motor, and motor patterning modalities interfere with learning"

The authors suggest that the MSSST be used as part of a program of progressive levels of screening:

1. Gross screening of all children by teacher rating and group tests
2. Finer individual screening of selected children with instruments such as the MSSST
3. Intensive individual diagnostic assessment for a few children

The authors stress that the MSSST scores alone should not be used to label a child as "learning disabled."

In addition to the sound background of the MSSST, the test has several other strengths:

• The sections of the manual on interpretation of test results, including the graphic profile and the behavioral rating scale, are excellent. Case studies are used to illustrate test interpretation.

• Studies related to content and predictive validity of the MSSST are reported in the manual, and although they are poorly reported and somewhat incomplete, they show a moderate degree of predictability.

• The MSSST has good test-retest reliability and interscorer reliability over a two- to four-week period.

• The MSSST is designed so that it can be given by trained paraprofessionals.

• The three subtests are constructed so that they have equal numbers of items and the same scaled score mean (10) and standard deviation (3).

LIMITING FACTORS OF THE MSSST

• Strangely, in such a complete monograph, there is no description of the norming sample. Extensive research is reported that gives the numbers of children in different schools and their IQs and achievement levels, but there is no information on such variables as age, sex, racial background, or socioeconomic class. This is a serious deficit if one attempts to use the mean scaled scores for interpretation or the cutoff point for identification of children at risk.

• The cutoff score of 39 points or below for kindergarteners is not well substantiated by research. The cutoff score of 55 for first graders was not validated at all.

• The Language subtest is the weakest of the three subtests. It does not include any measure of receptive or expressive vocabulary or articulation. The placement of counting tasks in the Language subtest is questionable, and there is no task assessing auditory discrimination. Although the skilled examiner can pick up information on both articulation and discrimination throughout the test administra-

Table 24. MSSST Subtests

Subtest	Purpose	Tasks	Task Points (total: 87½)	Skills
1. Motor Patterning	To survey bilateral sequential movement patterns and spatial awareness	Gait Patterns	5	Unilateral and bilateral body movement patterns, such as hopping and skipping
		Clap Hands	6	Unlearned sequential spatial patterns
		Hand Patterns	6	Unlearned sequential spatial patterns
		Follow Directions I	6	Comprehension, memory, and translation of verbal directions involving spatial concepts
		Touch Fingers	6	Coordination of hands and fingers in rapid bilateral patterned movements
			Total: 29	
2. Visual-Perceptual-Motor	To survey visual discrimination, visual memory, design copying, and comprehension of spatial and directional concepts on paper	Block Tapping	6	Memory for spatial sequences
		Visual Matching	5	Discrimination of form and spatial orientation
		Visual Memory	6	Short-term memory for geometric and letter forms
		Copy Forms	8	Eye-hand coordination
		Follow Directions II	5	Spatial and directional concepts through drawing
			Total: 30	
3. Language	To survey listening comprehension, auditory memory, and language formulation	Repeat Words	5½	Discrimination and repetition of speech sound sequences
		Repeat Sentences	5	Auditory memory for words
		Counting	7	Ability to sequence numbers
		Tell-a-Story	5	Ability to formulate and express thoughts
		Language Sequencing	6	Comprehension of time concepts
			Total: 28½	

tion, there is no place to record this critical information, and it is not included in the score. Both Follow Directions subtests include a large component of language comprehension, but these scores are not included in the Language subtest.

• The authors state that the cutoff scores of 39 and 55 points "identify those children whose information processing skills are not sufficient to allow them to meet the curriculum demands of the grade" (manual, p. 15). Obviously, this depends somewhat on the curriculum being offered. More information is needed regarding the relationship between MSSST subtest scores and curriculum areas (reading, spelling, writing, and math) and instructional techniques.

Compton Speech and Language Screening Evaluation

Arthur J. Compton
Carousel House, 1978
P.O. Box 4480, San Francisco, CA 94101

Purpose	To provide a quick estimate of speech and language development in children
Major Areas Tested	Articulation and language development
Age or Grade Range	3–6 years
Usually Given By	Special education teacher Psychologist Speech/language clinician Paraprofessional
Type of Test	Individual
Scores Obtained	Age level
Student Performance Timed?	No
Testing Time	6–10 minutes
Scoring/Interpretation Time	10 minutes
Normed On	500 children
Alternate Forms Available?	No

FORMAT

The materials for the Compton Speech and Language Screening Evaluation consist of a collection of small objects (glass, sock, badge, doll, frog, and others), the manual, and individual response forms. All of the materials are packaged in a carrying case shaped like a lunch box.

The instrument includes the following tasks:

1. *Articulation and Vocabulary.* The child is asked to name each of the 14 objects. Two responses are required for each object, which provides a check on the consistency of articulation. Initial and final consonant sounds are assessed.

2. *Naming Colors.* The child is asked to identify six colors: red, green, blue, orange, yellow, and purple.

3. *Recognition of Shapes.* The child is asked to identify three shapes: circle, square, and triangle.

4. *Auditory-Visual Memory Span.* The child is asked to remember which objects the examiner places in the carrying case; the examiner names and shows the child two, three, or four objects (depending on the child's age); as the examiner drops them into the case, the child repeats the names of the objects.

5. *Language.* Using the objects, the examiner elicits plurals, opposites, progressive and past tense, prepositions, and possessive pronouns. The child's ability to follow directions is also assessed.

6. *Spontaneous Language.* This task involves an informal observation of the child's conversational language, including the number of words in the longest utterance and the usual number of words per utterance.

The response form also contains sections to note observations of fluency, voice, and structure and function of the oral mechanism.

STRENGTHS OF THE COMPTON SPEECH AND LANGUAGE SCREENING EVALUATION

• This test is a quick but comprehensive instrument for screening preschool and early primary-grade children. It is intended to identify children with potential speech and language handicaps and to alert the professional that more extensive testing is needed. The test is easy to administer and score, and the manual is clear and concise.

• Children are attracted to the small toy objects, and spontaneous language is usually easy to elicit. This is an important factor in a quick screening test. Another advantage is that for some children the toy objects are more easily recognized than pictures.

• This evaluation provides a systematic and structured means of observing the speech and language behavior of children in a playlike situation, thereby increasing the chance that the examiner will have typical behavior to observe.

LIMITING FACTORS OF THE COMPTON SPEECH AND LANGUAGE SCREENING EVALUATION

• Despite the author's statement that no special training is required to give the screening test, it is clear that a person with a speech and language background would be able to use the instrument more effectively. As with any screening instrument used with young children, much of the value comes from informal observations of the child's behavior. In this case, the child's spontaneous language (or lack of it), voice quality, fluency, and articulation in connected speech are critical cues to potential speech and language problems. The trained examiner is much more alert to such cues.

• No information is provided on the sample of over 500 children that the author used to develop the test items. Age-level guidelines were taken from the child-development literature. Again, an experienced examiner is needed to avoid overidentification.

Kraner Preschool Math Inventory (KPMI)

Robert E. Kraner
Learning Concepts, Inc., 1976
2501 N. Lamar, Austin, TX 78705

Purpose	To determine the acquisition age of quantitative concepts of young children and to provide practical information for planning early childhood learning programs
Major Areas Tested	Mathematics
Age or Grade Range	3–6½ years
Usually Given By	Classroom teacher Speech/language clinician Special education teacher Paraprofessional Psychologist
Type of Test	Standardized Individual Criterion-referenced
Scores Obtained	Age level Receptive age Mastery age
Student Performance Timed?	No
Testing Time	30–40 minutes
Scoring/Interpretation Time	15–20 minutes
Normed On	273 suburban, middle-class children from one south central state
Alternate Forms Available?	No

FORMAT

Both the manual and test items for the Kraner Preschool Math Inventory (KPMI) are contained in a three-ring vinyl binder. The binder has a flip-page arrangement for presentation, with the examiner's instructions on one side, and the test materials on the side facing the student. The student responds verbally or by pointing to the test items, which are presented in conjunction with pictorial material using common shapes and animals. The animals are black-and-white, cartoonlike figures. The majority of the KPMI test items have a multiple-choice format.

The KPMI is an untimed test administered on an individual basis. The examiner uses a separate scoring form to record individual responses. To facilitate the use of test data, a classroom record form and an individual record form are also provided.

The KPMI evaluates mathematics skills and concepts in seven areas: Set Comparison, Counting, Cardinal Numbers, Sequence, Position, Direction, and Geometry/Measurement. Three performance exercises are provided for each of the test items. If successful performance is achieved on Trial A and B of an item, credit is given. If the student fails one trial and succeeds on the other, the Optional trial is given to determine if credit is allowed.

Because the KPMI is a criterion-referenced inventory, testing sessions do not demand the rigid constraints of norm-referenced tests. No required testing sequence must be followed; that is, the seven areas may be given in any order. However, to avoid confusing the student, the items within an area should be given in order.

Before testing begins, the warm-up exercises should be administered to the student. These exercises contain the key words and symbols used throughout the test and help to make certain that the student will understand the test directions and material.

STRENGTHS OF THE KPMI

• Many features of the KPMI are advantageous. The test is easy to administer, is applicable for very young students, and permits evaluation of a student's comprehension of such mathematical concepts as quantity, number, and space (dimension, direction, location, and orientation). No specific training is needed to administer the KPMI, which extends its use to paraprofessionals.

• The test items consist of familiar pictures and shapes, selected because of their inclusion in most preschool instructional materials. Each test plate is clear and uncluttered; numerals are printed in large-sized type, appropriate for young students. The multiple-choice format for most items reduces the demands on memory and recall, because the correct answer can be identified by recognition.

• Requiring the student to give two correct responses out of three trials is an especially good feature. Young students

often respond inconsistently in testing situations because their attention may wander. Giving a student a second chance assures the examiner of a more valid estimate of the student's abilities. The warm-up exercises are also helpful because they familiarize the student with the test demands.

• Although the KPMI is not intended for use with students beyond age 6½, it does have value as a clinical evaluation tool for older students who are having difficulty in arithmetic. The KPMI is useful for assessing the concept formation of slow learners and learning-disabled, mentally retarded, and language-impaired students.

• Comparing a student's performance in the seven skill and concept areas provides important diagnostic information. A pattern of errors at times gives information regarding the nature of specific vocabulary and concept-formation problems. For example, the student may fail most items that have a spatial reference but correctly answer items that have a quantitative reference. The analysis of error patterns may suggest areas for instructional emphasis, especially if the concept is within a student's mastery age.

Mastery age refers to the earliest age interval at which 80 percent of the students in the norming sample responded correctly to an item. The mastery age indicates the age level at which students can be expected to know the skill or concept. Individual instruction is warranted for the student who fails a mastery-age item.

Receptive age, on the other hand, represents the earliest age level at which 50 percent of the students responded correctly to an item. The receptive age represents the age level at which the skill or concept may be appropriately included in the instructional program for normal learners. The manual presents forms for receptive and mastery ages at six-month intervals between the ages of 3 and 6½ years.

• The KPMI, built on the criterion-referenced model, identifies specific skills and concepts required for learning mathematics. When the test has been completed, the examiner can clearly see what the student knows and needs to learn. Thus the test can aid in curriculum planning, diagnostic teaching, and program evaluations.

LIMITING FACTORS OF THE KPMI

• Although the KPMI is a criterion-referenced measure, the inventory contains some normative data. The test was normed on a middle-class suburban population from only one state. The sample size was quite small (273), with several age intervals represented by less than 15 students. Evidently, students from different ethnic groups are not represented in the sample. Caution must be used when applying the norms to students from low socioeconomic and minority groups. Students from a culturally different background may receive low scores on the test because they have not had adequate language stimultion and experience at home. Measures of validity and reliability are not available for the KPMI.

- The quantitative concepts behind the test items were selected from research studies, curriculum guides, national study reports, and other sources. The concepts were included because they are required by entering first-grade students. However, no specific information is provided that describes how all entries into the item pool were screened and ultimately accepted or rejected for the final version of the test.

- The aesthetic quality of the black-and-white line drawings is mediocre, and the shapes (hearts, balls, and stars) are used repeatedly throughout the test. Although there are advantages in using familiar shapes, after a while many students find the items uninteresting. The inclusion of colorful and stimulating materials would help to sustain students' interest in the KPMI.

- The KPMI requires the student to give the correct response on two out of three performance exercises. This is a good test feature. However, the drawback from the student's viewpoint is a long, repetitive testing session. The bright student, especially, may become bored quickly.

- The basic concepts tested in the KPMI are assessed at the receptive level only. An example of an item: "Show me the star on top." Understanding a word and pointing to the correct picture is a very different task from following such directions as "Sit on top of the box." If a student performs poorly on the KPMI, the examiner may want to examine mastery of spatial prepositions through direct physical experience. This can be accomplished by having the student act out verbal commands to place an object or position himself or herself in different locations in space ("Sit on/under/behind the desk.")

Slingerland Pre-Reading Screening Procedures

Beth H. Slingerland
Educators Publishing Service, Inc., 1968; revised 1976, 1977
75 Moulton St., Cambridge, MA 02188

Purpose	To identify bright children with difficulties in the auditory, visual, and kinesthetic modalities that may indicate specific language disability
Major Areas Tested	Auditory, visual, and kinesthetic skills related to beginning reading
Age or Grade Range	Grades K–1
Usually Given By	Classroom teacher Special education teacher Psychologist Administrator
Type of Test	Informal Group
Scores Obtained	Rating scale (guidelines for evaluating test performance)
Student Performance Timed?	Yes
Testing Time	20–25 minutes each for three test sessions
Scoring/Interpretation Time	15–20 minutes
Normed On	Not normed
Alternate Forms Available?	No

FORMAT

The materials for the Slingerland Pre-Reading Screening Procedures consist of student booklets, cards and charts for three subtests, and a teacher's manual. Practice pages and markers are also provided. The tests are designed to be used with groups of kindergarten children who have not yet been introduced to formal reading. The recommended group size is 15 children. At least one monitor is needed to help the children locate the right page and to prohibit them from copying each other's work. The students use pencils without erasers and are taught to bracket their errors so that self-corrections can be noted.

The recently revised Slingerland Pre-Reading Screening Procedures contain 12 subtests to be given to the group and a set of individual auditory tests. The 12 subtests are:

1. *Visual Perception* requires matching single-letter and two-letter combinations (Figure 61).

2. *Visual Perception* requires visual matching of three-letter combinations (Figure 62).

3. *Visual Perception and Memory* requires visual memory of geometric and letter forms (Figure 63).

4. *Near-Point Copying* requires copying geometric and letter forms (Figure 64). Space is provided on both sides of the geometric and letter forms for left-handed and right-handed students.

5. *Auditory-Visual Association* requires listening to a spoken direction and marking the appropriate picture. In Figure 65 the examiner says, ''Mark the picture of the bird flying to its nest.''

6. *Letter Recognition* requires marking the visual symbol of the letter name pronounced by the examiner. In Figure 66 the examiner says, ''Mark the *f*.''

7. *Visual-Kinesthetic Memory* requires visual perception and memory of geometric forms. The student draws the forms from memory after being shown a model (Figure 67).

Figure 61. Slingerland Pre-Reading Screening Procedures, Procedure 1, Visual Perception

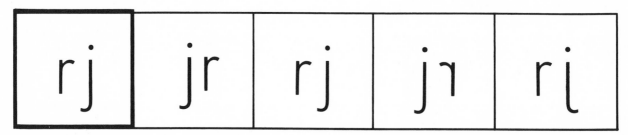

Figure 62. Slingerland Pre-Reading Screening Procedures, Procedure 2, Visual Perception

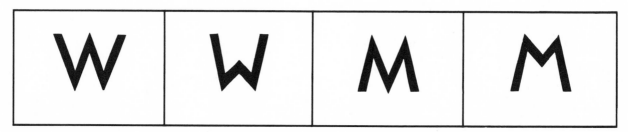

Figure 63. Slingerland Pre-Reading Screening Procedures, Procedure 3, Visual Perception and Memory

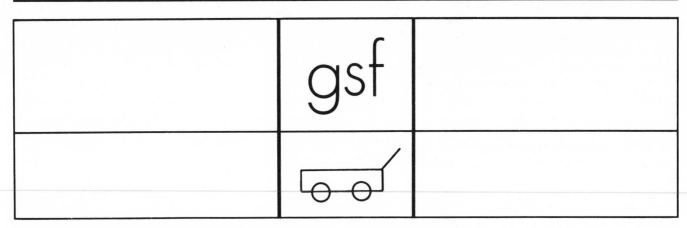

Figure 64. Slingerland Pre-Reading Screening Procedures, Procedure 4, Near-Point Copying

Figure 65. Slingerland Pre-Reading Screening Procedures, Procedure 5, Auditory-Visual Perception

Figure 66. Slingerland Pre-Reading Screening Procedures, Procedure 6, Letter Recognition

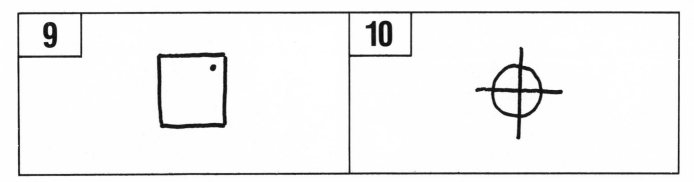

Figure 67. Slingerland Pre-Reading Screening Procedures, Procedure 7, Visual-Kinesthetic Memory

8. *Auditory Perception with Comprehension* requires listening to a story and indicating comprehension by marking a picture. In Figure 68, the examiner would tell the following story: *Jane said to her little sister, "I wish you would go to the big table and get the little box for me. Something for you is in the little box." Mark the picture that shows where Jane wanted her sister to go.*

9. *Far-Point Copying* requires copying geometric and letter forms from a wall chart (Figure 69).

10. *Auditory Discrimination* requires listening to sets of three words and indicating if the words are the same or different. In Figure 70 the examiner says, "Slap, slap, slab." The student marks XX in the space between the two balloons, because the three words do not sound the same. When the words all sound the same, the student marks / / in the space.

11. *Auditory-Visual-Kinesthetic Integration* requires listening to the name of a letter, selecting it from three printed letters, and copying it. In Figure 71 the examiner says, "Copy the letter *B* in the last box in the row."

12. *Auditory-Visual Association* requires identifying pictures that begin with a specific sound pronounced by the examiner. In Figure 72 the examiner says, "You see a book, a pencil, and a table. Mark the picture of the one that begins with the sound *t*."

The individual auditory tests include the following:

1. *Echolalia* requires repeating a word several times.
2. *Reproducing a Story* requires listening to and retelling a story.

The Slingerland Pre-Reading Screening Procedures are not normed for age or grade-level scores. However, a five-point rating scale (high, high-medium, medium, low-medium, and low) for evaluating student performance is given, as well as specific guidelines for scoring the tests. Alternate forms for test-retest purposes are not available, but because many of the subtests assess the same processes as the higher-age-level Slingerland Tests, the series of tests can be used as a measure of progress.

STRENGTHS OF THE SLINGERLAND PRE-READING SCREENING PROCEDURES

• The Slingerland Pre-Reading Screening Procedures are a well-planned battery of readiness tests. They have been carefully designed to include tasks that assess a student's skills in all modalities: auditory, visual, and kinesthetic, alone and in combination. The teacher's manual is well organized, and the directions are very clear. The idea of using practice pages to train the students in the proper procedures is excellent. One part of the practice pages

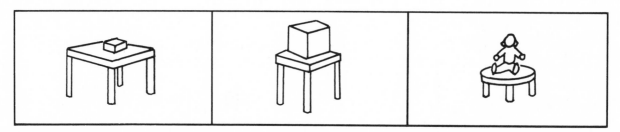

Figure 68. Slingerland Pre-Reading Screening Procedures, Procedure 8, Auditory Perception with Comprehension

Figure 69. Slingerland Pre-Reading Screening Procedures, Procedure 9, Far-Point Copying

is a ''This is Me'' picture, which yields a great deal of information about the student's readiness skills. Although the subtests are timed, this is primarily to keep the group testing moving along and does not put serious constraints on the students. The teacher's manual gives excellent discussions of the subtests and the skills being measured by each. The Slingerland Pre-Reading Screening Procedures are an excellent contribution to the field when used as a group screening measure (1) to give the first-grade teacher extensive information on the modality strengths and weaknesses of a class of beginning readers and (2) to identify specific children who may need further individual testing.

LIMITING FACTORS OF THE SLINGERLAND PRE-READING SCREENING PROCEDURES

- The Slingerland Pre-Reading Screening Procedures must be considered informal tests at this time. No age or grade norms are provided. The five-point rating scale is based on the test results of several hundred children just entering first grade in school districts throughout the United States, but no further information about the sample is given.

- The Slingerland Pre-Reading Screening Procedures were designed to identify children who would enter first grade using the Slingerland adaptation of Orton-Gillingham techniques as a curriculum. The teacher's manual interprets student test performance from the Orton-Gillingham point of view. This is not a serious problem in using the tests, but the teacher should be aware that such statements as ''The brighter the child, the more opportunities there have been for language learning'' is an opinion, not a statement of fact.

- The author suggests that the Slingerland Pre-Reading Screening Procedures be used with the Pinter-Cunningham Primary Test of general intelligence (1966). This suggestion points up the need to be cautious about diagnosing any child's learning disabilities on the basis of one test.

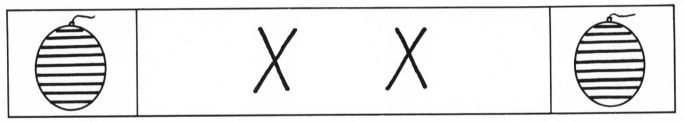

Figure 70. Slingerland Pre-Reading Screening Procedures, Procedure 10, Auditory Discrimination

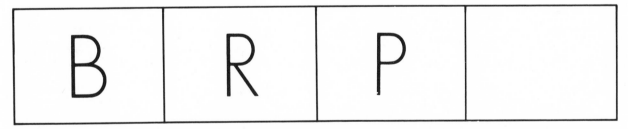

Figure 71. Slingerland Pre-Reading Screening Procedures, Procedure 11, Auditory-Visual-Kinesthetic Integration

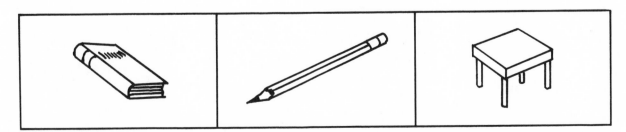

Figure 72. Slingerland Pre-Reading Screening Procedures, Procedure 12, Auditory-Visual Association

PART III

General Intelligence Tests and Developmental Scales

No other area of assessment has caused so much controversy as the area of intelligence testing, or IQ tests. Debates rage over such topics as the meaning of intelligence, the use of IQ tests as predictors of school achievement, the cultural biases of standard IQ tests, and the interpretation (or misinterpretation) of IQ scores. There may never be any widespread agreement about whether IQ tests should be given, what they measure, or what they mean, but they continue to be used regularly in the field of special education.

In this section, individual IQ tests are viewed as another source of information about a student that may be used in planning an instructional program. Teachers who are familiar with the format and content of general intelligence tests can use information about the student's performance to plan a curriculum.

The most commonly used individual test of general intelligence, the Wechsler Intelligence Scale for Children—Revised, is reviewed in depth and contrasted with the Wechsler Preschool and Primary Scale of Intelligence and the Wechsler Adult Intelligence Scale. The oldest and best-known intelligence test, the Stanford-Binet Intelligence Scale, is also reviewed. Three less familiar tests are included: The Slosson Intelligence Test for Children and Adults, a short screening test patterned after the Stanford-Binet; the Leiter International Performance Scale and the Arthur Adaptation, for language-impaired students; and the McCarthy Scales of Children's Abilities, a new test for preschool and primary students.

Developmental scales are measures of a particular process in a maturing child. Language and visual perception are examples of processes that mature without specific teaching.

Because they are age-related, developmental scales are often indicators of advanced development or immaturity. The Goodenough-Harris Drawing Test is reviewed in this section because it is most often used as a test of cognitive development and intellectual maturity. Several other tests in the book can be considered developmental in nature. Because of the specific nature of their content, the Marianne Frostig Developmental Test of Visual Perception and the Beery-Buktenica Developmental Test of Visual-Motor Integration are reviewed in Chapter Two: Perception and Memory Tests. For the same reason, the Developmental Sentence Scoring system is included in Chapter Three: Speech and Language Tests, and the Denver Developmental Screening Test, the Brigance Diagnostic Inventory of Early Development, and Developmental Indicators for the Assessment of Learning are reviewed in Part II: Preschool and Kindergarten Tests.

Wechsler Intelligence Scale for Children— Revised (WISC-R)

David Wechsler
The Psychological Corporation, 1974
757 Third Ave., New York, NY 10017

Purpose	To measure specific mental abilities and processes
Major Areas Tested	General intelligence
Age or Grade Range	6–17 years
Usually Given By	Psychologist
Type of Test	Standardized Individual
Scores Obtained	Verbal IQ Scaled Performance IQ Test ages Full-scale IQ
Student Performance Timed?	Yes (seven subtests)
Testing Time	50–75 minutes (10 subtests)
Scoring/Interpretation Time	30–40 minutes
Normed On	2,200 children, including 100 boys and 100 girls at each age level, balanced for race, geographic regions, urban and rural residence, and occupation of the head of household, conforming to the 1970 census
Alternate Forms Available?	No

FORMAT

The Wechsler Intelligence Scale for Children—Revised (WISC-R) is an individually administered test designed to assess the global aspects of general intelligence. To probe intelligence in as many different ways as possible, the WISC-R includes 12 subtests that emphasize various types of ability. These subtests, by representing different ways in which intelligence may manifest itself, contribute to a composite view of intellectual functioning.

The WISC-R is divided into two main parts, a verbal scale and a performance scale, each having five mandatory subtests and one subtest usable as a supplement or an alternate. IQs are calculated on the basis of the five verbal and five performance tests listed below. The numbers indicate the order in which the tests are given. Most examiners find it convenient to give the tests in the following order; however, the examiner is free to change the prescribed order to meet the needs of the testing situation.

Verbal Scale	Performance Scale
1. Information	2. Picture Completion
3. Similarities	4. Picture Arrangement
5. Arithmetic	6. Block Design
7. Vocabulary	8. Object Assembly
9. Comprehension	10. Coding (or Mazes)
11. Digit Span (supplement or alternate)	12. Mazes (supplement or alternate)

Digit Span on the verbal scale and Mazes on the performance scale have been retained as supplementary tests to be given when time allows or as substitutes if a regularly administered test is invalidated or cannot properly be administered. It is always permissible to administer all 12 subtests. The supplementary tests add useful qualitative and diagnostic information.

Because the WISC-R is appropriate for students from 6 to 17 years of age, different starting points for each subtest have been specified, depending on the student's age and estimated level of ability. The directions for starting and discontinuing each subtest are conveniently indicated on the record form as well as in the WISC-R manual. Rules for establishing a basal level on each subtest are given in the manual. A basal must be established in order to assume credit for easier items not given.

Test materials for the WISC-R are packaged in a briefcase-sized kit. They include the manual, individual record forms, and the cards, blocks, puzzles, and booklets necessary for the various subtests. The examiner must supply a stopwatch.

The specific items within each subtest on the WISC-R are arranged in order of increasing difficulty. A general idea of the kinds of abilities assessed by each subtest, along with other descriptive information, is given in Table 25. The examples given in the table are similar, but not identical, to those found on the WISC-R.

In scoring the WISC-R, raw scores on each subtest are first transmitted into scaled scores within the student's age group. Tables of such scores are given for every four-month interval between the ages of 6 years and 16 years, 11 months. The subtest scaled scores are expressed in terms of a distribution with a mean of 10 and a standard deviation of 3. Thus, if Bobby obtains a score of 10 on a subtest, he is average for his age. If Joey obtains a scaled score of 7 on a subtest, he is 1 standard deviation below the mean for his age.

After obtaining the subtest scaled scores, the next step is to add these scores together to produce an overall verbal score, an overall performance score, and a full scale score. Finally, using the norm tables, the scores are converted into verbal, performance, and full scale IQs; each IQ has a mean of 100 and a standard deviation of 15. Thus, an IQ of 100 on any of the scales defines the performance of the average student of a given age on that scale. An IQ of 130 on any of the scales defines the performance of the very superior student, falling 2 standard deviations above the mean for that age group. With equal standard deviations, IQs are directly comparable for various ages—a particular advantage of the test.

It is also possible to obtain test ages on the WISC-R. This allows comparison of WISC-R scores with age norms of other scales and facilitates the interpretation of scores from a developmental viewpoint.

STRENGTHS OF THE WISC-R

• The WISC-R is a convenient, reliable instrument that is modern in construction and contains materials intrinsically interesting to students. The test materials are compact and very accessible. The WISC-R manual is efficiently arranged and contains clear directions and tables. An improvement in the WISC-R manual that facilitates administration is the use of brown boldface type for the test directions to students and black boldface type for the examiner's instructions.

• The WISC-R record form gives adequate space for recording answers. Some minor improvements in the record form ease administration. For instance, the directions for starting and discontinuing each subtest are printed directly on the form. The front of the form also contains a profile (see Figure 80) that can be filled in to show graphically a student's strengths and weaknesses on the WISC-R subtests.

• Changes made in the WISC-R over the original edition have strengthened the test. One principal change involves the age range of the battery: The WISC-R spans the age range 6 through 17 years, whereas the 1949 WISC was appropriate for students aged 5 through 15 years. Another change involves the sequence in which the tests are given. The verbal and performance tests are now administered in

Table 25. WISC-R Subtests

Verbal Scale
Requires auditory-verbal input and verbal output. Questions are read aloud by the examiner; the student responds orally.

Subtest	Description	Sample Test Items
Information	30 basic fact questions	"Name the month that comes after June." "Why does the moon look larger than the stars?" "On what continent is Argentina?"
Comprehension	17 questions requiring the practical knowledge needed to make judgments about social situations	"What are some reasons why we need an army?" "What is the thing to do if you have a bloody nose?"
Arithmetic	18 arithmetic word problems requiring mental computation	"Tommy had three pennies and his mother gave him two more. How many pennies did he have altogether?" "A salesperson earned $35; she was paid $5 an hour. How many hours did she work?"
Similarities	17 pairs of words requiring recognition of likenesses (critical or superficial) between concrete objects, substances, facts, or ideas	"In what way are a *sweater* and a *coat* alike?" "In what way are *happiness* and *sadness* alike?"
Vocabulary	32 words (20 nouns, 7 verbs, and 5 adjectives) requiring definition; the list progresses from concrete words representing objects to more abstract words	"What is a *wagon*?" "What does *isolate* mean?"
Digit Span	14 series of numbers: numbers are given at a rate of one per second; no digits are repeated within a series; digit series must be repeated without error and in correct sequence after a single presentation	
Digit Forward	7 series of unrelated digits requiring the student to repeat three to nine digits in two trials	Trial 1: 4-3-1-7 Trial 2: 5-8-1-6
Digit Backward	7 series of unrelated digits requiring the student to repeat backward two to eight digits in two trials	Trial 1: 7-5-3-1-4 Trial 2: 2-5-8-7-9

alternating order, as in the Wechsler Preschool and Primary Scale of Intelligence. Alternating verbal and performance tasks helps to maintain a student's interest in the test.

Another change allows the examiner to demonstrate the solution to a problem or to provide the correct answer to a question when a student fails the first item of any test. Giving the correct response to at least the first item helps ensure that the student understands the nature of each test. This modification is especially important for young students and for those who are mentally deficient.

Other important changes in the WISC-R involve modifying or eliminating ambiguous or obsolete test items

and dropping items that were allegedly unfair to minority populations. For example, in the Information subtest, such questions as "What does COD mean?" were eliminated. To strengthen the reliability of each test, some new items were added. In Picture Completion, additional items include more pictures of female and black subjects. But overall, an effort was made to retain as much of the 1949 WISC as possible because of its widespread use and established credibility as a clinical and diagnostic tool.

In terms of reliability, the coefficients for the WISC-R are quite high across the entire age range. Split-half coefficients in the .90s have been reported for the verbal, performance,

Timed?	Areas Measured	Notes
No	General information acquired from experience and education, remote verbal memory, understanding, associative thinking	The socioeconomic background and reading ability of the student may influence the subtest score.
No	Social judgment, commonsense reasoning based on past experience, practical intelligence	Compare with Picture Arrangement subtest.
Yes	Mental alertness, concentration, attention, arithmetic reasoning, reaction to time pressure, practical knowledge of computational facts	This is the only subtest directly related to the school curriculum.
No	Abstract and concrete reasoning, logical thought processes, associative thinking, remote memory	
No	Understanding of spoken words, learning ability, general range of ideas, verbal information acquired from experience and education, kind and quality of expressive language	This subtest is relatively unaffected by emotional disturbance, but it is highly susceptible to cultural background and level of education. It is also the best single measure of intelligence in the entire battery.
No	Attention, concentration, immediate auditory memory, auditory attention, behavior in a learning situation	This subtest correlates poorly with general intelligence.

and full scale IQs. The reliabilities for the individual subtests are generally satisfactory, with the average coefficients ranging from .77 to .86 for the verbal subtests and from .70 to .85 for the performance subtests.

Special studies have indicated good correlations between the WISC-R and other individually administered intelligence tests. The Stanford-Binet Intelligence Scale and the WISC-R tend to be highly correlated despite the differences in test items. As might be anticipated, the verbal and full scale IQs on the WISC-R generally correlate higher with the Stanford-Binet than do the performance IQs (.71, .73, and .60 respectively).

The correlation between the full scale IQs of the WISC-R and the Wechsler Preschool and Primary Scale of Intelligence is .82. The WISC-R and Wechsler Adult Intelligence Scale full scale IQs show a .95 correlation coefficient.

• The WISC-R is a particularly well standardized test. The 1974 revision used the data from the 1970 census. The test was carefully normed on 2,200 boys and girls of wide geographic distribution, and the procedures were fully reported. Attention was given to including race as a variable, which makes the WISC-R one of the better standardized tests for current use with nonwhite students. There is also a Spanish-language adaptation of the WISC

Table 25 —*Continued*

Performance Scale

Presented visually; require motor, nonverbal output. Although brief verbal directions for each task are given by the examiner, the student receives the information visually and nonverbally, and the motor response demands no verbalization.

Subtest	Description	Sample Test Items
Picture Completion	26 line drawings on cards (15 objects, 7 human figures, 4 animals) each requiring the student, after a 20-second exposure, to identify verbally or by pointing a missing element	"What is missing in this picture?" (see Figure 73 on p. 234)
Picture Arrangement	12 comic-strip picture sequences of three to five pictures requiring logical rearrangement	"Put these pictures in the right order." (see Figure 74 on p. 234)
Block Design	11 two-color block designs requiring reproduction either from an actual block model or from a picture	"Make a block design like this one." (see Figure 75 on p. 235)
Object Assembly	5 puzzle pictures of four to eight pieces depicting familiar objects; the name of the object is given on the first two pictures only	"Put these pieces together to make a star." (see Figure 76 on p. 235)
Coding Coding A (under 8 years)	45 symbols in the test booklet requiring the student to match shapes and write the proper symbols inside	"Put the right mark inside each of these shapes." (see Figure 77a on p. 235)
Coding B (8 years and above)	93 symbols with numerals in the test booklet requiring the student to match numerals and write the symbols below	"Put the right mark in the box below each number." (see Figure 77b on p. 235)
Mazes	9 mazes to be followed by the student without lifting the pencil	"Draw a line from the circle to the X without lifting your pencil." (see Figure 78 on p. 235)

(*Escala de Intelligencia Wechsler Para Niños* 1951), also available from The Psychological Corporation.

• One of the primary strengths of the WISC-R is the wealth of diagnostic information it provides. For example, analysis of the size of the difference between the verbal IQ and the performance IQ may be of clinical significance. Wechsler claims that a discrepancy of 15 points or more is important and warrants further investigation. Generally, a student's verbal and performance IQs do not differ significantly. A large difference between them suggests a true difference in ability. On the WISC-R record form shown in Figure 79, one can easily see how low verbal scores have depressed this particular student's full scale IQ. Thus, a student's differential ability in verbal and nonverbal

tasks can be assessed objectively on the WISC-R.

It is important for an examiner to know how large a difference there must be between a student's scaled scores on two separate subtests for that difference to be considered meaningful. As a general rule, Wechsler states that a difference of three or more scaled-score points between any pair of tests may be considered significant at the 15-percent level of confidence. It is thus possible to analyze intersubtest scatter to determine a student's strengths and weaknesses and to help answer such questions as "What particular educational deficits are handicapping Mary?" In the WISC-R profile shown in Figure 80, one can readily see a significant imbalance between verbal and performance skills and the great degree of intersubtest scatter

Timed?	Areas Measured	Notes
Yes	Visual alertness to surroundings, remote visual memory, attention to detail, visual perception (closure ability), ability to isolate essential from nonessential detail, perceptual and conceptual skills	This subtest may indicate word recall problems or inadequate vocabulary if the student points to the missing part but is unable to give the word.
Yes	Visual perception, comprehension, and synthesis of environmental experiences used to anticipate and size up a total situation; logical sequencing of events; attention to detail; ability to see cause-effect relationships	This is considered a test of social intelligence. Compare with Comprehension subtest.
Yes (bonus points given for quick perfect performance at the higher levels)	Ability to perceive, analyze, synthesize, and reproduce abstract forms; visual perception; nonverbal concept formation; capacity for sustained concentration; visual-motor coordination; abstract and concrete reasoning applied to spatial relationships; general ability to plan and organize	This is considerd the best single nonverbal measure of general intelligence in the battery, because it is little influenced by cultural factors.
Yes (bonus points given for quick perfect performance)	Immediate perception of a total configuration; understanding the relationship of individual parts; visual perception and anticipation of part-whole relationships; visual synthesis abilities; visual-motor-spatial coordination; simple assembly skills; ability to work flexibly toward a goal	This subtest does not correlate highly with general intelligence.
Yes (bonus points given for perfect score)	Ability to associate meaning with symbol, visual-motor dexterity (pencil manipulation), flexibility and speed in learning tasks when stimuli are visual and kinesthetic, ability to memorize rapidly	This subtest does not correlate highly with general intelligence.
Yes	Ability to shift attention and visual focus quickly and accurately, ability to use left-right progression	
Yes	Ability to formulate and execute a visual-motor plan, pencil control and visual-motor coordination, speed and accuracy, planning capability, foresight	

suggestive of specific disabilities. The low Coding score, for example, may indicate poor visual-motor coordination; the depressed verbal scores probably indicate a language disability. On the plus side are the near-average Comprehension score and the superior Picture Arrangement score; these scores reflect strengths in commonsense knowledge and social competence.

• In addition to analyzing scores and subtest patterns of the WISC-R, the examiner can consider the quality of a student's responses. By observing the student's behavior in the test situation, the examiner may gain valuable insights that may explain the student's difficulty. Why are some items passed and others failed? If, for example, a student fails questions dealing with temporal-sequential and spatial

relationships on the Information subtest, the examiner will want to investigate more thoroughly the student's mastery of such concepts. If a student begins a story in Picture Arrangement at the right instead of beginning at the left, other tasks requiring left-to-right progression should be investigated. If a student performs poorly on Mazes, the reason may be extremely slow working speed or perhaps a lack of foresight and planning ability.

The examiner will also need to assess a whole range of behavioral factors during testing. What is the student's relationship with the examiner: Cooperative? Self-reliant? Confident? Fearful? Negative? What is the student's reaction to tasks: Motivated? Persistent? Attentive? Impulsive? Reliant on trial and error? The testing situation

Figure 73. WISC-R Picture Completion

Figure 74. WISC-R Picture Arrangement

can provide the examiner with an excellent opportunity for clinical observations that may, in fact, be more significant in many cases than the actual test scores.

• Although considerable research has been carried out regarding the diagnostic significance of particular subtest patterns on the WISC (1949 version), the results are inconclusive. Nevertheless, certain generalizations seem warranted, because several studies have reported finding certain subtest patterns with some degree of regularity. For example:

1. Many mentally deficient students are likely to score higher on the performance than on the verbal section.

2. Many brain-damaged students are likely to score higher on the verbal than on the performance scale. They also show the most difficulty with Coding and Block Design.

3. Students classified as poor readers are likely to score higher on subtests not directly related to the school curriculum (Picture Arrangement, Object Assembly, and Block Design). They often score lowest on subtests related

to school instruction (Information, Arithmetic, and Digit Span).

4. Students with specific language disability (dyslexia) are more likely to score lower on the verbal scale than on the performance scale. Frequently the verbal IQ is significantly lower than the performance IQ.

• Finally, particular mention should be made regarding the usefulness of the WISC-R for the evaluation of the student suspected of having a learning disability. The dichotomy between verbal and performance skills is only one of the several ways the tests could be grouped. Other groupings have included:

1. *Meaningfulness versus Nonmeaningfulness of the Subtests.* In this grouping, all the verbal subtests, with the exception of Digit Span, are considered meaningful tasks. The meaningful nonverbal tests are Object Assembly, Picture Arrangement, and Picture Completion. The performance tests considered nonmeaningful (Block Design, Coding, and Mazes) are categorized as such because they

Figure 75. WISC-R Block Design

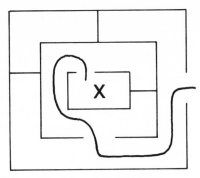

Figure 78. WISC-R Mazes

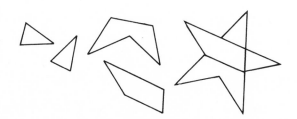

Figure 76. WISC-R Object Assembly

Figure 77a. WISC-R Coding A

	Year	Month	Day
Date Tested	77	11	9
Date of Birth	64	6	30
Age	13	4	

	Raw Score	Scaled Score
VERBAL TESTS		
Information	11	4
Similarities	15	8
Arithmetic	12	8
Vocabulary	30	7
Comprehension	14	5
(Digit Span)	(8)	(5)
Verbal Score		32
PERFORMANCE TESTS		
Picture Completion	22	11
Picture Arrangement	31	10
Block Design	38	10
Object Assembly	27	12
Coding	57	11
(Mazes)	( )	( )
Performance Score		54

	Scaled Score	IQ
Verbal Score	32 *	78
Performance Score	54 *	105
Full Scale Score	86	89

*Prorated from 4 tests, if necessary.

Figure 79. WISC-R Record Form

Coding B symbols:
1 ÷	2 +	3 V	4 X	5 ⌐	6 ⊣	7 (	8 ⊡	9 ⌐
8	4	1						

Figure 77b. WISC-R Coding B

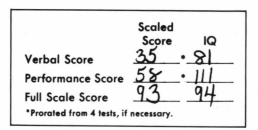

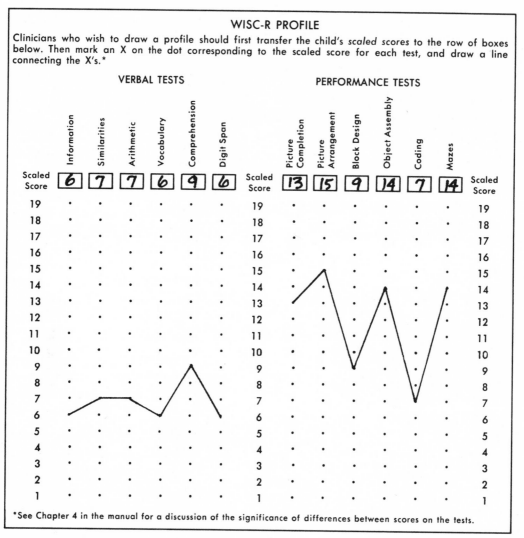

Figure 80. WISC-R Profile

deal with material that is not generally within the typical experience of the student. Analyzing WISC-R subtests within this framework may show a student's ability to process meaningful information successfully and inability to deal with nonmeaningful material (or vice versa).

2. *Social versus Nonsocial Tasks*. The verbal subtests all involve social perception, with the exception of Digit Span and Similarities. Only the Picture Arrangement subtest of

the performance tests entails this ability. The division into Social versus Nonsocial may be another useful way of viewing a student's WISC-R patterns in relation to learning disabilities.

3. *Spatial versus Conceptual versus Sequential Tasks*. Bannatyne (1968) has offered another way to analyze WISC-R subtest patterns, by categorizing them as follows:

Conceptual Score. Sum of scaled scores of Comprehension, Similarities, and Vocabulary. Language ability is required by these subtests.

Spatial Score. Sum of scaled scores of Block Design, Picture Completion, and Object Assembly. These subtests require the ability to manipulate objects in multidimensional space, either directly or symbolically.

Sequential Score. Sum of scaled scores of Digit Span, Coding, and Picture Arrangement. These subtests demand short-term memory of visual and auditory sequences.

The composite scaled score for each of these three groupings should average 30. Bannatyne compares a student's scores in the three areas to obtain information about particular strengths and weaknesses. Recently Bannatyne (1974) added a fourth category, *Acquired Knowledge,* composed of Information, Arithmetic, and Vocabulary.

In summary, the WISC-R is a high-quality general-purpose intelligence test that compares favorably with other individual scales and will likely remain the most commonly used measure of intelligence within the school system. It is a reliable and well-known instrument that usually provides scores correlating highly with school achievement.

LIMITING FACTORS OF THE WISC-R

• Caution must be exercised in interpreting WISC-R scores. The level of intellectual ability achieved on the test indicates only a small sample of the student's performance at one moment in time. An IQ is not immutable; it reflects the present capacity of the student and shows what can be expected if current conditions remain the same. Furthermore, the test may or may not be an adequate sample of a student's potential intellectual abilities. All tests give only a limited measure of a student's assets. The significance of an IQ score for a particular student can accurately be assessed only when it is compared to other data: the student's social-emotional maturity level, the amount of schooling, achievement levels, and cultural or language background. The testing situation itself is important, because emotional reactions such as anxiety can significantly diminish a student's performance. Thus, the examiner must weigh a number of factors and check for discrepancies and congruencies in order to better understand the meaning of the IQ results and test scatter obtained.

• It is clear that the verbal scale is more closely related to academic achievement than the performance scale. The verbal score also predicts much more accurately than the performance score how successful an individual is likely to be in future school situations. This fact should be borne in mind when evaluating the protocols of students showing high nonverbal scores but poor verbal facility. Although the performance score may reflect average intellectual functioning, this score alone cannot be taken at face value

when assessing a student's chances for future school success.

• The WISC-R shows limits for the tabled IQs. Verbal and performance IQs range from 45 to 155; the full scale IQ ranges from 40 to 160. There is also no breakdown or diagnostic classification of mental deficiency in terms of severity (mild, moderate, severe). All IQs below 69 are simply classified as "mentally deficient." The WISC-R is not a particularly sensitive instrument for students at either end of the intelligence distribution.

• Of concern to many investigators is that most of the WISC-R's content was based on a test for adults, the Wechsler-Bellevue Intelligence Scale (1947). The question researchers pose is, Should a children's intelligence scale simply be a downward extension of an adult scale? Wechsler himself comments that we cannot assume that similar tests tap identical skills at all ages.

• Several of the WISC-R subtests have limitations that the examiner should be aware of.

Vocabulary. Scoring of vocabulary items contains some subjectivity, although the revised manual includes expanded sample answers. If a student fails to express a definition of a word, there is no procedure the examiner can follow to find out if the student has at least a passive familiarity or understanding of the word.

Picture Completion. The difficulty level of this subtest increases unevenly, because success is influenced by the student's familiarity with the objects pictured.

Digit Span. Digit Span is the only test of short-term memory on the WISC-R. Serial presentation of such items as the repetition of digits forward and backward tires children easily. The fatigue factor is increased on the WISC-R because both trials of each of the items must be administered. Furthermore, Digit Span is the least reliable of the verbal subtests. It may be more useful to include a meaningful verbal memory test, such as sentence, phrase, or story repetition, in a diagnostic evaluation.

Coding. This subtest is frequently purported to reflect a memory factor, but it should be stressed that it is not designed as a memory test. The scale would benefit from the inclusion of a nonverbal memory test.

Arithmetic. The oral presentation of the word problems stresses concentration, memory, and facility in mental arithmetic. This subtest should not be regarded as an index of a student's achievement level in arithmetic.

WECHSLER PRESCHOOL AND PRIMARY SCALE OF INTELLIGENCE (WPPSI)

The WPPSI is intended for use with children between the ages of 4 and 6½ years. There are 11 subtests, but only 10 are used in computing the IQ. Verbal and performance subtests are alternated during administration to provide variety, which is helpful in holding the young child's attention.

The subtests are listed below in order of administration:

Verbal Scale	Performance Scale
1. Information	2. Picture Completion
3. Comprehension	4. Block Design
5. Arithmetic	6. Animal House
7. Similarities	8. Mazes
9. Vocabulary	10. Geometric Design
11. Sentences (alternate)	

The verbal scale is essentially the same as the WISC-R. Sentences is a new subtest, replacing Digit Span. The student listens to sentences read by the examiner and repeats them. Although both tasks assess rote automatic auditory memory, the memory for words in a sentence appears to be less abstract and less demanding of the student's attention. The Sentences subtest is used only as an alternate to another verbal subtest.

On the performance scale, Picture Arrangement, Coding, and Object Assembly from the WISC-R have been dropped; Mazes has been made a required subtest, and two new subtests have been added—Animal House and Geometric Design. Animal House, like Coding, is an associative learning task. The student places a particular colored peg in the board under the picture of one of four animals. For example, the student is asked to place all the red pegs under the picture of the pig, the blue pegs under the horse, and so forth. Attention and concentration are enhanced by the gamelike quality of this subtest, which is more appropriate for preschoolers than is the pencil-and-paper task, Coding. Visual-motor coordination is measured by the Geometric Design subtest. Geometric Design requires the child to copy 10 designs made up of circles and straight lines.

As on the WISC-R and the Wechsler Adult Intelligence Scale, verbal, performance, and full scale IQs are obtained, with a mean of 100 and a standard deviation of 15.

WECHSLER ADULT INTELLIGENCE SCALE (WAIS)

The WAIS is almost identical in organization, administration, and scoring to the WISC-R. It may be used with students from age 16 to adult. The verbal scale consists of six required subtests, and the performance scale has five required subtests. There are no alternate or supplemental subtests. The subtests are given in the following order:

Verbal Scale	Performance Scale
1. Information	7. Digit Symbol (equivalent to WISC-R, Coding)
2. Compehension	8. Picture Completion
3. Arithmetic	9. Block Design
4. Similarities	10. Picture Arrangement
5. Digit Span	11. Object Assembly
6. Vocabulary	

Verbal, performance, and full scale IQs with a mean of 100 and a standard deviation of 15 are obtained, as on the WISC-R.

Stanford-Binet Intelligence Scale (Stanford-Binet)

Lewis M. Terman and Maud A. Merrill
Houghton Mifflin Company, third revision (Form L-M), 1960; renorming 1972
Test Department, Box 1970, Iowa City, IA 52240

Purpose	To measure general intellectual ability
Major Areas Tested	General intelligence
Age or Grade Range	2 years–adult
Usually Given By	Psychologist
Type of Test	Standardized Individual Norm-referenced
Scores Obtained	Mental age IQ
Student Performance Timed?	Yes (some items)
Testing Time	30–90 minutes (depending on age and ability)
Scoring/Interpretation Time	30–45 minutes
Normed On	2,100 urban and rural students from various geographic locations, with a wide range of intellectual abilities; 100 individuals at each age level
Alternate Forms Available?	No

FORMAT

The materials for the Stanford-Binet Intelligence Scale (Stanford-Binet) consist of an examiner's manual, individual record booklets, and a variety of pictures and manipulative materials necessary for administration of the individual test items. All of the materials are packaged in a suitcase-style carrying case.

The test items are arranged by age level. At each age level, six tests are administered. They assess a variety of abilities, such as vocabulary, memory, abstract reasoning, numerical concepts, visual-motor skills, and social competence. Testing begins at an age level where the examiner thinks the student will be challenged but successful, usually about one year below age level. The manual defines the basal age as "that level at which all tests are passed which just precedes the level where the first failure occurs" (p. 60). Testing is discontinued when the student fails all of the tests at a given age level. One alternate test is available at each age level, to be substituted when a test is invalidated by examiner error.

Table 26 gives examples at different age levels that illustrate the types of test items. (These items are similar but not identical to test items.) Often an item such as Vocabulary is listed at several age levels. The item is administered once, the first time it is listed. Scoring criteria differ, and more correct answers are required to pass the item at each higher age level. For example, in the Vocabulary section, the criteria change as follows:

Year	Correct Answers Required to Pass
6	6
8	8
10	11
12	15
14	17
AA (Average Adult)	20
SA, I (Superior Adult, I)	23
SA, II (Superior Adult, II)	26
SA, III (Superior Adult, III)	30

Each item is scored pass or fail according to the specific instructions in the manual. A specified number of months' credit is given for each item passed. All items below the basal are assumed passed; all items above the ceiling are assumed failed. The number of months credited is totaled to get a mental age. Tables are used to convert mental age to IQ.

STRENGTHS OF THE STANFORD-BINET

• The Stanford-Binet is the grandfather of individual intelligence tests. The original Binet scales were developed in 1905; in 1916 they were revised and extended for use in the United States. They were revised again in 1937 and 1960. The current 1972 edition is a renorming of the 1960 edition.

• The Stanford-Binet is the only intelligence scale available for the age range between 30 months, when the Bayley Scales (1969) end, and 48 months, when the Wechsler Preschool and Primary Scale of Intelligence begins. It remains the favored test for assessing the preschool child because of its better coverage at the lower end of the scale. Because of its emphasis on verbal skills and its greater reliability at the extremes of IQ, the Stanford-Binet also continues to be a favorite of psychologists for testing students with very high intellectual ability.

LIMITING FACTORS OF THE STANFORD-BINET

• The Stanford-Binet was designed as a test of general intellectual ability, not as a differential measure of several aspects of mental ability. It is based on a unitary concept of intelligence. With the gain in popularity of the Wechsler Scales (WISC-R, WAIS, WPPSI) and other tests yielding profiles of subtest performances, the Stanford-Binet has become less frequently used. Several attempts (Meeker 1969; Sattler 1965; Valett 1964) have been made to develop systems for classifying the kinds of items on the Stanford-Binet. These classification systems have had little agreement and no attempts at validation. The Stanford-Binet was not designed as a test of differential skills and any attempt to use it in that way yields questionable results. However, the teacher benefits when the psychologist lists the tests that were passed and failed at each level with some description of their content. Because the Stanford-Binet yields a single score, the Wechsler Intelligence Scale for Children—Revised is usually selected for exceptional children when knowledge of their particular pattern of skill development is essential for proper placement and program planning.

• Salvia, Ysseldyke, and Lee (1975) demonstrated that the 1972 edition does not have items placed appropriately for the age levels. In earlier editions, an item was placed at the 8-year-old level because a majority of 8-year-olds answered it correctly. When the test was renormed, items were not changed in relationship to new data. The result is that students must perform above age level to earn average IQs.

• Reliability and validity for the 1972 edition are not reported. The assumption is that, because earlier editions were reliable and valid, this one is too.

• The Stanford-Binet is a difficult test to learn to administer correctly. The variety in items and materials requires the psychologist to practice the test many times

Table 26. Stanford–Binet Sample Test Items

Age Level	Test	Materials	Procedure
2.6	Identifying Objects by Use	Card with small objects attached (bed, boat, pencil, hat, stove)	Present the card and say: "Show me what… a. we sleep on." b. goes in the water." c. we can write with." d. we can cook on."
3	Copying a Triangle	Printed triangle in the record booklet	Give the child a pencil and point to the triangle and say: "Make one like this."
4.6	Three Commissions	Any available book	Say: "Here is a book. I want you to put it under the desk, touch the window curtain, and sit down in that chair."
6	Vocabulary	Vocabulary card	Say: "When I say a word, you tell me what it means." a. "tomato" b. "hay" c. "acrobat" d. "abundance"
8	Similarities and Differences	None	Say: "Tell me how these two things are alike and how they are different." a. "tennis ball and a tire" b. "fish and a submarine" c. "mountains and desert"
10	Abstract Words	None	Say: "What do we mean by… a. suffering?" b. astonishment?" c. patriotism?"
11	Memory for Designs	Card with two designs	Show the card to the student for 10 seconds. Take it away and have the student draw the designs.
13	Copying a Bead Chain from Memory	48 kindergarten beads	Make this bead chain while the student watches: ○ □ ○ ○ □ ○ □ ○ ○ □ Show it to the student for five seconds, then remove it. Say: "Make one just like it."

on individuals of various ages and types before assuming that a test is valid. One feature that increases the difficulty of test administration is the placement of the scoring standards at the back of the manual. The examiner needs to check almost every response to determine when a basal and ceiling level have been reached.

Slosson Intelligence Test for Children and Adults (SIT)

Richard L. Slosson
Slosson Educational Publications, Inc., 1961; reprinted 1975
140 Pine St., East Aurora, NY 14052

Purpose	To evaluate mental ability
Major Areas Tested	Mental ability
Age or Grade Range	5 months–adult
Usually Given By	Classroom teacher Counselor Special education teacher Principal Psychologist Nurse
Type of Test	Standardized Individual Norm-referenced
Scores Obtained	Mental age IQ
Student Performance Timed?	No
Testing Time	15–30 minutes
Scoring/Interpretation Time	10 minutes
Normed On	Urban and rural students in New York state with a wide range of intellectual levels
Alternate Forms Available?	No

FORMAT

The materials for the Slosson Intelligence Test for Children and Adults (SIT) are contained within a single manual. The manual includes the test questions; instructions for administration, scoring, and interpretation; information on test construction; and SIT score sheets. An IQ Finder, to aid in calculating IQ, is also included. No other materials, except a pencil, are needed to administer the test with preschool students through adults. For infant testing, some simple toys (rattle, ball) are needed.

The SIT is a question-and-answer test; no reading or writing is required. The examiner asks the student a series of short-answer questions. The items are very similar to those on the Stanford-Binet tests. The following questions illustrate the types of content areas assessed. (These questions are similar but not identical to test items.)

Math Reasoning: A boy was carrying a box of four dozen eggs. He dropped the box and broke a third of them. How many eggs did he break?

Vocabulary: If you heard that the old man was *frugal,* what would that mean?

Auditory Memory: Say these letters backwards for me. For example, if I should say *a, b, c,* you would say *c, b, a.* Say these letters backwards: *m, r, b, v, t.*

Information: Name the three months of the summer season.

The testing usually begins with a question about a year below the student's chronological age and continues forward until the student answers 10 consecutive questions correctly. This constitutes the basal age. If necessary, the examiner goes backward, asking easier questions, until the basal age is obtained. Testing continues until a ceiling level of 10 consecutive errors in a row is achieved.

The answers to each item are printed immediately following the item; all correct items are marked + on the score sheet, and all incorrect items are marked √ or −. In this way, scoring is completed as the test is administered. In field testing by teachers and others inexperienced in intellectual testing, all items that were difficult to administer or score were eliminated.

After the test is completed, the examiner finds the mental age by multiplying the number of correct answers above the basal age by a specific number of months' credit; that is, 0 to 2 years equals .5 months' credit per item, 2 to 5 years equals 1 month credit per item, and so forth. The total months are added to the basal age to obtain the mental age. This procedure is well described in the manual and indicated on the score sheet. For example:

Basal age = 6 years, 8 months = 80 months
Credit for items over basal = 30 months
                                                            110 months or
            Mental age = 9 years, 2 months

IQ is then found by the traditional formula:

$$\frac{\text{Mental age}}{\text{Chronological age}} \times 100$$

An IQ Finder (a dial graph that eliminates the division process) is also provided.

Because this is a screening test, the examiner is directed to encourage and support the student and to repeat items as many times as needed to obtain as accurate an indication of the student's ability as possible. No time limits are imposed.

Items for the infant section of the test were taken from the *Gesell Developmental Schedules* (1949). The items require observation of the infant sitting, playing, walking, and "talking." (Obviously the question-answer format is not appropriate for an infant.) The author cautions the examiner about overinterpretation of infant IQ scores, which have questionable reliability.

STRENGTHS OF THE SIT

• The SIT is a brief individual test of intellectual ability. It was designed as a screening test to be used by professionals relatively untrained in individual testing. It can be administered and scored in 30 minutes. As a quick screening device, it can provide useful information about a student's probable level of mental ability and can identify students in need of more intensive intellectual assessment.

• The format and test items were selected because they were unambiguous to administer and score. Test-retest reliability is high. The printing of the correct answers next to each question allows the scoring to be accomplished during the administration. Computation for calculating the IQ is minimal. The fact that the test is individually administered and untimed allows the very distracted or deliberate student more opportunity to demonstrate knowledge and ability than a group test does. Also, group intelligence tests often require reading and writing, which the SIT does not. The wide age range of items allows even the young or very disabled student an opportunity to experience success.

• Although the SIT was not intended to give a profile of a student's strengths and weaknesses, it is possible to identify areas that need further assessment by analyzing the student's error pattern. Some students, for example, make errors on most of the math reasoning problems, whereas others have particular difficulty with vocabulary. Such information can be used to plan further diagnostic procedures.

LIMITING FACTORS OF THE SIT

• The norming sample for this test is not well described. It is unclear how many students the SIT was standardized on or the composition of the norming sample. The author describes a diverse group of individuals but gives no information about the breakdown by age, sex, race, socioeconomic class, or ability range. Without this information, the examiner has no idea whom the student is being compared to.

• The author reports validity studies correlating SIT scores with the Stanford-Binet. High correlations are to be expected, because many of the items are the same. However, on the SIT, standard deviations are very large (ranging from 16.7 at age 17 to 31.2 at ages 18 and above). Validity studies on the Wechsler Scales are on very small numbers of students. Because the SIT is a screening instrument, comparisons with group IQ tests would be interesting.

• The author mentions the lack of reliability and validity for infant intellectual assessment. His criticism includes the SIT. Many items in the infant section would be difficult to observe during a brief testing session. No provision is made for parent report or for correcting the scoring for items not observed. For infants, other screening tests, such as the Denver Developmental Screening Test (p. 201), would be more appropriate.

• The SIT for preschoolers also has serious limitations. The items are too verbal for children with delayed language or with language problems due to cultural or physical factors.

• The SIT manual states that it can be used with blind and deaf students, yet for the blind, the only advice given is to eliminate the items the student needs to see. No procedure is given for correcting the scoring for the omitted items, and no data is provided on the validity of the test with blind students. If the deaf student cannot read, it is recommended that another test be given.

• The content of the SIT is limited to items that can be presented in a question-and-answer format. No performance tasks are included, other than a few design-copying items. Thus, students with excellent visual-spatial skills have no opportunity to demonstrate them, and students with deficits in these areas will go unidentified. In terms of content and type of test, the SIT is more clearly a substitute for the Stanford-Binet Intelligence Scale than for the Wechsler Scales.

• The SIT is a screening test, and under no circumstances should it be substituted for the in-depth intellectual assessment needed for such critical educational decisions as special education class placement or termination, retention, or acceleration.

Leiter International Performance Scale and the Arthur Adaptation (Leiter Scale)

Russell Leiter and Grace Arthur
C. H. Stoelting Company, 1948; revised 1969; Arthur Adaptation, 1950
424 North Homan Ave., Chicago, IL 60624

Purpose	To assess nonverbal intellectual functioning in children with difficulties in verbal expression
Major Areas Tested	Nonverbal intellectual functioning
Age or Grade Range	2–18 years
Usually Given By	Psychologist
Type of Test	Standardized Individual Norm-referenced
Scores Obtained	Mental age IQ
Student Performance Timed?	No
Testing Time	30—60 minutes
Scoring/Interpretation Time	30 minutes
Normed On	289 students from a homogeneous middle-class, midwestern, metropolitan background (Arthur Adaptation)
Alternate Forms Available?	No

FORMAT

The history of the Leiter International Performance Scale (Leiter Scale) is long and complex. Constructed in 1929 by Russell Leiter for the purpose of assessing deaf and non-English-speaking students, the test was revised several times. In 1950, Grace Arthur published an adapted version of the test for children between the ages of 2 and 12 years. Only minor changes in instructions were made in the Arthur Adaptation, and the test materials remained almost identical. Because it seemed impractical to manufacture two sets of materials, one for the Leiter Scale and one for the Arthur Adaptation, the five additional response blocks necessary for the Arthur Adaptation were added to the Leiter Scale materials. As a result, the examiner ordering either the Leiter Scale or the Arthur Adaptation receives the same materials for children from 2 to 12 years old.

The following materials are available: (1) wooden response form with adjustable card holder (see Figure 81); (2) trays of response blocks with corresponding stimulus cards (two trays for the 2- to 12-year-olds and an additional tray for the 13- to 18-year-olds); (3) individual record cards for recording scores; and (4) a carrying case.

The Leiter Scale manual is organized into two parts. Part I contains general instructions for the Leiter Scale, including directions for obtaining basal age, ceiling, mental age, and IQ scores. Part II is the examiner's manual, which includes directions for administering and scoring test items. The Arthur Adaptation manual includes directions for administering and scoring the test and some information on test construction.

The Leiter Scale consists of 68 items arranged in order of increasing difficulty. There are four items at each year level from ages 2 to 18 years. Each item is administered in the same manner. The examiner places the stimulus card in the adjustable card holder on top of the wooden response form. The blocks for the item are placed in front of the student in the manner described in the manual. The student places each block in the correct slot in the wooden response form.

The items range from simple tasks of color and form matching to more complex tasks that require an understanding of spatial relationships, sequencing, and numer-ical and verbal reasoning. Most of the items require visual discrimination and perceptual organization.

The following illustrates the types of items used at various age levels (these examples are similar but not identical to the test items):

Year Level	Task
3	*Number Discrimination* (Figure 82). A card with the top design is placed on the card holder. The student places each block in the holder under the picture with the same number of objects.
6	*Analogous Progression* (Figure 83). The student arranges the blocks in descending order, analogous to the arrangement of the triangles.
10	*Block Design* (Figure 84). The student arranges four triangular blocks to make a square identical to the one on the picture card and places them in the corresponding slot in the card holder.

Because the test was devised for language-impaired students, all directions are given in pantomime. The examiner is instructed to keep busy with clerical work rather than to watch the child's performance. No time limits are imposed (except on the block-design items). When the student is finished, the examiner scores the item and puts the blocks away. Last-minute corrections are allowed.

Testing begins with the first item at an age level two years below the student's estimated mental age. There are no verbal directions, so the task must be simple enough for the student to understand what to do. If that item or any other in that age level is missed, the examiner goes back to the first item at the next-lower age level. Testing continues in this manner until a basal age is reached; that is, until all items at a given age level are passed. Once the basal age is obtained, the examiner moves forward again, repeating items failed during the establishment of the basal age. Before the basal age is established, it is not certain whether the student fails an item because he or she does not understand what to do or because the student does not have the ability to do it. But

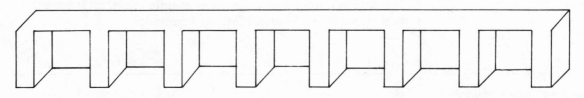

Figure 81. Leiter Scale Card Holder

before the blocks are put away. The mental age is found in the same manner as on the Stanford-Binet. A specified number of months' credit is given each item passed. All items below the basal are assumed passed; all items above the ceiling are presumed failed. The total number of months credited yields a mental age. The formula

$$\frac{\text{Mental age}}{\text{Chronological age}} \times 100$$

is used to calculate IQ.

The mean IQ on the Leiter Scale is 95; the standard deviation is 16. In order to compare the IQ of the Leiter with the Stanford-Binet Intelligence Scale or the Wechsler Scales, which have a mean of 100, 5 points are added to the Leiter IQ. This adjusted IQ is always the IQ reported from the Leiter. Tables are used to adjust the mental-age score.

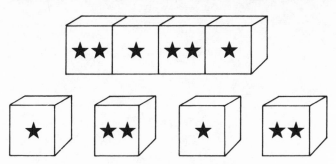

Figure 82. Leiter Scale Number Discrimination

STRENGTHS OF THE LEITER SCALE

• The Leiter Scale is unique because it enables intellectual assessment of students with difficulties in verbal expression, such as hearing-impaired and non-English-speaking students. The pantomimed instructions and nonverbal response format is also very useful in evaluating students with language disorders such as aphasia, students with delayed language due to retardation or emotional disturbance, and bilingual students. The materials are highly interesting to young children and older students alike. The test is designed for children as young as 2, and the beginning items seem to allow them to learn the process as they take the test.

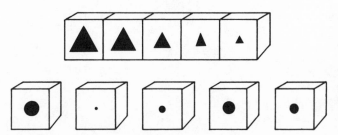

Figure 83. Leiter Scale Analogous Progression

LIMITING FACTORS OF THE LEITER SCALE

• It is difficult to find information on standardization, reliability, and validity of the Leiter Scale. Leiter published this information in the 1952 manual, but it is not available in either the 1969 manual or in the Arthur Adaptation manual.

Arthur's standardization was based on only 289 students from a middle-class midwestern urban background. No exceptional children, for whom the test was designed, were in the sample.

No reliability data is published in either the 1969 manual or Arthur's manual. Such data is seriously lacking. Validity studies indicate moderate correlations with the Stanford-Binet Intelligence Scale (169–193) and the Wechsler Intelligence Scale for Children—Revised (179–180 performance scale, .40–.78 verbal scale). The studies were presumably conducted with normal children.

Because the Arthur Adaptation was intended for a specific group of students, reliability and validity studies on that population need to be carried out.

• The test has no evidence of construct validity. There is no information explaining how the test items were selected. The level of difficulty of the items seems uneven, and this

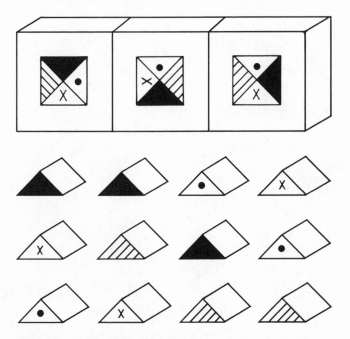

Figure 84. Leiter Scale Block Design

after the basal age is established, it is safer to assume that the student fails because of a lack of ability.

Testing continues until all tests at two consecutive year levels have been failed. Each item is scored pass or fail makes the process of obtaining a basal age and a ceiling difficult and lengthy.

• Some of the Leiter Scale items are outdated. For example, on Year V, Test 3, Clothing, many students make errors because they do not recognize the styles. Because there are only four items at each age level, poor items can seriously affect scores.

• Fine visual discrimination is needed to do many of the items. Children with organically based hearing or language deficiencies often have problems with visual perception as well. Thus, a low score on the Leiter Scale may be the result of inadequate visual perception.

• The manuals are very confusing. Because only black-and-white pictures are used, the examiner must read the full description of each item to determine how to set up the blocks. Colored illustrations would facilitate this process.

• No answers are given to the test items. The examiner must go through the test, performing each task and coding the blocks, to facilitate efficient scoring.

• Although the test manual states that the Leiter Scale extends to age 18, Leiter sets 13.0 years as the maximum chronological age for determining mental age and IQ. This is based on the questionable assumption that the ability to visually organize new materials does not increase after age 13, as verbal learning does.

• Items on the scale are scored pass or fail; credit is all or none. This penalizes the child who understands the concept but does not complete the whole item correctly. Partial credit would seem to reflect many students' abilities more fairly.

McCarthy Scales of Children's Abilities
(McCarthy Scales)

Dorothea McCarthy
The Psychological Corporation, 1972
757 Third Ave., New York, NY 10017

Purpose	To measure intelligence and to identify children with possible learning disabilities
Major Areas Tested	General intellectual ability
Age or Grade Range	2½–8½ years
Usually Given By	Special education teacher Psychologist
Type of Test	Standardized Individual Norm-referenced
Scores Obtained	Mental age Standard Percentile
Student Performance Timed?	Yes (some subtests)
Testing Time	1 hour
Scoring/Interpretation Time	30 minutes
Normed On	1,032 urban and rural children stratified by age, sex, race, father's occupation, and geographic region
Alternate Forms Available?	No

FORMAT

The materials for the McCarthy Scales of Children's Abilities (McCarthy Scales) consist of an examiner's manual, individual scoring sheets, and a kit of attractive manipulative materials (ball, blocks, puzzles, xylophone, and others).

The McCarthy Scales consist of 18 subtests grouped into six scales. The organization and content of the test is shown in Table 27. The sequence of subtests has been carefully organized to facilitate and maintain the interest and attention of the young child. The test begins with two manipulative tests and then gradually increases the demand for a verbal response. The three motor tests are grouped in the middle of the sequence to provide a natural activity break. The drawing tests come next to refocus attention, and the battery ends with three tests requiring minimal verbal response. Examples are given on most subtests, and in many cases "second chances" secure the child's best performance.

Using an eight-step process clearly outlined in the manual, the following scores are obtained and recorded on the individual scoring sheet:

- The general cognitive scale raw score is converted into a standard score with a mean of 100 and a standard deviation of 16. This score is called the general cognitive index and is the equivalent of an IQ score.
- Separate scale indexes on each of the other five scales have a mean of 50 and a standard deviation of 10.
- Percentile ranks for each of the scaled scores.
- An estimated mental-age score for the general cognitive index.

STRENGTHS OF THE McCARTHY SCALES

- The McCarthy Scales are a well-designed, theoretically based instrument to assess the intellectual functioning of preschool and primary-aged children. The tasks include a variety of different activities of interest to young children, and the colorful and interesting materials naturally engage the children in the tasks. Particular attention has been given to the sequence of the subtests and to procedures for providing feedback and support to the child during the testing situation. The well-written manual explains the test administration and scoring procedures very clearly.
- The McCarthy Scales include a number of subtests particularly appropriate for children with suspected learning disabilities. The Motor Scale includes an assessment of gross motor ability, which is not included on any other individual IQ test. The subtests that measure verbal and nonverbal short-term memory are also good.
- The McCarthy Scales were normed on a representative standardization sample stratified by age, sex, race, father's occupation, and urban or rural residence. Good test-retest reliability is reported, and although more validity studies are needed, those reported by Kaufman and Kaufman in

Clinical Evaluation of Young Children with the McCarthy Scales (1977) show promise. The Kaufman and Kaufman book contains an excellent critique of the McCarthy Scales as well as helpful information on administration, scoring, and interpretation.

- The field of assessment is greatly in need of valid instruments for assessing Black children. The McCarthy Scales were constructed with this in mind, and the items were selected to avoid cultural bias. Kaufman and Kaufman report studies of good construct validity of the McCarthy Scales for both racial groups. Kaufman also reports that the Black preschool children did not differ significantly from the white children on mean general cognitive index; but for school-aged children, the Black children obtained a lower mean general cognitive index.

LIMITING FACTORS OF THE McCARTHY SCALES

- The McCarthy Scales should be administered by examiners experienced in the clinical assessment of young children. The test may only be given by psychologists, learning-disabilities specialists, or other professionals well trained in individual testing. The test requires a fair amount of time to administer, score, and interpret. The computational process for scoring is long and offers many opportunities for error.
- The McCarthy Scales cover a very limited age range. The tasks and materials are clearly designed for young children; there is no test form for older children. This presents some problems for using the test with children who require periodic reevaluations. The ceiling is too low for most children older than 7 years.
- The McCarthy Scales are lacking in items that assess social and practical judgment as well as abstract problem-solving skills. This is another reason why the McCarthy Scales are more appropriate for preschool children.
- More studies of predictive and concurrent validity are needed, particularly with exceptional children. No exceptional children were included in the sample, and no research has been done on the validity of the test for retarded or learning-disabled children.
- Research reported by Kaufman and Kaufman (1974) indicated that learning-disabled children obtained general cognitive index scores about 15 points lower than their IQ scores on the Wechsler Preschool and Primary Scale of Intelligence and the Stanford-Binet Intelligence Scale. Given the rigid criteria for qualifying a child for a learning-disability program in some schools, the McCarthy Scales may need to be supplemented with another IQ test or an adaptive-behavior scale to document a significant discrepancy between ability and achievement.

Table 27. McCarthy Scales Subtests

Scale	Content/ Process	Response	Subtests	Task
Verbal	Words	Verbal	3. Pictorial Memory	Recalling pictured objects
			4. Word Knowledge	Identifying and naming objects; defining words
			7. Verbal Memory	Repeating words, sentences, and story
			15. Verbal Fluency	Naming things within four categories
			17. Opposite Analogies	Completing verbal analogies
Perceptual-Performance	Concrete materials	Nonverbal	1. Block Building	Copying block structures
			2. Puzzle Solving	Assembling two- to six-piece puzzles
			6. Tapping Sequence	Repeating sequences of three to six notes on xylophone
			8. Right-Left Orientation	Recognizing right and left on self and on picture
			12. Draw-a-Design	Copying geometric designs
			13. Draw-a-Child	Drawing a child of the same sex
			18. Conceptual Grouping	Demonstrating concepts of size, color, and shape; discovering rules
Quantitative	Digits	Verbal and Nonverbal	5. Number Questions	Answering questions about number facts and quantitative concepts
			14. Numerical Memory	Recalling sequences of digits, forward and backward
			16. Counting and Sorting	Counting and sorting blocks into groups using concepts such as *equal*
Motor	Motor coordination	Nonverbal	9. Leg Coordination	Walking, tiptoeing, and hopping
			10. Arm Coordination	Bouncing, catching, and throwing
			11. Imitative Action	Performing three tasks of eye and hand preference
			Subtests 12 and 13	
Memory	Short-term memory	Verbal and nonverbal	Composite of subtests 3, 6, 7, and 14	
General Cognitive			Composite of Verbal, Perceptual-Performance, and Quantitative scales	

Goodenough-Harris Drawing Test (Goodenough-Harris)

Dale B. Harris
Harcourt, Brace & World, Inc., 1963 (revised extension of the Goodenough Draw-A-Man Test by Florence Goodenough, 1926)
757 Third Ave., New York, NY 10017

Purpose	To assess cognitive development and intellectual maturity
Major Areas Tested	Conceptual and intellectual maturity and personality characteristics
Age or Grade Range	3–15 years
Usually Given By	Special education teacher Psychologist
Type of Test	Standardized Individual Group
Scores Obtained	Standard Percentile Quality scale
Student Performance Timed?	No
Testing Time	10–15 minutes
Scoring/Interpretation Time	10–15 minutes
Normed On	275 urban and rural children from the South, West Coast, Upper Midwest, Middle Atlantic, and New England; sample representative of 1950 United States population in regard to father's occupation
Alternate Forms Available?	No

FORMAT

Materials needed for the Goodenough-Harris Drawing Test (Goodenough-Harris) consist of a test booklet, with separate pages for three drawings, and a pencil. Plain white typing paper may be used in lieu of a test booklet, but crayons should not be substituted for a pencil. Very simple oral instructions are required. The student instructions read, "Make a picture of a man. Make the very best picture that you can. Be sure to make the whole man, not just his head and shoulders." After drawing a picture of a man, the student is instructed in a similar fashion to draw a picture of a woman. The student's final drawing is a self-portrait.

The Goodenough-Harris is administered with no time limit, but most students rarely take more than 15 minutes to complete all three drawings. The test can be given individually or in groups. Individual administration is necessary for preschool children and for students being examined clinically. Group administration requires an assistant to help proctor the test. Erasing, redrawing some features of a figure, or starting completely over again is allowed on the Goodenough-Harris. If given individually, the examiner may question the student about any unclear aspects of the drawings. Responses are recorded on the drawing itself. The examiner may encourage the students with praise. However, the examiner must refrain from offering any suggestions that might influence the nature of the drawing.

No alternate, equivalent forms of the test are available. However, because the correlation of the man and woman scoring scales is about as high as the split-half reliability of the man scale, Harris suggests that the two drawings be considered alternate forms.

The test manual for the Goodenough-Harris contains detailed, exact scoring instructions, with examples of items marked for credit or no credit. Illustrative scored drawings are also provided. There is a total of 73 scorable items, chosen on the basis of age differentiation, relation to total scores on the test, and relation to group intelligence scores. Credit is given for such features as the inclusion of individual body parts, clothing detail, proportion, and perspective.

After carefully studying the instructions, scoring may be accomplished by teachers or paraprofessionals. Separate sections for scoring the man and woman scales are provided. In addition, separate norms for boys and girls and for the man and woman scales are given.

A short scoring guide for both the man and woman point scales is contained in the manual. This guide should only be used by experienced scorers, however.

The total raw score for each drawing is obtained first. The raw score, representing the total points earned, is then converted into a standard score with a mean score of 100 and a standard deviation of 15. The standard score is particularly useful, because it expresses a student's relative standing on the test in relation to the student's own age and sex group. Thus a standard score of 130 indicates that the student's performance is two standard deviations above the average of his or her age and sex group.

Another advantage of standard scores is that they can be averaged. Averaging the standard scores on the man and woman drawings results in a more reliable estimate of maturity than is found when using the scores on either test alone. To score the self-drawing, the examiner uses the point scale of the appropriate sex.

An alternative method of evaluating performance on the Goodenough-Harris is the use of the quality scale. The examiner selects one of 12 sample drawings that most closely resemble the student's drawing and then assigns the scale value of that sample to the drawing. The quality scale value is converted into a standard score, which can ultimately be converted into a percentile score. The quality scale is advantageous for school psychologists who wish to screen large groups of students efficiently. Separate quality scales are provided for man and woman drawings.

STRENGTHS OF THE GOODENOUGH-HARRIS

• The Goodenough-Harris is an easy-to-administer test that is generally nonthreatening and appealing to students. It is valuable as a measure of intellectual maturity, providing indications of development in the areas of self-perception and body concept.

• The results of extensive reliability studies with the original Goodenough Draw-A-Man Test have been encouraging. Both interscorer and same-scorer correlations were found to be high. The effect of art instruction on test scores was found to be negligible, as was examiner effect. The majority of correlations with other intelligence tests are adequate. In addition, the Goodenough-Harris has been used in many studies of different cultures and ethnic groups.

• The results of the Goodenough-Harris give the classroom teacher some information about the intellectual maturity of students. The psychologist may use the test as a screening device to gain a quick impression of a student's general ability level. The test identifies students needing further clinical evaluation.

• If administered individually by an experienced examiner, the Goodenough-Harris may provide valuable clinical information from observations of the student's behavior. For example, spontaneous comments made while drawing, excessive erasing, the sequence of drawing the figure, or using the examiner or self as a model are all important diagnostic indicators. Although the test is not designed to be a measure of visual-motor integration per se, comparisons of the drawings with other tests measuring visual-motor skills is often useful.

• Helpful to the examiner who uses the Goodenough-

Harris is Harris's *Children's Drawings as Measures of Intellectual Maturity* (1963). It contains a comprehensive survey of literature dealing with the psychology of children's drawings, as well as a wealth of other information.

LIMITING FACTORS OF THE GOODENOUGH-HARRIS

• Any adult can learn to reliably score the Goodenough-Harris, but psychological training is necessary to adequately interpret the test results. Clinical observations of the student, together with the score, lead to valuable diagnostic insights.

• Although the author does not recommend using the Goodenough-Harris as a personality or projective test, it is often used in this way by psychologists. The student's self-portrait is used for projective purposes. Harris includes an experimental qualitative checklist for evaluating the self-drawing by comparing it with the other two drawings. The self-drawing is not standardized and is therefore regarded as a tentative measure of intellectual maturity. To date, the projective uses of the self-drawing have been disappointing. Thus, one should be cautious in making generalizations about the usefulness of drawings in personality assessment.

• Neither the 1926 nor the 1963 versions of the Goodenough-Harris report any correlation studies with academic achievement.

• The Goodenough-Harris is most useful for assessing the conceptual maturity of the elementary-age student. Beyond grade school, the test has only limited applicability. The mean raw scores increase sharply between the ages of 5 and 14. Above 14 years, however, the scores level off for both sexes on both the man and woman scales. For older students, the point scale is a better scoring method than the quality scale, because the latter shows less age differentiation at the upper ages. The test can also be given to 3- and 4-year-olds. Harris provides tentative guides for interpretation.

• The manual, which is Part 2 of Harris's book, is reproduced in its entirety and published separately. It contains, however, only the instructions for administration and scoring. For specific information on construction and technical properties of the Goodenough-Harris, the examiner must consult the book.

Appendix A

A GUIDE TO SPECIFIC TESTS FOR ASSESSING ACADEMIC SKILL AREAS

Skill Area	Tests
Reading	
Decoding	
Phonic skills	Brigance Diagnostic Inventory of Basic Skills
	Spache Diagnostic Reading Scales
	Durrell Analysis of Reading Difficulty
	Gates-McKillop Reading Diagnostic Tests
Sight-word recognition	Wide Range Achievement Test
	Peabody Individual Achievement Test
	Spache Diagnostic Reading Scales
	Durrell Analysis of Reading Difficulty
	Gates-McKillop Reading Diagnostic Tests
	Woodcock Reading Mastery Tests
	Diagnostic Word Patterns
Oral paragraph reading	Gray Oral Reading Tests
	Gilmore Oral Reading Test
	Spache Diagnostic Reading Scales
	Durrell Analysis of Reading Difficulty
	Gates-McKillop Reading Diagnostic Tests
Comprehension	
Oral reading	Gray Oral Reading Tests
	Gilmore Oral Reading Test
	Spache Diagnostic Reading Scales
	Durrell Analysis of Reading Difficulty
	Gates-McKillop Reading Diagnostic Tests
Silent reading	Peabody Individual Achievement Test
	Spache Diagnostic Reading Scales
	Durrell Analysis of Reading Difficulty
	Woodcock Reading Mastery Tests
	Gates-MacGinitie Silent Reading Tests
	Durrell Listening-Reading Series
Listening	Spache Diagnostic Reading Scales
	Durrell Analysis of Reading Difficulty
	Durrell Listening-Reading Series
Comprehension in specific content areas	Durrell Listening-Reading Series
Writing	
Penmanship	Durrell Analysis of Reading Difficulty
(Manuscript, Cursive)	Slingerland Screening Tests for Identifying Children with Specific Language Disability
	Malcomesius Specific Language Disability Test
Written Expression	Myklebust Picture Story Language Test
(Fluency, Syntax, Mechanics, Content)	

A GUIDE TO SPECIFIC TESTS FOR ASSESSING ACADEMIC SKILL AREAS —*Continued*

Skill Area	Tests
Spelling	
Written	Wide Range Achievement Test
(Phonic words, Irregular words)	Brigance Diagnostic Inventory of Basic Skills
	Larsen-Hammill Test of Written Spelling
	Diagnostic Word Patterns
Recognition of Sight Words	Peabody Individual Achievement Test
Oral	Gates-McKillop Reading Diagnostic Tests
Arithmetic	
Concepts	Peabody Individual Achievement Test
	Brigance Diagnostic Inventory of Basic Skills
	KeyMath Diagnostic Arithmetic Test
Computation	Wide Range Achievement Test
(Addition, Subtraction, Multiplication, Division)	Brigance Diagnostic Inventory of Basic Skills
	KeyMath Diagnostic Arithmetic Test
Word Problems	Peabody Individual Achievement Test
(Oral, Written)	Brigance Diagnostic Inventory of Basic Skills
	KeyMath Diagnostic Arithmetic Test
Oral Language	
Receptive	
Vocabulary	Gates-McKillop Reading Diagnostic Tests
	Durrell Listening-Reading Series
	Peabody Picture Vocabulary Test
	Assessment of Children's Language Comprehension
Listening comprehension	Spache Diagnostic Reading Scales
	Durrell Analysis of Reading Difficulty
	Durrell Listening-Reading Series
	Illinois Test of Psycholinguistic Abilities
	Assessment of Children's Language Comprehension
	Test for Auditory Comprehension of Language
	Boehm Test of Basic Concepts
	Northwestern Syntax Screening Test
	Sequenced Inventory of Communication Development
Expressive	
Articulation	The Fisher-Logemann Test of Articulation Competence
	The Goldman-Fristoe Test of Articulation
	The Templin-Darley Tests of Articulation
	Compton-Hutton Phonological Assessment
Language	Illinois Test of Psycholinguistic Abilities
(Morphology, Syntax, Semantics)	Northwestern Syntax Screening Test
	Developmental Sentence Scoring
	Language Sampling, Analysis, and Training

Appendix B

PROCESS-MODALITY CHART

Modality	Process				
	Reception (initial receiving of information)	**Perception** (initial organizing of information)	**Association** (relating new information to other information)	**Memory** (short-term, sequential memory)	**Expression** (output)
Auditory (primary stimuli are auditory)	ACLC Boehm Detroit ITPA NSST PPVT SICD TACL	Detroit GFW ITPA LAC Malcomesius Test Slingerland Tests Wepman	Detroit ITPA Malcomesius Test Slingerland Tests	Detroit ITPA LAC Malcomesius Test Slingerland Tests	**Verbal expression** Compton-Hutton Detroit DSS Fisher-Logemann Goldman-Fristoe ITPA NSST Slingerland Tests TACL Templin-Darley Tyack and Gottsleben
Visual (primary stimuli are visual)	Detroit ITPA PPVT	Detroit DTVP ITPA Malcomesius Test MVPT SCSIT Slingerland Tests Survey	Detroit ITPA Malcomesius Test Slingerland Tests	Detroit ITPA Malcomesius Test MVPT Slingerland Tests	**Written expression** Bender Detroit DTVP Malcomesius Test PSLT Slingerland Tests VMI
Tactile/Kinesthetic (primary stimuli accompanied by motoric output)	SCSIT	SCSIT		Malcomesius Test SCSIT Slingerland Tests	**Motoric expression other than written or verbal** ITPA SCSIT

Key

ACLC: Assessment of Children's Language Comprehension

Bender: The Bender Visual Motor Gestalt Test

Boehm: Boehm Test of Basic Concepts

Compton-Hutton: Compton-Hutton Phonological Assessment

Detroit: Detroit Tests of Learning Aptitude

DSS: Developmental Sentence Scoring

DTVP: Marianne Frostig Developmental Test of Visual Perception

Fisher-Logemann: The Fisher-Logemann Test of Articulation Competence

GFW: Goldman-Fristoe-Woodcock Test of Auditory Discrimination

Goldman-Fristoe: The Goldman-Fristoe Test of Articulation

ITPA: Illinois Test of Psycholinguistic Abilities

LAC: Lindamood Auditory Conceptualization Test

Malcomesius Test: Malcomesius Specific Language Disability Test

MVPT: Motor-Free Visual Perception Test

NSST: Northwestern Syntax Screening Test

PPVT: Peabody Picture Vocabulary Test

PSLT: Myklebust Picture Story Language Test

SCSIT: Southern California Sensory Integration Tests

SICD: Sequenced Inventory of Communication Development

Slingerland Tests: Slingerland Screening Tests for Identifying Children with Specific Language Disability

Survey: Purdue Perceptual-Motor Survey
TACL: Test for Auditory Comprehension of Language
Templin-Darley: The Templin-Darley Tests of Articulation
Tyack and Gottsleben: Language Sampling, Analysis, and
    Training
VMI: Beery-Buktenica Developmental Test of Visual-Motor
    Integration
Wepman: Wepman Auditory Discrimination Test

Appendix C

EDUCATIONAL EVALUATION, SAMPLE 1

Student's Name: Anne
Grade: 5th
Birth Date: 8/10/68
Chronological Age: 10.4
Date of Testing: 12/10/78

REFERRAL

Anne was referred for educational evaluation by her parents following some testing at school that indicated weaknesses in auditory skills. Anne is currently having difficulty with reading, and retention has been suggested by her classroom teacher.

BEHAVIOR DURING TESTING

Anne was cooperative and hardworking throughout the testing session. She was somewhat quiet and nervous but responded well and gave good effort to all tasks.

TESTS ADMINISTERED / RESULTS

Spache Diagnostic Reading Scales
This test measures a variety of reading skills, including word recognition and oral reading.

Word Recognition—ability to read single words in isolation — Mid-fifth grade

Oral Reading—ability to read paragraphs aloud and to answer comprehensive questions — Mid-fifth grade

Gates-McKillop Reading Diagnostic Tests
Anne was given one subtest from this battery of reading subskills.

Recognizing the Visual Form of Sounds—ability to choose from four nonsense words the one pronounced by the examiner (example: *dopery, poding, bobary, podery*) — 3.7 grade level

Slingerland Screening Tests for Identifying Children with Specific Language Disability

Visual Perception Memory—ability to recall word and select it from a group of visually similar words (example: *unbrella, umdrella, uwbrella, umbrella*) — 93 percent correct

Auditory Kinesthetic Memory—ability to recall and write dictated sentences — 80 percent correct

Wide Range Achievement Test

Spelling—ability to write single words in isolation from dictation — 3.5 grade score

Detroit Tests of Learning Aptitude

Verbal Absurdities—ability to listen to a complex sentence and to identify and express the foolish part (example: *The farmer was afraid to let his ducks out in the rain for fear they would get their feet wet, take cold, and die.*) — 13.6 age score

Verbal Opposites—ability to give the word opposite in meaning to a common word (example: *strong-weak, love-hate*) — 9.6 age score

Auditory Attention Span for Unrelated Words—ability to remember and repeat a series of unrelated words — 8.0 age score

Visual Attention Span for Objects—ability to recall sequences of spoken words or pictures of familiar objects — 7.6 age score

DISCUSSION

Recent testing at school indicated that Anne demonstrated a clear pattern of modality strength on the ITPA. She obtained scores at or above age level on tests requiring visual processing, but tests requiring auditory skills were significantly lower. Reading testing indicated that Anne was functioning at high fourth-grade level in both silent and oral paragraph reading, but silent reading of isolated words was at low third-grade level.

Current testing indicates that Anne is having some difficulties in the reading process. She tries to work out new words quickly, frequently guessing from the general configuration rather than sounding out each phoneme. Anne does not monitor what she reads and does not seem to perceive that her pronunciations do not make sense. Examples:

slince for *slice*
postphone for *postpone*
windshide for *windshield*
circumstrances for *circumstances*

Anne reads paragraphs rapidly with frequent omissions of little words and, again, with little monitoring. Comprehension is spotty, partially due to poor monitoring and partly due to inability to understand the question. For example, Anne read *calm* as *clam,* so I pointed it out to her and we discussed its meaning. Later, when I asked, "What kind of trip did the ship have?" she did not know what the question meant. I explained it meant "weather," and she replied, "not very much rainy," indicating her difficulties in verbal expression.

Anne demonstrated some reading problems at the perceptual level. For example, she confused *umbrella* and *unbrella* on the Slingerland Tests and had difficulty matching auditory stimuli with visual forms of nonsense words on the Gates-McKillop. Examples:

gobsill for *gopsel*—auditory discrimination
telgest for *telagest*—auditory discrimination
pedigren for *pettigrade*—auditory discrimination
intichtome for *inchitome*—visual sequencing

Anne's difficulties show up most clearly in spelling, where she is performing at third-grade level. She has poor visual recall of some basic sight words *(thay/they; babby/baby; gril/girl)* and weaknesses in the phonic skills necessary for word analysis. Examples:

kition for *kitchen*—*tion*
inter for *enter*—*e/i* confusion
addvic for *advice*—silent *e*
rezalt for *result*—*u/a* confusion

Deficits in verbal expression are also seen. Anne had difficulty thinking of the exact word needed for verbal opposites, even when she knew the concept. For example, for *laugh* she said *sad* rather than *cry;* for *north* she said *west* rather than *south.* For *same* she said *uneven* and for *after* she said *began.* Her score on this test was at the 9-year-old level. On Verbal Absurdities her score was quite high, indicating good verbal reception and concept development. However, Anne used phrases like "Cars are more faster," which reflect her immature language patterns.

On both rote memory tests of the Detroit, Anne functioned below age level. On the auditory test, some discrimination errors were seen *(nice/night, told/toad).* On the picture recall test, Anne had difficulties naming the objects. She asked me the names of such common pictures as *lamp, tub,* and *horn.* This dysnomia may play a role in her difficulties in verbal expression.

SUMMARY
Areas of Strength
Visual processes, including discrimination, closure, and picture interpretation; fine and gross motor coordination; verbal reception and concept development

Areas of Weakness
Verbal expression, word naming, auditory discrimination and sequencing; spelling

RECOMMENDATIONS
1. Screening for learning-disabled program with tutorial assistance in reading comprehension, spelling, and verbal expression
2. Individual IQ testing at school or clinic
3. Individual or small-group help in speech and language program at school to focus on auditory discrimination and verbal expression

REMEDIAL SUGGESTIONS
Reading
1. Small-group instruction on word-attack skills, focusing on structural analysis. Prefixes, suffixes, root words, little words in big words, and other visual cues should be emphasized.
2. Preparation for reading that includes pronunciation of multisyllabic words in a story. Otherwise, Anne hurries over them and does not learn either their pronunciation or meaning.
3. Instruction using materials geared to teach reading for meaning. Anne needs to develop a more cautious, self-monitoring style. Particular attention is needed to assure she understands the comprehension questions.

Spelling
1. Specific practice on words with short *e, i,* and *u* and soft *g* sounds.
2. Drill on two- and three-syllable words with common endings such as *tion, sion,* and *en* and words that have a silent *e.*
3. Emphasis on visual similarities among such words as *watch, catch,* and *fetch.* Color-coding silent letters will increase their visual impact.

Verbal Expression
1. Develop small-group games that require thinking up specific names of things quickly, such as naming things to eat that begin with the letters *f, p,* and *t.* Other games might include Password (giving one-word clues to guess a given word) and Brainstorming ("How many girls can you name in one minute?").
2. Develop games that require giving verbal cues, such as Twenty Questions, I Spy, and Password.
3. Help Anne develop a format for rehearsing a book report to be given orally or for describing current events.

EDUCATIONAL EVALUATION, SAMPLE 2

Student's Name: Maria
Grade: 9th
Birth Date: 8/26/64
Chronological Age: 13.2
Date of Testing: 9/24/77, 10/1/77

REFERRAL

Maria was referred for an evaluation of her spelling skills by her English teacher. Maria has a history of spelling difficulties, which have been resistive to remediation.

BEHAVIOR DURING TESTING

Maria entered cooperatively into the evaluation procedures. She described at length the various methods that have been used to teach her spelling and her frustration in this area. According to Maria, her spelling is a problem to her in two respects. First, working on it takes time from her other subjects, and second, being unable to spell hinders her ability to express her ideas in writing. In the second testing session, it became clear that Maria is really more concerned about the time she is spending on spelling and her seemingly slow progress.

TEST RESULTS

Wide Range Achievement Test—Spelling (Level I)

Grade Score: 5.5

On this measure of written spelling, Maria obtained a fifth-grade score. She was given the lower level of the test in order to give her more words she could spell correctly before reaching a ceiling and more opportunities to make errors so that they could be analyzed. Error analysis:

Word	Maria	Error Type
grown	growen/gron	visual memory
explain	explian	visual sequencing
edge	eage	visual memory
kitchen	kiten	omitted sound (ch)
surprise	suripre	auditory sequencing
advice	addvice	visual memory
success	sucksess	visual memory

Although most of Maria's errors reflect weaknesses in visual memory, errors in auditory processing are also seen. In her cursive writing, the letters *u* and *v* were formed incorrectly, suggesting weaknesses in kinesthetic memory as well.

Peabody Individual Achievement Test—Spelling

Grade Score: 6.7

The PIAT requires the student to look at four spellings of a word and to identify the correct spelling. Examples include *vegatable, vegetabel, vegetable, vegatabol*. Maria's score was a year higher than her written spelling. Although

it is still a difficult task for her, visual memory for words is somewhat stronger when writing is not required.

Beery-Buktenica Developmental Test of Visual-Motor Integration

Age Score: 14.10

This design-copying test assesses a student's skills in visual-motor integration. Although she obtained an appropriate age score, Maria had to put forth great effort on the task. She measured distances carefully and used dots to outline figures. Design-copying skills often reflect a student's abilities in handwriting. In an informal test of eye-hand skill, Maria was more accurate with her left hand. This may have been because she did the left-handed task very casually, whereas on the right-handed task she became tense with effort.

Malcomesius Specific Language Disability Test

Visual Perception and Recall: no errors
Visual Kinesthetic Recall: no errors

These subtests assess visual memory for words with and without a written response. The student looks at a word for 10 seconds and then either finds it in a list or writes it from memory. Maria made no errors on either task. She used her favorite spelling strategy of isolating a small word in a big word to aid recall. Maria made one interesting error: She wrote a *b* for a *d* in *dandelions* and then corrected herself. Such *b/d* confusions are often seen in children with reading and spelling problems.

Wide Range Achievement Test—Reading (Level II)

Grade Level: 9.1

Although she reportedly has excellent reading skills in content material, Maria's word recognition skills are just a little above grade level. In addition to those words she read incorrectly, she hesitated on many others. Error pattern:

Word	Maria	Error Type
aboard	abroad	visual sequencing
alcove	aclove	visual sequencing
protuberance	protubulance	incorrect syllable
irascible	irriseribable	extra syllables
covetousness	conventuous	incorrect syllable

Maria's errors reflect the same visual sequencing problems and weaknesses in systematic word attack that were seen in her spelling.

Picture Story Language Test

Productivity:
    Total Words: tenth percentile for age and sex
    Words per Sentence: eighty-fifth percentile for age and sex
    Syntax: ninety-ninth percentile for age and sex
    Abstract-Concrete: seventieth percentile for age and sex
When asked to write a paragraph about a picture, Maria

did quite well. Her scores reflect her high-level thinking ability and creative writing skills. The struggle that this task involved—the crossed-out words and rewritten sentences—suggest that fluency in written expression is difficult for Maria. She has much to say and the language skills to say it, but the mechanics of written expression are not fluent.

SUMMARY

Maria is a gifted child in many areas. Her overall intellectual ability, superior verbal skills, and conscientious effort have enabled her to do well in school in all areas except spelling. Spelling brings out her difficulties in visual processing, auditory-visual integration, and kinesthetic memory. It is important to realize that Maria's spelling problems are not an isolated skill deficiency but rather the only observable area in which she has not been able to compensate through superior intellectual ability. As a younger child, Maria may have shown more of the symptoms of specific language disability, but it is probable that even at a young age she was able to compensate for weaknesses in perceptual skills with superior cognitive abilities.

RECOMMENDATIONS

1. If Maria chooses to continue with remedial spelling help, the method should focus on

    a. Improvement of word analysis through syllabication to make her spelling more systematically phonetic.

    b. Programmed spelling techniques designed to teach rules and their applications.

    c. De-emphasis on word-tracing techniques, which require integration of the kinesthetic modality, a relatively weak channel for Maria.

2. It would be equally as valid to simply ignore the spelling problem and to allow Maria to continue to develop her own compensations for weak spelling, such as

    a. Creative writing with no emphasis on spelling, proofread by her parents, and recopied before handing in.

    b. Use of phonetic dictionaries.

Appendix D

A COMPARISON OF READING TESTS

	WRAT	PIAT	Gray Oral	Gilmore Oral	Spache	Durrell Analysis	Gates-McKillop	Woodcock	Gates-MacGinitie	DLRS
Features of the Test										
Standardized	X	X	X	X	X	X	X	X	X	X
Battery					X	X	X	X		
Alternate forms available			X	X	X		X	X	X	X
Student performance timed			X			X			X	X
Grade range	K–12	K–12	1–12	1–8	1–8	1–6	1–6	K–12	1–12	1–9
Skills Assessed										
Oral paragraph reading			X	X	X	X	X			
Silent paragraph reading					X	X		X	X	X
Word reading	X	X			X	X	X	X	X	X
Reading subskills					X	X	X	X	X	
Oral comprehension			X	X	X	X				
Silent comprehension		X			X	X		X	X	X
Listening comprehension					X	X				X

Key
DLRS: Durrell Listening-Reading Series
Durrell Analysis: Durrell Analysis of Reading Difficulty
Gates-MacGinitie: Gates-MacGinitie Silent Reading Tests
Gates-McKillop: Gates-McKillop Reading Diagnostic Tests
Gilmore Oral: Gilmore Oral Reading Test
Gray Oral: Gray Oral Reading Tests
PIAT: Peabody Individual Achievement Test
Spache: Spache Diagnostic Reading Scales
Woodcock: Woodcock Reading Mastery Tests
WRAT: Wide Range Achievement Test

Appendix E

A COMPARISON OF ARTICULATION TESTS

	Compton-Hutton	Fisher-Logemann	Goldman-Fristoe	Templin-Darley
Features of the Test				
Screening function		X		X
Diagnostic function	X	X	X	X
Easy-to-use manual	X	X	X	
Stimuli that easily elicit response	X	X	X	
Easy-to-record response forms	X	X		
Developmental norms for phoneme acquisition		X		X
Provision for geographical variants and foreign dialects		X		
Distinctive-feature analysis	X	X		
Skills Assessed				
Consonants, vowels, diphthongs, clusters	Consonants only	X	Consonants and vowels	X
Phonemes in three syllable positions	Initial, final only	X	X	Initial, final only
Articulation in connected speech		X	X	
Coarticulation factors		X		
Imitation and stimulability			X	X

Key
Compton-Hutton: Compton-Hutton Phonological Assessment
Fisher-Logemann: The Fisher-Logemann Test of Articulation Competence
Goldman-Fristoe: The Goldman-Fristoe Test of Articulation
Templin-Darley: The Templin-Darley Tests of Articulation

Appendix F

10 TESTS FOR ASSESSING BILINGUAL STUDENTS
The major function of testing should be to improve instruction; that is, to diagnose learning difficulties and prescribe educational activities appropriate to individual learning needs. Unfortunately, tests often are used to label and classify students into discrete groupings to meet administrative needs. As a result of the Civil Rights movement in this country, examiners have become more aware of the discriminatory nature of some assessment practices. Testing a student in his or her native language or dialect, accounting for cultural biases in test content, and providing appropriate representation for minority groups in normative samples have all become important considerations in the assessment process.

This is particularly true in the area of language testing. Bilingual testing must be carried out with two types of students: those whose first acquired language is other than English and those for whom the language most often spoken in the home is not English. Competency in both linguistic systems must be evaluated and compared to discriminate between a pervasive language disorder and a deficit in English skills due to bilingual interference.

Several new measures that have been developed reflect the abilities and characteristics of native Spanish speakers more adequately. These Spanish assessment procedures fall into two categories:

• *Translations*. These tests are direct translations of existing English-language tests (often without normative data).

• *Spanish versions*. These assessment tools were independently developed using the Spanish linguistic system (usually include normative data). The accompanying table outlines the primary areas of language assessment and lists the English-Spanish instruments currently available.

English-Spanish Language Assessment Instruments

Area	English Instrument	Spanish Instrument	Translation or Spanish Version
Receptive language	Peabody Picture Vocabulary Test	Peabody Picture Vocabulary Test	Translation
	Test for Auditory Comprehension of Language	Test for Auditory Comprehension of Language	Translation

	Del Rio Language Screening Test
	Subtests:
	  Receptive Vocabulary
	  Story Comprehension
		Del Rio Language Screening Test	Spanish version

	Boehm Test of Basic Concepts	Prueba Boehm de Conceptos Basicos	Translation
Syntax and morphology	Test for Auditory Comprehension of Language	Test for Auditory Comprehension of Language	Translation
	Northwestern Syntax Screening Test	Screening Test of Spanish Grammar	Spanish version
	Developmental Sentence Scoring	Developmental Assessment of Spanish Grammar	Spanish version
Articulation	The Goldman-Fristoe Test of Articulation	Austin Spanish Articulation Test	Spanish version
	The Fisher-Logemann Test of Articulation Competence	Medida Español de Articulacion (MEDA)	Spanish version

Auditory Processing	Del Rio Language Screening Test
	Subtests:
	  Sentence Repetition
	  Oral Commands
		Del Rio Language Screening Test	Spanish version

	Detroit Tests of Learning Aptitude
	Subtests:
	  Oral Commissions
	  Auditory Attention Span for Unrelated Syllables
	  Auditory Attention Span for Related Syllables
		Del Rio Language Screening Test
		
		  Oral Commands
		
		  Sentence Repetition
			Spanish version

	Wepman Auditory Discrimination Test	Spanish Accent Auditory Discrimination Test	Spanish version
Language dominance*	James Language Dominance Test	James Language Dominance Test	Spanish version
	Del Rio Language Screening Test	Del Rio Language Screening Test	Spanish version

*These tests can be used to help determine the student's preferred language by comparison of scores on English and Spanish subtests.

Caution should be exercised in interpreting the scores on these tests. Instruments that are only Spanish translations have limited usefulness because they are based on knowledge of language acquisition and conceptual development in English. These tests should be used to obtain descriptive information on the student's functioning in Spanish or to aid in determining bilingual proficiency by comparison of raw scores in Spanish and English. The absence of normative data from a Spanish-speaking population severely limits the usefulness of these tools.

Independently developed Spanish versions, on the other hand, have added value because they use vocabulary that is more appropriate to Spanish speakers and assess the grammatical concepts crucial to the Spanish linguistic system. Many of these Spanish versions have accounted for dialectal differences of Mexican-American and Puerto Rican students by including appropriate vocabulary for these two groups.

More detailed information on the most widely used Spanish language tests follows.

Peabody Picture Vocabulary Test*

American Guidance Service, Inc. (publication pending; contact publisher for details)
Publishers' Building, Circle Pines, MN 55014

Age Range	2–18 years
Description	Format and content the same as the English version.
Norms	Normative data presently being collected.

*See review of the Peabody Picture Vocabulary Test, p. 152.

Test for Auditory Comprehension of Language*

Elizabeth Carrow
Learning Concepts, 1974
2501 N. Lamar Blvd., Austin, TX 78705

Age Range	3–7 years
Description	Evaluates comprehension of nouns, verbs, adjectives, adverbs, prepositions, and various morphological and syntactic forms through a picture format.
Norms	Not available.

*See review of the Test for Auditory Comprehension of Language, p. 156.

Prueba Boehm de Conceptos Basicos*
The Psychological Corporation
304 E. 45th St., New York, NY 10017

Grade Range	Grades K–2
Description	Measures knowledge of concepts needed for achievement in school through a picture format.
Norms	Not available.

*See review of the Boehm Test of Basic Concepts, p. 159.

Del Rio Language Screening Test
A. Toronto, D. Leverman, C. Hanna, P. Rosenzweig, A. Maldonado
National Educational Laboratory Publishers, Inc., 1975
PO Box 1003, Austin, TX 78767

Age Range	3–7 years
Description	Language screening instrument that assesses English and Spanish skills in the areas of: 1. *Receptive Vocabulary.* Comprehension of single nouns and verbs through picture format 2. *Sentence Repetition (Length).* Memory for utterances gradually increasing in length 3. *Sentence Repetition (Complexity).* Memory for utterances ranging in syntactic complexity 4. *Oral Commands.* Memory for sequential motoric commands presented verbally This test can be used to determine degree of bilingual proficiency or as a measure of functioning in a student's native language.
Norms	Standard deviations and percentile scores at one-year intervals for ages 3 to 7 years are included for each separate subtest. The second to third percentile is the second standard deviation below the mean and should be used as a cutoff point for deviant performance. Standardized for predominantly Spanish-speaking Mexican-American children and for Anglo-American children.

Screening Test of Spanish Grammar*

Allen S. Toronto
Northwestern University Press, 1973
1735 Benson Ave., Evanston, IL 60201

Age Range	3–7 years
Description	Evaluates Spanish receptive and expressive grammar in the same format as the Northwestern Syntax Screening Test, but items were independently selected on the basis of the Spanish syntactic system. Some substitutions in vocabulary may be used for Puerto Rican and Mexican students.
Norms	Standard deviations and percentile scores at one-year intervals for ages 3 to 7 years. A score at or below the second standard deviation from the mean on either subtest (receptive or expressive) indicates probable need for language remediation. Standardization included equal numbers of Mexican-American and Puerto Rican children.

*See review of the Northwestern Syntax Screening Test, p. 162.

Developmental Assessment of Spanish Grammar*

Allen S. Toronto
Entire assessment procedure described in Journal of Speech and Hearing Disorders,
Vol. 41, 1976

Age Range	3–7 years
Description	Systematic grammatical analysis of a conversational language sample. Similar format to Developmental Sentence Scoring but based on knowledge of Spanish langue acquisition. The purpose is to describe a student's grammatical deficiencies and to serve as a model for structuring speech and language therapy.
Norms	Percentile scores at one-year intervals for ages 3 to 7 years. Normative population included equal numbers of Mexican-American and Puerto Rican children.

*See review of the Developmental Sentence Scoring, p. 169.

Austin Spanish Articulation Test
Developed under supervision of Elizabeth Carrow
Learning Concepts
2501 N. Lamar Blvd., Austin, TX 78705

Age Range	3–12 years
Description	Picture articulation test that evaluates single production of consonants, vowels, and blends in initial, medial, and final positions. Phonemes chosen for test on basis of Stockwell and Bowen's Spanish phonetic classification system (1965). Target words are elicited by a sentence-completion format with corresponding pictorial stimuli.
Norms	Not available.

Medida Español de Articulacion (MEDA)
M. H. Mason, B. F. Smith, M. M. Hinshaw
San Ysidro School District, 1974
2250 Smythe Ave., San Ysidro, CA 92173

Age Range	4–9 years
Description	Picture articulation test evaluating production of consonants, vowels, and blends. Provides suggested developmental levels for phonemes.
Norms	Not available.

Spanish Accent Auditory Discrimination Test*

Peter Proul
Merced County Department of Education, 1971
632 W. 13th St., Merced, CA 95340

Age Range	Above 5 years
Description	Assesses auditory discrimination through a "same-different" format using minimal pairs, similar to the Wepman Auditory Discrimination Test. Measures discrimination of consonants and vowels most commonly confused by native Spanish speakers.
Norms	Not available.

*See review of the Wepman Auditory Discrimination Test, p. 92.

James Language Dominance Test

Peter James
Learning Concepts, 1974
2501 N. Lamar Blvd., Austin, TX 78705

Grade Range	Grades K–1
Description	Set of 40 pictorial stimuli designed to yield a measure of a student's language dominance or bilingualism in both reception and expression. Results in a language classification as "Spanish dominant," "bilingual with Spanish as home language," "English dominant but bilingual in comprehension," or "English dominant."
Norms	Raw scores on English and Spanish sections determine language classification. Standardized on a mixture of language backgrounds—Mexican-American, Anglo, and Black American.

Appendix G

A COMPARISON OF GROSS MOTOR TESTS

	Survey	Bruininks-Oseretsky	Frostig	SCSIT
Features of the Test				
Age scores		X	X	
Percentiles		X		
Standard scores		X	X	X
Individual administration	X	X	X	X
Group administration		X	X	
Short form for screening		X		
Skills Assessed				
Gross motor				
Running		X	X	
Balance	X	X	X	X
Bilateral coordination		X		X
Strength	X	X	X	
Upper-limb coordination	X	X		
Crossing the midline	X		X	X
Flexibility			X	
Fine motor				
Response speed		X		
Cutting		X		
Copying	X	X		X
Eye-hand speed		X	X	X
Motor sequencing	X		X	X
Aiming accuracy			X	

Key

Bruininks-Oseretsky: Bruininks-Oseretsky Test of Motor Proficiency
Frostig: Frostig Movement Skills Test Battery (Experimental Edition)
SCSIT: Southern California Sensory Integration Tests
Survey: Purdue Perceptual-Motor Survey

Appendix H

**A LIST OF TESTS APPROPRIATE FOR
PRESCHOOL CHILDREN**

PART I: SKILL AREA TESTS
Chapter Two: Perception and Memory Tests
Marianne Frostig Developmental Test of Visual Perception
Motor-Free Visual Perception Test
Beery-Buktenica Developmental Test of Visual-Motor
   Integration
Chapter Three: Speech and Language Tests
The Fisher-Logemann Test of Articulation Competence
The Goldman-Fristoe Test of Articulation
The Templin-Darley Tests of Articulation
Compton-Hutton Phonological Assessment
Illinois Test of Psycholinguistic Abilities
Peabody Picture Vocabulary Test
Assessment of Children's Language Comprehension
Test for Auditory Comprehension of Language
Boehm Test of Basic Concepts
Northwestern Syntax Screening Test
Sequenced Inventory of Communication Development
Developmental Sentence Scoring
Language Sampling, Analysis, and Training
Chapter Four: Gross Motor Tests
Bruininks-Oseretsky Test of Motor Proficiency
Southern California Sensory Integration Tests

**PART III: GENERAL INTELLIGENCE TESTS AND
DEVELOPMENTAL SCALES**
Wechsler Preschool and Primary Scale of Intelligence
Stanford-Binet Intelligence Scale
Slosson Intelligence Test for Children and Adults
Leiter International Performance Scale and the Arthur
   Adaptation
Goodenough-Harris Drawing Test

Glossary of Testing Terms

Words set in italics are defined elsewhere in the glossary. The glossary contains six sections: General Terms, Diagnostic Categories, Academic Terms, Visual and Visual-Perceptual-Motor Processing, Oral Language and Auditory Processing, and Fine and Gross Motor Skills.

GENERAL TERMS

AGE NORM (Age score). A score indicating average performance for students classified according to *chronological age*. Generally expressed in terms of *central tendency, standard score, percentile rank,* or *stanine.* In an *achievement test,* the age equivalent for grades.

AGE SCORE. See *age norm.*

ALTERNATE FORMS. See *equivalent forms.*

BASAL LEVEL. The level at which all items of a test are passed, just preceding the level where the first failure occurs. All items below the basal point are assumed correct. Contrast with *ceiling level.*

BATTERY. A group of carefully selected tests administered to a student, the results of which are of value individually, in combination, and/or totally.

CEILING LEVEL. The maximal level of a test. The highest item of a sequence in which a certain number of items has been failed. All items above the ceiling item are assumed incorrect. Contrast with *basal level.*

CENTRAL TENDENCY. A statistical measure used to describe typical values in a set or distribution of scores. The most common such measures used in educational testing are the *mean, median,* and *mode.*

CHRONOLOGICAL AGE (CA). Age from birth expressed in years and months; for example, 7 years, 6 months.

CORRELATION COEFFICIENT (r). A statistical index that measures the degree of relationship between any two variables (for example, sets of scores). It ranges in value from −1.00 (a perfect negative correlation) to +1.00 (a perfect positive correlation). An example is the high positive correlation between vocabulary and *intelligence.*

DERIVED SCORE. Any score that has been converted from a qualitative or quantitative unit on one scale into the units of another scale, thereby allowing a direct comparison of the student's performance on different tests or a comparison of his or her performance to the performance of others. Examples of derived scores are *percentile rank, age norm,* and *standard score.*

DIAGNOSTIC TESTING. An intensive, in-depth evaluation process using formal, *standardized tests* and *informal tests* designed to determine the nature and severity of specific learning problems. Generally provided by an interdisciplinary team of specialists.

EQUIVALENT FORMS (Alternate forms). Two comparable or parallel forms of a test that measure the same skill or trait to the same degree and are standardized on the same population. Useful for *pretest* and *posttest* measurement.

EXTRAPOLATION. A process of estimating the scores of a test beyond the range of available data.

FREQUENCY DISTRIBUTION. A tabulation of scores from low to high that indicates the number of individuals who obtain each score.

INTELLIGENCE. A global construct or entity composed of several functions. The abilities constituting intelligence are such factors as cognitive skills or processes, abstract verbal and numerical aptitudes, comprehension and memory functions, and the abilities to learn, reason, and solve problems.

INTELLIGENCE QUOTIENT (IQ). An index of mental ability, expressing a student's performance on an intelligence test. If a student's *mental age* and *chronological age* are equal, his or her IQ is 100 (which represents average performance). Thus IQ is a *standard score* with a *mean* fixed statistically at 100 and the *standard deviation* fixed according to the test author's discretion.

DEVIATION IQ. Indicates the amount by which a student's performance on an IQ test is above or below the average performance of students of his or her age group.

RATIO IQ. A *derived score* that expresses the student's *mental age* in relation to *chronological age,* according to the formula:

$$IQ = \frac{MA}{CA} \times 100$$

INTERPOLATION. A process of estimating an intermediate value between two known points. In the example, a *raw score* value of 55, by interpolation, would be assigned a *grade norm* of 4.9.

Raw Score	Grade Norm
52	4.5
54	4.8
56	5.0
58	5.2

MEAN (M). The sum of a set of scores divided by the number of scores. The value of the mean can be strongly influenced by a few extreme scores.

MEDIAN (MD). The middle point in a set of ranked scores. The value that has the same number of scores above it and below it in the distribution. For example, the median in the following set of scores is 10: 17, 13, 11, 10, 9, 9, 8. In a distribution of scores such as 9, 8, 6, 5, the median, by *interpolation,* would be 7.

MENTAL AGE (MA). A measure of a child's level of mental development, based on performance on a test of mental ability and determined by the level of difficulty of the test items passed. If a child, no matter what age, can pass only those items passed by the average 8-year-old, the child will be assigned a mental-age score of 8.

MODE (MO). The score that occurs most frequently in a distribution. In the distribution 18, 14, 12, 11, 10, 10, 7, the mode is 10. Its value is entirely independent of extreme scores.

NONVERBAL TEST. See *performance test.*

PERCENTILE RANK. A type of converted score that expresses a student's score relative to his or her group in percentile points. Indicates the percentage of students tested who made scores equal to or lower than the specified score. If a score of 82 has a percentile rank of 65, this means that 65 percent of the students who took the test had a score of 82 or lower than 82.

PERFORMANCE TEST (Nonverbal test). Designed to evaluate the general intelligence or specialized aptitudes of students. Consisting primarily of motor test items or perceptual items in which verbal abilities play a minimal role. Contrast with *verbal test.*

PROJECTIVE TECHNIQUE. A test situation in which the student responds to ambiguous stimulus materials, such as pictures, inkblots, or incomplete sentences, thereby projecting personality characteristics.

PROTOCOL. The original record of the test results.

RANK ORDERING. The arrangement of scores from highest to lowest.

RAW SCORE. The basic score initially obtained by scoring a test according to the directions in the manual. Generally equal to the number of right answers—but may be the number of incorrect responses, the time required for a task, or some other criterion.

RELIABILITY. The degree to which a student would obtain the same score if the test were readministered (assuming no further learning, practice effects, or other change). Stability or consistency of scores.

ALTERNATE-FORM RELIABILITY. A method of estimating test reliability by the *correlation coefficient* between two equivalent or comparable forms of the test. The student is tested with one form on the first occasion and with another, parallel form on the second.

INTERSCORER RELIABILITY. A method that requires a sample of tests to be scored independently by two examiners. The two scores are correlated, and the resulting *correlation coefficient* is an estimate of interscorer reliability.

SPLIT-HALF RELIABILITY. A method for determining the reliability coefficient for a test by obtaining the *correlation coefficient* for two halves of the same test. Usually items are split odd-even to provide the two comparable halves.

TEST-RETEST RELIABILITY. A method of establishing reliability that involves readministering the same test to the same sample of students and then determining the degree of correlation between the two sets of test scores.

SCATTER. The extent of variation among a student's scores on all subtests of a single test or on several different tests. May indicate whether all aspects of a student's ability are developing evenly or whether the student has an unusual facility or handicap in a certain area. Wide discrepancies in a student's profile of abilities do not necessarily suggest underlying pathology.

STANDARD DEVIATION (SD). The most commonly used measure of variation. A statistic used to express the extent of the distribution's deviations from the *mean.* In the normal distribution, about 68 percent of the scores lie within one SD above or below the mean.

STANDARD ERROR OF MEASUREMENT (SE_M, Standard error, Test error). A statistic that indicates how chance errors may cause variation in the scores that a given student might obtain if he or she were to take the same test an infinite number of times. If the SE_M is 3, the chances are 2 to 1 that any given student's score will fall within a range of three points of the obtained score. For example, if Jerry gets a score of 160, his "true" score lies somewhere between 157 and 163.

STANDARDIZATION. In test construction, refers to the process of trying the test out on a group of students to determine uniform or standard scoring procedures and methods of interpretation.

STANDARDIZATION SAMPLE. Refers to the section of the reference population that is chosen for use in establishing test norms. Should be representative of the reference population in main characteristics, such as sex, race, age, grade, geographical location, socioeconomic status, and other factors.

STANDARDIZED TEST. Contains empirically selected materials, with specific directions for administration, scoring, and interpretation. Provides data on *validity* and *reliability,* and has adequately derived norms.

STANDARD SCORE. *Derived score* that transforms a *raw score* in such a manner that it has the same *mean* and the same *standard deviation.* The standard score scale is an equal-interval scale; that is, a difference of, say, five points has the same meaning throughout the scale.

STANINE. A weighted scale divided into nine equal units that represent nine levels of performance on any particular test. The stanine is a *standard score.* Thus the intervals between different points on the scale (for example, the difference between 8 and 5 and between 4 and 1 on the scale) are equal in terms of the number of correct test responses they represent. The *mean* is at stanine 5 in the example.

Stanine	1	2	3	4	5	6	7	8	9
Percent in									
Stanine	4	7	12	17	20	17	12	7	4

TEST ERROR. See *standard error of measurement*.

VALIDITY. The extent to which a test measures what it is designed to measure. A test valid for one use may have negligible validity for another.

CONCURRENT VALIDITY. How well scores on a test correspond to performance on some criterion data available at the time of testing. For example, comparing end-of-course achievement test scores with school grades.

CONSTRUCT VALIDITY. Reports the extent to which the test measures a theoretical construct or trait. *Intelligence,* verbal fluency, and mechanical comprehension represent theoretical constructs.

CONTENT VALIDITY. How well the content of the test samples the behavior domain or subject matter about which conclusions are to be made. This concept is used principally with *achievement tests*.

FACE VALIDITY. The idea that the test appears as if it should be valid. That is, a test is assumed to be valid simply by definition. For example, a scale is a valid instrument of weight, by definition of what constitutes weight.

PREDICTIVE VALIDITY. How effectively predictions made from the test are substantiated by data obtained at a later time. An example is the correlation of intelligence test scores with school grades.

VERBAL TEST. Designed to evaluate the general *intelligence* or specialized aptitudes of students. Consists primarily of items requiring the use of language. Contrast with *performance test*.

DIAGNOSTIC CATEGORIES

A-, AN-. A prefix equivalent to un- or in- that signifies absence, lack, -less, not. Contrast with *dys-*.

ACALCULIA. See *dyscalculia*.

AGNOSIA. Lost or impaired ability to identify familiar objects or events in the absence of a defective sense organ.

AUDITORY AGNOSIA. Impairment of the ability to recognize sounds or sound combinations (for example, nonrecognition of the ring of an alarm clock).

TACTILE AGNOSIA (Astereognosis). Impaired ability to recognize objects through the sense of touch.

VISUAL AGNOSIA. Inability to recognize objects, persons, or places by sight.

AGRAPHIA. See *dysgraphia*.

ALEXIA. See *dyslexia*.

APHASIA. See *dysphasia*.

APRAXIA. See *dyspraxia*.

BRAIN DAMAGE. Any structural damage or insult to the brain, whether by accident or disease.

DYS-. In medicine, a prefix denoting difficult or painful, faulty or impaired, abnormal or morbid.

DYSCALCULIA. Disturbed or impaired ability to calculate, to manipulate number symbols, or to perform simple arithmetic.

DYSFUNCTION. Abnormal or impaired behavior of any organ.

DYSGRAPHIA. A type of *dyspraxia* affecting the visual-motor system. Results in the inability to remember the kinesthetic patterns that go into writing. That is, an inability to relate the mental image of words or symbols to the motor movements necessary for writing them.

DYSLEXIA. Partial inability to read. Generally thought to be associated with neurological dysfunction.

DYSNOMIA (Word-finding difficulty). Weakness in the ability to name objects or to recall and retrieve words. Generally the individual knows the word, recognizes it when spoken, but cannot retrieve it at will.

DYSPRAXIA. Impairment of the ability to recall and perform purposeful, skilled movements. Contrast with *praxis*.

MOTOR DYSPRAXIA. Weakness in the ability to plan and execute unfamiliar motor tasks, even though coordination may be adequate for familiar tasks.

ORAL DYSPRAXIA. Severe impairment in the ability to perform voluntary movements involving the speech musculature, even though automatic movements of the same musculature appear to be intact.

MINIMAL BRAIN DAMAGE. See *minimal brain dysfunction*.

MINIMAL BRAIN DYSFUNCTION (Minimal brain damage, Minimal cerebral dysfunction). A mild neurological abnormality that causes learning difficulties in the child with near-average or even above-average intellectual potential. Common behavioral characteristics may include hyperactivity, distractibility, impulsivity, and poor motor functioning.

MINIMAL CEREBRAL DYSFUNCTION. See *minimal brain dysfunction*.

NEUROSIS. Behavior disturbance characterized by emotional conflict and anxiety but not a loss of contact with reality. Represents the milder forms of mental illness. Contrast with *psychosis*.

PERSEVERATION. The tendency to continue a specific act of behavior after it is no longer appropriate (for example, repeating a word over and over again, continuing a movement such as letter writing, prolonging laughter). Related to difficulty in shifting from one activity to another.

PSYCHOSIS. The class of the more severe mental disorders, in which there is a departure from normal patterns of thinking, feeling, or acting. Commonly characterized by loss of contact with reality, distortion of perception, disruptions of cognitive and emotional processes, and abnormal mental content, including hallucinations and delusions. Contrast with *neurosis*.

SPECIFIC LANGUAGE DISABILITY (SLD). Refers to those who have great difficulty learning to read and spell but who are otherwise intelligent. Generally applies to any language deficit impeding learning (oral, visual, or auditory). Sometimes used interchangeably with *dyslexia*.

WORD-FINDING DIFFICULTY. See *dysnomia*.

ACADEMIC TERMS

ACHIEVEMENT TEST. An objective test that measures how much a student has learned or knows about a specific subject.

ACTUAL GRADE PLACEMENT. The student's grade and month-in-grade at the date of testing. A tenth of a grade-placement unit is added for every month of school finished. For example, a first-grade student tested in late October has an actual grade placement of 1.2.

CHANNEL. The sensorimotor route through which language flows (for example, visual-motor, visual-vocal, auditory-motor). Theoretically, many combinations are possible.

CLOZE FORMAT. A procedure used in teaching and testing reading comprehension in which certain words are deleted from the text, leaving blank spaces. Measurement is made by rating the number of blanks that the student can accurately fill.

CRITERION-REFERENCED TEST (CR). Objective test yielding a *ratio score* and designed to assess a student's development of certain skills in terms of absolute levels of mastery. CR devices are made up of a specified set of sequential skills (criterion behaviors) arranged in a hierarchical order. These tests provide answers to specific questions such as, "Can Billy identify the topic sentence in at least three out of four paragraphs?" Contrast with *norm-referenced test*.

DECODING. In reading, refers to the ability to translate the printed symbol into language. Entails visual perception and discrimination, preceded by auditory perception and discrimination.

DISCRIMINATION. The process of detecting differences among stimuli.

AUDITORY DISCRIMINATION. Ability to determine whether two acoustic stimuli (either speech sounds or nonspeech sounds) are the same or different.

TACTILE DISCRIMINATION. Central response to stimuli presented only to the tactile sense. The ability to recognize differences and similarities in shape and pattern by touch alone.

VISUAL DISCRIMINATION. Ability to distinguish between different objects, forms, and letter symbols presented visually.

ENCODING. In writing, refers to the ability to translate verbal language into graphic symbols. The act of

committing one's thoughts to the written form encompasses the ideational use of language, as well as visual, auditory, and visual-motor abilities.

GESTALT PSYCHOLOGY. A German school of psychology that places emphasis on a whole perceptual configuration and the interrelations of its component parts.

GRADE EQUIVALENT. See *grade norm*.

GRADE NORM (Grade equivalent, Grade score). The average test score obtained by students classified at a given grade placement. For example, a grade score of 3.4 indicates that the student performed as well on the test as an average student who has been in the third grade for four months.

GRADE SCORE. See *grade norm*.

INFORMAL TEST. Nonstandardized test, often teacher-constructed, useful in analyzing a student's learning style and thinking processes. Indicates what the student does and how he or she does it.

MODALITY. A pathway for acquiring sensory information. Auditory, visual, tactile, and kinesthetic are the most common modalities through which learning occurs.

MULTISENSORY APPROACH. Generally refers to teaching methods that rely simultaneously on several sensory modalities—visual, auditory, kinesthetic, and tactile.

NORM-REFERENCED TEST. Objective test standardized on groups of individuals. Compares a student's performance to the performance of other students who are the same *chronological age*. Using norm-referenced tests, for example, Jill's reading can be assigned a grade-level score of 3.2 on a standardized reading test. In other words, the test tells how Jill is doing compared with other students. Contrast with *criterion-referenced test*.

ORTON-GILLINGHAM TECHNIQUE. A method of teaching reading that is highly structured and phonetically oriented and that stresses a *multisensory approach* (visual, auditory, and kinesthetic).

PRETEST. A preliminary test used to establish a baseline of performance in a specified area.

POSTTEST. A terminal evaluation of the student's status on completion of specific instruction or training. *Pretests* and posttests make it easier to measure progress in the course of remedial work.

RATE OF READING. A speed-of-reading score comparing the time required for a student to read a selection with standard rates obtained from cases in the standardization population. Generally expressed as the number of words read per minute.

RATIO SCORE. Refers to *criterion-referenced* testing, where the score can be expressed as a ratio. The total number of skills mastered divided by the total number of skills required:

$$\frac{\text{Number of skills mastered}}{\text{Number of skills required}} = \text{Score in percent}$$

For example, if Mary has learned 180 words out of a total of 200 words on a reading test, her score would be 180/200, or 90 percent.

SCREENING. A fast, efficient measurement for a large number of students. The purpose of screening is to identify students from the general population who need further diagnostic testing because of suspected deviance in a specific area.

SEQUENCING. A distinctive, fairly automatic function of the mind related to the serial ordering of stimuli. For example, remembering a series of movements within a skill, recalling the pattern of letters in a spelling word, or remembering the sequence of sounds within a word.

STRUCTURAL ANALYSIS. Breaking a word into its component parts, such as word families, rhyming aspects, roots, prefixes, and suffixes.

TACHISTOSCOPE. An apparatus that exposes visual material for brief, controllable periods of time. Practice with this device is designed to improve rate and span of the visual perception of words and phrases.

WORD ANALYSIS. A reading term that refers to the analysis of an unlearned word in terms of known elements for the purpose of identification.

WORD RECOGNITION. Identification of a word presented in isolation, either through the use of form configuration or skill in phonetic analysis. Indicates accurate decoding ability, but does not tap knowledge of word meaning.

VISUAL AND VISUAL-PERCEPTUAL MOTOR PROCESSING

COPY. Direct reproduction of a form with a pencil. Involves the ability to look at a figure and reproduce it without any additional clues. Contrast with *imitation*.

FAR-POINT COPYING. Copying with constant access to a model placed at a distance (for example, copying from a blackboard). Requires visual perception in association with a kinesthetic-motor response. Contrast with *near-point copying*.

IMITATION. A process used in learning copying skills by demonstration. First the student watches the examiner demonstrate how to draw the form; then the student imitates the examiner's movements. Contrast with *copy*.

NEAR-POINT COPYING. Copying with constant access to a model placed close at hand (for example, copying from a textbook). Requires visual perception in association with a kinesthetic-motor response. Usually an easier task than *far-point copying*. Contrast with *far-point copying*.

VISUAL-MOTOR INTEGRATION. The ability to associate visual stimuli with motor responses. Coordinating vision with the movements of the body or parts of the body.

VISUAL PERCEPTION. Ability to identify, organize, and understand sensory stimuli received through the eye.

ORAL LANGUAGE AND AUDITORY PROCESSING

AUDITORY PERCEPTION. Ability to identify, organize, and understand external auditory stimuli, such as environmental sounds, music, or speech.

DISTINCTIVE FEATURE. A distinguishing acoustic or articulatory feature of a *phoneme,* such as voicing, stop, nasality, or place of articulation.

DYSPHASIA. Impairment of the ability to acquire symbols for a language system. The partial or complete loss of ability to comprehend spoken words (receptive dysphasia) or to speak words (expressive dysphasia). Associated with injury, disease, or abnormality of the speech centers.

ECHOLALIA. The parrotlike, senseless repetition of sounds, words, phrases, or sentences spoken by another person, without understanding the meaning of the language.

EXPRESSIVE LANGUAGE. The ability to produce language for communication purposes. Speaking and writing are the expressive language skills.

GRAMMAR. The study of word classes, their inflections, and their functions and relationship in sentences. A part of *syntax.*

HEARING VOCABULARY. Recognition vocabulary, generally measured through a picture vocabulary test. More heavily weighted with *receptive language* than with *expressive language*. Provides a rough estimate of verbal *intelligence*.

LANGUAGE. A conventionalized system of audible and visible signs (symbols) by which thoughts are conveyed.

LINGUISTICS. The scientific study of the form and function of *language*.

MORPHEME. The smallest unit of speech that is meaningful. For example, *farm,* the *er* in *farmer,* and the *ing* in *farming* are all morphemes.

MORPHOLOGY. The aspect of *linguistics* that deals with the study of and the rules for the formation of words in any particular language (for example, the formation of plurals, possessives, and compounds).

PHONEME. The smallest unit of sound in a language. Each phoneme is made up of a set of *distinctive features*. Each individual letter sound or blend, such as /p/ or /ch/, are phonemes.

PHONOLOGY. The study of the linguistic system of speech sounds in any language.

PSYCHOLINGUISTICS. The study of the psychological and linguistic aspects of the language process.

RECEPTIVE LANGUAGE. The ability to comprehend the spoken or written word. Listening and reading are the receptive language skills.

SEMANTICS. The study of meaning in language, including the relationship among language, thought, and behavior.

SYNTAX. The study and science of the grammar system of a language. The linguistic rules of word order and the function of words in a sentence (sentence structure).

FINE AND GROSS MOTOR SKILLS

BILATERAL INTEGRATION. Integration of the sensorimotor function of the two sides of the body, including such factors as the ability to smoothly coordinate the two hands (or two legs) in bilateral (two-sided) motor activities. The tendency to cross the midline of the body, and the ability to distinguish the right side of the body from the left.

BODY IMAGE. The concept and awareness of one's own body. Includes the impressions one receives from internal data as well as feedback resulting from contact with others.

FINE MOTOR SKILL. The development of small muscle skills (for example, the use of eye-hand coordination in cutting, writing, tying shoes, and other tasks).

GROSS MOTOR SKILL. The development of large muscle skills (for example, walking, running, climbing, throwing, and other activities).

KINESTHESIA. Movement sense. Perception of position, direction, and speed of movement of the body or part of the body. Principal receptors are in the joints, ligaments, and inner ear.

MOTOR PLANNING. See *praxis*.

POSTURAL MECHANISMS. Motor responses, generally automatic, that allow an individual to maintain a desired position in relation to gravity and the earth's surface. An example is the shifting of body weight necessary to maintain sitting balance on a moving object.

PRAXIS (Motor planning). The ability to plan and to execute unfamiliar skilled motor tasks.

SENSORY INTEGRATION. The organization of incoming sensory information by the brain. Also a specific type of perceptual-motor training.

TACTILE PERCEPTION. The ability to recognize and give meaning to sensory stimuli that are received through the sense of touch.

VESTIBULAR SYSTEM. Detects sensations related to equilibrium and position. Sensitive to both movement (linear, angular, and rotational, acceleration and deceleration) and position of the head in relation to the pull of gravity.

References

Anastasiow, Nicholas J., *et al.* 1973. *Educational Psychology: A Contemporary View.* Del Mar, Calif.: CRM Books.

Ayres, A. Jean. 1973. *Sensory Integration and Learning Disorders.* 2nd ed. Los Angeles: Western Psychological Services.

Bannatyne, Alex. 1968. Diagnosing Learning Disabilities and Writing Remedial Prescriptions. *Journal of Learning Disabilities* vol. 1.

————. 1974. Diagnosis: A Note on the Recategorization of the WISC Scaled Scores. *Journal of Learning Disabilities* vol. 7.

Bateman, Barbara. 1963. *Reading and Psycholinguistic Processes of Partially Sighted Children.* Council for Exceptional Children Monograph Series A, no. 5.

Bayley, Nancy. 1969. *Bayley Scales of Infant Development.* New York: The Psychological Corporation.

Betts, Emmett A. 1946. *Foundations of Reading Instruction.* New York: Atlantic.

Blank, Marion. 1968. Cognitive Processes in Auditory Discrimination in Normal and Retarded Readers. *Child Development* vol. 39.

Bliesmer, Emery P. 1962. Evaluating Progress in Remedial Reading Programs. *The Reading Teacher* vol. 15.

Bloom, Lois. 1970. *Language Development: Form and Function in Emerging Grammars.* Cambridge, Mass.: MIT Press.

Brown, Roger. 1973. *A First Language: The Early Stages.* Cambridge, Mass.: Harvard University Press.

Chaney, C. M., and Kephart, Newell C. 1968. *Motoric Aids to Perceptual Training.* Columbus, Ohio: Charles E. Merrill.

Chomsky, Noam. 1957. *Syntactic Structures.* The Hague: Mouton.

————. 1965. *Aspects of the Theory of Syntax.* Cambridge, Mass.: MIT Press.

Cratty, Bryant J. 1970. *Perceptual and Motor Development in Infants and Children.* New York: Macmillan.

Curr, W., and Gorlay, N. 1960. The Effects of Practice and Performance in Scholastic Tests. *British Journal of Educational Psychology* vol. 30.

de Hirsch, Katrina; Jansky, Jeanette J.; and Langford, William S. 1966. *Predicting Reading Failure.* New York: Harper & Row.

Dembinski, Raymond J., and Mauser, August J. 1977. What Parents of the Learning Disabled Really Want from Professionals. *Journal of Learning Disabilities* vol. 10.

Elkins, J. 1972. Some Psycholinguistic Aspects of the Differential Diagnosis of Reading Disability in Grades I and II. Ph.D. dissertation, University of Queensland.

Farr, Roger. 1969. *Reading: What Can Be Measured?* Newark, Delaware: International Reading Association Research Fund.

Ferrier, E. E. 1966. An Investigation of the ITPA Performance of Children with Functional Defects of Articulation. *Exceptional Children* vol. 32.

Fillmore, Charles. 1968. The Case for Case. In *Universals in Linguistic Theory,* edited by Emmon Bach and Robert T. Harms. New York: Holt, Rinehart and Winston.

Foster, S. 1963. Language Skills for Children with Persistent Articulation Disorders. Ph.D. dissertation, Texas Women's University.

Gesell, Arnold, and Amatruda, Catherine S. 1949. *Gesell Developmental Schedules.* New York: The Psychological Corporation.

Gillingham, Anna, and Stillman, Bessie W. 1960. *Remedial Training for Children with Specific Language Disability in Reading, Spelling, and Penmanship.* 6th ed. Cambridge, Mass.: Educators Publishing Service.

————. 1965. *Remedial Training for Children with Specific Language Disability in Reading, Spelling, and Penmanship.* 7th ed. Cambridge, Mass.: Educators Publishing Service.

Hallahan, Daniel P., and Cruickshank, William M. 1973. *Psychoeducational Foundations of Learning Disabilities.* Englewood Cliffs, N.J.: Prentice-Hall.

Hammill, Donald D., and Weiderholt, J. L. 1972. Review of the Frostig Visual Perception Test and the Related Training Program. In *The First Review of Special Education* vol. 1, edited by L. Mann and D. Sabatino. Philadelphia: JSE Press, Grune & Stratton.

Harris, Dale B. 1963. *Children's Drawings as Measures of Intellectual Maturity.* New York: Harcourt Brace Jovanovich.

Hejna, R. 1959. *Hejna Developmental Articulation Test.* Ann Arbor, Mich.: Speech Materials.

Johnson, Wendell; Darley, Frederic L.; and Spriestersbach, D. C. 1963. *Diagnostic Methods in Speech Pathology.* New York: Harper & Row.

Karlin, Robert, and Jolly, Hayden. 1965. The Use of Alternate Forms of Standardized Reading Tests. *The Reading Teacher* vol. 19.

Kaufman, Nadeen L., and Kaufman, Alan S. 1974. Comparison of Normal and Minimally Brain-Dysfunctioned Children on the McCarthy Scales of Children's Abilities. *Journal of Clinical Psychology* vol. 30.

————. 1977. *Clinical Evaluation of Young Children with the McCarthy Scales.* New York: Grune & Stratton.

Keogh, Barbara, and Becker, Laurence D. 1973. Early

Detection of Learning Problems: Questions, Cautions and Guidelines. *Exceptional Children* vol. 40.

Kephart, Newell C. 1960. *The Slow Learner in the Classroom*. Columbus, Ohio: Charles E. Merrill.

Kirk, Samuel A., and Kirk, Winifred D. 1971. *Psycholinguistic Learning Disabilities*. Urbana: University of Illinois Press.

————. 1978. Uses and Abuses of the ITPA. *Journal of Speech and Hearing Disorders* vol. 43.

Koppitz, Elizabeth M. 1964. *The Bender-Gestalt Test for Young Children* vol. 1. New York: Grune & Stratton.

————. 1975. *The Bender-Gestalt Test for Young Children* vol. 2. New York: Grune & Stratton.

Lee, Laura, and Canter, Susan M. 1971. Developmental Sentence Scoring: A Clinical Procedure for Estimating Syntactic Development in Children's Spontaneous Speech. *Journal of Speech and Hearing Disorders* vol. 36.

Lee, Laura, and Koenigsknecht, Roy A. 1974. *Developmental Sentence Analysis*. Evanston, Ill.: Northwestern University Press.

Lindquist, E. F., and Hieronymus, A. N. 1956. *Iowa Test of Basic Skills*. Boston: Houghton Mifflin.

Lorge-Thorndike Teacher's Word Book of 30,000 Words. 1944. New York: Teacher's College of Columbia University.

McCarthy, Joseph M. 1965. Patterns of Psycholinguistic Development of Mongoloid and Non-mongoloid Severely Retarded Children. Ph.D. dissertation, University of Illinois.

Meeker, M. 1969. *The Structure of Intellect*. Columbus, Ohio: Charles E. Merrill.

Menyuk, Paula. 1969. *Sentences Children Use*. Cambridge, Mass.: MIT Press.

Morehead, Donald, and Ingram, David. 1973. The Development of Basic Syntax in Normal and Linguistically Deviant Children. *Journal of Speech and Hearing Research* vol. 16.

Moriarity, Alice E. 1972. Denver Developmental Screening Test. In *Buros' Seventh Mental Measurements Yearbook*, edited by Oscar K. Buros. Highland Park, N.J.: Gryphon Press.

Morrissey, Patricia. 1979. Pre-Academic Predictors of Success in a Multisensory Reading Program. Ed.D. dissertation, University of San Francisco.

Myklebust, Helmer R. 1973. *Development and Disorders of Written Language, Volume Two: Studies of Normal and Exceptional Children*. New York: Grune & Stratton.

Orton, Samuel T. 1937. *Reading, Writing and Speech Problems in Children*. New York: Norton.

Osgood, Charles E. 1957. A Behavioristic Analysis. In *Contemporary Approaches to Cognition*. Cambridge, Mass.: Harvard University Press.

Osgood, Charles E., and Sebeok, T. A., eds. 1965. *Psycholinguistics*. Bloomington: Indiana University Press.

Paraskevopoulos, John, and Kirk, Samuel. 1969. *The Development and Psychometric Characteristics of the Revised Illinois Test of Psycholinguistic Abilities*. Urbana: University of Illinois Press.

Pascal, G. R., and Suttrell, B. J. 1964. *The Bender-Gestalt Test: Quantification and Validity for Adults*. New York: Grune & Stratton.

Pintner, Rudolf; Cunningham, Bess V.; and Durost, Walter N. 1966. *Pintner-Cunningham Primary Test*. New York: Harcourt Brace Jovanovich.

Ratusnik, Daniel L., and Koenigsknecht, Roy A. 1975. Internal Consistency of the Northwestern Syntax Screening Test. *Journal of Speech and Hearing Disorders* vol. 40.

Rockowitz, Ruth J., and Davidson, Phillip W. 1979. Discussing Diagnostic Findings with Parents. *Journal of Learning Disabilities* vol. 12.

Salvia, John, and Ysseldyke, James E. 1978. *Assessment in Special and Remedial Education*. Boston: Houghton Mifflin.

Salvia, John; Ysseldyke, James E.; and Lee, M. 1975. 1972 Revision of the Stanford-Binet Intelligence Scale: A Farewell to the Mental Age. *Psychology in the Schools* vol. 76.

Sattler, J. M. 1965. Analysis of Functions of the 1960 Stanford-Binet Intelligence Scale, Form L–M. *Journal of Clinical Psychology* vol. 21.

Satz, Paul, and Friel, Janette. 1974. Some Predictive Antecedents of Specific Reading Disability: A Preliminary Two Year Follow-up. *Journal of Learning Disabilities* vol. 7.

Satz, Paul; Friel, Janette; and Goebel, Ron A. 1975. Some Predictive Antecedents of Specific Reading Disability: A Three Year Follow-Up. *Bulletin of the Orton Society* vol. 25.

Sequential Tests of Basic Skills. 1958. Palo Alto, Calif.: Educational Testing Service.

Shaftel, F., and Shaftel, G. 1970. *People in Action: Role-Playing and Discussion Photographs for Elementary Social Studies*. New York: Holt, Rinehart and Winston.

Smith, Judith M.; Smith, Donald E.; and Brink, James R. 1977. *A Technology of Reading and Writing* vol. 2. New York: Academic Press.

Stockwell, R. P., and Bowen, J. D. 1965. *The Sounds of English and Spanish*. Chicago: University of Chicago Press.

Tiegs, E. W., and Clark, W. W. 1970. *California Achievement Tests*. New York: CTB/McGraw-Hill.

Toronto, Allen. 1972. A Developmental Spanish Language

Analysis Procedure for Spanish-speaking Children. Ph.D. dissertation, Northwestern University.

Valett, Robert E. 1964. A Clinical Profile for the Stanford-Binet. *Journal of School Psychology* vol. 2.

Wallace, Gerald, and Larsen, Stephen C. 1978. *Educational Assessment of Learning Problems: Testing for Teaching*. Boston: Allyn and Bacon, Inc.

Wechsler, David. 1947. *Wechsler-Bellevue Intelligence Scale*. New York: The Psychological Corporation.

_____. 1951. *Escala de Intelligencia Wechsler Para Niños*. New York: The Psychological Corporation.

Wepman, Joseph, and Morency, Anne. 1973*a*. *Auditory Memory Span Test*. Los Angeles: Western Psychological Services.

_____. 1973*b*. *Auditory Sequential Memory Test*. Los Angeles: Western Psychological Services.

Index

Stanford-Binet Intelligence Scale, 239–241
   277
Stark, J., 154
Stillman, Bessie W., 61

T

Teachers College Press, 42, 49
Teaching Resources Corporation, 96
Templin, Mildred C., 133
The Templin-Darley Tests of Articulation,
   133–135, 256, 257, 265, 277
Terman, Lewis M., 239
Test for Auditory Comprehension of
   Language, 156–158, 256, 257, 268,
   269, 277
Tiegs, E. W., 1
Tobin, A., 166
Toronto, Allen S., 172, 270, 271
Tyack, Dorothy, 173

U

University of Illinois Press, 141
University of Iowa, The, 133
University of Washington Press, 166

V

Valett, Robert E., 240

W

Wallace, Gerald, 2, 5, 204
Wechsler, David, 228
Wechsler Adult Intelligence Scale, 238
Wechsler-Bellevue Intelligence Scale, 236
Wechsler Intelligence Scale for
   Children—Revised, 228–238, 240
Wechsler Preschool and Primary Scale of
   Intelligence, 238, 277
Weiderholt, J. L., 105
Wepman, Joseph M., 92, 93
Wepman Auditory Discrimination Test,
   92–95, 257, 268
Western Psychological Services, 191
Whittlessey, John R. B., 100
Wide Range Achievement Test, 7, 9, 10,
   19–21, 25, 255, 256, 259, 261, 263
Woodcock, R. W., 46, 94
Woodcock Reading Mastery Tests, 4,
   46–48, 255, 263

Y

Ysseldyke, James E., 2–3, 105, 106,
   151, 240